MONETARY THEORY

Conventionally, monetary problems have been examined with reference to a monetary framework which has little to do with the real world of banking. The purpose of this volume is to provide an alternative analysis to monetary economics based on the distinctive properties of bank money.

In *Monetary Theory: National and International* the author argues that a new approach is needed which will be capable of providing modern analytical instruments based on the intrinsic nature of bank money. This analysis is based on the principles of book entry money and monetary problems are investigated from a structural point of view.

The book:

- analyses money by referring directly to banks' book entries;
- shows that the distinction between money and income is rooted in the everyday practice of central and secondary banks;
- examines exchange rate instability and financial crisis;
- puts forward an alternative proposal for European Monetary Union.

Alvaro Cencini is Professor of Monetary Economics at the Centre for Banking Studies, Lugano, Switzerland and at the University of Varese, Italy. He is also a member of the Centre d'études monétaires et financières at the University of Bourgogne, France. He has extensive research and practical experience.

MONETARY THEORY

National and International

Alvaro Cencini

ROUTLEDGE

London and New York

First published 1995
by Routledge
11 New Fetter Lane, London EC4P 4EE

Simultaneously published in the USA and Canada
by Routledge
29 West 35th Street, New York, NY 10001

Typeset in Garamond by LaserScript, Mitcham, Surrey
Printed and bound in Great Britain by
Mackays of Chatham PLC, Chatham, Kent

British Library Cataloguing in Publication Data
A catalogue record for this book is available from the British Library.

Library of Congress Cataloguing in Publication Data
Cencini, Alvaro.
Monetary theory: national and international/Alvaro Cencini.
p. cm.
Includes bibliographical references (pp.) and indexes.
ISBN 0-415-11054-8.
1. Monetary policy. 2. International finance. 3. Banks and banking, Central – European Union countries. 4. Foreign exchange – European Union countries. 5. European Monetary System (Organization). 6. Debts, External – European Union countries. 7. Debt service – European Union countries. I. Title.
HG230.3.C4 1994
332.4'6 – dc20 94-33804
CIP

ISBN 0-415-11054-8

To Marco and Massimo

CONTENTS

Part II Money and international transactions

Part III Towards the creation of a supranational money

ACKNOWLEDGEMENTS

During the preparation of this book I have greatly benefited from the participation of the students in my classes and seminars at the Centre for Banking Studies in Lugano and from critical discussions with the members of the Centre d'études monétaires et financières of the University of Bourgogne and with Bernard Schmitt. I am indebted to them as well as to Adrian Pollock for his invaluable contribution in improving the style of the English manuscript, to Paola Bernasconi for plotting all the figures and tables and to Nicole Martinez for helping me to prepare the bibliography. Finally, I am grateful to the Cultural Commission of Canton Ticino for having financially supported my research.

INTRODUCTION

Since the science of economics began, money has been defined as a unit of account and its main task identified as the measurement of produced goods and services. Thus, money was immediately conceived of as a numerical standard of no intrinsic value. Avoiding the vicious circle implicit in the claim that the value of real output is expressed in terms of the value of money, Adam Smith introduced a crucial distinction between nominal and real money, showing that it is as a nominal standard that money is issued by the banking system. If money could be created already endowed with a positive value, then the wealth of a given nation would be measured by the sum of the values of its real production and its quantity of money. By arguing that wealth cannot be artificially increased by the simple creation of (nominal) money, Smith was thus able to prove that money is not an element of the set of commodities. His analysis was to be corroborated by Marx, whose concept of 'form of value' provided a further insight into the nature of money. Starting from the problem of how to determine the value of commodities, Marx showed that money is the key element in the very existence of value. Without money it would not be possible to give value its social expression. In other words, only money can give its form to the value of goods and services since it does not itself pertain to the world of real output (if money were itself a commodity it would have a value of its own and it would be necessary to find another 'form' in order to express the value of money). According to the classical works in this field (in particular those of Smith, Ricardo and Marx), money is therefore perceived as the numerical form of goods and services, that is, as their a-dimensional standard of value.

Even the great economists who went on widening the analytical horizon of the classical approach confirmed the function of money as a unit of account and its essentially numerical basis. As Walras's concept of the *numéraire* clearly indicates, and as is implicit in the neoclassical dichotomy, money has no intrinsic value of its own. It is a kind of veil which adds nothing to the value of the real world of production. Reiterating what had been repeatedly maintained by Smith, the neoclassical authors stressed the non-cumulativeness of money and output up to the point of claiming that real variables are all that count (or, at least, all that should count) in economics. Yet Smith himself was well aware of the fact that money also plays the role of a unit of payment and that, as such, it has to be endowed with positive purchasing power. The problem of determining the value of money is therefore as old as the concept of money itself. Ricardo's search for an invariable unit of measure is a well-known example of the efforts which were made in order to conciliate the unit-of-account definition of money with the necessity of attributing a positive value to a purely numerical standard. The author of the *Principles* was trapped in a cul-de-sac: he was looking for his constant unit in the world of commodities forgetting that, as a form of value, money cannot itself have a value (and cannot, therefore, pertain to the world of real goods). The problem remains. Even if as a unit of account money is an a-dimensional standard, it is certain that, as a unit of payment, it is able to exert a positive purchasing power over real output. To maintain, as is brilliantly done by Tobin (1980) and again by Hahn (1982), that, like language, money is a means of communication which owes its value to its general acceptance by individuals, does not seem to be a satisfactory answer. Indeed, if money is socially accepted it is because it is endowed with a positive purchasing power and not the other way around. Another solution was proposed of defining money as a net asset issued as such by the banking system. However, once again, the way out of the dilemma is worryingly close to a *petitio principii*. To claim that money has a positive value since it is issued with it amounts to maintaining that banks have the supernatural power of creating out of nothing.

Although still far from being totally adequate, the net asset definition of money has the merit of highlighting the problem. As all the great economists who were interested in analysing this subject point out, money has its origin in the banking system and it is through a careful examination of the way it is issued by banks that the mystery of its twofold nature can be finally understood. It is in the works of Keynes that the key elements of the solution can be found. Elements which, when properly understood, allow for the working out of a theory of bank money to which several economists have already contributed and which, though still in the making, seems solid enough to give a clear explanation of some of the main difficulties which hamper the further development of our economic systems. In particular, there is still too much confusion about such worrying phenomena as inflation and deflation, and the time has come to make it clear that the rise of the price index cannot be taken as the manifestation of inflation (a much more complex concept than the cost of living) and that the understanding of unemployment is strictly related to that of Keynes's distinction between voluntary and involuntary unemployment, a distinction which, by confining the concepts of structural and conjunctural unemployment to the first category, points out the deflationary nature of the second category, by far the most worrying of the two.

In the first part of this work we have tried to show how the genesis of money can be explained through a careful analysis of the entries recorded by banks when acting as an intermediary between firms and workers, savers and consumers, savers and investors, consumers and public institutions, and so on. A distinction is made between the monetary intermediation carried out by banks and their role of financial intermediation. It is the coexistence of these two roles which explains how money can simultaneously be a numerical entity and be endowed with positive purchasing power. Properly understood, the analysis of the circular flows of money and income tells us that banks can only create a vehicular and a-dimensional means of payment whose content, the purchasing power proper, comes from people engaging in the activity of production. Banks, therefore, are entrusted with the double function of issuing the vehicular (nominal) money required for the circulation of output, and of lending the income (real money) generated by production and entered by them as a bank deposit.

The process of money creation is sometimes wrongly perceived as an act of income creation and, as such, it is the work of Central Banks. By this reasoning, if Central Banks were sufficiently well equipped to operate the miracle of spontaneous generation implied in the concept of income creation, the supporters of this metaphysical approach to money would attribute to banks the medieval right of printing real money (seigniorage). They seem to be aware, however, of the fact that their use of this right has the annoying consequence of producing inflation, and this is why they want it to be limited to Central Banks. Had they paid attention to the teaching of the classic authors, they would have understood that what can effectively be created by banks is only a numerical standard, a vehicular form with no intrinsic power over real output; which means that the creation of money is not an act of seigniorage and can thus be carried out by any secondary bank. Facts fully support this conclusion. In our monetary systems private banks currently issue money in the form of bank deposits, and it is unanimously recognised that these deposits represent the greater part of what is called the quantity or the mass of money. Moreover, the mechanisms of the payments carried out by secondary banks and the rules these institutions have been implementing in order to settle their mutual indebtedness have practically reduced to nil the danger of their emissions being used in order to finance the final purchase of real goods and services (which, of course, would have introduced the pathology of seigniorage into the system).

To claim that the emission of money is the work of secondary banks does not undermine the role played by Central Banks. Besides their marginal interventions as the source of bank notes, Central Banks have their fundamental *raison d'être* in the necessity to create a common 'space of measure' for all the secondary currencies issued by the commercial banks of a given country. In other words, it is through the workings of Central Banks that nations come into an economic existence defined by their own monetary systems. A country can enjoy its monetary sovereignty only if it benefits from the services of a Central Bank which, by acting as a multilateral clearing house between secondary banks, allows for the homogeneity of the currencies issued at secondary level. The banking system adopted by our countries develops at two interrelated levels, the first being made up of secondary issuing banks, and the second of a Central Bank which takes them under its aegis, allowing for their currencies to become part of a unique mass called national money. Now, the analysis of the way Central Banks intervene in the clearing system is essential to the understanding of the laws pertaining to bank money. Indeed, while it represents a particularly useful means for the critical appraisal of the interventions carried out by monetary authorities, it also allows us to work out the logical criteria which should be applied at the international level in order to build up a common monetary system between countries without forcing them to give up their monetary sovereignty.

As the recent shortcomings of the European Monetary Systems (EMS) have clearly shown, the attempt to control or even reduce exchange rate fluctuations between national currencies is bound to be unsuccessful unless the entire mechanism is fundamentally revised. It is through a reappraisal of the analyses of Keynes, Rueff and Triffin, and by examining the main events and theories put forward before and after Bretton Woods, that, in the second part of the book, we try to show what is wrong with the present system of international payments. Let us consider, for example, the huge amount of Eurocurrencies which are daily traded on the international market and whose erratic movements are a persistent cause of monetary instability. Are these Eurocurrencies compatible with the vehicular definition of money? Are they perfectly in line with the use of money as a means of payment?; or do they not represent factual proof that currencies are being used as if they were real goods? And, finally, is it not true that, by trying to transform a means of payment into its real content, the system is allowing a few (strong) countries to pay their debts by becoming indebted, and that their IOUs are thus the object of a duplication which makes them into Eurocurrencies? If the analysis proposed here has some elements of truth, then it is immediately evident that our international monetary system is far from having the same internal consistency as our national systems. In particular, the lack of an international institution acting as the Central Bank of national Central Banks does not allow for the existence of a common monetary area between sovereign countries. Keynes pinpointed this: without an international clearing system, national currencies are bound to remain heterogeneous and countries will have to settle their commercial deficits both financially and monetarily.

If an international Central Bank existed, it would be correct to claim that the settlement of deficits amongst countries is not fundamentally different from the one taking place amongst regions of the same country. Currencies would pertain to the same monetary system, and payments would only require the payer to find the necessary amount of real income to transfer to the payee. The only problem countries would be faced with would be a financial one, and their payments would not put any strain on their national currencies.

The kernel of the analysis is again the distinction between the monetary and the financial aspects of every transaction. Being a purely numerical means of exchange, money should be made available free of cost to the economic agents who need it to convey their payments. And, surprisingly as at first sight it may appear to be, this is precisely what happens at the national level. What the debtor needs in order to pay for its net real purchases is a positive amount of income, the money necessary for its transfer to the creditor being circularly issued by the banking system. If we examine the accounting relationships involved in the transaction, we can easily verify that the payment amounts to the transfer of a bank deposit (income) carried out on behalf of the debtor. The vehicular money required for the transfer is instantaneously created by the bank of the payer and destroyed by this same bank as it flows back to its point of origin. In a way, the monetary problem is so well solved by our national banking systems that, except in the case related to the investment of profits, there is hardly any need to worry about it. However, what is true at the national level cannot be taken for granted at the international one. Payments between countries are not simply a matter of finding the income needed for their financing. If national currencies were perfectly homogeneous (a state of affairs which implies the existence of a true system of international payments and, therefore, of a Bank carrying out multilateral clearing) then we would not be confronted with what Keynes called 'the transfer problem'. Unfortunately, given the persistence of monetary heterogeneity, countries have to deal with the double requirement of earning the income they owe to their partners (Keynes's budgetary problem) and of finding the vehicular money which actually conveys it to them (the transfer problem).

The more we analyse the working of the key-currencies standard system, the further we understand the implications of the distinction between money and income. These implications are investigated in the second part of the book and aim to show that the building up of an international monetary system requires the institution of an international Central Bank allowing for the transformation of the actual regime of *relative exchange rates* into a new system of *absolute exchange rates*. What is meant by absolute exchange rates and how currencies can effectively be put into an absolute relationship without there being the need for a constant intervention of monetary authorities is explained in the third part by analysing the possibility of creating a European monetary area endowed with a common currency without countries having to give up their monetary sovereignty. A case can indeed be made for the creation of a multilateral clearing system at the EC level. This would imply the institution of a European Central Bank with the task of issuing a European currency (ECU) whose main functions would be to represent a common standard for inter-European transactions and to vehiculate their real payments. Unlike what has sometimes been maintained (and is also partially present in the project proposed by Keynes at Bretton Woods), the new international unit would not be endowed with any intrinsic value, and would not be used for the settlement of any real imbalance. In accordance with its own nature, bank money can never be the content of any payment. Appearances to the contrary arise only because payments are effectively made using money. But its use as a means of payment does not mean that money is also the object conveyed by money. Thus, according to the plan outlined here, the ECU would only be used circularly amongst the European countries and the ECB, which would act as a monetary intermediary. The instantaneous flowing back of the ECU to its point of departure would be all that is needed in order to guarantee the transfer of the real output (goods, services and financial bonds) required for the real payment of commercial imbalances. The system would have to work in such a way so as to avoid money being the final object of (monetary) payments; which means, let us repeat, that the ECU would have to convey real goods so that countries would finally pay for their net commercial purchases with the net sale of bonds. The mechanism of inter-European payments would thus achieve the double result of avoiding real purchases being paid for by the transfer of a sum of IOUs (one should not forget, of course, that money is a simple acknowledgement of debt of the banking system which issues it) from the debtor to the creditor country, and not including money in the set of real goods. The main reason for the instability of the present system of exchange rates is the erroneous belief that currencies pertain, as such, to the world of real goods and, therefore, that they can be purchased and sold as if they had a positive intrinsic value. The application of the law of supply and demand to the world of currencies is a consequence of this dangerous confusion between a numerical vehicle and its real content, and the end of the disruptive fluctuations caused by the erratic investment of speculative capital will become a reality only when currencies are integrated into a system allowing for their circular (vehicular) use.

The examples analysed in the third part of the book should clarify this line of argument and provide some elements for the construction of a system of international payments compatible with the traditional (but so often abused) concept of the neutrality of money. Another strong piece of evidence against the key-currencies standard regime under which we live is given by the analysis of the international debt problem. Despite the great efforts which have been made in order to reduce the burden that lies so heavily on less developed countries (LDCs), the debt crisis is far from being brought under control. The fact is that the remedies adopted so far are more or less adequate to cure the main symptoms but not the disease itself. A definitive release can obviously be obtained only by getting rid of the very cause of the disorder. Unfortunately too little has been done in this respect. It is enough to read through the latest reports of the IMF experts to get a discouraging picture of the actual level of understanding of the problem. The discrepancies between the aggregate commercial imbalances of the main indebted countries and their effective indebtedness are so huge that it is vain to impute it to 'errors and omissions'. Moreover, even when some of them have been able to pay interest and principal to their foreign creditors, their debt has not decreased correspondingly. We thus get the impression that external debt servicing takes place through a mechanism which reduces it to a self-defeating process. The analysis confirms this astonishing result: the servicing of external debt (interest and principal) within the key-currencies standard system can only take place through a double payment. This double payment is all the more surprising in that it never occurs at the national level. The servicing of a debt between residents of different regions of the same country requires only a single payment: the transfer of positive income from the debtor to the creditor. However, it has to be kept in mind that inter-regional payments take place within a single monetary system. Monetary homogeneity is what allows for a unique payment of debts; monetary heterogeneity, on the contrary, entails their double payment, since they require a transfer of income and the purchase of the vehicle necessary for the transfer in order to be effective. The point is that international debts have to be serviced, cumulatively, by the residents who have incurred them and by their own countries. The institution of a supranational Bank acting as a monetary intermediary between countries would avoid the double payment, since the Bank would prevent the purchase of the vehicular money by the indebted countries. Until then, external debts are bound to be serviced twice, the payment of the residents having to be backed by an equivalent payment of their nation.

The distinction between residents and nation is all-important here. As the analysis shows, nations cannot be reduced to the sum of their residents and their existence has to be correctly taken into account by the system chosen for the settlement of international transactions. The difficulty could be avoided, of course, if we were all prepared to give up national sovereignties in order to give birth to the United States of the World. Much as some of us would like it to happen, this event is still very far from being more than a utopian dream. If a solution has to be found, and of this no one can be in doubt, it has to be entirely compatible with the survival of national sovereignties. The aim of the institution of an international clearing system is precisely that of providing countries with a monetary structure which will allow them to be part of a unique monetary area without giving up their national currencies. In a system such as this, countries will carry out their external debt servicing on behalf of their residents, and not additionally to them.

Developed throughout the book, the distinction between monetary and financial aspects of payments finds its last application in the analysis of the external debt problem. The double servicing of external debt is a corollary of the confusion between these two aspects, a confusion which leads to the transformation of bank money into a net asset and, therefore, to the need to buy it as if it were a commodity. The source of the endemic instability of our system and of its most worrying manifestations (such as the constant growth of Eurocurrencies, the unpredictable fluctuations of exchange rates and the persistence of the debt crisis) is therefore the same, and will only be removed through the same monetary reform. It is towards the working out of the elements of this reform that our efforts have been aimed. They represent only a few steps in this direction. Other and more important contributions are needed if a new monetary theory is to see the light, and we can only hope that those which have already been made (particularly by Bernard Schmitt) will elicit the interest they deserve and that many others will soon follow.

Part I

MONEY, PRODUCTION AND THE BANKING SYSTEM

1

ON MONEY

The aim of this introductory chapter is to provide a rigorous definition of bank money. As is well known, money has its origin in the banking system and is issued as a spontaneous acknowledgement of debt. There is also a fundamental convergence of opinions as to the means used to represent it. It is generally recognised, in fact, that bank notes represent only a decreasing fraction of the currency issued by the various national banking systems. Moreover, bank notes are nothing other than claims against the Central Bank, which makes it easy to conclude that the totality of money is of a book-keeping nature. Money is thus created by banks through a book-keeping entry, and it is this entry that provides the point of departure for our short introductory analysis.

FROM MONEY TO INCOME

Money as an asset-liability

Let us consider a bank, B. If it is to be a possible point of emission of money it is necessary to endow it with the faculty to enter in its book-keeping its spontaneous acknowledgement of debt to the economy, represented here by its client C (Table 1.1). By incurring a debt to C, the bank is thus creating a deposit, in favour of C, whose object is the same IOU issued by it. As double entry book-keeping requires, this entry has to be balanced by another, equivalent, on the asset side of B's balance sheet (Table 1.2). Bank B is thus simultaneously the creditor and the debtor of a sum of money created *ex novo*. Now, what has to be determined is the nature of the asset allowing for the bank to spontaneously incur a debt to its client C.

According to one of the solutions often put forward, the bank would issue its debt in exchange for a non-monetary asset deposited by C. The traditional example is that of treasury bonds given by the State in exchange for the money issued by the Central Bank, while other examples referring to secondary banks and to their clients could be easily thought of. Since the

Table 1.1

B			
Liabilities			*Assets*
Client C	x		

Table 1.2

B			
Liabilities			*Assets*
Client C	x		x

claims to the new bank deposits would be offered in exchange for those corresponding to the assets supplied by the public, the creation of money would be defined, therefore, as an exchange of claims.

> The bank deposits – i.e. the debts of the bank to the public – are always covered by the assets people have offered to the bank in exchange for deposits claims against the bank. The process of 'creation' of bank deposits is essentially an exchange of claims. The member of the public offers a claim of some sort – such as legal tender State money, or a government bond, or a mere promise – and the bank offers a book debt called a bank deposit.
>
> (Sayers 1958: 12)

Yet this solution cannot be endorsed, since the purchase of bonds or of any other non-monetary asset requires the disposability of a positive income and not that of a simple IOU. In other words, it is mistaken to explain the origin of money by resorting to an operation that implies the existence of income, and which, therefore, necessarily presupposes the very existence of money. If money creation took place according to this circular mechanism, it would inevitably be inflationary and the only way out of this disastrous situation would be to give up the monetary system altogether.

There is another obvious argument against the identification of monetary emission with an exchange of assets (the monetary credit of the bank and the non-monetary asset deposited by its clients). In fact, the creation of a net asset is a process that can be ascribed to B only under the condition of endowing it with the supernatural power of creating something positive out of nothing. Metaphysical considerations notwithstanding, creation is conceivable only as an event whose result is simultaneously positive and negative. The emission of money, therefore, has to give rise to a bookkeeping entry defining, at the same time, a debt and an equivalent credit to the same person.

Let us consider the entry in Table 1.3. This time the exchange between two distinct assets is replaced by the entry of an *asset-liability* totally consistent with the concept of creation. Hence, the bank is simultaneously a debtor to C, for C is the beneficiary of the monetary emission, and a creditor to C, to which the money just issued is lent. Reciprocally, C is the holder of a credit and of an equivalent debt with the bank, precisely because money is created to be lent.

Table 1.3

B			
Liabilities			*Assets*
Client C	x	Client C	x

It is important to note that, despite appearances to the contrary, this operation does not give rise to a self-defeating result since, although they are concomitant, the causes that give rise to the entry of the debt and of the credit of C (and of B) are distinct. The credit of C is the result of bank monetary creation (its spontaneous incurring of a debt to C), while the debt of C is due to its acceptance of the obligation to give back the money lent to it by the bank. Thus, the double entry defining the emission of an *asset-liability* does not imply a vicious circle that would bring about its cancellation.

It is true that the quantitative result of emission is zero, but this does not mean that the entire operation is absurd or meaningless. On the contrary, in the same way as the discovery of the number zero marked an important advance in the field of mathematics, identification of bank money with an *asset-liability* is a considerable step towards understanding the laws ruling our economic systems.

Nominal money and real money

The idea that money is a purely numerical unit of account comes from the impossibility of endowing banks with the faculty of creating a monetary asset *ex nihilo*, and from the logical necessity to explain the origin of money without having recourse to income. Being a unit of account, money is neither a net asset nor a net liability, but simultaneously an asset *and* a liability whose function is that of 'counting' the products and not that of defining their valuable counterpart. The classical economists had already distinguished nominal from real money, where the second term stands for income and the first for money proper. They had clearly perceived that money is a form, a numerical container bound to get so closely connected to real goods as to become identified with them, and be thus transformed into income. On the other hand, even Léon Walras, the father of neoclassical theory, spoke of money, identifying it with the *numéraire*, and every economist knows that Keynes made bank money the core of his whole theory.

Money has to be seen, first of all, as a *numéraire*, i.e. as the standard of measure required for the counting of goods and services currently produced by the real economy. The task of banks is that of providing the economy with this unit of account through the emission and the lending of their acknowledgement of debt. In order for the *asset-liability* issued by banks to represent real output it is necessary, however, that the emission of money reaches the sector of real production. In other words, money has to be associated to real output if it is to play the role of 'form' or 'numerical container' of goods. This means that monetary emission cannot be confined to the banking sector, but has to be linked to a payment allowing for the transformation of nominal into real money.

Now, the only payment that is not concerned with the purchase of a product, and that does not require the presence of a positive income, is that defining the remuneration of labour. In fact, while the payment of all the other 'factors of production' implies the pre-existence of money both as a unit of account and as an income, the remuneration of labour is completely original: it is this operation that allows for the transformation of (nominal) money into income (real money). If logic required wages to be paid out of a positive income, that is, if the payment of wages consisted in a relative exchange between two distinct assets, the integration between money and output would be bound to remain a mystery, and money creation would pertain to the category of miracles. The task of carrying them out would be ascribed to banks, while economists would have to establish their limits on the basis of random and unreliable calculations. Fortunately, reality is more prosaic. The distinction between labour and output is a factual one, and it shows very rigorously that it pertains to labour to create output (where creation has to be understood as the attribution to matter and energy of a new utility form). Hence, the payment of wages is neither identical with the purchase of output nor with the purchase of labour (which, being totally different from any kind of good, cannot logically be purchased).

In order to understand more clearly the peculiarity of the payment of wages, let us refer to its book-keeping representation (Table 1.4). The first entry (1) defines the creation of x units of nominal money by bank B in favour of firm F. As we know, this creation refers to an *asset-liability*, to a unit of account which the bank lends to F and which is created by B incurring a debt to the firm. From a practical point of view, this operation corresponds to the opening of a line of credit, and its purpose is confined to defining the limits of the bank's possible intervention. The second entry (2) is concerned with the payment of wages carried out by the bank for the benefit of workers and on behalf of the firm. This time, the credit entered

Table 1.4

	B			
	Liabilities			*Assets*
(1)	Firm	x	Firm	x
(2)	Workers	x	Firm	x

in the bank account is net, as is the debt entered on the assets side of the same account. Workers obtain a bank deposit without getting indebted, while the firm obtains no monetary deposits in exchange for its debt.

Thus, the payment of wages defines the birth of an income benefiting workers which has the form of a bank deposit. Yet, what is the meaning of this creation? In order to understand it, it is enough to remember that money is essentially a numerical form with no axiologic value. Through the payment of wages, money and output meet, fusing in a unique object called 'income'. By putting money and output together, money acquires a real content, and output is given a monetary form. In other words, money measures (numerically) goods, and goods define the real content of money.

The exchange between money and output pertains to the category of absolute exchanges

Let us reason by analogy and consider the example of cloakroom tickets. Irrespective of the material of which they are made, it is immediately clear that, before being exchanged with the objects deposited, they have no value. It is only when the clients deposit their belongings that the tickets acquire a positive value. By taking the place of the objects deposited, they become their new definition; so much so that the objects are still owned by those who have deposited them, precisely because they hold them under the form of immediately convertible drawing rights. In a certain sense, the deposited objects disappear in the cloakroom to get metamorphosed into the tickets. Then, when the deposited objects are withdrawn, we observe the opposite metamorphosis: the tickets become again a simple set of numbers, a numerical form deprived of its real content, whereas the deposited goods recover their physical consistency. By analogy, money is a numerical container bound to be identified with the products it is associated with, until its drawing rights are exerted and real output definitively purchased.

It is important to observe that both the exchange between tickets and deposited objects, and that between money and current output, pertain to the category of absolute exchanges, and not to the traditional category of relative exchanges. If the cloakroom tickets had an intrinsic value equal to that of the deposited goods, and were given to the clients as their effective counterpart, then we would witness an exchange between real assets, distinct and equivalent, and we would have to conclude that the clients of the cloakroom will not get the very object that they have apparently deposited, but an asset that they will be able to exchange against any other real good whatsoever, irrespective of the nature of the objects initially deposited with the cloakroom. In this case, the hypothetical deposit will correspond to a (relative) exchange between objects of equal intrinsic value. If the bank emission as such could end up with a positive creation of income, the same conclusion would be also valid for the exchange between money and output. Money would then be a real good, distinct from the products it would be exchanged with at par value. The observation of facts, however, does not corroborate this analysis: neither tickets nor money have a positive value of their own. To pretend the contrary would amount to maintaining that banks and cloakrooms have the power of creating something out of nothing, or else to erroneously mix up money and tickets with the material of which they are made. In reality, the value of money and tickets is defined by the real goods and services they are associated with, and not by their own materiality.

Unlike relative exchange, which requires the presence of two distinct objects, absolute exchange refers to a unique object. When the deposited item gets changed into a ticket, it no longer exists in the form of a commodity (even though, as a mere material object, it maintains its initial physical aspect), but takes up the numerical form of the ticket. In the same way, money takes the place of the physical product and becomes its numerical form, so that the exchange between money and output defines their integration: money and output become the two complementary faces of a unique object.

Let us reconsider the book-keeping entry corresponding to the payment of wages (Table 1.5). As owners of a deposit of x units with bank B, workers are the true owners of the real output temporarily deposited with the firm. This result can be arrived at either by remembering that goods are the real content of wages, or by observing that neither the firm, since it is indebted for a sum equal to x, nor the bank, simple intermediary between workers and firm, own a drawing right over current output. Hence workers are, at least initially, the sole owners of produced goods, since they alone own the income necessary for their purchase. This does not mean that workers will necessarily be the final owners of these goods, since wages can be the object of a distribution allowing for other economic agents to take the place of workers as final users of the product. The determining point, however, is still represented by the fact that the whole output is measured by wages, direct and indirect, and that it is wages that define the purchasing power necessary for its global sale (Table 1.6). Let us suppose (entry (3) of Table 1.6) that wages have already been distributed among their final owners (through mechanisms that vary from market to fiscal

Table 1.5

	B		
Liabilities			*Assets*
Workers	x	Firm	x

Table 1.6

		B		
	Liabilities			*Assets*
	Workers	x	Firm	x
(3)	IH	x	Firm	x
(4)	Firm	x	IH	x

imposition), and let us call them IH (income holders). Entry (4) shows how the bank will register the operation once IH takes advantage of this income in order to withdraw the output initially deposited by workers. As is immediately evident, the last two entries, (3) and (4), cancel out. The final purchase of current output thus entails the destruction of the income originated in the payment of wages, and the final economic appropriation of goods.

THE VEHICULAR NATURE OF BANK MONEY

If we consider the whole economic process from the monetary point of view, we can ascertain that its three stages, i.e. creation, transfer and destruction of income, imply the presence of money both as a unit of account and as an instrument or 'vehicle' of circulation. Adam Smith had already clearly perceived the vehicular nature of money when he defined it as 'the great wheel of circulation', and assigned it the task of allowing for the circulation of goods among the various economic agents. Expounded when it was still usual to identify money with gold, Smith's analysis was not entirely orthodox and only a handful of economists were able to understand its great importance, both from a theoretical and from a practical point of view. With regard to the great classical economists' contemporaries, we are now in the favourable position of having to analyse a monetary system that has definitively gotten rid of any commodity-money, and whose operation makes it much easier to perceive the purely vehicular nature of money.

Let us consider, separately, the three categories of monetary transactions just referred to (Figure 1.1). Money and goods do not move in opposite

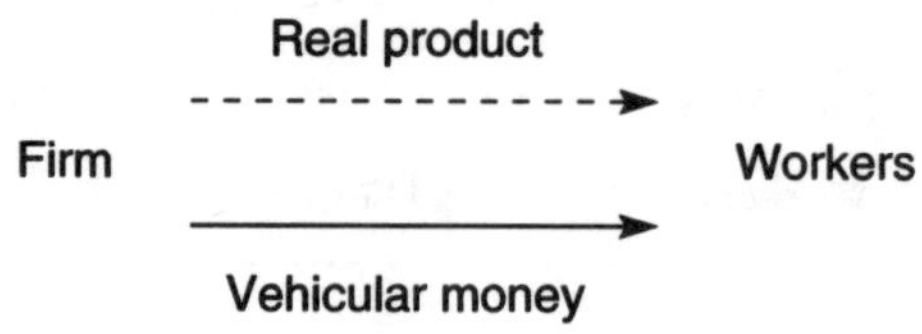

Figure 1.1

directions since they are not two distinct objects being exchanged one for the other. The neoclassical idea according to which (monetary) payments would pertain to the category of relative exchanges is based on the metaphysical assumption that banking assets can be created *ex nihilo* and is definitively denied by reality. In fact, nominal money has no intrinsic value and its task is confined to the circulation of the goods and services it is associated with.

Neither the classical authors nor Walras nor Keynes were fooled by the true, vehicular, nature of bank money. How is it then possible to go on assuming that the emission of money corresponds to an exchange of value? How can it still be claimed that the circulation of money can be stopped and money hoarded? Bound as they are by a 'materialistic' conception of money, these assumptions are not supported by facts. Fundamentally, bank money is a pure unit of account with no axiologic dimension. Moreover, its dual nature of asset and liability prevents it from moving except in a circular way. The instantaneous flow of money to its point of origin, therefore, is not a condition of equilibrium but a logical imperative. Let us verify it by analysing another category of monetary transactions: (reversible) transfers of income.

In this case, it is a matter of allowing for the transfer of income from the one who saved it to the one who wants to borrow it. A present income is thus exchanged against a claim to a future income (Figure 1.2). Through the intermediation of the bank, workers transfer to client C a part of their income and get a financial bond in exchange. As for the payment of wages, money intervenes as a numerical vehicle, conveying the monetary output from W to C. Hence, client C becomes the new owner of the bank deposit previously owned by workers, who exchange their drawing rights over current output against the engagement of C to give them equivalent rights to a new product in the future. The real product stored in the firm is now owned by C, who holds it under its monetary form (Figure 1.3). Once the transfer of the bank deposit between W and C has taken place, money disappears leaving its place to a book-keeping entry – the 'memory' of its tripolar circulation (Table 1.7). The analysis of the third category of payments is analogous to that we have just expounded.

The final purchase of output by income holders takes place through the

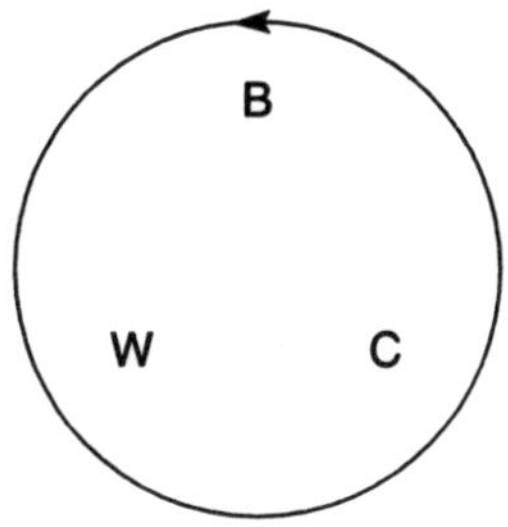

Figure 1.2

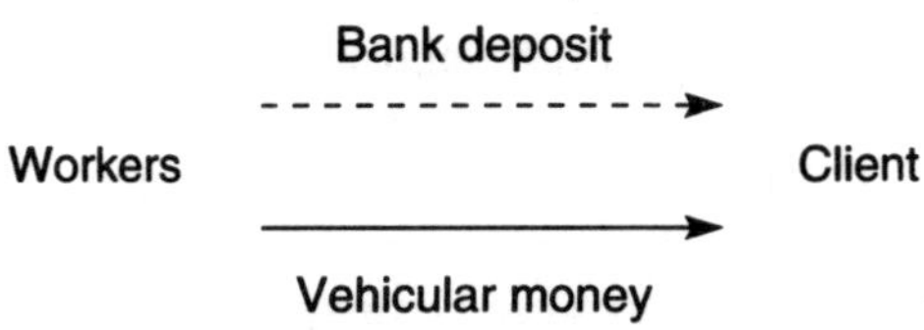

Figure 1.3

(irreversible) transfer of their bank deposits to the firm. And since income and product are one and the same thing, this is another operation defining an absolute exchange. However, whereas in the payment of wages money takes the place of real output, in the final expenditure of income, real goods get rid of their monetary envelope and recover their form of physical objects. As in the other cases, money displays its vehicular function in a circular movement that has the bank as its point of departure and of arrival (Figure 1.4). Bank B provides the income holders (IH) with the vehicle necessary for the transfer of their deposit to the firm (F) (Figure 1.5).

Now, while the payment of wages integrates money and output, giving rise to a positive income, the final purchase of output brings forth its

Table 1.7

	B			
	Liabilities			*Assets*
(1)	Workers	x	Firm	x
(2)	Client C	y	Workers	y
(3)	Workers	x – y	Firm	x
	Client C	y		

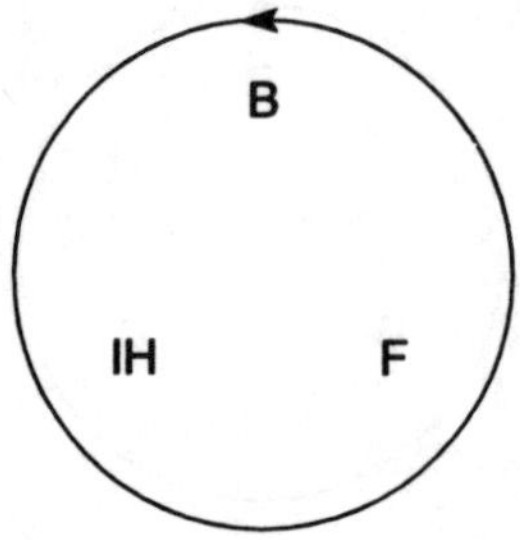

Figure 1.4

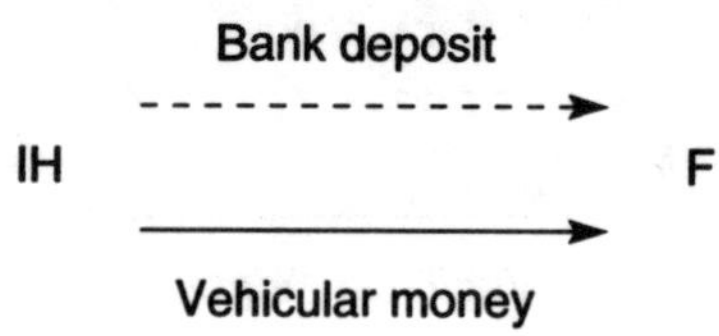

Figure 1.5

destruction through the dissociation of the monetary form from its real content. Goods, that had temporarily been metamorphosed into income, quit their monetary form in order to recover their purely physical one and be used, thus, as 'values in use'. From an economic point of view, therefore, consumption corresponds to the cancellation of income and must be clearly distinguished from physical consumption. In the analytical book-keeping of the bank, the operations of income creation (1), income distribution (2) and income final destruction (3) are entered in the following way (Table 1.8). As can easily be noticed, entries reciprocally cancel out, thus confirming that final expenditure entails the destruction of the income created through the integration of money and output. In the same way as cloakroom tickets lose their value as soon as they exert their drawing right over the deposited objects, income disappears at the very instant its purchasing power is spent for the acquisition of the real product stored with the firm.

Table 1.8

	B			
	Liabilities			*Assets*
(1)	Workers	x	Firm	x
(2)	IH	x	Workers	x
(3)	Firm	x	IH	x

Summarising, we can observe that each operation is carried out through the circular use of money, whose instantaneous circular flow leaves behind entries that define, successively, the creation, the transfer and the destruction of income. Vehicular and financial aspects are, thus, the two faces of every monetary transaction. Banks play the role both of supplying the economy with the numerical vehicle required for the measurement and the circulation of current output, and of fostering its (economic) consumption through the loan of the deposited income. In the first case they create vehicular money, in the second they transfer income.

MONETARY AND FINANCIAL INTERMEDIATION

As we have been trying to prove, every payment involves the banking system in its dual function of monetary and financial intermediary. From a purely monetary point of view, banks provide the economy with the instrument necessary to carry out its various transactions. Nominal money is, first of all, a unit of account, whose function is to make real output homogeneous by providing it with a purely numerical expression. The first intervention of banks, therefore, consists in issuing the numerical units required for the monetisation of current output. It is only if they are monetarily defined that real goods acquire the common characteristic that places them in a unique 'space of measure'.

Monetary intermediation consists in supplying the economy with the numerical instrument (the ticket) by means of which goods can be (economically) 'counted'. Hence, since numbers have no intrinsic value, it is not surprising that banks can freely issue any amount of nominal money required by the economy. The problem of over-emission would arise only if banks created wealth by issuing money. Yet, as claimed by Adam Smith, the emission of money must not be mixed up with the creation of income. The task of (nominal) money is limited to the measurement and circulation of an income that is generated through people's working activity, and not through an alleged and metaphysical intervention of banks.

The integration between money and output implicates banks in acting as monetary intermediaries precisely because money is a spontaneous acknowledgement of debt. This means that money flows back to its point of origin at the very instant it is issued. Thus, in the process of monetary integration money is simultaneously created, associated with current output and destroyed, in a circular movement that leaves a book-keeping mark defining the value of currently produced goods and services. As monetary intermediaries, banks confine themselves to supplying the economy with a numerical instrument that they immediately take back. Their acknowledgement of debt is lent to firms, who transfer it to workers, who earn it as a claim to a bank deposit. Hence, workers do not hold money, whose instantaneous circular flow is definitively opposed to its hoarding.

It is well known that people are still deeply bound to some manifestations of a fetishist nature. In the collective unconscious, gold has long been the symbol of wealth and, although it has rapidly been understood that it can be replaced advantageously by a simple piece of paper, it is still difficult nowadays to dissociate the idea of money from that of net assets. Thus the temptation to identify money both with the physical object used to represent it and with the value derived from its purchasing power is still very strong. From this viewpoint, hoarding seems to recover a meaning analogous to the one it had at the time when precious metals were used as means of payment, and it seems to be perfectly justified to assume that money has a velocity of circulation that varies according to the habits of its holders.

The simple observation that the mass of money is mainly made up of scriptural money should be enough, however, to show how the notions of hoarding and of velocity of circulation are related to an archaeological conception of the monetary instrument. Moreover, bank notes and book-keeping entries must conceptually be kept separate from what they represent. Their materiality does not identify with the essence of money, whose true nature is totally immaterial (as is the true nature of numbers). It is certainly possible to hoard precious metals, as it is possible, though not very rational, to hoard bank notes. This does not mean, however, that it is also possible to hoard money. Hidden under the fatal mattress or locked in a safe, bank notes are not money but bearer bonds whose difference with other kinds of bonds consists in their greater liquidity (balanced by the non-payment of interest). Being of a banking origin, money can only be deposited with the banking system. The public cannot hold and hoard money as such but only deposit bills, more or less secure and remunerative bonds. It follows that even the assumption that money can circulate more or less quickly must be abandoned in favour of the one according to which the circulation of money takes place instantaneously. Since it cannot exist outside the banking system, money can leave it only to go immediately back to it, in a movement that, precisely because it is made up of the simultaneous to and fro, defines a monetary circuit. To stop a monetary circulation would mean to prevent the instantaneous flowing back (into the banking system) of a money that, by definition, exists only as a bank deposit.

If the nature of bank money remains partially mysterious it is because we are still tempted to identify the vehicular instrument (purely numerical) with its content. The distinction between (nominal) money and money's value (real money) is crucial. If it is true that nominal money is a mere acknowledgement of debt with no value, it is also true that, once issued and associated with current output, it is transformed into real money. Workers do not obtain a simple deposit of nominal money from the firm, but a drawing right over the newly produced goods and services, a purchasing power that defines the value they have produced. Through banks' monetary intermediation, goods and services acquire a common form of value, and get metamorphosed into money thanks to an absolute exchange (analogous to the one that takes place between the tickets and the objects deposited with the cloakroom).

At this point, the object of bank deposits is no longer an empty sum of money, but the content of real money: the real output momentarily transformed into income. In accordance with Adam Smith's teachings, (national) income cannot be added to (national) product, for monetary and physical aspects are only the two faces of the same coin. As tickets define the object deposited in the cloakroom, income is the definition of real output, so much so that the final owner of the product is the income holder. In order to own the produced goods and services it is enough to hold the income necessary for their final purchase. In this context it is irrelevant whether output is physically deposited with the firm or not. The firm has a debt (to the banks or to its own circulating fund) equivalent to the income generated by production, and can face its obligations only through the sale of output. If it is true that, by selling the product, the firm itself can become the owner of a positive purchasing power (profit), it is also true that in this case the firm partially takes the place of the initial income holders, and that, as an owner of an income, it has to be kept separate, logically, from the productive firm.

In every circumstance, current output defines, before its final sale, the content of real money (income) deposited with the banking system. Now, from the moment income appears for the first time, banks are present as financial intermediaries between income holders and firms. Let us consider again the case when wages are paid by a secondary bank, SB, on behalf of firm F (Table 1.9). Income holders (IH) own a credit of x units with SB. This means that income is effectively deposited with the bank, and that they own it only in the form of a deposit certificate. Consistent with what we have been claiming about the true nature of bank money, income comes into existence as a bank deposit. It is immediately evident, then, that the income deposited by IH is lent to F. The fact that the bank owes IH what F owes the bank is proof that the credit granted by the bank to the firm is backed by income holders. The payment of wages does not presuppose the existence of a positive income, for the very reason that it gives rise to a new deposit that allows for the financial covering of the whole operation.

Table 1.9

SB_W			
Liabilities			*Assets*
IH	x	F	x

The bank operates, therefore, in order to integrate money and output, and to transfer, from IH to F, the income that defines it. The financial intermediation is added to the monetary one, so that the final object of the firm's debt is a sum of real money (the income lent to it by IH) equivalent to that earned by the owners of the bank deposit.

Let us dwell for a moment on the meaning of the credit implicit in the financing of current output. According to traditional terminology, the credit to production consists in a loan granted by banks to firms. This means that banks must have at their disposal the income necessary to cover the operation; income that can only be derived from an equivalent deposit. Now, to assume the pre-existence of this deposit would amount to a *petitio principii*, entirely gratuitous and logically unacceptable. Having ascertained that in order to explain the formation of income it is necessary to start from production, it would be a vicious circle to claim that the financing of this very production requires the availability of an already existing income. Unless we want to trace back the formation of income to the creation of the universe or even to God (in an infinite Cartesian-like recurrence), we have to give up any attempt of explaining income by relating its formation to its expenditure. If production cannot be financed by a pre-existent income, what is then the meaning of the credit granted by banks to firms?

Let us remind the reader that the credit we are analysing is related to the financing of new production and not to the purchase of already produced goods (purchase that is made possible precisely by the income whose formation we are trying to explain). Thus, costs of production are covered by the payment of wages since, unlike machinery, raw materials and all the other means of production, the work of man (or woman) does not pertain to the category of commodities. The fact that its remuneration effectively generates a new income is a proof, therefore, that human labour is the sole true factor of production. Finally, it is the work of people that generates the income necessary to cover its costs.

The financing of production takes place through the intermediation of banks, but does not have its original source in the banking system. Banks act as intermediaries, transferring to the debtor what has been deposited by the creditor. The income generated by production is instantaneously deposited and lent to firms, whose costs are covered by the credit granted to them by workers and by all the other economic agents who take their place as income holders.

The monetary circulation corresponding to the payment of wages has the dual effect of giving IH the drawing rights over the production physically stored by the firm, and of lending to W the income deposited with the bank by IH. The credit that income holders grant the firm defines the (implicit) loan of their deposit (Figure 1.6).

Besides the intermediation in favour of firms, banks carry on numerous other financial intermediations allowing for the transfer of the income

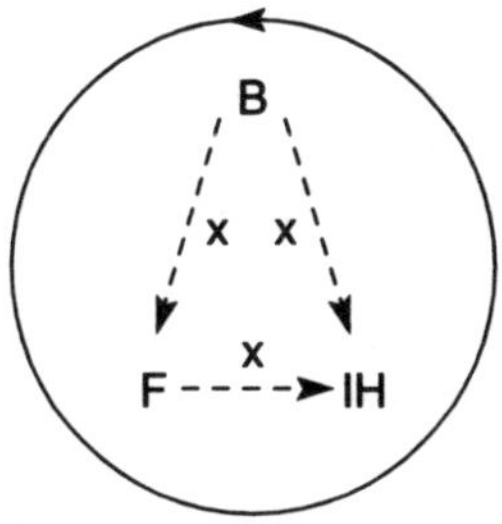

Figure 1.6

deposited by its initial holders to all who, upon the necessary guarantees, want to take advantage of a loan. This was clearly stated by Keynes: 'If an individual hoards his income, not in the shape of gold coins in his pockets or in his safe, but by keeping a bank deposit, this bank deposit is not withdrawn from circulation but provides his banker with the means of making loans to those who need them' (1973, vol. XXV: 273). Let us suppose that the entire amount of income corresponding to current production is lent to clients C. Thanks to the intermediation of banks, firm F will be able to sell its goods and refund its initial debt without having to wait for the decision of the initial income holders to spend their deposit. The transfer to C of IH income, whether explicit (purchase of non-monetary claims by IH) or implicit ('purchase' of a deposit certificate), ends up with the purchase of the real goods stored with the firm. Now, as is shown by the balance sheet entries of the bank, the final expenditure of income entails its destruction (Table 1.10).

Surprising as it may be, this result is the necessary consequence of the utilisation of the purchasing power generated by the integration of money and current output. Income expenditure implies the exertion of the right to draw real products out of the firm's stock. It is perfectly justified, therefore, to claim that, once it has been made use of, this right dies out. In the same way as the cloakroom ticket recovers its valueless numerical form once the deposited object has been withdrawn, money loses its purchasing power and again becomes a mere unit of account as soon as it is spent. This means

Table 1.10

B			
Liabilities			*Assets*
IH	x	F	x
C	x	IH	x
F	x	C	x

that, having been spent by C, the income earned by IH is no longer available. In order to get back a purchasing power equal to (or greater than) the one it has saved, IH will have to wait for C to be able to repay the bank or for other clients to make an equivalent deposit, In other words, the income IH will finally spend will be that determined by new production and not that which it has initially deposited with the bank. Hence, through the financial intermediation of banks, today's income can easily be replaced by a right to an equivalent income in the future, making it possible for some (C) to spend today the income saved by others (IH), who, in their turn, will spend tomorrow (when the loan is repaid or when it is renewed through new deposits) the income of the first ones.

By developing a whole series of more and more sophisticated instruments of credit, banks multiply the possibility of combinations deriving from the non-concomitance of economic agents' decisions relative to savings and income expenditure. Their capacity for intermediation goes even beyond the immediate availability of income. For example, it is always possible for banks, through the creation of money, which is perfectly licit in so far as it does not definitively take the place of income, to lend more than they get as deposits. The operation is monetarily neutral and does not alter, therefore, the internal equilibrium between output and money, provided that income which is spent in advance is not spent again when it is effectively formed. Accelerating the sale of products it reduces their stocking period and increases the degree of elasticity of the whole economic process.

ANOTHER LOOK AT BANK MONEY

Even though the a-dimensional conception of money is not of recent origin (it can be traced back to the works of Adam Smith, David Ricardo, Karl Marx, Léon Walras and John Maynard Keynes), the reader may find it difficult to get rid of a 'material' vision identifying the purchasing power with an intrinsic quality of the means of payment. Being accustomed to the physicality of our relationship with the surrounding world, we are driven to an interpretation of reality implying its dimensional measurement. Apart from intellectual speculation, there seems to be no room for nominal quantities in the context of an eminently real activity such as production. Hence, the idea that in economics the unit of account is always endowed with a positive intrinsic value follows quite naturally. If bank money had the same consistency as material money (for example gold), we would easily be driven to identify it with the precious metal used as means of exchange. The circulation of money would thus be mixed up with that of gold, and concepts such as hoarding, velocity of circulation and relative exchange would find a fertile soil to assert their general validity.

Let us consider the exchange between gold and goods carried out by two economic agents, P (purchaser) and S (seller) (Figure 1.7). With reference to two distinct objects, the exchange between gold and real goods pertains to the category of relative exchanges and is defined by two opposite and reciprocal flows. Thus, as in barter, money is apparently circulating in the opposite direction to real goods. The crucial point is precisely this. What allows for the passage from simple barter to monetary exchange? The fact of choosing a commodity as a means of exchange is not enough to monetise transactions. The exchange between gold and a real good is bound to remain an exchange of commodities even if we give gold the appellative of money. The problem is fundamental. The passage from barter to monetary exchange requires the intervention of a totally dematerialised money.

A major difficulty lies in the necessity to distinguish money from its material support. Money-gold cannot be reduced to commodity-money except by giving up the possibility to monetise exchanges. This means that commodity-gold itself has to resort to money-gold in order to be measured and conveyed in its exchange with real goods (Figure 1.8). The passage from the barter of Figure 1.7 to the monetised exchange of Figure 1.8 is possible on condition that money-gold becomes the common denominator of every commodity, commodity-gold included. Thus, before being exchanged against any other real good, commodity-gold has to acquire a

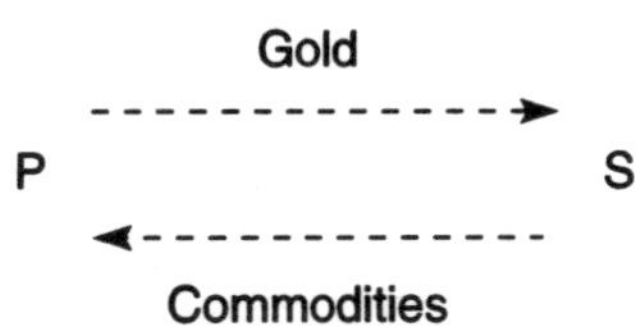

Figure 1.7

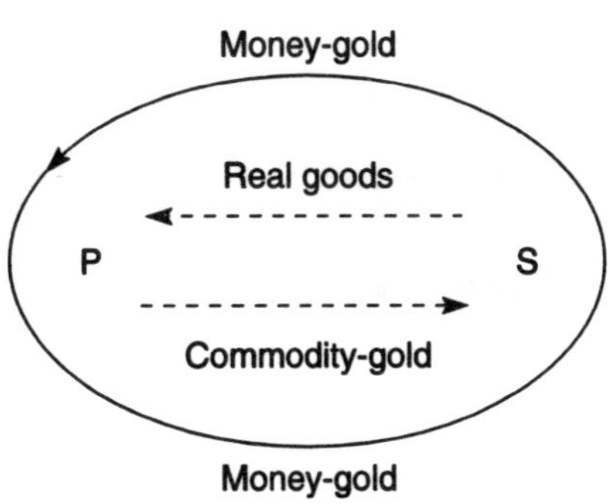

Figure 1.8

monetary form, an operation that requires its transformation into money by means of an *absolute exchange* (Figure 1.9). If money were a commodity, the transformation of commodity-gold into gold-money would not make sense. The physical object would be the sole reality, and its exchange with other commodities could only pertain to the category of barter.

The evolution of the banking system has greatly contributed to clarifying the terms of the problem. The almost complete de-materialisation of commodity-money (reduced to a simple electrical impulse) shows that the value of currencies has nothing to do with their 'intrinsic' value. The monetary transformation of real goods and services takes place through their association with a purely numerical unit of account. Money can be identified with goods (which are actually changed into money) precisely because it has no value of its own. Money's purchasing power derives from this identification. The value of money is not added to that of commodities. Through the metamorphosis of money and real goods, money becomes the numerical expression of goods, while they become its real content.

The passage from material money to a-dimensional money is made easier by the use of double entry book-keeping. The book-keeping instrument, indeed, has the advantage of letting the numerical nature of bank money appear clearly, and the analysis of the entries relative to its emission leaves no doubt as to the origin of its purchasing power.

Let us start from zero and ask how it is possible, first, to issue money through book-keeping entries and, second, to endow it with positive purchasing power. The emission of money in favour of client F makes the bank indebted to F. Yet, to the positive deposit of F (entered on the liability side of the bank's balance sheet) corresponds a negative deposit of the same amount (asset side of the balance sheet), since F incurs a debt to the bank (which lends him the sum just created) equivalent to the debt that the bank incurs to it (Table 1.11).

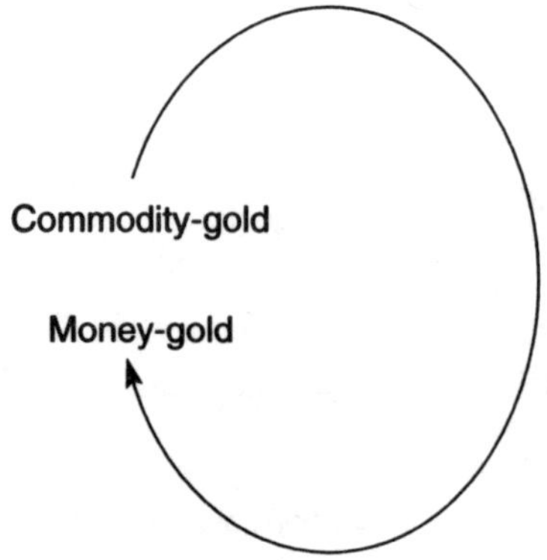

Figure 1.9

Table 1.11

	B		
Liabilities			*Assets*
F	x	F	x

What has to be determined now is the object of the debt and credit of F (and, respectively, of the bank). If it were maintained that the object of the debt is real and that the object of the credit is monetary, the emission would correspond to the bank's creation of the monetary counterpart of the real asset deposited by F. The total wealth would then be of 2x (x real asset + x monetary asset), and the emission would correspond to a proper instantaneous generation which is an absurd conjecture. Therefore the only possible solution is to enter the same object on both sides of Table 1.11. Starting from this first result it is necessary, then, to establish if the nature of this unique object is monetary or real or simultaneously monetary and real.

By identifying money with the object of the reciprocal indebtedness of F and B (bank) emphasis is put on the fact that money is issued by the banking system as a spontaneous acknowledgement of debt. To the extent that bank B owes F a sum of (nominal) money defining a simple IOU, the object of its debt is the acknowledgement of debt itself.

If we want to emphasise the fact that the emission of money becomes totally meaningful only when it is extended to the real world of goods and services, we simply have to observe that the object of the credit-debit is the product deposited by F. The object of F's monetary deposit (entered on the liability side) is the same output entered on the asset side of the bank's balance sheet. Through its emission, the bank gives a monetary form to F's output, which represents both the object of F's negative monetary deposit and that of its positive monetary deposit. Hence, F is the beneficiary of a drawing right over the real output monetarily deposited with the bank.

The analysis confirms the dual character of every monetary emission. Carried out independently of any pre-existent deposit, the creation of (nominal) money implies the creation of a new positive bank deposit and, correspondingly, of an equivalent new negative bank deposit. Simultaneously, the issued money is associated with real production, and the monetary deposits are transformed into financial deposits. For example, if F (firm) pays W (workers) by transferring its banking credit, W becomes the holder of a deposit whose real content is defined by the goods that cover the debt incurred by F. Monetary and financial aspects are thus the two faces of a reality that can be correctly interpreted only by starting from the analysis of the operations carried out by banks.

The obstacle that still hampers the understanding of the true nature of bank money is of a conceptual order. The a-dimensionality of money is so well masked by its value as to lead us to believe that value is indeed ingrained into money. To overcome this difficulty it is necessary to look more closely at the area of positive and negative numbers in order to discover that, consistent with the rules of double entry book-keeping, the emission of money entails the simultaneous creation of equivalent positive and negative deposits. The discovery of negative numbers goes back to the seventh century. It does not seem over-optimistic, therefore, to forecast that, thanks to the analysis of the numerical and vehicular nature of money, we shall soon understand the laws of its circulation better and that, by endowing the economic system with an appropriate monetary structure, we shall be able to eradicate the causes of the monetary disequilibria that restrain its further development.

2

THE MONETARY SYSTEM AND THE CENTRAL BANK

In this chapter we shall deal with the functions traditionally carried out by Central Banks, trying to assess critically the impact of some of their monetary policy interventions in the light of the distinction between monetary and financial intermediations. The analysis so lucidly elaborated by Ricardo and the important contributions of Keynes notwithstanding, this distinction has not yet found an effective application in our monetary systems, so that the confusion between money and income hampers the understanding of the mechanisms that govern them and that make their evolution so aleatory. In order to work out what the effective consequences of the monetary and financial policies adopted by Central Banks are, it is necessary, therefore, to elicit those concepts that explain analytically the working of the monetary system, leaving aside the merely descriptive approach which has characterised modern economic pragmatism for so long.

THE CENTRAL BANK AS THE BANK OF SECONDARY BANKS

Ricardo had already clearly perceived the necessity of making the national monetary system homogeneous through the institution of a Central Bank whose money would act as a common denominator of those issued by the various secondary banks operating in the market. The first function of a Central Bank, therefore, is to create a common monetary system within the country. Thus, by making the currencies issued by secondary banks homogeneous, Central Banks have worked, since their creation, as Banks of banks; a role that was bound to increase with the expansion of banking credit and with the abolition of convertibility (and the subsequent spreading of the financial intermediation carried on by Central Banks on behalf of secondary banks).

Through the management of the accounts held for settlement purposes, the Central Bank bestows a common status on the currencies issued by different secondary banks, inserting them in a unique 'space of measure'. In this function the Central Bank acts as a catalyst, transforming fundamentally heterogeneous currencies into undifferentiated elements of a set called national money. Every single money acquires the central currency character that the Central Bank ascribes to it by acting as an intermediary between the different secondary issuing banks.

Now, it is certain that, whether under a scriptural form or under the more traditional metal or paper aspects, money issued by the Central Bank does not increase a nation's wealth. As we have seen, a country's wealth does not consist in the currency as such, but in its real content: the real output money is given the task of measuring and conveying. Money creation, whether carried out by secondary banks or by the Central Bank, is an operation free of cost that should never be mixed up with income creation, an operation that requires the association of (vehicular) money with production. On the other hand, besides providing the economy with the instrument necessary for the definition of its own 'object' (real output), the banking system facilitates its repartition through direct and indirect transfers of income carried out as a mediator between the various economic agents. Thus, like secondary banks, the Central Bank acts both as a monetary and as a financial intermediary. It is in the context of this double function that the activity which it carries out within the interbank system as the Bank of banks must be analysed.

Bank clearing as monetary intermediation

As already seen, it is the Central Bank's intervention that makes currencies issued by the secondary banks operating nationally homogeneous. Without a Central Bank, in fact, secondary currencies would be entirely heterogeneous. For example, money issued by a secondary bank SB_1 would have nothing in common with the one issued by another secondary bank whatsoever, and this would prevent the very existence of an authentic national monetary system. It being impossible to establish an absolute relationship between the different secondary currencies, it would also be impossible to exchange them in an orderly fashion, and the 'system' would be reduced to a set of aleatory relations.

Since money issued by SB_1 defines its spontaneous acknowledgement of debt, its deposit in another secondary bank, SB_2, elicits a debt of the first bank to the second. Reciprocally, every deposit with SB_1 of money issued by SB_2 defines a debt of the second bank to the first. A question arises here. According to which principle can the mutual debts of the two secondary banks be, totally or partially, offset? It is immediately obvious that, without a common denominator between the two currencies, their heterogeneity makes the problem insoluble. The Central Bank's intervention within the clearing system is decisive. It is the Central Bank, in fact, that provides secondary banks with the common denominator of their respective acknowledgements of debt. Central money works as a catalyst and conveys its homogeneity to the various currencies of a secondary origin. 'Borio, Russo and Van den Bergh (1991) show that all the G-10 central banks offer settlement services to their national clearing systems, eight out of eleven operate clearing systems directly and nine set and enforce rules' (Angelini and Passacantando 1992: 456).

Clearing between the currencies issued by SB_1 and SB_2 can take place because they are both transformed into central money. The same status is thus ascribed to the acknowledgements of debt issued by the two banks; an operation that transforms them into constitutive elements of a unique set. The Central Bank is entrusted with the task of collecting secondary banks under its aegis, giving their currencies the homogeneous form of its own acknowledgement of debt (central money).

By operating as a clearing house, the Central Bank plays a role of monetary intermediation between secondary banks. In our example, it provides both SB_1 and SB_2 with the central money necessary to carry out the clearing of their reciprocal acknowledgements of debt. At the end of the operation, central money is destroyed, and it is re-created every time the Central Bank is called upon to carry out a new intermediation.

Let us represent the clearing carried out by the Central Bank on behalf of SB_1 and SB_2 by means of three bank entries (Table 2.1). As can be observed, we have used different indices to represent the currencies issued by the two secondary banks, as before Central Bank intervention they define two essentially heterogeneous objects. In its work of intermediation, the Central Bank takes over the debts between SB_1 and SB_2 generated by the payments made by their respective clients. Hence, SB_1 gets rid of its debt to SB_2 and becomes indebted to the Central Bank which, in turn, acknowledges a debt to SB_2 of an equivalent sum of central money. The money issued by the Central Bank therefore takes the place of both the currency issued by SB_1 and that issued by SB_2. Both secondary currencies give up their place to central money in a movement that transforms them into undifferentiated components of the same monetary mass (which we have represented by the symbol NM, national money).

The clearing is then completed by the Central Bank taking over the debt of SB_2 to SB_1 (which we assume to be equal to the debt of SB_1 to SB_2) (Table 2.2). Once clearing has taken place – reciprocal cancellation of the first and last entries – secondary currencies become elements of a unique set. By establishing a relationship of absolute exchange between them and central money, the Bank makes them perfectly homogeneous, turning their issuing banks into organs of a common monetary system: the national monetary system.

Finally, through Central Bank intervention part of the money issued by SB_1 is replaced by an equivalent sum of money issued by SB_2. If secondary

Table 2.1

SB_1

Liabilities		*Assets*	
SB_2	x M_1	Clients	x M_1
CB	x CM	SB_2	x M_1
CB	x CM	Clients	x NM

SB_2

Liabilities		*Assets*	
Clients	x M_2	SB_1	x M_1
SB_1	x M_1	CB	x CM
Clients	x NM	CB	x CM

CB

Liabilities		*Assets*	
SB_2	x CM	SB_1	x CM

Table 2.2

SB_1

Liabilities		*Assets*	
CB	x CM	Clients	x NM
Clients	x M_1	SB_2	x M_2
SB_2	x M_2	CB	x CM
Clients	x NM	CB	x CM

SB_2

Liabilities		*Assets*	
Clients	x NM	CB	x CM
SB_1	x M_2	Clients	x M_2
CB	x CM	SB_1	x M_2
CB	x CM	Clients	x NM

CB

Liabilities		*Assets*	
SB_2	x CM	SB_1	x CM
SB_1	x CM	SB_2	x CM

currencies pertain to a unique set it is because Central Banks assign them the common characteristic of national monies. In the clearing process analysed here, SM_1 is transformed into central money to be successively transformed into SM_2 through an operation in which central money is the common form of secondary bank currencies. Through CM, money S_1 disappears to come back under the form of SM_2. It is, fundamentally, a metamorphosis, in which SM_1 leaves its place to an equivalent sum of SM_2 created by SB_2. SM_2 creation and SM_1 destruction are the two sides of a unique operation, central interbank clearing, allowing the assembly of SB_1 and SB_2 in the same monetary area (Figure 2.1).

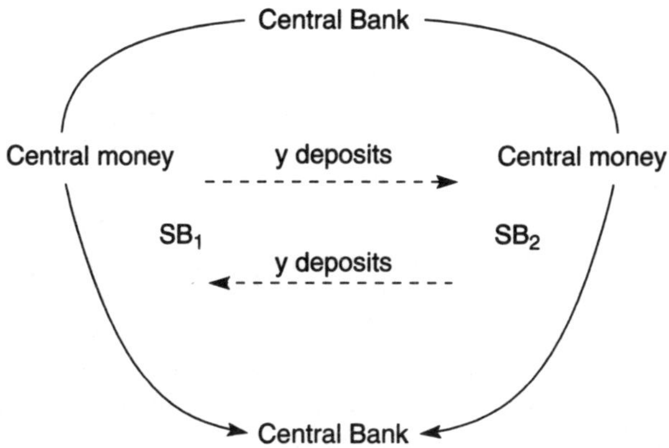

Figure 2.1

Another example of monetary intermediation: the emission of bank notes

From the beginning, Central Banks were empowered to mint coins and were given the monopoly of issuing bank notes. Even though the quantity of bank notes today represents a decreasing part of the total amount of money, it is important to analyse its emission in order to avoid confusion regarding the nature of money (central as well as secondary). Thus, let us consider the working of the Central Bank within this context and try to determine the nature of the money which it creates to the benefit of the entire economic system.

From a purely material point of view it is obvious that bank notes are only a very small part of national output, and that their intrinsic value is but a trifle compared to the extrinsic value they are endowed with as money. Considered as a simple piece of paper, the bank note is a negligible object, and its production has an extremely limited impact within the magnitude of national income. The cost of production of bank notes does not explain either their meaning or their (extrinsic) value. From this simple observation it can be induced that, in issuing bank notes, the Central Bank only provides the economy with a numerical container or, in the words of Adam Smith, a means of circulation whose value is not added to that which is defined by national production. To claim the contrary would amount to endowing the Central Bank with the metaphysical faculty of creating value *ex nihilo*. In reality, it does not take the place of either God or man, but confines itself to providing the economic system with a mere sign of value, a form whose content has to be derived from real production.

Having ascertained that this operation does not result in the creation of value, we have only to analyse the book-keeping entries it entails to realise that its main objective is to allow for the substitution of one form of money for another. For example, the holders of x units of income under the form of bank deposits can decide to retain part of it in the form of bank notes, forcing their secondary bank to ask the Central Bank to provide it with bank notes in exchange for part of the debt incurred to its clients. From a real point of view nothing has changed: income holders own the same purchasing power as before (even though it is now partially carried by claims, bank notes, formally different from the previous ones, deposit certificates), and their bank benefits from the same credit with the agents on whose behalf it has carried out the initial payment. As far as income is concerned, creditors and debtors remain the same, and so does its book-keeping relationship. What changes is the relationship between Central and secondary banks, since the secondary bank owes the Central Bank what it previously owed its clients and it is now owed them by the Central Bank (as bank notes holders, the secondary bank's clients own an acknowledgement of debt spontaneously issued by the Central Bank).

The initial situation is represented as shown in Table 2.3. The payment carried out on behalf of some of its clients makes the bank a creditor to them and a debtor to the income holders. Since no payment can be financed through a mere monetary creation, the object of this first transaction is part of national output. In other words, the credit of income holders has a real content (current output) that is not generated by the banks' emission of money, but by an operation, production, that 'invests' money with a positive purchasing power. It is confirmed, thus, that money as such is an acknowledgement of debt spontaneously issued by the banking system, the content of which comes from the real sector of production. Now, assuming that the bank's creditors want to transform part of their deposit claims into bank notes (i.e. into monetary claims on the Central Bank), the supply of bank notes would give rise to the following entries (Table 2.4). The meaning of the operation is clear. The reciprocal indebtedness of secondary and Central banks reveals the perfect substitutability of the currencies issued by the whole banking system. As is known, it is the Central Bank that, by reducing them to the same denominator, makes currencies issued by the other banks perfectly homogeneous. And it is as the Bank of banks that it can replace the acknowledgements of debt issued by private banks with its own acknowledgement of debt

Table 2.3

Secondary bank			
Liabilities			*Assets*
Income holders	x	Debtors	x

Table 2.4

Central Bank				*Secondary bank*			
Liabilities			*Assets*	*Liabilities*			*Assets*
Secondary bank (bank notes)	y	Secondary bank	y	Central bank	y	Bank notes	y

(represented here by bank notes). In other words, through Central Bank mediation the form under which (a right to) income is held can change and the initial relationship between creditors and secondary banks transformed into a relationship between them and the Central Bank. What changes then is not income (which, let us repeat, is never created by banks straightaway), but what is used to represent it or, if one prefers, the type of claim chosen by the income owners to hold their right to make use of it. Current account credits and bank notes are not fundamentally different, so much so that they can be used indifferently as means of payment by the simple operation of substitution we have just described and that, in our example, would give rise to the following entries (Table 2.5). The function of the currency issued by the Central Bank, therefore, is that of providing the economy with an alternative to the certificate of deposit and not that of taking the place of the bank deposit itself which, as is stressed by the accounting relationships synthesised here, is essentially due to an extra-banking operation, production, and is not modified by Central Bank intermediation. On the whole, the deposit with the secondary bank (the object of which is the output corresponding to the income holders' activity) is still entirely owned by the beneficiaries of the payment initially carried out by the bank on behalf of those we have called debtor agents. What the secondary bank owes the Central Bank is effectively owed by the latter to those clients who have decided to hold their drawing rights over current output under bank note form. Thus, if on one hand the real sector activity provides the content (or the object) of the deposit, the banking sector activity of creation provides the monetary form necessary to give physical output the numerical expression that, alone, can grant its homogeneity.

Table 2.5

Central Bank				*Secondary bank*			
Liabilities			*Assets*	*Liabilities*			*Assets*
Clients of the secondary bank	y	Secondary bank	y	IH	x – y	Debtors	x
				Central bank	y		

ON THE SUPPOSED CAPACITY OF THE CENTRAL BANK TO ACT AS A LENDER OF LAST RESORT

We have already shown that, through Central Bank intermediation, currencies issued by secondary banks are made perfectly homogeneous and that the Central Bank gathers the different banks in a unique ensemble called the national monetary system which includes institutions that, although they are not classified as banks, carry on activities of financial intermediation (in Switzerland, for example, where internal payments are partly carried out through a system of postal current accounts, the National Bank is an intermediary between the post office (PTT) and private banks, and allows for the daily banking credit of current assets accumulated in the postal current accounts).

To these functions of the Central Bank, it seems that we should add that of lender of last resort which it plays towards the secondary (or commercial) banking system. In order to guarantee the financial market's equilibrium – it is claimed by some economists – the Central Bank intervenes by providing secondary banks, in exchange for an equivalent sum of their assets, with the amount of bank notes or deposits necessary to cover the excess of credit granted to the private sector.

> Thus, the monopoly of the note issue in a nonconvertible system created a second form of open commitment of the Central Bank's balance sheet, now known as the 'lender of last resort' function, requiring the provision of deposit liabilities or notes against the assets of private banks in order to preserve the stability in private financial markets required if the Central Bank wanted to limit its agency commitment to government. Central Bank thus acquired both an obligation to be the lender of first resort to the Treasury and the lender of last resort to the private banking system.
>
> (Kregel 1988: 40)

The idea that seems to justify this kind of intervention is that there could be an emission of bank deposits greater than the amount of deposits the public is willing to hold. How is it possible to reach this disequilibrium? Let us suppose that secondary banks grant credits to the private sector in exchange for assets they are unable to sell in the financial market. Hence, deposits created in favour of the private sector seem to increase the banks' monetary liabilities without increasing their (monetary) assets. The result would be a decrease in the liquidity banks could balance through the intervention of the Central Bank, which would provide them with the bank notes necessary to restore monetary equilibrium. It is obvious, however, that the excess of credit cannot be ascribed to the monetary system considered as a whole. Loans granted by banks are necessarily deposited within the banking system, so that a disequilibrium can concern only some of the banks relative to the rest. Hence, if it is certainly possible for one or more private banks to grant credits greater than the deposits their clients want to hold with them, it is impossible for the totality of credits granted by banks not to be deposited with them.

The lender-of-last-resort conception of the Central Bank seems to be inherent to the role it plays within the interbank system. According to the classification proposed by Andrea Ripa di Meana and Mario Sarcinelli (1990), the credit of last resort (CLR) granted in the context of interbank clearing would represent the ordinary CLR, while those credits related to the safeguard of internal monetary and financial equilibrium would pertain to the category of extraordinary CLR. The conditional tense is used here not in relation to the choice of classification criteria adopted by the authors, but with respect to the presumed credit nature of Central Bank intervention. The lender-of-last-resort concept, in fact, suggests the idea that Central Banks could be given the faculty of granting loans without having to back them with any equivalent deposit (actual or advanced). Through a mere monetary creation they could be asked to supply the banking system with the assets necessary to cover imbalances of interbank (clearing) or conjunctural (financial deficits and particular situations of insolvency) nature.

In the following sections we shall try to prove how the lender-of-last-resort notion has to be substituted with that of intermediation, whether Central Bank intervention is concerned with clearing or with meeting increased liquidity needs.

Interbank indebtedness requires the Central Bank to intervene as a pure intermediary

To be able to analyse the problem of the alleged intervention of the Central Bank as lender of last resort in the best conditions we shall not consider the particular clearing structures adopted by various countries. Whether clearing is carried on through CHAPS (clearing house automated payments system), CHIPS (clearing house interbank payments system) or SIC (Swiss Interbank Clearing) is irrelevant regarding the role of Central Banks and the necessity to assure the effective payment of interbank balances.

Let us examine, step by step, the formation of a debt between two private banks, SB_1 and SB_2, the intervention of the Central Bank and the operation's final conclusion.

In the first stage SB_1 grants credits for a sum of x units, of which y are deposited with SB_2. The issuing bank thus incurs a debt of y units to bank SB_2 (Table 2.6). At this point the Central Bank intervenes, acting as intermediary between the two secondary banks. SB_1 debt is thus taken over by the Central Bank, which becomes simultaneously a creditor to SB_1 and a debtor to SB_2 for an amount of central money (CM) equivalent to y units of secondary money 1 (SM_1) (Table 2.7).

Table 2.6

SB1				*SB2*			
Liabilities			*Assets*	*Liabilities*			*Assets*
SB_2	y SM_1	Clients	y SM_1	Clients	y SM_2	SB_1	y SM_1

Table 2.7

SB1				*SB2*			
Liabilities			*Assets*	*Liabilities*			*Assets*
SB_2	y SM_1	Clients	y SM_1	Clients	y SM_2	SB_1	y SM_1
CB	y CM	SB_2	y SM_1	SB_1	y CM	CB	y CM

Bank SB_2 now owns y units of central money, while it owes the holders of the deposit generated by the credits initially granted by SB_1 y units of secondary money 2 (SM_2). However, clearing is not yet concluded. Central money, in fact, does not bear interest; it is thus immediately given back by SB_2 to the Central Bank, which, tracing the operation back to SB_1, destroys the whole amount of central money used as an instrument of clearing (Table 2.8). At the very moment it is paid by the Central Bank, SB_2 spends its deposit in order to acquire (either directly or through a clearing account) bonds issued by SB_1. From the monetary point of view, interbank clearing requires the intervention of the Central Bank in an operation defining a perfect circuit of central money (Figure 2.2). Monetary intermediation ends up with the necessary flowing back of central money to its point of emission. Yet, through this circulation of purely nominal money, the Central Bank allows for the transfer of bonds from SB_1 to SB_2. Financial

Table 2.8

SB1				*SB2*			
Liabilities			*Assets*	*Liabilities*			*Assets*
CB	y CM	Clients	y SM_1	Clients	y SM_2	CB	y CM
SB_2	bonds y	CB	y CM	CB	y CM	SB_1	bonds y

CB			
Liabilities			*Assets*
SB_2	y CM	SB_1	y CM
SB_1	y CM	SB_2	y CM

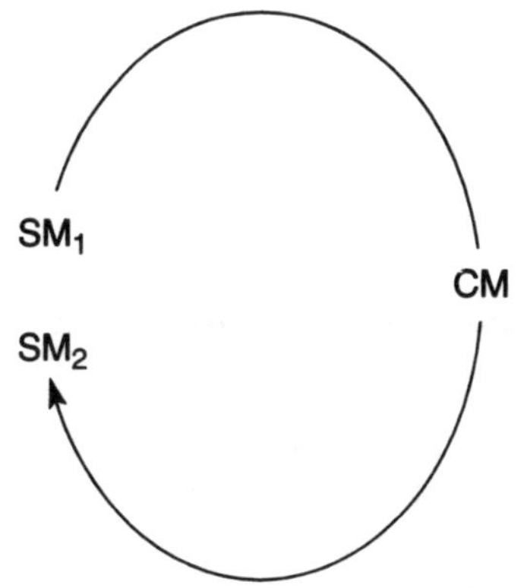

Figure 2.2

intermediation is thus grafted onto the monetary one, allowing for the carrying out of the whole process of clearing without any variation of internal equilibrium between money and output.

As required by the banking nature of money, its circulation defines its necessary flow to and from its point of origin. The object of every payment is the real content of vehicular money, and this is also true with respect to interbank clearing: SB_1 debt is settled through a transfer of bonds (or claims on clearing account deposits) implied in the circular intervention of the centrally issued currency. It is perhaps useful to specify that even when interbank clearing is carried on by private banks organised in a clearing house system, the settlement of balances requires a transfer of real assets. Whether these assets are deposited within the clearing house's accounts as 'real securities' of the member banks, or supplied when final settlements are due, is irrelevant. In any case the fact is that no debt can be settled through a pure creation of money or credit. In the case we are examining, the excess of credit granted by SB_1 to its clients is financed by an equivalent loan of SB_2. The clients of SB_1 spend (and destroy) the income saved by the clients of SB_2; it is thus normal that SB_1's debt towards SB_2 is settled through a transfer of financial claims: having spent the income saved by SB_2's clients, the clients of SB_1 give them a claim over their future income.

The passage from SM_1 to SM_2 (operated, let us remind ourselves, through SM_1 destruction and SM_2 creation) takes place by means of Central Bank intermediation. It is not surprising, therefore, that having completed its task, CM disappears. Hence, while the Central Bank is in a position of perfect equilibrium, both monetary and financial, private banks settle their imbalances through a transfer of securities (or deposit claims). The entire operation is carried through without Central Bank intervention leading to a net creation of national money: SM_1 transformation into SM_2 does not increase the quantity of money and is perfectly neutral relative to internal income distribution. It is clear, therefore, that the simple role of monetary intermediation carried out by Central Banks is openly opposed to the function of lender of last resort that some experts would like to bestow upon it.

Central Bank discounting as an operation of intermediation

Let us reason *ad absurdum* and accept momentarily the assumption that Central Banks can effectively act as lenders of last resort. How would transactions occur and what would be their consequences if Central Banks issued money in exchange for non-monetary claims deposited by secondary banks? According to our assumption, monetary assets issued by Central Banks should cover the financial deficits of secondary banks, allowing them to recover the necessary level of liquidity. However, as already observed, private banks considered as a whole would suffer a monetary deficit only if money were not of a banking nature: money which is deposited in the banking system cannot be withdrawn from circulation so that Central Banks are called upon only to allow for the correct working of interbank clearing.

As for the currency issued through Central Bank discounting in favour of secondary banks or of private and public firms, results are fundamentally the same. By discounting bank assets or commercial bills, Central Banks replace secondary currencies with central money without modifying the global amount of money required to measure and circulate current national output. For example, let us suppose that any secondary bank whatsoever, SB_w, applies to its Central Bank to discount a part of the assets derived from the monetisation of a new product. Initially SB_w pays x units of money on behalf of firm F_w, which makes it a debtor to the new income holders, IH, and a creditor to F_w (Table 2.9). In order to satisfy IH withdrawal requests, SB_w discounts part of its credit with the Central Bank, CB, which transfers to it an equivalent sum of central money in, let us say, bank notes (discount can be thought of as interest, thus justifying the purely didactic assumption of equivalence between discounted assets and the amount of central money given in exchange by the Central Bank) (Table 2.10). The Central Bank replaces SB_w, leaving the quantity of money totally available unchanged. A part y of total income has now the form of central money (bank notes, in our example), while the remaining part, $x - y$, maintains its initial form of secondary money. It is obvious, then, that Central Bank intervention does not modify the system's financial assets since it only gives a new form to the income which firms will pay back as bills fall due and that will then be destroyed at Central Bank level (Table 2.11). These examples are particularly important since they show how the empirical

Table 2.9

SB_W

Liabilities		*Assets*	
IH	x	F_W (output)	x

Table 2.10

SB_W

Liabilities		*Assets*	
IH	x – y	F_W	x
CB	y		
IH bank notes	y	Bank notes	y
IH	x – y	F_W	x – y

CB

Liabilities		*Assets*	
SB_W bank notes	y	F_W trade bonds	y
IH bank notes	y	F_W trade bonds	y

Table 2.11

SB_W

Liabilities		*Assets*	
F_W bank notes	y	IH bank notes	y
CB bank notes	y	F_W bank notes	y
F_W trade bonds	y	CB trade bonds	y

CB

Liabilities		*Assets*	
IH bank notes	y	F_W trade bonds	y
SB_W trade bonds	y	SB_W bank notes	y

development of our monetary systems is perfectly coherent with the analytical distinction between money and income (between monetary and financial intermediation). Reducing Central Bank intervention to a simple financial intermediation between secondary banks, the system avoids financing its institutions through a monetary creation whose inflationary nature only escapes those who obstinately take the emission of money for a creation of income.

The fact that several Central Banks only discount commercial bills is further proof that they are extremely cautious in granting credits that could support, even though indirectly, a too generous credit policy of the private banks. Referring to the emblematic example of the Swiss National Bank, directives adopted by the Federal Bill of 1978 clearly show how discounts are put under severe control both to avoid them being carried out on the deposit of financial bonds, and to prevent private banks, attracted by a possible gap between market and discount rates, from resorting to them in order to benefit from the positive margin of arbitrage.

> The National Bank requires bills presented for discount to satisfy very high qualitative criteria. It accepts only national bills of exchange guaranteed by at least two trustworthy and independent signatures, provided they are commercial bills; financial bills are excluded [. . .]. In the course of years, the National Bank has tendentially tightened access to rediscounted credit [. . .]. On several occasions the National Bank refused access to discount when it was very likely the applicant was asking for it not to cope with a temporary lack of liquidity, but to profit from the positive difference between market and discount rates.
>
> (BNS 1981: 169)

The same caution has been adopted when private banks apply to Central Banks to refinance their credits through advances against pledged securities. Limited to the need to intervene to counter temporary liquidity shortages, these advances are not fundamentally different from discount. Hence, the conclusions previously reached remain valid whether advances are related to commercial bills or are granted through the pledging of financial claims.

In the last analysis, the banking system, both central and secondary, is structured in such a way as to avoid almost completely the risk of confusion between monetary creation and financial intermediation. Central Banks, therefore, are only apparently playing the role of lenders of last resort. If they were playing it effectively, their intervention would pertain to seigniorage and would have unavoidable inflationary effects. By not financing commercial bank deficits through monetary creation, Central Banks act consistently with the logical rules of money. The problem of credit over-extension is thus restricted to private banks. Through the mechanism of clearing, every bank whose credits overcome its deposits has to transfer an equivalent amount of securities to the other banks it is indebted to. Whether this operation is carried out through Central Bank intermediation or not is totally irrelevant from a financial point of view. What is essential is the fact that interbank debts are cleared through a flows of bonds (or of deposit claims with the clearing account). Secondary banks are thus induced to comply as rigorously as possible with the principle of the daily balance of credits and deposits, limiting the risk that their activity could lead to an over-emission capable of modifying, albeit temporarily, the money–output relationship.

Besides, as is stressed in the next example, if they are included within the context of interbank clearing, advances lead to an over-emission of money only if the income advanced is deposited with the same bank granting the initial loan. If this is not the case, advances are immediately 'covered' and amount to simple financial intermediations.

Let us suppose again that Central Banks agree to finance, in the short term, the deficits of private banks. As in the example previously examined, our starting point is represented by a plethoric emission of money carried out by any secondary bank whatsoever. Let us call it SB_1 and suppose that it grants loans greater than the deposits made by its clients (Table 2.12). In order to provide for the increased demand of liquidity, SB_1 turns to the Central Bank handing over its financial assets in exchange for an equivalent amount of central money (bank notes) which it pays out to its clients C_1 (Table 2.13). At this point, the central money spent by C_1 and earned by C_2 is deposited with C_2's private bank (Table 2.14). SB_2 now owns a credit in central money which, as we know, does not bear interest, and a debt in secondary money on which it has to pay positive interest. As a logical consequence of this situation, SB_2 will quickly return its credit (bank notes) to the Central Bank, obtaining in exchange the financial assets handed over by SB_1 (Table 2.15). The result is analogous to the one determined by interbank clearing. The Central Bank intervenes only as an intermediary

Table 2.12

SB_1

Liabilities		*Assets*	
IH	x	Firms	x
Clients C_1	y	Financial assets	y

Table 2.13

SB_1

Liabilities		*Assets*	
IH	x	Firms	x
C_1	y	Financial assets	y
Financial assets	y	CB bank notes	y
Bank notes	y	C_1	y
IH	x	Firms	x

CB

Liabilities		*Assets*	
SB_1 bank notes	y	Financial assets	y

Table 2.14

SB$_2$				*CB*			
Liabilities		*Assets*		*Liabilities*		*Assets*	
IH	z	Firms	z	SB$_2$ bank notes	y	Financial assets	y
C$_2$	y	CB bank notes	y				

Table 2.15

SB$_2$				*CB*			
Liabilities		*Assets*		*Liabilities*		*Assets*	
IH	z	Firm	z	SB$_2$	y	Financial assets	y
C$_2$	y	CB	y	Financial assets	y	SB$_2$	y
CB	y	Financial assets	y				

and what seemed to be a financial credit of central origin appears to be a loan between private banks. Central money issued in the discount of financial bills is not added to that issued by secondary banks: there is a reciprocal substitution of one currency with the other and not a cumulation of the two.

THE CENTRAL BANK AS SECONDARY BANK OF THE STATE

That Central Bank currency has no intrinsic value is proven 'historically' by the fact that public deficit financing is no longer carried out through a simple creation of money or, when it is (in particular situations or countries), that everybody knows it is bound to generate inflation. No economic agent should be allowed, indeed, to buy part of national output without having to give in exchange an equivalent amount of income (obtained as remuneration of his own activity or through the sale of bonds). This principle, certainly valid for the whole of the private sector (whose members cannot pay by issuing a mere acknowledgement of debt, i.e. their own IOU), applies also to public authorities and their monetary institutions. Hence, the progress of banking tends to emphasise the distinction between monetary emission (and intermediation) and financial intermediation.

Let us consider more closely the activity of the Central Bank as bank of the State or of the Exchequer. As is well known, the Central Bank also acts as an intermediary to the profit of the Exchequer, whose activity is partially financed through fund-raising in the capital market. The possible mechanisms of this financing seem to be of two kinds, according to whether treasury bonds are first bought by the Central Bank to be successively sold to the public or directly subscribed to by the public. In reality, however, these two methods are substantially similar since in both cases treasury bills are finally purchased by the public who, in so doing, transfer part of their income to the State vaults. Central Bank intervention as first purchaser has to be seen as the initial stage of a transaction ending up with the transfer of treasury bonds to their final purchasers. In other words, the Central Bank confines itself to advancing the income that the public will effectively transfer to the State: it is only if the Central Bank were unable to sell part of the treasury bills it has monetised that public financing would amount to an inflationary creation of money. Analogously, if the Central Bank were prepared to buy the treasury bills nobody wants to purchase, we would witness an inflationary financing of public debt: from a simple intermediary between State and income holders, the Central Bank would then be changed into a lender of last resort to the public sector.

Let us suppose that clients of any secondary bank whatsoever, SB_w, are granted a credit in exchange for a deposit of financial securities. Now, whether issued by the same clients or by a third party, these securities are nothing other than intermediate goods whose sale implies a transfer of income from buyer to seller. SB_w intervention in the capital market allows the seller of bonds to get the desired loan before having sold them, or the buyer to be refunded in advance. In both cases the bank advances its clients the income they will obtain once the operation is completed. Let us now suppose that the Exchequer urges Central Bank intervention in order to transform state securities into monetary assets: the emission of central money would take the place of that of secondary money. It would be the Central Bank, then, which advances the income sought by the SB_w client (Table 2.16). When the loan falls due, the Central Bank would then be paid back and the bonds returned to the Exchequer (Table 2.17). The advance carried out by the Central Bank is obviously not a credit of last resort.

Table 2.16

CB			
Liabilities			*Assets*
State	y	Bonds	y

Table 2.17

CB			
Liabilities			*Assets*
State	y	Bonds	y
Bonds	y	State	y

The loan to the State does not arise out of monetary creation, but is financed by future income originating in the process of production.

Acting as a financial intermediary between the public sector and income holders, the Central Bank carries out the function of transferring income from its initial owners to the State. If it took the place of the public as the final purchaser of treasury bonds, the Central Bank would not only stop acting as a mere intermediary, but would also finance its purchase through a monetary emission equivalent to downright seigniorage. The absurdity of such an operation is striking if it is kept in mind that the emission of central money is practically gratuitous for the Bank.

The relationship between creation and intermediation can be illustrated by looking at bank financing of production. Let us consider the case in which firms are granted loans simply through acknowledgements of debts that are entered on the assets side of a commercial bank's balance sheet. The use of bank credit for the factors of production payment gives rise to an entry (on the liabilities side of the bank's balance sheet) benefiting those we shall call again the income holders (Table 2.18). Money creation does not correspond, in this case, to the purchase of any real or financial good by secondary banks, but to the simple monetisation of production, which is entirely owned by income holders. The latter are indeed the owners of the bank deposit granting them the purchasing power over current output, i.e. over the very object of their credit and of the firm's debt. Now, this business financing finds its real origin within production and its monetary origin in the emission carried out by banks. At this level the intervention of the Central Bank as lender of last resort would be totally absurd, no discrepancy being possible between the deposits generated by the emission of money and those the public wants to hold. The whole income earned through production is immediately deposited with banks precisely because it sees the light as a bank credit and, then, as a right to a deposit whose amount (defining the producers' earnings) cannot be smaller than the amount effectively owned by income holders.

The same argument applies to the monetisation of public sector activity. Whether it is carried out by Central or private banks, the monetary creation implied in the payment of those who work for the collectivity (State employees) is not inflationary since it does not entail any purchase by the issuing banks. Through remuneration of productive activity, money (whether of central or secondary origin) is associated with physical output, and

Table 2.18

SB			
Liabilities			*Assets*
Income holders	x	Firm	x

it is only then that it acquires a positive purchasing power. Contrary to what is still claimed by some economists, who consider money creation as an exchange of two assets (one deposited by firms and the other issued by banks), it is production that 'invests' money with positive value.

Autogenesis lies outside the faculties of banks so that it would be both mistaken and extremely dangerous to identify newly issued money with a net asset. As we have seen, this does not happen when emission coincides with the monetisation of production. The purchase of treasury bonds is a different case, since it is not related to the problem of giving production a monetary form. Our concern here is how to arrange the transfer of an already formed income from its initial owners to the Exchequer. The Central Bank (as the State's private bank) acts as an intermediary and, since its occasional creation of money in favour of the Exchequer only amounts to advances, the entire purchase of treasury bonds is finally financed by income holders. It is only if, being unaware of the 'nominal' nature of money, the Bank financed the final purchase of securities through a monetary emission that inflation would intervene to re-establish *equilibrium within disequilibrium*.

Difficulties related to the intermediations carried out by the Central Bank on behalf of the Exchequer, and by secondary banks on behalf of the private sector, cannot be overcome through simple monetary creation. Whether money takes the form of bank notes or of bank credits it remains, fundamentally, an IOU and nobody, not even the Central Bank, can be given the privilege of paying with an acknowledgement of debt. Thus, it is necessary to work out a book-keeping system in which no monetary creation can definitively be introduced within any intermediation process. Only by avoiding the mixing up of these two processes is it possible to conform to the very nature of bank money, and to prevent Central and secondary banks' activity from becoming a source of inflation. Now, the observance of this distinction is already implicit in the measures adopted both at the interbank regulation level and at Central Bank intervention level. What has still to be done is to extend the principle in which the distinction between money and income is based on the whole of bank activities. In this context, the following chapters can be seen as a modest contribution towards a better understanding of why and how our monetary system could be further improved.

3

INTERNATIONAL MONETARY DISEQUILIBRIA: INFLATION

The discovery of inflationary and deflationary disequilibria is not recent. The Ricardian study of inflationary wheat price increases is emblematic, and there are many examples showing how the classical authors point out deflation as the main cause of recession. In Keynes's works the analysis of these disequilibria acquires a centrality that is nowadays unanimously acknowledged by all experts in monetary problems. The fact that our economic systems are characterised by their constant presence should not lead us, however, to the conclusion that they will always be a necessary (though unwelcome) component of our everyday life. In reality, inflation and deflation are neither part of, nor functional to, the capitalistic system of production: on the contrary they represent an anomaly that seriously hampers its development. Thus, though both disequilibria are unavoidable consequences of the workings of our monetary systems (including that characterising the present stage of capitalistic development), neither of them can be considered an essential element of any of these systems. Indeed, the ineluctability of the pathology Americans started calling *stagflation* cannot be simply derived from its renewed presence in our economic systems. If it is true, therefore, that stagflation is more and more generally widespread, it is also true, as we shall try to show in the next two chapters, that it is generated by a pathological mechanism related to a particular structure of monetary payments, and not by a 'functional disorder' inherent in the systems of production and distribution adopted in the world up to now.

After stressing the need to distinguish the concept of cost of living from the concept of inflation (point 1), we shall point out how this disequilibrium cannot generally be ascribed to any economic agent's behaviour (point 2). Having removed the alleged 'behavioural' cause of inflation (which, if confirmed, would imply the need to consider it as potentially present in every economic system), we shall try to discover its 'structural' origin (point 3), deferring the analysis of deflation and its 'symbiotic' relationship with inflation (stagflation) to Chapter 4.

INFLATION AND COST OF LIVING: TWO CONCEPTS THAT MUST BE RIGOROUSLY KEPT SEPARATE

Following tradition, let us start by defining inflation as a loss of money's purchasing power. Despite its generality, this definition is sufficiently rigorous to avoid erroneously equating inflation with the increase in the cost of living. In fact, while inflation implies a loss of purchasing power for a given country's money relative to current output, an increase in the cost of living can have negative repercussions for one or more groups of residents without necessarily modifying the relationship between national money and national output (the relationship that defines the purchasing power of national money). Being usually referenced to the houswife's shopping basket, the cost of living index has more or less impact on consumers' purchasing power according to the income bracket they belong to. It is obvious, therefore, that its increase brings about a reduction in their real income. Yet, the decrease in the real income of consumers does not necessarily imply a reduction in the purchasing power of national money. As we shall see, there are cases where the increase in the cost of living index is caused by public or private decisions entailing a simple income transfer which does not modify the relationship between money and current output. The transfer of income entails its new distribution among economic agents, so that some of them earn what is lost by others; on the whole the available purchasing power remains unchanged and it is not possible, therefore, to call this inflation.

Analogously, it would be wrong to claim that the stability of the cost of living index is an unmistakable symptom of the absence of inflation. As shown in the section on price index stability (p. 55), the stability of prices or even their decrease can mask their inflationary rise, thus giving the (false) impression that an improvement in the standard of living is incompatible with the decrease in money's purchasing power. In reality it is perfectly possible to witness an improvement in the standard of living despite the presence of inflation. This does not mean that money does not lose part of its purchasing power, but that this loss is made up for (onerously) as far as physical consumption is concerned. And the cost of this compensation consists in the fact that, without inflation, the increase in consumption would have been greater. In other words, inflation always provokes a rise in prices, but it is possible that the increase simply compensates for, either totally or only partially, the real decrease caused by a reduction in the costs of production and circulation. In this case, however, we should not give way to the temptation to play it down since it is illusory to think that it is possible to prosper when there is a disequilibrium that keeps on diminishing the national money's purchasing power.

If it is easy to mix up inflation and the increase in the cost of living it is because the first always leads to the second. But the opposite is not always true. It is this asymmetry that elicits the necessity to examine inflation thoroughly in order to clarify its specificity. A first step in this direction consists in critically investigating the relationship between inflation and the price index expounded by traditional analysis.

Inflation and price index

Let us try to prove that neither the stability nor the variation of the price index are indisputable signs of the presence or absence of inflation.

The variation of the price index does not necessarily mirror that of the purchasing power of money

Three examples can help clarify the distinction between inflation and the cost of living index. The first refers to the decision taken by the State to increase tax receipts by raising indirect taxes. Such a decision will certainly have a negative effect on the purchasing power of the majority of consumers, hitting harder those categories of residents who make a large use of the taxed goods. The increased selling price of these goods will provide the State with new receipts corresponding to the increased transfer of income obtained from tax-payers. As it is due to a new tax provision, the loss of purchasing power suffered by some residents implies a new distribution of income in favour of the State, whose purchasing power will grow by the same amount. Independently of how the State utilises these new funds (which can be redistributed among consumers or invested to their direct or indirect benefit), it is plain, therefore, that the transfer of income caused by the introduction of new indirect taxes will not decrease the purchasing power of national money at all. In this first case the increased cost of living is not caused by a pathology of the national currency, but to a measure intended to improve the standard of living of certain categories of residents (pensioners, unemployed, disabled), or the quality, quantity or variety of social goods and services.

The second example is concerned with a rise in the cost of living due to the decision, taken by a firm or by a group of firms, to increase the selling price of their products in order to increase their profit. Besides the fact that such a policy can be carried out only in particular circumstances and in particular kinds of market (monopoly or oligopoly), even in this case the decrease in consumer purchasing power is balanced by an equivalent growth in the income firms can dispose of. Defined as that part of income that consumers transfer gratuitously to firms, profit does not bite into the purchasing power of money at all; its variation only modifies the final distribution of income among the different categories of economic agents. After the transfer, firms own part of the income previously owned by consumers and can use it to exert an equivalent demand in their place. On the whole, the demand exerted by income holders on the market of goods and services remains unchanged, as does the global supply of products.

The cost of living index changes every time the price of the commodities making up the houswife's shopping basket varies. *Ceteris paribus* the variation of the price of a single commodity leads to an increase or a decrease in the index. In the two examples we have just analysed the price increase of a product, whether public or private, increases the price of the basket and is considered, therefore, a reason for the rise in the cost of living. In both cases, however, the new prices do not cause a decrease in money's purchasing power, but only that of some residents. What is lost by some is earned by others (State or firms), a compensation that does not account for any inflationary increase in the quantity of money.

The previous argument applies with respect to either an increase or a decrease in prices. Let us verify this second possibility by means of a third example where the price index decreases following a variation of external origin.

Let us suppose that the national currency of a given country appreciates relatively to the currencies of its commercial partners. The diminished cost of imported goods will affect (at least partially) their prices, provoking a decrease in the cost of living index. Let us recall that this index is usually calculated relatively to a basket of commodities of which imported goods and services are integral parts. Making imported goods less expensive, the depreciation of foreign currencies grants the country's residents an improvement in their standard of living via an increase in their purchasing power. Does this mean, perhaps, that the national currency's purchasing power is thus increased?

As we know, the national currency's purchasing power defines its real content, and the real content of a currency is determined by its association with national output. For example, the value of sterling is defined by British domestic output and corresponds to the drawing right of income holders over this output. Now British sterling can only be issued by the British banking system and is associated only with British national product. Variations occurring to foreign products cannot modify, even marginally, the relationship between money and national output. The purchasing power of sterling is given by the relationship (of equivalence) between British money and British production, and can neither increase nor decrease because of variations totally external to this relationship.

Once again it is necessary to distinguish between the purchasing power of money and the purchasing power different categories of economic agents can dispose of. The fact that imports become less expensive does not mean that the real content of national money is necessarily increased. Although every single resident can buy more imported goods, it is only current national output which can define the content of national money.

To maintain that a change in the price of imported goods can modify the purchasing power of national money would amount to the assumption that commercial transactions with foreign countries have necessarily an impact on the relationship between money and internal product. In reality, as we shall verify in the second part of this work, international transactions cannot modify the banking nature of money and the logical rules governing it. As it is impossible for the currency of a given country to be issued by the banking system of another country, it is likewise impossible for it to leave its own banking system. All the pounds issued in Great Britain are deposited in the British banking system, all the liras in the Italian one and so on. In the specific case we are analysing, the purchase of imported goods does not modify either the quantity of national money available in the country, or the national output associated with it. Whether the owners of national income (entirely deposited in the country's banks) are residents or not is not important here. In every case, the total amount deposited remains unaltered and keeps defining the same commodities which generated its monetisation.

From this point of view, the purchase of imported goods corresponds to that of second-hand commodities: they both leave national income unaltered. As we observed in the first chapter, the purchase of output necessarily implies the destruction of the income defining it monetarily. This destruction, however, takes place only as far as the *final* purchase of output is concerned, i.e. so far as the expenditure of income covers the costs of production of the purchased goods. Hence, if costs were already covered, the repeated sale of the same product would have no effect on income, except its new distribution between buyers and sellers (Table 3.1).

Analogously to what happens for second-hand commodities, the purchase of imported goods does not imply any destruction of domestic income since the costs of production of imported goods can only be covered by an equivalent sum of the exporting country's national money. Income spent by the purchasers of foreign goods is therefore only transferred from its initial owners to its new holders (residents and non-residents).

Table 3.1

Banking system

Liabilities			*Assets*
Workers	100 NM	Firms (current output)	100 NM
Retail sellers	10 NM	Workers	10 NM
Workers	80 NM	Firms	100 NM
Retail sellers	10 NM		

On the whole, the income still available after the purchase of imported goods is unaltered; and, since a country's income is determined by the relationship between national money and current output, it follows that the purchasing power of national money is independent of the price variation of foreign goods.

Thus, even acknowledging that the reduction in prices of imported goods gives the importing country's residents a better standard of living, we have to conclude that this happens in full compliance with the internal relationship between money and output, that is, without modifying the purchasing power of national money at all.

The three cases we have analysed show how a change in the price index does not necessarily mirror a variation in money's purchasing power. To go on identifying one with the other would lead to serious confusion which would hamper our correct understanding of monetary disequilibria. Hence, if it is true that inflation causes a price increase, it is not always true that this rise is necessarily a symptom of inflation. Reciprocally, it would be wrong to interpret the price index stability as irrefutable evidence of the absence of inflation. Let us briefly verify this.

Price index stability is neither a necessary nor a sufficient condition for the absence of inflation

It is almost superfluous to note that if the general price index stability was a necessary condition to verify the absence of inflation, a reduction in prices would have to be understood as a sign of negative inflation. Now, a careful observation of facts shows that neither stability nor a decrease in the price index can allow us to rule out, a priori, the presence of positive inflation. The reality of our economic systems is characterised by the importance of technological progress. As is well known, one effect of technological progress is that of reducing the cost of producing goods. The evolution of our productive systems implies, therefore, the almost constant reduction of prices, and it is with this potential decrease that variations in the price index have to be compared.

Let us reason *ad absurdum* and suppose that the economy of an industrialised country does not suffer from any inflationary pressure. In such a case internal prices should decrease (because of technological progress), entailing a proportional decrease in the price index; for example from 100 to 90. Thus, if the statistical calculation of the index led to a different result, of 100 or 95, we should conclude that prices have been submitted to an inflationary increase that has made them rise from their 'natural' level to the one effectively verified on the commodity market (Figure 3.1). Without inflation, the price index would have moved from 100 to 90; the fact that it has settled at the level of 100 or 95 is thus a clear sign of the presence of an inflationary disequilibrium that determines its relative

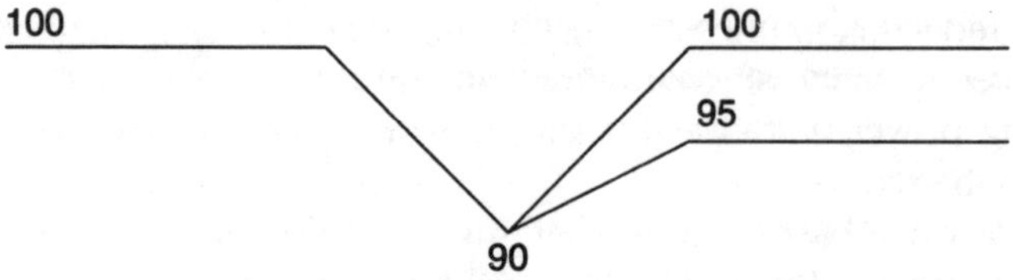

Figure 3.1

increase. The simple observation of absolute price levels would bring us to a wrong assessment of the situation, excluding the presence of an anomaly which, in reality, subtracts purchasing power from national money and, by way of a necessary consequence, from its owners.

The benefit that residents should derive from technological progress is both of a qualitative and quantitative order. Without biting into the profits of firms, the reduction in costs should allow consumers to buy a greater quantity of products, thus improving their living standard. Inflation, instead, deprives them of part of the advantages deriving from technological progress. The inflationary rise in prices conflicts with the technological increase of their purchasing power, reducing (or even nullifying) the 'quantitative' increment of their real income.

In this respect it is useful to observe that, while it is possible to evaluate the standard of living in quantitative terms, the pathological variation of the purchasing power of money is independent from the quantity of goods it is associated with. Let us suppose that in period p_0 ten tables are produced at a cost of 100 units of national money (NM), and that in the following period, p_1, productivity increases thanks to new techniques so that twelve tables are produced at the same cost as the previous ten. From a quantitative point of view it is obvious that the 100 income units of period p_0 purchase fewer tables than the 100 units of period p_1. Yet, does this mean that from p_0 to p_1 the economic system witnesses an increase in the purchasing power of national money and, therefore, negative inflation? Certainly not. Inflation, whether positive or negative, defines a variation of the purchasing power of money relative to a unique period of reference. Independently of the quantity of goods produced in every period, if the relationship between money and output of every single period remains unchanged it is impossible to speak of inflation. Thus, for example, inflation would be present in p_1 if the 100 units of money initially associated with twelve tables allowed only for the final purchase of eleven tables, the remaining table being bought through the expenditure of the 9 units of money added to the initial 100 units by inflation.

Although it limits the quantitative repercussions of inflation, technological progress is not a true remedy against this monetary anomaly. The loss of purchasing power is only apparently compensated for by the technological reduction in prices. In reality, this reduction leads to the subtraction of a greater quantity of goods from income holders. After all, the loss of purchasing power will not be measured in quantitative terms, but in proportion to the reduction in money's real content (in terms of value).

The obvious observation that without inflation prices would decrease, shows that price index stability is not a necessary condition for its absence. Could it be its sufficient condition? The correlation between price stability and monetary equilibrium would be true only if prices were not affected by variations determined either by technological progress or public and private redistributive needs. Since these variations are integral parts of our economic systems, the price index calculated by referring to the traditional commodity basket is only a very approximate indicator of monetary disequilibria.

In order to have a better grasp of inflation, let us analyse it beginning with the arguments usually portrayed by traditional theory.

THE 'TRADITIONAL' ANALYSIS OF INFLATION

Assuming that inflation necessarily leads to an increase in the level of prices, several authors have tried to ascribe its causes to the behaviour of various economic agents. Others, instead, have preferred to stress the 'structural' aspect of inflation, looking for its causes within the inelasticities of our economic systems. Gathered into two broad categories, demand-induced and cost-induced inflation, the hypothetical causes that should bring about a reduction in money's purchasing power are assumed to be linked to the decisions taken (singularly or collectively) by individuals or institutions whose behaviour would directly influence the determination of macroeconomic variables.

In order to analyse this 'traditional' approach it is useful to start by defining the basic principle according to which it is possible to ascribe the cause of price increases to inflation.

Let us start from two firmly held beliefs on monetary theory:

1 inflation is determined by an increase in global demand relative to global supply;
2 national income is the measure of national production.

According to what is claimed in point 1, an inflationary increase in prices (and thus an absolute or relative variation in the price index) occurs every time that money supply inflates, that is, every time its increase is not matched by an equivalent growth of real production. Now, since demand originates from the income available in a given economic system, the causes of inflation must be looked for in all those operations that entail a growth in demand without modifying supply to the same extent.

Point 2 teaches us, on the contrary, that total demand (national income) is always necessarily equal to total supply (national output). Since the works of Adam Smith it has been known that national income and national output are one entity since the first measures the second, and the second defines the real content of the first. The determination of one is therefore simultaneous to that of the other. To claim, as some economists seem tempted to do, that the quantity of money and the quantity of products are two distinct objects determined according to partially autonomous criteria is in open contradiction both with the principles of double accounting (in national accountings domestic output and domestic income are the two faces of the same coin), and with the nature of bank money (the numerical form of real output).

How can we conciliate the apparently contradictory teachings of points 1 and 2? How is it possible for demand to be greater than supply given that demand and supply are parts of an inseparable unity?

The answer is based on the distinction between nominal and real money, or, according to modern terminology, between *empty* and *full* money. If we consider an orderly process of production, the association of empty money with current output leads to the birth of a full money in which form and content define the two aspects, monetary and real, of the same production (Figure 3.2). In a case like this it would be useless to look for a gap between demand and supply. Let us suppose, however, that empty money can be added to full money, that is, for example, that demand grows from 100 to 120 units while output remains unaltered at the level of 100 (Figure 3.3). This time the product initially associated with 100 units of money is confronted with a global monetary demand (full money + empty money) of 120 units. It thus becomes possible to claim, without contradicting oneself, that total demand is simultaneously greater than and equal to total supply. Greater because, in terms of value, the measure of current output is always of 100 units, equal because the same output is now uniformly distributed over 120 units of money: 20 units of empty money are

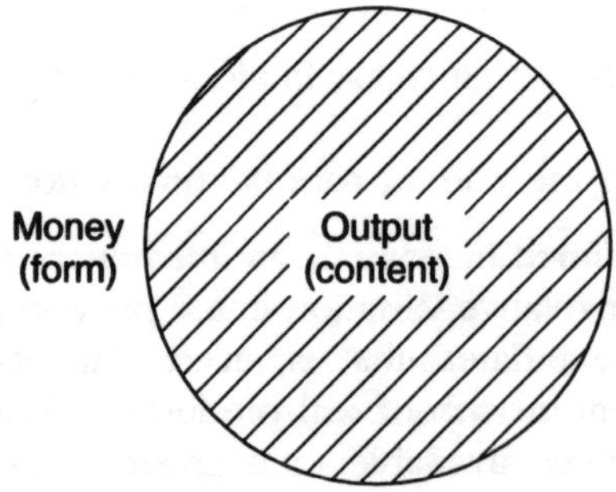

Figure 3.2

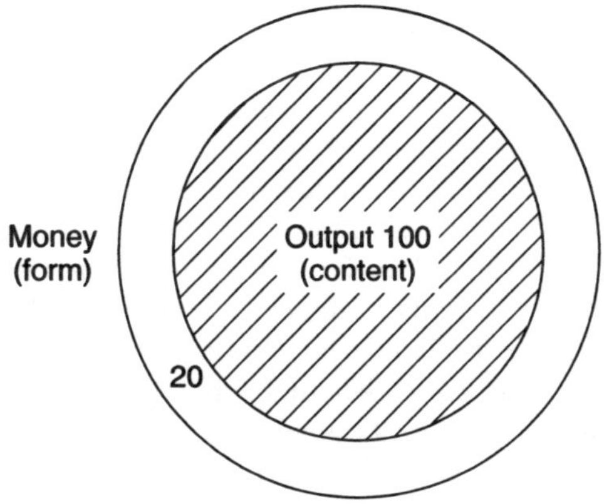

Figure 3.3

assimilated to the 100 units of full money whose initial purchasing power is correspondingly diminished. As a consequence of inflation, the content of money, unchanged in real terms, acquires a new numerical expression. A greater quantity of money is needed, therefore, to purchase the same product.

At this point we have at our disposal a principle which is rigorous enough to critically assess the different explanations of inflation proposed by traditional analysis. If behavioural or structural inelasticities bring about a variation in the internal relationship between money and current output, we shall be justified in classifying them among the possible causes of inflation: if not, we shall be forced to acquit them of any such imputation and to look elsewhere for the origin of the inflationary gap between total demand and total supply.

Demand-pull inflation

Following the order usually adopted in textbooks, let us analyse, successively, the role played by consumers, secondary banks, the State, and by public sector structural rigidities.

Consumers' behaviour is monetarily neutral

The traditional argument runs as follows. Let us suppose that during particular periods, such as wartime, consumers are forced to save an important part of their income, and that, once restrictions have been lifted, they decide to spend the amount previously saved. In this latter period, expenditure would be financed both out of current income and out of that saved during wartime. Thus, total demand would increase relative to current supply causing a rise in retail prices that would reduce the purchasing power of total national income.

Now this argument assumes that the income saved by consumers can only be spent by them (when the changing socio-economic conditions allow them to do it). This means we are forgetting, however, that savings necessarily take the form of bank deposits and that bank deposits are always lent by banks. The book-keeping entry that defines deposits as a banking debt has to be balanced, in fact, by an equivalent entry defining the credit of banks to the economy (Table 3.2). Income saved by C_2 is thus lent to C_1 precisely because the bank SB_w acts as an intermediary both at a monetary and at a financial level. Whether lending takes place with the explicit or implicit consent of deposit owners, the result is unchanged: what is saved by C_2 is spent by C_1 in order to finance its debt to the banking system.

This implies that, when C_2 resolves to spend his savings, his purchases will be financed by an equivalent income out of C_1's savings. A twofold substitution between C_1's and C_2's incomes takes place, therefore, through the bank's intermediation. In the first period C_2's current income takes the place of C_1's future income, allowing him to spend it in advance, while in the second period C_1's (new) income takes the place in C_2's assets of that previously spent by C_1.

Let us apply these principles of monetary book-keeping to forced wartime savings. First of all, it is obvious that, for consumers, rationing entails an accumulation of savings at least equivalent to the amount of military expenditure. Production of weapons, for example, provides a source of income which is not directly spent on the purchase of these weapons. Yet, does this mean perhaps that the income thus saved is not spent in order to cover the costs of production of weapons? The fact that weapons (or investment goods) are not directly purchased by consumers is irrelevant. There can be no doubt, indeed, that arms-producing firms must 'sell' them in order to meet their financial obligations. It is the State that, as commissioner, has to pay for the production of weapons, and to be able to do so, it has to find the necessary financial resources. However, as book-keeping entries relative to the monetisation of arms production show, the income required to finance their purchase is precisely that saved by consumers (Table 3.3). Coverage of the costs of production of weapons is provided by income holders, whose savings are lent to the arms industry.

Table 3.2

	SB_W		
Liabilities			*Assets*
Client C_2	x NM	Client C_1	x NM

Table 3.3

Banking system

Liabilities		*Assets*	
Income holders	100 NM	Firms	100 NM
Income holders	x NM	Arms-producing firms	x NM
Firms	100 NM	Income holders	100 NM
Income holders	x NM	Arms-producing firms	x NM

The subsequent intervention of the State only determines the form of savings. If financing is obtained through the sale of public bonds, consumers transfer their income temporarily to the State; if, however, it is granted through an increased tax burden, the transfer is final. In the latter case, income is entirely spent and will no longer be available to finance new purchases at the end of wartime. In the first case, income is also totally spent, and consumers will obtain an income equivalent to the one they have lent only when the public bonds fall due and on condition that the State can benefit from a new transfer out of current production. Supposing that at the end of war production amounts to 1,000 units and that taxes are equal to x, the maximum amount of income consumers can spend if the State honours all its debts is 1,000 – x + x, a sum equal to the current value of production.

Unless the State covers arms production through simple monetary creation, forced savings cannot be the source of an inflationary disequlibrium. In more general terms, consumers' behaviour is not capable of modifying the rules inherent in the use of bank money. Although they reflect an unlimited number of behavioural decisions, book-keeping entries have to respect a criterion (of double entry) sufficiently rigorous to safeguard (with regard to behavioural changes) the relationship between money and output determined by the monetisation of production.

Secondary banks, credit facilities and inflation: a groundless causal relationship

The private banks are another suspect in the case of the presumed causes of inflation. Granting credits too easily, private banks would contribute to an increase in the demand for consumer goods, thus bringing about an inflationary rise in their prices. In order to assess the significance of this argument more carefully we need to analyse the activity of intermediation, monetary and financial, carried out by secondary banks.

Let us start from financial intermediation. As shown in Chapter 1, from the financial point of view banks can lend only what they get as deposits. It is true that a bank can get it wrong and grant credits that will not be matched by equivalent deposits, but it is also true that for all the banks taken together loans cannot exceed deposits. Through the Central Bank's intervention as clearing house, the excess of credit granted by any secondary bank whatsoever, SB_w, gives way to a transfer of bonds (either directly or indirectly, through claims on clearing accounts), so that SB_w's overdraft credit is balanced by equivalent new deposits formed in other banks (Table 3.4).

Now, despite the perfect correspondence between loans and deposits, SB_w's overdraft could bring about an over-emission of money relative to current output. In this case, the money issued by SB_w and its partners would amount to 120 units whereas output would be only equal to 100, the remaining 20 units being represented by bonds. Thus, on a first analysis, we should conclude that an excess of credit modifies the relationship between money and product, giving rise to an inflationary increase in prices. Yet this conclusion does not take into account the fact that non-monetary claims pertain to the category of real goods. If we keep this in mind we can immediately realise that the total amount of money is equal to the total amount of real goods (real output + financial claims). The meaning of this observation is clear: the working of our banking systems is such that overdrafts of private banks are reduced to an advance. In other words, what clients C_2 can spend today is part of the income that will be produced tomorrow. Advances are not in conflict with the rules of the game. An inflationary growth in demand requires the presence of an empty money that is definitively added to the mass of full money. In the case we

Table 3.4

SB_W				*Other banks*			
Liabilities			*Assets*	*Liabilities*			*Assets*
Clients	x	Firms	x	Clients	z	Firms	z
Other banks	y	Clients	y	Clients	y	SB_W	y
Clients	x – y	Firms	x	Clients	z + y	Firms	z
CB	y					CB	y
Bonds	y	CB	y	CB	y	Bonds	y
Clients	x – y	Firms	x	Clients	z + y	Firms	z
Bonds	y					Bonds	y

are analysing, this is not what happens. The empty money apparently added by SB_w's over-activity is merely a part of the full money of tomorrow advanced by the banking system. The non-inflationary nature of overdrafts is confirmed by another simple observation related to reimbursement. When loans fall due, clients must refund their banks, and when they do so global demand is correspondingly decreased. The increase in demand generated by SB_w's over-emission in period 1 is matched, therefore, by an equivalent decrease in demand taking place at maturity (interests are irrelevant in this context since they define a net transfer of income from payer to payee). Over the two periods, total demand is equal to total supply, which proves that the gap formed in period 1 is not cumulative in time.

Hence, even if we claimed that private bank overdrafts are a cause of inflation since they modify the relationship between money and current output, we would have to add that the discrepancy between demand and supply which it causes is not seriously worrying, for it is bound to be compensated for in the following periods. Moreover, since firms usually make their decisions on the basis of business forecasts spanning several periods of time, the compensated increase in demand will not affect the determination of prices. If we also take into consideration the fact that our complex monetary systems work in such a way that in each period new bank overdrafts take place simultaneously with the reimbursement of outstanding loans (so that the positive gap between demand and supply caused by bank overdrafts is normally balanced in each single period by an equivalent gap of the opposite sign), we can conclude that inflation (conceived as a monetary pathology) is not generated by secondary bank financial intermediation.

As far as monetary intermediation is concerned, it is certain that, by monetising current output, secondary banks contribute to the growth of the quantity of money. On the other hand, it is likewise certain that this growth is matched by an (equivalent) increase of produced output. More precisely, the new money is 'filled' with the new product and defines, therefore, both a demand and a supply of equal value.

It is also possible to disprove the inflationary nature of money creation by considering the fact that the monetary intermediation relative to the monetisation of current output is coupled with financial intermediation. Since the income generated by the monetisation of produced goods and services has the form of a bank deposit, it is immediately lent to firms, which can use it in order to finance their debt to the banking system or to restore their circulating capital, that is, in more general terms, to cover their costs of production.

Finally, bank activities cannot be taken to be the cause of any serious inflationary gap between demand and supply. It is true that, being a monetary anomaly, inflation can only find its origin in the banking system. Yet, this does not mean that inflation can be caused by the behaviour of any of the members of this system. As we shall soon see, the pathological variation of the relationship between money and current output is due to an imperfection in the actual system of payments and can only be dealt with through a reform of this monetary structure.

Inflation and public intervention

The argument according to which the State could be the origin of an inflationary increase in demand is supported both by those who claim that inflation is caused by monetary factors and by those who stress its structural causes. Fundamentally, while the former maintain that an economic policy based on State intervention would entail an inflationary growth of demand, the latter claim that the massive infrastructural intervention of the State necessary for the development of less industrialised countries is only too often financed through money creation.

Let us briefly analyse these two theses, starting with the alleged inflationary effect of public intervention on the relationship between national money and national output. As we have already observed with respect to the production of weapons, it would be wrong to maintain that State intervention affects the relationship between domestic money and domestic output.

If public intervention merely consists in the redistribution of income, it is obvious that it cannot modify the amount of global demand (which is determined by the sum of income available in the system, independently of the identity of its holders). Again, the observation of book-keeping entries is of great help (Table 3.5). Whether IH_1 is the unique owner of the income corresponding to current output (1), or whether after the intervention of the State (2) part of this income is transferred to IH_2, is of no importance as far as the total amount of bank deposits is concerned. Hence, since bank deposits define disposable income, and since disposable income defines global demand, the relationship between money and current output cannot be altered by the simple redistribution of income.

Table 3.5

	Banking system			
	Liabilities			*Assets*
(1)	IH_1	x	Firms	x
(2)	State	y	IH_1	y
	IH_2	y	State	y
(3)	IH_1	x – y	Firms	y
	IH_2	y		

The wrong impression that income redistribution can cause a discrepancy between demand and supply is derived from the belief that what is saved is, temporarily or definitively, not spent. If this were the case, income distribution to residents with a low propensity to save (high propensity to spend) would obviously cause an increase in demand. Yet, the banking nature of money is opposed to the deeply 'material' concept of hoarding. As we have already seen, savings are immediately lent by banks. Through their financial intermediation income is thus entirely spent for the direct or indirect purchase of current output.

If the State is involved in some sort of productive intervention, the conclusion will not change substantially. Besides increasing the amount of disposable income (and, therefore, of global demand), the production of public goods also increases global supply. With regard to the process of monetisation, public production does not differ from private production. They both elicit financial obligations which firms have to meet by selling their products, and they both lead to the formation of the amount of income necessary and sufficient to cover their costs. To claim that commodities produced by the State are not necessarily bought by consumers, can cause confusion. Whether it is a matter of weapons, welfare services or mere holes, public enterprise output is an integral part of national product and plays a part in the determination of global supply in the same way as wages paid out by public firms do in the determination of global demand.

Let us now consider the argument put forth by the authors who attempt to provide a 'structural' theory of inflation starting with State productive intervention. According to the supporters of this point of view, development in poor countries requires State intervention (in order to provide for the huge infrastructural works necessary to attract private investment) even when production is not backed by a monetary and fiscal system able to provide for the coverage of costs. In other words, despite the fact that the production of new infrastructures elicits a new income, in some countries the State is not able to find (through taxes and selling treasury bonds) the income required to cover its costs of production. In a case like this the State would have to refer either to foreign investment, or to the Central Bank, asking for a new emission of central money. In this second event new empty money would be added to that previously associated with national output, generating an inflation that would reduce its purchasing power.

Infrastructural expenditures are meant to improve the productive capacity of a country and are paid for by all its residents. However, this does not imply any monetary disadvantage for the collectivity, since the costs of infrastructural output are entirely covered by the income generated from its production. Difficulties are not related to the decision taken by the State to engage in public utility works, but to the inadequacy of the means it can rely on for the 'selling' of its products. Thus, being unable to cover all its costs of production through the usual transfers of income, the State asks for

Central Bank intervention. Finally, therefore, infrastructural output is paid for by residents through the inflationary decrease in their purchasing power. Being added to 'full' money, the empty money issued by the Central Bank alters 'pathologically' the relationship between national product and the quantity of money. The fact is that the public deficit is covered by the creation of money, which brings about an inflationary growth of prices, and not by the entrepreneurial intervention of the State.

In conclusion, the cause of inflation cannot be ascribed to decision-taking since economic agent behaviour leaves the relationship between money and output totally unaffected.

In the case against the alleged causes of inflation there are still at least two 'excellent' defendants; let us analyse the charges brought against them.

Cost-push inflation

In this second category, the causes of inflation are imputed to those factors whose behaviour affects total supply modifying price through a change in the conditions of production or sale. According to experts in monetary inflation, workers and trade unions would be the main defendants together with countries producing staple commodities, whereas, according to experts in structural inflation, they should be identified with agriculture sector rigidities and with recurrent deficits in trade balances. Let us proceed by distinguishing between the most symptomatic cases.

Wage increases as an alleged cause of inflation

Traditional arguments have developed along two complementary lines of thought. It can be claimed either that an unjustified rise in wages (i.e. an increase greater than the increase in the productivity of labour) leads to a rise in costs and prices, or that it brings about an increase in total demand relative to total supply. Now, both these reasonings are not entirely correct since they do not pay due attention to the distinction between inflation and price index variation.

Nobody can deny that a rise in the cost of production brings about, *ceteris paribus*, a rise in prices. However, this does not allow us to conclude that this increase is of an inflationary nature. As we have seen, it is only when a variation in the relationship between money and national output is observed that we can be certain of the presence of an inflationary disequilibrium. Now, how is it possible to verify such a variation given that the relationship between money and product is determined by the payment of wages?

The analysis of bank money leaves no room for doubt. The only operation defining the monetisation of production is the remuneration of labour. Every change in the sum paid to workers simply leads to a change in the way production is measured.

Whether this scale goes from 1 to 100 or to 1,000 is of no importance. What matters is that, once chosen, it is no longer modified *relative to the same product*. For example, if a table is 'worth' 100 units of money and *the same table* is successively valued (and 'vehiculated') at 110 units, the variation in the money/output relationship is the mark of an inflationary gap of 10 per cent (Figure 3.4). However, if *another table* (physically similar to the first) is produced at a labour cost of 110, we observe a simple change in scale that leaves the relationship between money and each of the two products totally unaltered (Figure 3.5).

In this second case, although being physically similar the two tables are economically associated with two nominally distinct sums of money. Now, it is obvious that the repeated variation of the measurement scale makes the system more complicated numerically. In other words, without serious motivations justifying its change, it would be more rational to keep the scale of wages unaltered. Technological progress and the fall in prices deriving from it would account for a continuous increase in *real* wages despite the stability of *nominal* wages. If, in spite of this, we witness the

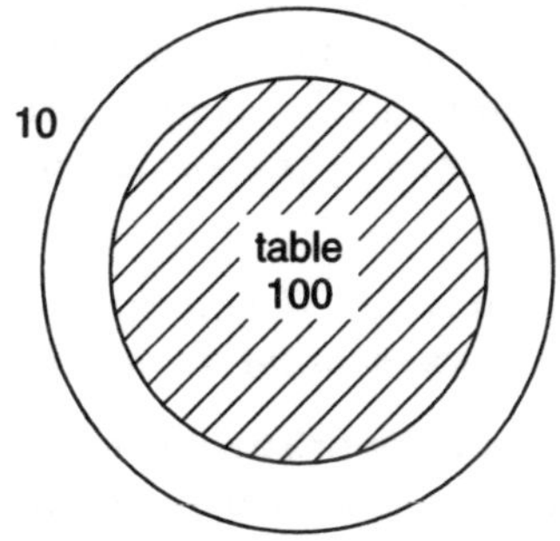

Figure 3.4

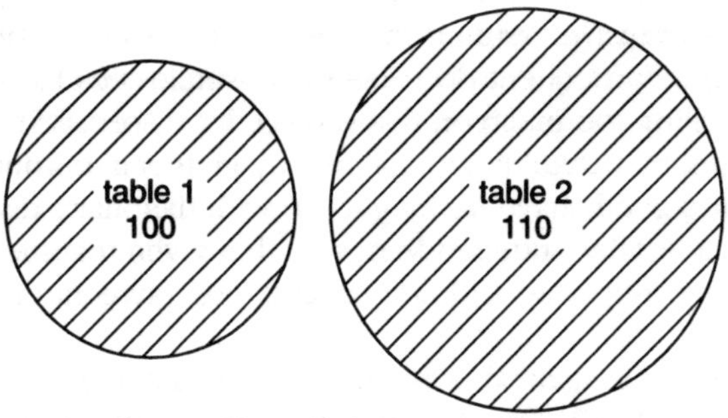

Figure 3.5

renewed variation in wage levels it is because the presence of a serious monetary disequilibrium precludes the growth in real wages, by eroding their purchasing power. Hence, it is because of inflation that nominal wages are regularly adjusted.

Finally, wage increases are never a cause of inflation since either

1 they are implemented in order to limit income holder losses due to inflation, in which case it is impossible to understand how the cost of living adjustment can be considered the cause of the same increase which has given rise to it, or
2 they simply modify the ratio of real wages to profits to the benefit of workers, or
3 they induce firms to raise their selling prices, without altering, in any of these events, the relationship between money and output.

It is only in the third case that we could get the impression that the purchasing power of money is decreased because of the rise in wages. Yet, as we have proved, the rise in the price index must be separated from the loss of money purchasing power. Other things being equal, if firms increase the selling prices of goods consumers will buy fewer of them, but firms will take their place. Globally, the loss of consumers is matched by a growth in profits, so that this new distribution of national output does not cause the slightest decrease in national money purchasing power.

The incidence of exchange rate fluctuations and imported goods prices on inflation

Whether they stress the monetary or structural origin of inflation, authors agree in claiming that exchange rate fluctuation can have a negative impact on the purchasing power of internal income. Their argument is linear and sounds like the one we have recalled in the first part of this chapter (on the variation of the price index, p. 52). Since it is calculated starting from a basket in which imported goods are usually included, the price index varies when exchange rates vary. If national money is devalued, imported goods become more expensive, leading to a rise in the price of the commodity basket and to the consequent decrease in consumer purchasing power.

Without dwelling too much on this subject, let us remind the reader that inflation is an anomaly hitting national money in its relationship to *national* output. Imported goods have nothing to do with this relationship. They are monetised in a totally independent way from the process of internal association between money and output, and their price cannot influence it at all.

Confusion is once again due to the lack of distinction between price index variation and inflation. Causing an increase in prices, devaluation entails a new distribution of real income among the different categories of economic agents (residents and non-residents), but it does not in the least reduce the purchasing power of national money. As we know, the latter is determined only by the internal 'charge' that the productive system commits to money and which money takes care of conveying. Thus, since the relationship between money and output is independent from income distribution, no inflationary effect can be ascribed to devaluation.

Consider the following example. Let us suppose that in two successive periods, p_1 and p_2, internal production is defined by the same amount of national money, equal to 100 NM, and that the price of imported goods, expressed in terms of NM, rises from 10, in p_1, to 15, in p_2. Assuming that the purchase of imported goods is not reduced, consumers have to pay out a larger share of their income, thus having less to spend on internal output. Now, if the income spent on purchasing imported goods were destroyed we would observe a reduction in the price of national output that would not allow us to ascertain the presence of either inflation or a price index increase. Yet, modern bank money theory shows that what is spent on the market of imported goods remains entirely available for financing the purchase of internal product. Income destruction only takes place relative to the final coverage of production costs, and as far as imported goods are concerned it can only apply to the exporting country's currency. The fact that the whole of national money is deposited in the country's banking system is sufficient to prevent a decrease in demand which is of external origin. Internal demand, therefore, remains perfectly equivalent to the supply defined by national production, which means that, albeit differently distributed, national income goes on defining the same relationship between money and output. Inflation is entirely avoided even though, relatively to p_1, a greater part of what is produced within the country is now in the (purchasing) power of non-residents.

The inelasticity of supply has nothing to do with the inflationary increase in prices

Among the hypothetical causes of inflation the rigidity of supply characterising the agricultural sectors is traditionally mentioned. Referring to the case of numerous underdeveloped countries, experts in structural inflation maintain that, because of the increased demand for food products related to increased urbanisation and industrial production, the inadequate productive capacity of agriculture generates an 'endemic' gap between demand and supply that leads to an inflationary increase in prices.

Since we have already dealt with this argument, we shall only recall here the main points of the analysis. Whether production is quantitatively abundant or scarce, its monetisation elicits the income necessary and sufficient for its final purchase (that is, for the final coverage of its costs). If the income formed in other sectors were spent in the agricultural sector, this would allow farmers to increase the selling price of their products, thus getting a profit proportional to the excess demand. Yet, let us repeat it, price index increases are not necessarily a symptom of inflation. To be able to correctly diagnose the presence of this monetary pathology we have to verify a change in the relationship between money and the internal output it is initially associated with. In the case we are examining, the new profits of farming do not define an increase in the quantity of money relative to output, but merely a new distribution of national income. Taking advantage of the new profits, farmers can now exert part of the demand that could have been exerted by consumers. As when indirect taxes are increased, the increased demand for goods produced in a given sector can cause a rise in the price index (on condition, of course, that it is not compensated for by a reduction due to the decrease in demand elicited in the other sectors), but leaves the purchasing power of national money unaltered.

TOWARDS A NEW ANALYSIS OF INFLATION

In this third part we shall try to provide the first elements of an alternative analysis of inflation. Giving up the search for the 'behavioural' causes of this monetary anomaly, we shall try to establish how the relationship between money and output can be pathologically modified by a simple accounting mechanism that does not pay sufficient attention to the banking nature of money and to its functional link with production and circulation. The explanation we are suggesting is therefore more 'structural' than 'behavioural', since it stresses the technical aspect of payments and the effects they can have on money purchasing power.

Unlike traditional structural analyses of inflation, the one embryonically proposed here is essentially monetary and can be applied to highly industrialised countries as well as to developing (or underdeveloping) countries.

On the necessity to conform 'empirically' to the logical distinction between money, income and capital

The principle on which the structural-monetary analysis of inflation is based is that of the coherence between the nature of money and the accounting mechanism of payments. This implies that a monetary system can avoid inflationary and deflationary disequilibria only if it works according to mechanisms which are perfectly consistent with the banking nature of money. Inversely, if the system of payments is logically 'disordered', that is, if it does not comply with the laws of bank money, inflation and deflation are the ineluctable sanction of the disconnection between theoretical and empirical reality.

The reader alert to this kind of problem certainly has no doubts about either the real existence of theories or the fact that, unless the theory is proven false (in which case, strictly speaking, it would not even be a theory), empirical reality must (necessarily) conform to it. Indeed, a theory is merely the 'revealer' of the laws governing particular events. Now, the fact that the absence of pathological symptoms derives from the perfect consistency between theory and practice, i.e. between laws and norms, is particularly evident in monetary economics. Being created (conceived) by man, money is an 'object' of which the theory can give a complete and clear explanation defining the logical laws of its working. If these laws are not matched by a monetary structure capable of ensuring their respect, they assert themselves anyway (a necessity due to the fact that the nature of laws is logical and not conventional), determining a conflicting situation bound to give rise to the monetary anomalies that are still hampering our economic systems.

Having established that the foundation of monetary order requires monetary structures to be adjusted to the laws of money, we now have to make them explicit.

Starting from modern monetary theory it is possible to show (see Chapter 1) how the banking nature of money compels us to distinguish between money and its content. Without repeating the whole analysis, let us simply remember that, as monetary intermediaries, banks only create a numerical form, an a-dimensional vehicle whose real charge is provided by the productive system. Even though it is carried out through a medium of no intrinsic value, the payment of wages endows money with positive purchasing power because it determines its association with real output. Theory teaches us first, therefore, that vehicular and real money must be kept clearly distinct.

The association between money and output elicits an income defined as a bank deposit. And it is precisely because it is formed as a bank deposit that income is immediately lent. Through the financial intermediation of banks, savings are instantaneously lent by their initial owners and spent by their borrowers. Income is thus transformed into capital, and it is as such that money can play the role of bridge between present and future so clearly enunciated by Keynes.

The category of capital has therefore to be added to those of money and income. The logical distinction between these three categories represents the second precept of monetary theory. Although the final expenditure of income implies its destruction, the existence of capital shows how part of income is destroyed *in advance*, so that those who benefit from the bank loan can spend today their income of tomorrow, while those who save today can spend their present income tomorrow. It is thanks to capital that this substitution is possible, which is why it is essential to keep it distinct from the other two monetary categories, whose task is to convey payments (money) and to define money purchasing power (income).

To summarise, the analysis of bank money and of its functions as a standard of measure, a means of payment and a reserve of value leads us logically to distinguish between:

1 vehicular money, a mere instrument of circulation present in every payment and defined by its instantaneous flow to and from its issuing bank;
2 real money or income, which defines the real content of payments and entails the financial intermediation of banks;
3 capital, which provides a bridge between present and future production through income saving.

Empty money as the result of the lack of distinction between money, income and capital

Once it has been proved that money must not be identified either with income or capital, it is necessary to establish (a) whether the actual monetary structure conforms to this distinction, and (b) what the consequences would be if it did not comply with it.

The criterion to be followed in order to answer to the first question is simple. Since money is of a banking and accounting nature, the practical implementation of the threefold distinction (between money, income and capital) requires banks to match each monetary category with a specific book-keeping entry. The observation of bank accounting shows, however, that payments are entered together in an indiscriminate fashion, so monetary and financial intermediations are mixed up and it is not always possible to distinguish capital from income. There is, therefore, a distortion between the logical requirements of a monetary system adequate to the nature of money and the techno-structural characteristics of the present system.

As for the consequences of the disconnection between theory and practice, it is important to observe that they are revealed by a pathological alteration of the money/output relationship. In order to corroborate this claim, let us examine two cases in which payments take place in contradiction with the threefold nature of money.

The clearest example of the violation of monetary laws is shown by the covering of public deficit through money creation. If the Central Bank of a given country issued its currency in order to re-establish the State budget we would witness an inflationary increase in the quantity of money, implying a pathological variation of the internal relationship between money and output. If, consistently with the laws on money, the public deficit were covered financially (that is, through income raising), everything would work according to logic. This is what happens in the countries which, having adopted a monetary system sufficiently rigorous to avoid financial intermediation being replaced by money creation, comply with the principles already expounded by David Ricardo since 1823.

> If Government wanted money, it should be obliged to raise it in the legitimate way; by taxing the people; by the issue and sale of exchequer bills, by funded loans, or by borrowing from any of the numerous banks which might exist in the country; but in no case should it be allowed to borrow from those, who have the power of creating money.
>
> (Ricardo 1951–5, vol. IV: 283)

Unfortunately, in some countries the inadequacy of the banking structure allows for advances to be replaced by money creation, the expenditure of income by that of empty money, thus bringing about an inflationary reduction in their national currency purchasing power.

The second example is slightly more complicated and refers to the opposite substitution, of an income to a simple nominal money. As we know, it is the payment of wages which, by associating it with production, transforms (nominal) money into income. Logically, this payment is carried out without having to use up any positive income. If, even though they are paid using purely vehicular money with no intrinsic value, wages define a positive asset, it is because they give rise to new income. The empty money out of which wages are paid is filled up with real output, and it is the drawing-right money acquires over this output that defines its purchasing power (Figure 3.6).

Yet, what would happen if, instead of being paid using empty money, wages were paid using a positive income (full money)? Let us suppose that a firm makes a profit of 20 units and decides to invest it in new production. The bank in which the profit is deposited carries out the payment of wages crediting workers and debiting the firm. Wages are thus paid out of profit, that is out of income that the firm obtains gratuitously through the selling of products. But then the payment of wages becomes a twofold operation: monetisation of new production on one side, and expenditure of pre-

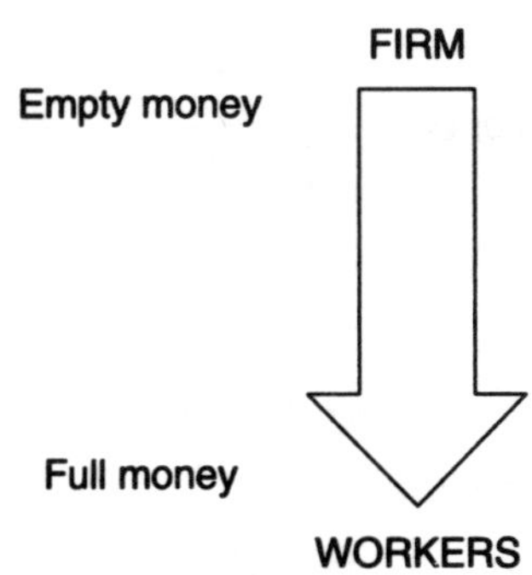

Figure 3.6

existent income on the other. Now, the final expenditure of a given income defines the purchase of an equivalent product. Included in the payment of wages, the expenditure of profit implies therefore the purchase of an equivalent amount of commodities produced by workers, whose salary is correspondingly emptied of its real content. By paying its workers out of profit, the firm removes the product from wages, so that the money workers are credited with is literally *empty* (Figure 3.7).

Let us try to avoid some possible misunderstandings. The anomaly that leads to empty money is not directly linked either to profit investment by firms, or to the intervention of banks taking place in this context. No one doubts that the development of our economic systems is based on saving (and profit is a form of collective saving) and on its investment in the process of production. Capital formation proceeds from this investment, and it would be absurd to require its suppression claiming that it is a cause of inflation. Effectively, it is not the investment of profit that has to be questioned, but the way its entry is recorded in bank accounting.

Though reasserting the fundamental neutrality of bank behaviour, we have to acknowledge that empty money would never take the place of income if the structure of accounting were consistent with the nature of money. It is the monetary system as a whole, therefore, that is responsible for the imbalances which the lack of distinction between money, income and capital leads to.

Referring the reader interested in a thorough study of inflation to the work of Bernard Schmitt (1984), let us very concisely show how to avoid wages being paid out of positive income (every time a firm invests part of its profit in a new process of production) by spreading the operations over three bank departments.

The three departments, I, II, III, are, respectively, the monetary, financial and capital department. The initial payment of wages requires the intervention of the first two departments: the monetary one since every

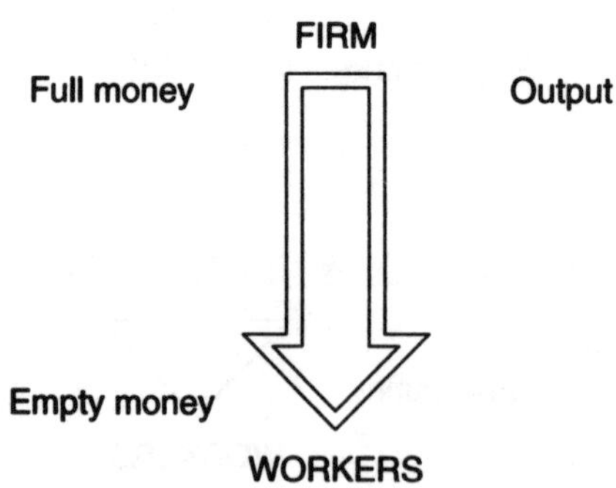

Figure 3.7

transaction must be carried out by money, and the financial one since the payment of wages gives rise to new income (Table 3.6). Since monetary and financial intermediations always go together, by the end of the week (or of any other period of time corresponding to the length of the firm's process of production) what is saved by income holders is lent to the firm, whose debt is transformed from a monetary one into a financial one. In this case, entries would be recorded in the balance sheets of the two departments as follows (Table 3.7). Cancellation of first department entries derives from the purely vehicular nature of money, whose 'mark' is financial and can be found in the bank's second department.

Supposing the firm makes a profit of y units, its entry has to be recorded in the third department since, being a form of saving (irreversible saving), profit defines the first type of capital (capital-time). Let us enter this transaction in the bank balance sheets, taking into account that, in order to get a profit, a firm's receipts must be greater than its costs of production and, therefore, the expenditure of other income holders (whose credit with the bank is matched by an equivalent new product P_2) has to be added to that of the first (Table 3.8). As is shown by the entry of department III,

Table 3.6

Department I			
Liabilities			*Assets*
II	x	Firm	x

Department II			
Liabilities			*Assets*
Workers	x	I	x

Table 3.7

Department I			
Liabilities			*Assets*
II	x	Firm	x
Firm	x	II	x

Department II			
Liabilities			*Assets*
Workers	x	I	x
I	x	Firm	x

Table 3.8

Department II			
Liabilities			*Assets*
Workers	x	Firm	x
IH	y	Output	y
Firm	x	Workers + IH	x + y
III	y		

Department III			
Liabilities			*Assets*
Firm	y	II	y

firm F owns capital by means of which it will be able to exert a drawing right over future output. Now, because of the three departments, the investment of profit no longer entails its destruction. The entry defining a new payment of wages (which we suppose to be equal to y units) is recorded in the first two departments, and leaves the profit accumulated by F and deposited with the third department unaltered (Table 3.9). Being paid in conformity with money's threefold distinction, wages define an income equivalent to the new products. Deposited with the bank's financial department, this income defines a purchasing power to the benefit of income holders. Money paid to workers is thus *full* money.

The positive deposit of workers corresponds to the negative deposit of F, whose debt towards the second department is equivalent to its credit with the third. Yet, the distinction between the three departments is sufficient to avoid the mechanical compensation of these two entries. The purchase of capital goods by F does not take place through the investment of profit on the labour market, thus avoiding part of the money paid out as wages being emptied of its real content.

As our book-entry reading shows, after the new payment of wages workers own y units of full money with which they can purchase the goods previously 'saved', leaving the handling of capital goods deriving from the investment of profit to F. The entry between second and third department defines the amount of this investment and prevents profit being spent within the payment of wages (Table 3.10).

The analysis of the monetary anomalies leading to inflation has to be further improved. The elements of reflection proposed in this chapter must be seen as a first step towards the understanding of a phenomenon erroneously ascribed to economic behaviour and whose eradication calls

Table 3.9

Department I				*Department II*			
Liabilities			*Assets*	*Liabilities*			*Assets*
II	y	Firm	y	Workers	y	I	y
Firm	y	II	y	I	y	Firm	y

Table 3.10

Department II				*Department III*			
Liabilities			*Assets*	*Liabilities*			*Assets*
III	y	Output	y	Firm	y	II	y
Workers	y	Firm	y				

for an adjustment in the structure of payments consistent with the banking (and incorporeal) nature of money.

Keeping within the limits of an introductory analysis, let us in the next chapter examine some controversial aspects of the debate concerning deflation and unemployment.

4

INTERNATIONAL MONETARY DISEQUILIBRIA: DEFLATION

UNEMPLOYMENT: REAL OR MONETARY CAUSES?

Widely studied by economists of different schools of thought, the problem of unemployment is of a particular theoretical relevance in Keynes's work. It is to the great English economist that the first contribution to its clarification is due. By introducing a neat distinction between 'voluntary' and 'involuntary' unemployment, Keynes provides the elements necessary for the understanding of the monetary aspect of a disequilibrium that, before him, economists had tendentially considered of a real nature. Let us reconsider the essential points of his analysis in order to show how, as in the case of inflation, unemployment cannot be ascribed either to economic behaviour or to the socio-productive structures of our economic systems.

The distinction between 'voluntary' and 'involuntary' unemployment

Right from the first pages of his *General Theory* (1936/1973) Keynes clearly distinguishes 'involuntary' from frictional and 'voluntary' unemployment, imputing the last two anomalies to real causes and the first one to essentially monetary factors. Let us first consider the behaviour of economic agents. The degree of uncertainty implicit in the previsions on which a firm's productive choices are based is a cause for miscalculations which, in particular cases, can lead to temporary unemployment. The same applies when firms undertake important restructuring of their productive machinery or when insufficient information or reduced worker mobility leads unemployed people to turn down jobs offered by firms.

> For example, unemployment due to a temporary want of balance between the relative quantities of specialised resources as a result of miscalculation or intermittent demand; or to time-lags consequent on unforeseen changes; or to the fact that the change-over from one employment to another cannot be effected without a certain delay, so

> that there will always exist in a non-static society a proportion of resources unemployed 'between jobs'.
>
> (Keynes 1936/1973: 6)

Defined as 'frictional' by Keynes, unemployment resulting from the flaws in decision-taking, from unforeseen events or from technological progress is not too worrying since it is essentially of a transitory nature. Firms can remedy miscalculated forecasts, and technological progress can contribute to the creation of new jobs, allowing, simultaneously, the freeing of people from part of the mechanical and repetitive activities to which they are still enslaved. If productive capacities in our economic systems could be entirely exploited, the problem of technical unemployment would be a marginal one and its cause would also provide its solution, through a reduction in working time that would become a real possibility because of the great increase in productivity. Today this is plain utopia, it is true, but why? What hinders the development of our productive forces? What restrains growth in economic welfare? Fundamentally, the answer is only one: unemployment. But of what unemployment should we be talking about, given that frictional unemployment is in a certain sense functional to economic development?

Keynes's analysis goes on to exclude another kind of unemployment, which he calls 'voluntary'.

> In addition to 'frictional' unemployment, the postulate is also compatible with 'voluntary' unemployment due to the refusal or inability of a unit of labour, as a result of legislation or social practices or of combination for collective bargaining or of slow response to change or of mere human obstinacy, to accept a reward corresponding to the value of the product attributable to its marginal productivity.
>
> (1936/1973: 6)

Due to social and legal structures that limit free competition, this unemployment seems to be of a monetary kind. However, the determinant element is not monetary wages but the relationship between wages and the marginal productivity of labour. This means that the cause of unemployment is still linked to real (physical productivity) and 'behavioural' factors (decisions taken by trade unions and employer organisations). Besides, since the relationship between wages and prices modifies the amount of profits, disagreement between trade unions and firms can lead to a variation in the distribution of income, but not to the indefinite protraction of unemployment. As such, a decrease in profits is not enough to induce firms to give up or seriously reduce production. Other factors have to play their role in order for the situation to deteriorate, but none of them pertains to the structural-behavioural category defining frictional and 'voluntary' unemployment.

Pushing the Keynesian classification a bit further, we could say that both categories of unemployment analysed so far can be defined as 'voluntary' in the sense that they are fundamentally implicit in the collective choice of an economic system based on capitalisation and, therefore, on agricultural and industrial production and on exchange. By choosing a system like this, we implicitly accept all its consequences, including those related to the implementation of technology and innovations. If to this we add the fact that even the decisions related to legislative structures forming the social and juridical framework of economic activity are part of this choice, then there can be no doubt about the 'voluntary' origin of frictional unemployment.

Taking into account what has just been said it is now easy to define 'by elimination' *involuntary* unemployment.

> Clearly we do not mean by 'involuntary' unemployment the mere existence of an unexhausted capacity to work. An eight-hour day does not constitute unemployment because it is not beyond human capacity to work ten hours. Nor should we regard as 'involuntary' unemployment the withdrawal of their labour by a body of workers because they do not choose to work for less than a certain real reward. Furthermore, it will be convenient to exclude 'frictional' unemployment from our definition of 'involuntary' unemployment.
> (1936/1973: 15)

Not being due either to collective or to individual choices, 'involuntary' unemployment is caused by the superposition of purely monetary factors on real ones. As has been clearly perceived by Keynes, it is at the level of effective demand that the problem arises. 'We have shown that when effective demand is deficient there is under-employment of labour in the sense that there are men unemployed who should be willing to work at less than the existing real wage' (1936/1973: 289). Hence, deflation is the main cause of 'involuntary' unemployment, and it is only by explaining the genesis of deflation that it is possible to provide a thorough definition of pathological unemployment and of the suitable instruments needed to eradicate it.

On the basis of Keynes's distinction it is easy to observe how what is nowadays called structural unemployment effectively pertains to the category of 'voluntary' unemployment. Changes introduced by firms at the productive level, whether they are due to technological progress, to international competition or to the attempt to evade norms or taxes judged too penalising, are not new. The capitalist economic system adopted by almost every country is founded on competition (more or less free) and on technological progress; it is obvious, therefore, that in choosing the one we also choose the others. To the extent that the development of the system entails a growth in unemployment it is perfectly licit to consider the latter as 'voluntary'. Yet, precisely because it is inherent to the evolution of the capitalist system it is difficult to maintain that the high level of unemployment the majority of industrialised countries are suffering from today (1995) is essentially of a structural kind. If unemployment were largely due to technological progress, it should be balanced (at least partially) by an increase in our standard of living. Yet, it is more and more evident that we are living through a phase of relative worsening of our living standard. If increasing productivity and reducing costs do not lead to a growth in production and to a higher standard of living (which would compensate for the growth of unemployment and provide the conditions for the implementation of new strategies capable of limiting its social costs), it is because real and structural factors are subjected to restrictions of a completely different kind. Analogously, if competition goes together with a generalised impoverishment it is because firms are faced with a deflationary decrease in demand (if this were not the case it would be impossible to understand why the production of the less competitive firm could not be taken over by the others, thus assuring its quantitative and qualitative growth).

Even the analysis of structural unemployment stresses the importance of monetary factors and, more precisely, of this pathological disequilibrium known as 'deflation'. Before trying to explain its origin, let us show in a few lines how 'involuntary' unemployment is a symptom of the disconnection between real and monetary sectors characterising our economic systems.

The dichotomy between the monetary and real world

The need to integrate monetary variables into 'real' models is a common feature of the economic theories preceding Keynes's work. Yet neither the attempts of classical nor those of neoclassical economists were successful, mainly because both theories were worked out in real terms (working time, physical quantities of goods) and money (itself material) was still essentially considered to be an object. Beyond the great intuitions of their leading representatives (Smith, Ricardo, Marx, Walras), these two schools of thought were unable to elaborate an a-dimensional conception of money which would have allowed them to transform the real world into a monetary one.

In this respect Keynes's contribution is crucial. Reversing the logical order of the analysis, he worked out his theory starting from money; and he never gave up his project of reaching a unitary formulation of the laws governing our economic systems. Taking over his teachings in the light of the most recent developments in banking, it is possible today to build up a theory of production and circulation which is entirely monetary. The material conception of money is definitively replaced by its purely numerical conception, the only one consistent with money's role of means (instrument) of exchange and payment. Thus, by taking bank money as its point of departure, modern economic theory is immediately conceived under a monetary form. Besides, since the emission of money defines a positive creation only if it is related to the payment of wages (see Chapter 1), production is immediately determined as the process giving money its real content. The two aspects, monetary and real, are therefore so deeply associated as to be defined a unique 'object'.

Let us now pass from theoretical to empirical evidence. If the actual system of payments complied with the vehicular nature of money, the labour market would be influenced only by real factors. The orderly working of the system of payments allows money to play its role of intermediary in a totally neutral way. Under these conditions if workers are partially unemployed it is because their decisions and those of firms do not coincide. Unemployment is purely 'voluntary' and can be eliminated or reduced either through an agreement between the two parties, an improvement of the techniques of prevision, management and information, or a whole series of measures aimed at improving the productive application of technological progress.

It is almost superfluous to stress how the high levels of unemployment, from which both underdeveloped and industrialised countries are suffering, are totally incomprehensible if we take into consideration only the 'real' aspect of the problem. The unsatisfied needs of the world population are so great as to grant full employment for many worker generations to come, and the exhaustion of resources, although it is a possibility to be taken into serious consideration, can efficaciously be forestalled by technological progress.

If, despite the enormous need for goods and services of every kind, production contracts, the reason has to be looked for at the monetary level. Demand, in fact, is not exerted by need, but by available income. Hence, it is a shortage in demand which causes the contraction of production and the growth in unemployment.

Let us consider for a moment the dichotomous representation of economic reality proposed by the quantitative theory of money. According to monetarism, deflation is defined by the inadequacy of the quantity of money with regard to the quantity of products – inadequacy that can be due either to a decrease in the quantity of money, or to a unilateral increase in the quantity of products (Figure 4.1). Given the fundamental autonomy of the two quantities assumed by monetarism, deflation can result from decisions taken by monetary authorities or by firms (public and private), or by a non-compensatory combination of the two. By modifying the discount rate, for example, the Central Bank of a given country could provoke or support a reduction in the quantity of money, causing a disequilibrium between total demand and total supply similar to that which could take place if firms suddenly increased their supply of goods and services.

An analysis of bank money totally invalidates this dichotomous vision of the economic world. As is shown by the working of our banking systems,

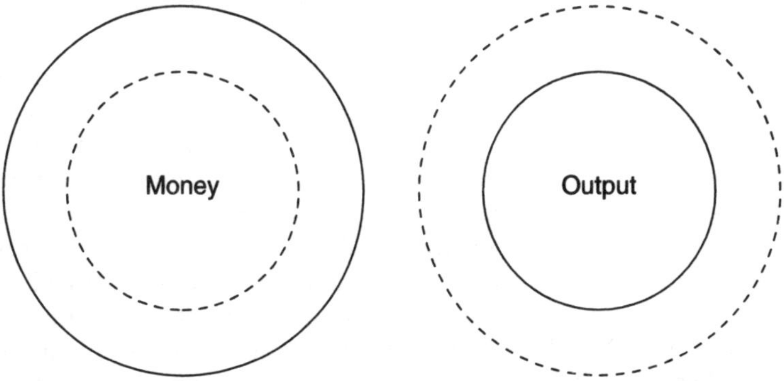

Figure 4.1

money is never issued independently from produced output, and all new output is immediately associated with money. Hence, it is impossible for interest rate policies to have an impact on the supply of money, since it is impossible for (a part of) income to disappear into nothing: bank bookkeeping entries are an irrefutable proof of it. The whole of income is necessarily lent as soon as it is created since its creation defines a bank deposit. On the other hand, the object of every bank deposit is an equivalent output entered on the assets side of bank balance sheets. An increase in total supply due to new production is thus matched by an equivalent increase in demand, i.e. in the money the new output is associated with.

At this point, however, the refusal of the neoclassical dichotomy between real and monetary variables makes it particularly difficult to explain how the system can suffer from a shortage in total demand.

As already pointed out by Keynes, 'involuntary' unemployment results from a reduction in demand which is of a pathological origin. If the increase in production is not matched by an equivalent increase in available income, the positive gap between total supply and total demand leads to a deflationary situation whose consequence on employment is only too well known. Let us try to point out the mechanisms which make it possible for the money–output relationship to be numerically modified.

The insufficiency of demand: a reality requiring a theoretical approach based on the banking conception of money

In this short section we shall attempt to show that Keynes's message becomes meaningful only if it is related to his own conception of money. To maintain that lack of demand is related to hoarding amounts to considering Keynes as a member of the large group of authors who have essentially identified money with a real good, reducing monetary theory to a mere superstructure of the one worked out in real terms.

In textbooks the insufficiency of effective demand is often attributed to the fact that income holders do not spend the totality of their income. Saving is seen, therefore, as a process potentially capable of withdrawing income from the system, reducing expenditure and creating a gap between output and demand that can be filled only through State or monetary authority intervention. Now, saving would withdraw income from expenditure only if money was material and could effectively be hoarded. Such a conception of money, however, lies completely in the past, and it is to Keynes that we owe the merit of having laid the foundations for the elaboration of an analysis where material money is definitively replaced by a purely numerical standard.

Right from the first pages of his *Treatise on Money* (1930/1973), Keynes makes bank money the core of his theory, clearly distinguishing between the vehicular function of money, the simple numerical form of output, and its purchasing power, the object of its holders' (income holders') bank deposits. 'Thus money of account is the term in which units of purchasing power are *expressed*. Money is the form in which units of purchasing power are *held*' (Keynes 1930/1973: 49). Starting from this 'banking' conception of money, the great Cambridge economist reaches the conclusion that everything that is earned in the production of goods and services is spent on the purchase of these same products.

> I propose, therefore, to break away from the traditional method of setting out from the total quantity of money irrespective of the purpose on which it is employed, and to start instead – for reasons which will become clear as we proceed – with the flow of the community's earnings or money income and with its twofold division (1) into the parts which have been *earned* by the production of consumption goods and of investment goods respectively, and (2) into the parts which are *expended* on consumption goods and on savings respectively.
>
> (1930/1973: 121)

From the previous quotation it is clear that, according to Keynes, saving must not be identified with hoarding since the income saved is necessarily *spent*. Acting as a financial intermediary, the banking system transfers to some what has been deposited by others, allowing those who benefit from the loan to spend their future income (by using savers' actual income) in advance. Keynes's teachings go even further. Not only is the income saved by some consumers spent by others, but even their global savings are spent, in particular on the purchase of investment goods. Whether global savings correspond to firm profits or not, they define the amount of income necessary and sufficient to cover the costs of production of the goods and services which are not bought by consumers. By lending to firms, who spend the money on purchasing these same goods and services, banks guarantee the equality of total supply and total demand.

Let us reason from the firm's point of view. Its decisions relative to production are influenced by its sales forecasting, which is elaborated by taking into account the role of intermediation played by banks. Thus, consumer savings do not create any particular difficulty to firms, unless they are the mark of serious flaws in sales forecasting. If consumers were no longer interested in buying goods produced by a given firm, it is obvious that this particular firm would suffer a loss and would have to stop or modify its production. This does not mean, however, that the ensuing unemployment would be caused by an insufficiency of effective demand. The income saved by consumers would be lent to the firm to cover its costs, and would define a forced purchase of unsold (and unsaleable) goods which would immediately restore equilibrium between total demand and total supply.

Let us reaffirm that the insufficiency of demand cannot be due to consumer or producer behaviour. For example, if consumers resolved to save an increased portion of their income, their decision would have no repercussion on the relationship between money and output. Formed as a bank deposit, the income saved remains entirely available and continues to exert a demand on its corresponding real output. Analogously, it is impossible for a firm to increase its production without contributing, through the payment of wages, to an equivalent increase in demand. If, nevertheless, there is an income shortage, it is because the decisions of firms are not matched by book-keeping entries which are perfectly neutral from the monetary point of view.

The attempt to explain unemployment by referring to economic agents' behaviour is part of those analyses which assume the problem of monetary neutrality to have been solved even before having been effectively stated. If money is identified with a particular good (for example gold) or with a net asset, its neutrality cannot be taken for granted. Yet, this seems to be an essential element in supporting the claim that consumer saving leads to a shortage in demand. Likewise, monetary neutrality is essential if it is to be maintained that unemployment is determined by real factors such as technological productive restructuring. In both cases unemployment is attributed to 'voluntary' causes that make it a practically unavoidable disequilibrium.

Unemployment that is assumed to be due to consumer behaviour is said to pertain to the category of *conjunctural* unemployment. On the basis of an analysis as linear and simple as it is widespread, it is maintained that a policy of high interest rates carried out by monetary authorities has a negative impact on the level of employment since it pushes entrepreneurs to reduce their investment (because of the high cost of money), and consumers to increase their savings. Besides the fact that this argument is in conflict with the argument, often supported by the same experts, according to which recession is due to a lack of savings and should be fought with a policy encouraging people to spend more (increasing interest rates?), the analysis of bank money clearly shows that demand is totally independent of income holder behaviour. Without repeating ourselves too much, it is important to stress that hoarding is a concept of the past, which is not supported by banking practice. To imagine that a person can decrease the sum of bank deposits without spending (and, therefore, without exerting an equivalent demand), amounts to assuming, erroneously, that money identifies itself with the material supports used to represent it. A person can hide bank notes in his garden or under his mattress, of course, but this does not mean that, by doing so, he destroys the book-keeping entries corresponding to the bank notes withdrawn from circulation and recorded by banks at the moment of their emission. Bank notes can be hoarded, money cannot. To hoard bank notes amounts to taking claims on bank deposits out of circulation, but not the bank deposits themselves. Since demand is determined on the basis of the income available to finance it, it immediately follows that it is fundamentally independent from the behaviour of those who deposit their income within the banking system.

Finally, since deflation is not related to consumer behaviour, the fight against unemployment does not require the adoption of measures suitable for modifying it. What we have called, following Keynes, 'involuntary' unemployment has its origins in the same anomalies of the structure of payments that we have identified as the cause of inflation. In order to verify this, let us first show that these two disequilibria are only apparently complementary. The strict relationship existing between them will then be clearer, showing unemployment to be a consequence of inflation.

FROM INFLATION TO DEFLATION

The apparent complementarity of the two disequilibria

The attempt to establish a complementary relationship between inflation and unemployment, verifying the hypothesis of their trade-off, is well known in the economic literature. The English economist A.W.H. Phillips is famous for having maintained that the two phenomena are inversely correlated, corroborating his thesis with a series of statistical observations concerning Great Britain over the period 1861–1957. Other economists followed his example and, before Friedman's critical intervention (which denies the existence of an inverse correlation only in the long term), several authors believed that unemployment could be reduced only at the price of an increase in inflation and that, vice versa, a reduction in inflation would necessarily have implied a growth in unemployment.

However, both the conclusions and the method followed by Phillips are highly questionable. The fact that he has used statistics referring to variations in nominal wages in order to evaluate inflation, and that he has not introduced any distinction between 'voluntary' and 'involuntary' unemployment, considerably reduces the significance of his analysis; not to mention the fact that simple statistical information cannot lead to the formulation of any theory not already a priori present in the researcher's mind. In reality, the presumed discovery of Phillips is an arbitrary matching of statistical information, an illusory attempt to use it in order to validate a hypothesis which is erroneously taken for granted. Facts have since proved the groundlessness of his analysis. As we all know, our economic systems are subject to *stagflation*, a situation in which inflation coexists with deflation.

All the experts are unanimous in observing that, since it defines an excess of total demand, inflation should characterise the upward phases of the economy, while downward phases, caused by an insufficiency of total demand, should be marked by a negative increase in prices. Unfortunately, facts do not corroborate this theoretical vision. Indifferent to the principle of the excluded middle, the actual economic situation proves the coexistence of inflation and deflation, systematically disavowing the forecasts of all those who persist in believing that the two disequilibria are necessarily complementary.

Even according to the analysis derived from Keynes's arguments, stagflation is determined by the simultaneous presence of inflation and deflation. Now, it is interesting to observe how the explanation of this phenomenon is not only out of reach of mainstream (neoclassical) economics, but also of 'Keynesian' economics. In the income determination model (resulting from an interpretation in terms of equilibrium of the original version formulated in Keynes's *General Theory* (1936/1973)), total supply can only be greater, equal or smaller than total demand, without it ever being possible to verify the simultaneous presence of an excess in demand (inflation) and of a shortage in demand (deflation).

To claim that complementarity is verified only at the global level whereas at the sectorial level only one disequilibrium or the other can prevail, is no satisfactory answer. If inflation and deflation could prevail in some sectors so as to be balanced globally, unemployment would be almost completely imputed to the insufficient mobility, professional and social, of workers, and the sectorial increase in prices would be largely compensated for by reductions taking place in the other sectors and by reductions in costs due to technological progress. Once again facts disprove the theoretical hypothesis. Apart from particular conjunctural situations applying to this or that sector, disequilibria are of a global nature. Moreover, if demand and supply could be effectively balanced, a given economy could never suffer, simultaneously, from an excess and a shortage in total demand; one of the two would prevail over the other and it would be impossible to justify the concomitant presence of deflation and inflation. Let us refer to the simple Keynesian model of income determination and to its famous diagram (Figure 4.2). On the axis of abscissa we have inscribed the values of three hypothetical national incomes, Y_e, Y_f and Y_1, corresponding to the income of equilibrium, of full employment and of period p_1. Given the values of consumption, C, and investment, I, it is easy to show that income Y_1 defines a situation in which total demand (C + I) is greater than total supply (represented in the diagram by the bisector). Now, since Y_f is greater than Y_1, current production does not allow for the full employment of the working population and seems to be characterised, therefore, by the simultaneous presence of inflation (D>S) and unemployment ($Y_1<Y_f$). We should not forget, however, that the unemployment hitting our economic systems is mainly of the 'involuntary' kind, i.e. it is essentially due to a shortage in total demand. The Keynesian model our example refers to can, at most, represent a situation in which inflation coexists with 'voluntary' unemployment (frictional or structural), but it is totally incapable of providing a suitable representation of reality. The coexistence of inflation and deflation would imply the determination of an income which would have to be inscribed to the right and to the left of the point of equilibrium simultaneously, a possibility that lies outside the logical capabilities of a model based on the strict distinction of the two disequilibria.

As we have already observed, the understanding of facts requires the elaboration of a theory allowing for the principle of the excluded middle to be disposed of, and which develops out of a totally dematerialised conception of money.

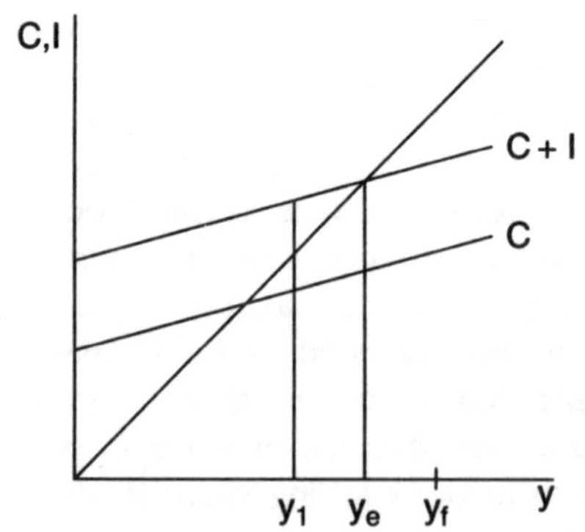

Figure 4.2

The problem of reconciling theory with facts is still open. From the analysis we have been carrying out we know that inflation results from the defective adjustment of our monetary structures to the laws of money. What we have to prove now is that inflation carries with it the seeds of deflation.

Capital over-accumulation as an 'effect' of inflation and a 'cause' of deflation

As recent research in the monetary field has shown, empty money generated through the investment of profit coincides with the formation of *fixed capital*, i.e. of the capital which, definitively lost for income holders, defines the property of 'de-personified' firms. Amortisation of this capital leads to an inflationary profit entailing the partial duplication of production. The working population is thus partially employed in producing consumption and amortisation goods on one side, and capital goods on the other. Besides the normal process of capital accumulation, inflation leads to an over-accumulation through the investment of the inflationary profit derived from the amortisation of fixed capital.

Let us reaffirm that this over-accumulation is the effect of a pathological process whose origin cannot be ascribed to economic agent behaviour. It is neither the existence of profit, nor its investment, which should be blamed, but the way in which entries related to these operations are recorded. The anomaly lies with a mechanism inappropriate to the nature of money, with a monetary structure still defective, and not with the decision to invest profit more or less productively.

If transactions took place consistently with the threefold distinction of money, income and capital, the system would suffer from no pathology of monetary order. In particular, capital would be owned entirely by 'personified' firms (shareholders and entitled persons), that is, by the whole of income holders. The formation of empty money would definitively be avoided and, with it, that of the pathological capital generated by the process of over-accumulation (i.e. by the investment of inflationary profit).

The pathological capital accumulated during the upward phase of our economic systems has obviously contributed to increasing our material welfare, thus limiting the negative effects of inflation. If our standard of living has increased despite the presence of inflation, it is thanks to capital which is technologically more and more productive and has brought about a reduction in the unit costs of production. Yet we should not forget that capital, the pathological as well as the 'sound', has to be remunerated. With the growth in capital we can also observe an increase in the income which has to be sacrificed to achieve it. The greatest difficulties arise from the moment pathological capital has reached such a dimension as to make its remuneration problematic.

In the actual phase of development of highly industrialised countries, for example, the remuneration of pathological capital has a negative impact on the level of employment. The current trend towards a decrease in the rate of profit relative to the rate of interest leads firms to vary the productive investment of their profits. Instead of financing the production of new machinery, they could invest them in the production of new consumption goods. By so doing, however, they would provoke an increase in the supply of these goods without matching it with an equivalent increase in demand. The subsequent deflation would force them to reduce their activity, and, with it, the level of employment.

Let us try to clarify the main lines of the argument. The analysis of inflation has shown that, given the actual monetary structure, the investment of profit inevitably leads to empty money. Without any real content, empty money is literally a *non-income*, and since an effective demand can only be exerted by a positive income, it is clear that a 'non-income' defines an additional demand of an inflationary kind.

In the case we are examining, along with the inflationary expenditure of an empty money, we observe a disequilibrium between supply and demand caused by a new production of consumption goods. By paying wages out of its profit, the firm buys the product of workers, reducing to zero the real content of their monetary remuneration. The consumption goods produced instead of capital goods are therefore purchased by the firm on the labour market (and not, as logic requires, on the commodity market), and workers are paid with empty money. The deflationary effect would not be present if firms invested their profits in the production of capital goods, since the capital goods purchased through the payment of wages would be fixed within the same firms. On the contrary, consumption goods are bound to be offered on the market. The supply of consumption goods grows to the extent that firms invest their inflationary profits in this production. Even though they have already been purchased on the labour market (giving rise to a destruction of income), consumption goods are offered again on the commodity market. Yet this new supply is not matched by a corresponding new income which could finance an equivalent demand: the gap cannot be filled and deflation manifests itself in all its dramatic force.

Let us analyse again the operations which lead to inflation and to deflation. In a first period, firms make a profit which they invest in the following period by financing a production of capital goods which are formed as fixed capital. As we have observed, this capital is never in the power of income holders since it is definitively fixed within 'de-personified' firms. Hence, from the moment workers are employed in the production of amortisation goods designed to 'nourish' this capital, the income corresponding to this production will necessarily be spent in the purchase of commodities produced by other firms. Let us call A_1 the firms producing amortisation goods meant for fixed capital and A_2 those producing consumption and capital goods, and let us suppose the production of A_1 to be equal to 100 units of money. Considering that the income generated by the production of A_1 can logically be spent only on A_2, it can be induced that the A_2 firms make a profit of 100 which nourishes part of their manufacturing expenses. In the wages paid out by A_2 is thus included an expenditure of income corresponding to the investment of profit. Besides normally paying wages out of a nominal money (which we suppose to be equal to 100), the A_2 firms remunerate their workers in a transaction implying the final purchase of output. This means that, out of the 300 wage units globally paid by A_1 and A_2, 100 units are emptied of their real content. Effectively, by spending the totality of their income IH (income holders) obtain a product whose value is only 200 (of which 100 correspond to the costs of production of consumption goods and 100 to those of the capital goods 'incorporated' in the production of these same consumption goods). Financed out of empty money, excess demand defines an inflationary gap equivalent to the profit made by the whole set of firms because of the amortisation of fixed capital.

At the book-keeping level, these operations would give rise to the following entries (Table 4.1). The balancing of book-keeping entries, perfectly in line with the rules of double entry book-keeping, should not lead us astray. As has been shown before, part of the income of IH is empty. The demand, equal to 300 units, exerted by IH on the commodity market is thus matched by a supply equal to 200 units, the remaining 100 units having already been purchased by A_2 on the labour market.

Let us suppose the development of our productive system to have reached a critical stage, where the reduction in the profit margin makes the remuneration of accumulated capital particularly difficult. In this case, as we have seen, the A_2 firms could decide to invest their profit in the production of consumption goods. If this happened, book-keeping entries would be similar to those of Table 4.1. Production and purchase of consumption, amortisation, and capital goods (which in this case would have the form of consumption goods) would take place according to the modalities that we have already analysed and, after having given rise to an

Table 4.1

Banking system			
Liabilities			*Assets*
IH	100	A_1	100
A_2	100	IH	100
IH	200	A_2	200
A_2	200	IH	200
A	100	A_1	100

inflationary increase in prices, the entries recorded on the banking system balance sheet would cancel out.

Independently of the form they can take on, capital goods produced through the investment of profit are purchased by A_2 firms on the labour market. However, if the form under which they are produced is that of consumption goods, firms will try to sell them, together with the other consumption goods, on the commodity market. A global supply of 400 units will then be faced with a global demand of only 300 units. The selling, by A_2, of the consumption goods additionally produced will thus generate a deflationary gap that will successively lead to a shrinkage in production.

All the income created by the production of consumption, capital and amortisation goods having being destroyed in the purchase of these same goods carried out by IH and A_2, the further supply of consumption goods is bound to remain unsatisfied (unless prices are proportionally decreased, which is a clear symptom of the fact that the whole production is faced with a shortage in demand). Thus, to the inflationary process related to the amortisation of fixed capital we have to add the deflationary process caused by the selling of capital goods produced under the form of consumption goods. Both disequilibria are essentially due to the lack of distinction between money, income and capital that we have already reported. In the absence of this distinction, the investment of profit leads to the formation of fixed capital, whose amortisation causes an emission of empty money (inflation) and whose remuneration, beyond a certain level of over-accumulation, entails an over-production of consumption goods (deflation). The over-accumulation of capital generated by inflation creates the conditions for a deflationary increase in supply. In this sense the over-accumulation of capital is a determinant factor for the unification of the two disequilibria, whose simultaneity thus acquires a precise significance, not only in the empirical description of facts, but also in their theoretical understanding.

The shortage in total demand is not due to conjunctural reasons, nor can it be attributed to the behaviour of one or more categories of economic agents. It is not because consumers resolve to increase their propensity to save that the income available for the financing of demand decreases, and it is not because monetary authorities follow a particular interest rate policy that firms' investments are reduced. As so clearly stated by Keynes, firms take their production decisions on the basis of the principle of effective demand. This means that the level of production is determined by the effective possibilities of selling the products. If it is implemented only by some countries, a policy of high interest rates can penalise their firms, inducing them to transfer part of their production abroad. But it is also true that, in the absence of a true deflationary process, firms would go on expanding, globally, their production; this is not to mention that, besides increasing the supply of savings (which drives interest rates down), the high cost of money could also be matched by a growth in self-financing or by an inflow of foreign capital. Consequently, in the same way that a policy of high interest rates is not a cause of deflation, a reduction of these same rates is not enough to re-launch a process of growth seriously hampered by a shortage in total demand. By lowering interest rates the profit margin increases, encouraging a new process of capital accumulation (investment of profit in the production of new capital goods), but, at the same time, the remuneration of accumulated capital is reduced, which pushes firms to invest in the consumption goods sector (reproducing the conditions for the renewing of deflation).

A theory is real only if it is confirmed by facts, if it allows us to 'read' the reality and not some hypothetical, abstract reconstruction of it. Then, if the reading of facts shows that they are inconsistent with logical reality, this means only that they are subjected to anomalous pressures which modify their evolution. Stagflation is the result of some of these pathological conditionings our monetary system is currently submitted to. To determine its genesis means having to explain the mechanisms through which it manifests itself. Theory can take on this task only on condition that it can first explain the laws on which the orderly (logical) working of the system has to be founded.

These laws are those which lead to the vehicular definition of money and to the determination of income and capital. Our brief analysis should have provided the reader with some of the elements necessary to look into the nature of this threefold distinction and to investigate the consequences deriving from the adoption of a monetary practice inconsistent with this distinction. Let us conclude this chapter by observing that the fight against stagflation will no longer amount to a mere heap of partially contradictory measures adopted on the basis of a fundamentally powerless pragmatism, only when it is definitively clarified that its origin is not 'real' and 'behavioural' but 'structurally monetary'.

5

THE MONETARY INTERVENTION OF CENTRAL BANKS

INTERNAL MONETARY POLICY

In order to preserve internal monetary stability, Central Banks have for a long time tried to control the quantity of money. Yet the attempt to control the quantity of money directly has proved to be inappropriate with regard to Central Banks' real capacity for intervention. Monetary authorities have since chosen to switch to controlling the monetary base, with the aim of indirectly regulating the growth in the quantity of money through a series of interventions which could influence the determination of its other components. The monetary base is made up of circulating bank notes and bankers' balances at the Central Bank. Control of the monetary base takes place either through the issuing of bank notes or through the granting of credit and the buying and selling of assets from the banking and non-banking sectors. For example, by modifying the giro account deposits of secondary banks, the Swiss National Bank tries to determine the evolution of demand deposits and publicly held currency (that is, of what is usually called the quantity of money *strictu sensu*: M_1).

Obviously, the critical considerations introduced in the previous chapters also apply here. Since they cannot create net assets out of nothing, Central Banks can only provide the economy with a currency with a simple numerical form; it is production that will then assume the task of giving money a value associating it with real output. As we already know, the emission of bank notes complies perfectly with this requirement. Taking the place of secondary bank deposits, bank notes are one of the possible representations of a drawing right over national output which originated from the association of money with the process of production. Thus, Central Banks create no income *ex nihilo*, but simply allow those who already own it to hold it in a different form from those supplied by secondary banks.

Seigniorage is also avoided when Central Banks discount assets coming directly from public or private sectors, even though, rigorously speaking, this kind of intervention does not pertain to those carried out by a Central Bank as such. Discounting of financial bonds or commodity papers handed over by private or public firms places the Central Bank at the same level as secondary banks. It is well known that every Central Bank plays the dual role of national Bank and bank of the State, and that when it acts on behalf of the State (one of the numerous elements making up an economic system) it does not differentiate from private banks. When granting loans to firms (to State-owned enterprises, for example) the Central Bank acts as any other private bank and it has to comply with the same rules governing their activity. Discounting of commodity papers and financial bonds corresponds to the simple advance of an income generated by production. In both cases the currency issued by the Central Bank is associated with new output, and the growth in the quantity of money is perfectly balanced by an increase in production.

Only the lack of distinction between the two roles played by Central Banks could lead to a plethoric emission of money. If a Central Bank made use of its right to print money in order to back blank granted credits, this would amount to resuming seigniorage, a practice that would inevitably cause an inflationary increase in the quantity of money. Central Banks can purchase bonds (or other assets) only if they do not finance the operation through money creation. For the purchase to be effective it is necessary for there to be a positive expenditure of income, and not that of an empty numerical form. Hence, buying and selling operations have to be carried out either on behalf of income holders, or from funds earned by Central Banks thanks to their activity of intermediation. Respect for the rule according to which 'nobody can pay by becoming indebted' does not allow for exceptions, and since central money is nothing other than the acknowledgement of debt spontaneously issued by the national Bank, it is obvious that Central Banks themselves have to comply with this rule on pain of provoking an inflationary disequilibrium.

Strictly speaking, the control of the quantity of money should be understood as the control of the rigorous application of this fundamental principle, according to which, let us repeat, nobody can get rid of his debt by issuing his own IOU. By avoiding the mixing up of money and income, Central Banks would allow for economic transactions to be monetised without creating any inflationary gap between demand and supply. It is also true, however, that inflation is generated by the working of mechanisms whose control is generally out of the reach of Central Banks. Thus their intervention seems to be necessary to restore the lost equilibrium by reducing the gap between quantity of money and product. However, monetary base policy does not seem to be up to the task. Because of the level of official interference on the workings of the banking system that this kind of control implies, it would be extremely difficult and dangerous to rely on monetary base policy to limit the growth of money supply. It seems therefore licit to maintain, with Dow and Saville, that 'in face of a continuing tendency for the aggregates to grow more rapidly than the authorities regard as desirable, base control would not be an effective way of controlling the growth of broad money, nor for long a practicable way of controlling the growth of narrow money' (Dow and Saville 1990: 152). Among the other principal instruments of intervention, which Central Banks make use of, are: foreign exchange dealings (purchase, sale, swaps), open-market operations (sale and purchase of bonds), control over exports and imports of capital, interest rate policies, and the levy and release of minimum reserves. Let us briefly analyse each of them.

Foreign exchange transactions

Foreign exchange transactions include both the buying and selling of foreign currencies, and the carrying out of swaps. Central Bank reserves are mainly made up of key-currencies (prevalently the American dollar), and the buying and selling of these currencies is related to international speculation. Central Bank intervention on the foreign exchange market can be aimed at controlling these speculative fluctuations (as we shall soon see when analysing the problems related to foreign monetary policy), or at stabilising internal monetary equilibrium.

As far as the effect of buying and selling of foreign exchange on the relationship between money and output is concerned, it is useful to distinguish the operations related to foreign currencies obtained through net commercial exports from those in which the flows of foreign currencies correspond to financial movements.

Foreign exchange transactions relative to financial flows do not modify the relationship between money and output

Let us consider the case in which a Central Bank intervenes by buying the foreign currencies (dollars for example) which secondary banks (SB) are credited with on behalf of their clients (C), who are exporters of bonds to the rest of the world. Supposing that private banks monetise x units of national output, we would have the following entries (Table 5.1). Let us now suppose that the credit in national currency granted to clients C is used to finance equivalent purchases on the domestic commodity market (if it were used to finance commercial imports it would imply the purchase of an amount of dollars equal to that transferred to the Central Bank) (Table 5.2). Secondary banks have a debt of x units with income holders, on which they have to pay interest, and a credit of the same amount, only part of which bears interest. Since the credit in central money is not remunerated, secondary banks avoid every risk of loss by giving it back to the Central Bank in exchange for monetary (dollars for example) or financial assets

Table 5.1

SB

Liabilities		*Assets*	
IH	x	Firms (output)	x
Clients	y	Dollars	y
Dollars	y	CB	y
IH	x	Firms	x
Clients	y	CB	y

CB

Liabilities		*Assets*	
SB	y	Dollars	y

Table 5.2

SB

Liabilities		*Assets*	
IH	x	Firms (output)	x
C	y	CB	y
Firms	y	C	y
IH	x	Firms	x – y
		CB	y

CB

Liabilities		*Assets*	
SB	y	Dollars	y

(Table 5.3). After compensation, we can still observe a positive gap between the amount of available income, x units, and that of saleable output, x – y units (Table 5.4). However, the fact that part of the income deposited by IH is backed by an equivalent amount in bonds (obtained either directly from the Central Bank or through the investment of dollars on the Euromarket), shows that the emission to the benefit of clients C corresponds to an advance. What is spent by C is the income saved by IH through their purchase of the bonds sold by secondary banks. Once this transfer (advanced, let us say it again, by the emission of SB in favour of C) has been taken into account, the situation is that of a perfect equilibrium between money and output (Table 5.5). We would have arrived at this result immediately if, as very often happens in practice, the dollars initially entered on the assets side of secondary banks had been fiduciary, purchased on behalf of income holders and placed on the Euromarket.

Whether the purchase of bonds or foreign currencies takes place directly, or through the Central Bank, the conclusion is fundamentally the same: the purchase of foreign exchange derived from the selling of financial securities leaves the relationship between money and output unaltered, further

Table 5.3

SB

Liabilities		*Assets*	
IH	x	Firms	x − y
		CB	y
CB	y	Dollars or equivalent assets	y

CB

Liabilities		*Assets*	
SB	y	Dollars	y
Dollars or equivalent assets	y	SB	y

Table 5.4

SB

Liabilities		*Assets*	
IH	x	Firms (output)	x − y
		Bonds	y

Table 5.5

SB

Liabilities		*Assets*	
IH	x	Firms	x − y
Bonds (IH)	y	Bonds	y
		IH	y
IH	x − y	Firms	x − y

evidence of the fact that Central Banks do not play the role of lender of last resort. As far as Central Bank selling of foreign exchange is concerned, its effect on the quantity of money has to be related to that caused by the initial formation of the Bank's foreign exchange reserves. From what we have just seen it follows that the selling of currencies obtained through the export of financial bonds confirms the advance of national income which has taken place at the moment of their purchase. The return of foreign currencies to secondary banks cancels the debt position of the Central Bank (and, therefore, its initial emission of central money) and restores, definitively, the initial relationship between money and output. Foreign currencies are immediately placed on the foreign exchange market by secondary banks, which, by selling their positions to C, obtain from IH the sum initially transferred to the sellers of bonds.

Finally, the buying and selling of foreign currencies amounts here to an open-market operation in foreign exchange which can only temporarily modify the supply of money, and which can mainly be used by Central Banks in order to help secondary banks to solve their liquidity problems

Foreign exchange transactions are monetarily neutral when they are concerned with net commercial exports

According to the analysis we have been developing, Central Bank intervention on the internal foreign exchange market does not alter the relationship between national money and national output, whose global stability (over the two periods) is provided by the mechanisms related to interbank payment rules. There is a case, however, in which the present monetary structure seems inadequate and, therefore, a cause of cumulative inflationary disequilibria: the growth of official reserves through Central Bank purchasing of the currencies obtained in exchange for net commercial exports.

As we shall observe again in the second part of this work, the increase in official foreign exchange reserves is financed by the Central Bank through an emission of central money. Does this mean perhaps that the purchase by monetary authorities of the foreign currencies earned through net commercial exports, while corroborating the phenomenon of duplication expounded by Jacques Rueff (see Chapter 7), leads to an over-emission of national money? If this were the case, the objective of increasing the quantity of money would be achieved at the price of an internal disequilibrium that would cancel its positive effects.

Let us represent the book-keeping entries relative to the monetisation of internal production by secondary banks (1), the payment of net commercial exports (2), and the increase in official reserves carried out by the Central Bank (3) (Table 5.6). Like the ones in the previous case (Table 5.2), book-keeping entries in Table 5.6 differ from them essentially to the extent that, in the case of net commercial exports, the payment of firms does not entail any transfer of income. Contrary to what happens when the monetisation of foreign currencies is related to a net export of bonds, secondary banks do not grant any new loans, and therefore do not have to balance entry (2) with an equivalent entry in national currency. In our example, the counterpart of the emission of national money is represented by dollars, a situation which defines a growth in the quantity of money. The emission is then definitively confirmed by Central Bank intervention, which sanctions the inclusion of the foreign exchange earned through net commercial exports within official reserves. A growth in official reserves cannot be obtained through the selling of national bonds, since the increased indebtedness due to the export of bonds and the new credits corresponding to the increase in reserves cancel each other out. In our case, the creation

Table 5.6

SB

	Liabilities		*Assets*	
(1)	IH	x	Firms (output)	x
(2)	Firms	y	Dollars	y
(3)	Dollars	y	CB	y
	IH	x	Firms (output)	x – y
			CB	y

CB

Liabilities		*Assets*	
SB	y	Dollars	y

of money carried out by the Central Bank defines an effective increase in the quantity of money available in the system.

Unlike what happens in the case analysed above (p. 96), foreign currencies obtained through net commercial exports are here definitively incorporated into official reserves and the Central Bank emission of money cannot be reduced to a simple advance. The final payment of exporting firms entails the destruction of an equivalent amount of national income. However, the income which is destroyed is not that of IH, whose amount is not modified by the internal monetisation, carried out by the Central Bank, of the income of external origin paid by foreign importers. Net commercial exports provide the country with a foreign income whose monetisation does not imply a reduction in the internal quantity of money. If exporting firms were paid by domestic income holders (albeit through CB advance), net exports would bring no gain to the country, and the lack of monetary creation would lead to a loss rather than to monetary equilibrium. The case that we are examining requires both that the Central Bank emission is not reduced to an advance, and that the money created against foreign exchange remains available within the system.

Another argument leads to the same result. By increasing total demand, net exports provoke an equivalent increase in the price of the goods still available on the market (Table 5.7). If the transfer of dollars into official reserves took place at the expense of internal income holders, that is, if the monetisation of foreign exchange corresponded to an advance, national output, whose price is equal to x units of national money, could not be sold entirely. Income holders would only dispose of x – y units in order to purchase an output valued at x units. Instead of encouraging the stability of internal equilibrium between money and output, the absence of the Central Bank emission would lead to a decrease in the income necessary for the purchase of current output (deflation). Fortunately this does not happen. The incorporation of foreign currencies into official reserves

Table 5.7

Banking system			
Liabilities			*Assets*
Income holders	x	Firms	x
Firms	y	Dollars	y
Income holders	x	Firms (output) *price x*	x – y
		Dollars	y

entails a creation of national money which avoids the danger of deflation and whose 'inflationary' effects are not cumulative in time. A monetary creation of x units, for example, is enough to build up a 'circulating fund' which, period after period, will allow for the monetisation of the successive earnings due to net commercial exports. A new intervention by the Central Bank in order to increase the quantity of money would be necessary only if net commercial exports were greater than the amount of this fund. Increments notwithstanding, the initial 'circulating fund' is automatically reconstituted and is perfectly able to avoid deflation without causing any cumulative process of expansion in the quantity of national money.

We still have to analyse what would happen if, in a second moment, the Central Bank sold part of its foreign exchange reserves on the internal market. First of all it has to be observed that while Central Banks currently make use of their foreign exchange in order to maintain the external stability of their national currencies, they do not intervene in order to provide funds to the exchange market. However, even if they did intervene, it is clear that the purchase of foreign currencies by secondary banks could take place only on the request of their clients, i.e. only if their clients wanted to spend part of their income on importing goods, services or bonds. In any case the selling of foreign currencies by the Central Bank would lead to a transfer of income carried out by secondary banks on behalf of their clients, a transfer which would take the form of a debit with the Central Bank, whose account would be credited with a deposit with the secondary banks (Table 5.8). As we can see from Table 5.8, the income available within the whole banking system does not decrease because of the selling of foreign currencies carried out by the Central Bank. Deposits with secondary banks remain equal to x units of national currency, their amount being totally indifferent to the fact that part of it can be owned by the Central Bank. Finally, even in this hypothetical case operations are fundamentally neutral and do not alter the relationship between money and output determined by national production.

Table 5.8

Secondary Bank			
Liabilities			*Assets*
Income holders	x	Firms	x
Central Bank	z	Foreign curr.	z
Foreign curr.	z	Income holders	z
Income holders	x – z	Firms	x
Central Bank	z		

Exceptionally the inflow of foreign capital can cause a temporary inflationary increase in the quantity of money

Analysis developed in the section on foreign exchange transactions (p. 96) shows that capital inflow is not a cause of inflation since it does not modify the internal relationship between money and output. National money issued in correspondence with the inflow of foreign exchange plays a purely vehicular function, transferring income from their initial holders to the sellers of bonds on the international market. Neither the intermediation of secondary banks, nor that of the Central Bank, leads to an increase in the quantity of money. Yet it is possible that, because of the repeated inflow of huge amounts of capital, banks are not able to fully play their role of financial intermediation. If in a given country (as happened in Switzerland in the 1970s) inflows of dollars were repeatedly higher than the amount residents were willing to invest in dollars or in bonds, their purchase by the Central Bank would bring forth an excessive growth in the quantity of money, which would force the Bank to intervene in order to avoid the consolidation of the surplus leading to an undesirable growth in internal prices.

In this case, the selling of currencies different from the dollar could be a useful instrument in fighting the increase in the quantity of money. By selling foreign currencies on the internal market, the Central Bank could re-absorb part of the national money created because of the plethoric inflow of dollars, thus contributing to the restoring of internal equilibrium. Let us note, moreover, that the use of swaps increases the efficacy of these interventions, limiting the period of their implementation and avoiding their unwelcome repercussions on exchange rates.

Among various examples which could well illustrate this kind of intervention let us refer to the one carried out by the National Swiss Bank which, in 1961, 'agreed with the Bank of England a line of gold–sterling swaps up to the amount of £40 million. The National Bank obtained sterling protected from exchange rate risks which it exchanged against francs (on the basis of swaps with private banks). The national Bank was thus able to reabsorb part of the liquidity created because of the inflow of foreign currencies related to the monetary crisis' (BNS 1981: 177).

Efficaciously tackled by Central Bank intervention, the growth in the quantity of money due to extraordinary inflows of foreign currency is not a source of serious worries, so much so that the growth is of a conjunctural nature and can be re-absorbed in a later period, thus avoiding persistent pressure on prices. The case of net commercial exports notwithstanding, the inflationary gaps originating from foreign currency flows are absolutely exceptional and never cumulative.

Let us conclude by observing that, apart from the increase in official reserves, foreign exchange transactions are fundamentally neutral as far as monetary stability is concerned. The Central Bank intervention does not definitively modify the money–output relationship and can be considered as a further instrument of financial intermediation whose utility is related to practical (liquidity requirements) and conjunctural needs. This is confirmed by the fact that foreign exchange transactions carried out by Central Banks take the form of swaps, i.e. of forward exchange deals allowing for the control of both exchange rates, and quantity of money growth. 'In this way the National Bank can prevent the final creation of liquidity, avoiding at the same time disturbances due to purely technical factors taking place on exchange markets' (BNS 1981: 175). In the same text we also read that:

> Since the beginning of free exchange rate fluctuation in 1973, swaps became the major instrument used for the control of bank liquidities, and for the drain of the liquidity created through foreign exchange interventions. Since in Switzerland there is an important market for the dollar, these transactions can practically take place in every moment without changing the exchange rate of the dollar too much. Moreover, swaps are an instrument that can be used in a flexible way as to amount, length and conditions, and they are convenient for the issuing bank since they allow it to determine the impact of the transactions on bank liquidities in advance.
>
> (BNS 1981: 177)

Open-market operations

Another intervention carried out by Central Banks is related to the so called open-market policy. It consists in the buying and selling of bonds operated on the monetary market and through which Central Banks attempt to preserve the internal equilibrium between money and current output. Transactions can concern different kinds of bonds, mainly State acknowledgements of debt (governmental securities), which can have various terms of redemption. Apart from a few exceptions, like Switzerland (where the monetary market is not very large), the buying and selling of short-term bonds is one of the instruments generally more used for quick and precise interventions.

If Central Banks own a substantial securities portfolio, their interventions on the monetary market can lead to variations in the quantity of money. In particular, they can drain money through the selling of short-term securities and they can increase the quantity of money through their buying of government securities. Now, it is important to note that the effects of these interventions are only temporary, and that they do not substantially modify the relationship between money and output. Let us consider the selling of government securities to the public. The result of this operation is a transfer of income to Central Banks. Yet does this necessarily lead to a correspondent decrease in the quantity of money? Being of a banking nature, money is always deposited within the banking system, and its transfer from one economic agent to another does not reduce its amount. The fact that what was previously owned by the public is presently owned by Central Banks is not enough to bring us to the conclusion that the supply of money is correspondingly reduced. In reality, the entire amount of money is still available and it is only if the deposits obtained by Central Banks (through their selling of bonds) are frozen that their intervention has a temporary effect on prices. The efficacy of this kind of open-market policy is thus essentially dependent on the ability shown by monetary authorities to sterilise part of the available income in periods of overheating, and not on their effective power in getting rid of inflation. The selling of (short-term) bonds by Central Banks has only a limited effect in time, and it would be illusory to believe that inflation can be eradicated through the repeated sterilisation of a part of national income.

Even though it is carried out through monetary creation, Central Banks' purchase of government securities does not give rise to any particular difficulty since it corresponds to the re-purchase of the same bonds previously sold to the public. 'An open-market purchase essentially replaces an interest-earning asset on the books of banks (either a government security or a loan to some entity holding a government security) with a claim on the central bank – that is, with a reserve balance that has been created for the purpose of acquiring the security' (Axilrod and Wallich 1992: 75). The money created by Central Banks to finance their re-purchase of government securites takes the place of the money spent by the public for its initial purchase of these same securities, so that, on the whole, the supply of money remains unchanged.

As far as the buying of privately issued bonds is concerned we must first observe that Central Banks can carry this out either through the creation of central money or through the selling of their own bonds. In the latter case, the amount of national money brought in by Central Banks is the same as that spent by the public in order to buy central bonds. The inflow of central money is compensated by an equivalent outflow of secondary money, and the whole operation has no effect on monetary equilibrium. Things are apparently quite different in the first case, where the purchase of bonds is financed through money creation. Instead of selling public bonds to get the income required for the purchase of privately issued bonds, Central Banks create money as their own acknowledgement of debt. If this corresponded to a final transaction, i.e. if Central Banks did effectively take undue advantage of their particular function, the principle governing monetary payments would not be complied with, and a mere promise (Central Banks' IOUs) would be given in exchange for a net asset (bonds). In this hypothetical case Central Banks would pay for their purchases with empty money, causing an inflationary increase in the quantity of money. The intervention of Central Banks on the monetary market would thus lead to the absurd result of trying to cure a disequilibrium (deflation) by creating another (inflation). Fortunately this is not what happens (at least in the great majority of industrialised countries). The creation of money by Central Banks has to be seen within the broader context of bank intermediations. Financed through money creation, the purchase of bonds loses its inflationary character as soon as it is integrated in the set of monetary and financial intermediations carried out by the banking system. What seemed to be an inflationary emission of empty money is reduced to a simple advance of income which does not fundamentally modify the relationship between money and output.

The sale of bonds allows for the transfer of income from buyers to sellers. Acting as simple intermediaries, banks foster the redistribution of income without modifying its amount. Yet, precisely because they play this role of intermediation very efficiently, banks can also allow the public to spend today tomorrow's income. Open-market interventions by Central Banks are part of these transactions. If it is carried out on behalf of the public, their purchase of bonds never leads to inflation. Indeed, the central money created today will be replaced (and destroyed) tomorrow by the money Central Banks drain through their open-market sales. On the whole, what is thrown into the system by Central Banks is equal to what is derived from it. The initial over-emission is covered by an equivalent flow of income from the public to Central Banks so that even their purchase of privately issued bonds is effectively financed by the economy and not by empty money. It is by advancing the future income of the public that Central Banks can carry out their net purchases of bonds without having to worry about the inflationary nature of their intervention.

Finally, open-market operations can be a useful instrument in temporarily modifying the distribution of income as well as the supply of money without altering the relationship between money and output. That is to say that, if open-market transactions are properly carried out (i.e. without causing an inflationary emission of empty money), they cannot represent a true remedy against either inflation or deflation. Since both these disequilibria entail a variation in the money–output relationship, they can be fought only by means of instruments capable of restoring the correct level of this relationship. It would be illusory, therefore, to believe that inflation can be definitively neutralised through the sale of bonds operated by Central Banks. In fact, the reduction in the quantity of money would take place only if Central Banks sterilised the income derived from the public, an operation which would have an impact on the effects of inflation but not on its cause. Hence, despite the onerous intervention of monetary authorities, inflation would go on provoking successive increases in the quantity of money which would call for further interventions of draining and strerilisation, in an endless spiral which would soon become too burdensome for the State.

The control over capital imports and exports

Besides their foreign exchange interventions, Central Banks have often endeavoured to control capital exports and imports in order to avoid internal disequilibria. Though still in force, the measures adopted are much less severe nowadays, and it is widely acknowledged that their efficacy is extremely limited. Despite the scarce success of this kind of intervention, it is useful to analyse the influence exerted by capital flows over internal monetary equilibrium.

If we consider the symptomatic case of Switzerland, it is immediately evident that the important inflow of foreign capital which has characterised various periods of international monetary instability has always been seen as the cause of a dangerous growth in the quantity of money. To slow down this inflow of capital, the Swiss government and secondary banks did not hesitate to agree upon the non-payment of interest on foreign deposits (they went as far as to impose negative interest on these deposits) and decided to forbid investment in Swiss assets and bonds. The measures adopted by the Swiss National Bank were intended to discourage the inflow of capital, since it was believed that, once deposited in the Swiss banking system, they would lead to inflation. As we can see from the following quotation, the increase in the quantity of money was considered the unavoidable consequence of the growth in the monetary base. 'Within a system of fixed exchange rates, the huge inflows of funds forced the bank of emission to purchase foreign currencies, thus determining an undesired expansion of the monetary base' (BNS 1981: 234). The situation did not improve with the passage to flexible exchange rates, since the inflow of foreign currencies pushed the Swiss franc upward, forcing monetary authorities to intervene to protect export industries.

As for secondary banks, it must be observed that the deposit of foreign currencies does not increase their capacity of emission, which is limited by the amount deposited in national money with each of them. Thus, if it is true that secondary banks create national money on the basis of foreign currencies (invested, for example, in the purchase of national bonds), it is also true that this creation has to be covered by an equivalent deposit in national currency and that each bank is bound to respect the equilibrium between credits and deposits. This rule, as we have already stressed, is sufficient to avoid secondary banks' activity being a cause of serious and cumulative inflation.

Even if the same rule does not apply to Central Banks, their purchase of foreign currencies is also not a cause of inflationary growth in the quantity of money. In spite of this, in some particular cases (like the Swiss one we have just been recalling) the repeated purchase of foreign currencies by the Central Bank can lead to a constantly renewed modification of the relationship between money and output. In the presence of a strong and persistent inflow of foreign currencies, secondary banks are effectively forced to refer to central authorities to be able to meet their new obligations incurred in national money. The Central Bank monetary emission maintains or even increases the inflationary gap between total demand and total supply, a situation that entirely justifies the adoption of measures capable of discouraging the excessive investment of foreign capital.

If, under the present system of international payments, the constant inflow of foreign capital can be considered dangerous for the safeguarding of monetary equilibrium, the same cannot be said about capital exports, since money is always deposited within the banking system from which it is issued. Dollars are all deposited within the American banking system, sterling within the English, lira within the Italian, Swiss francs within the Swiss, and so on. It is true that the successive international deposits of the dollars paid by the United States give rise to their duplication, but this does not modify the fact that, by crediting foreign banks with dollars, American banks do not decrease the amount of dollars deposited within the United States. What changes is the owner of the deposit, not its banking seat (Table 5.9). From these simple entries it can be verified that the transfer of dollars carried out by an American bank on behalf of its client A decreases the deposit of A with his bank (or, which is the same, increases the debt of A to the bank), not the deposit in dollars which, always equal to \$x, is now

Table 5.9

American Bank				*Foreign Bank*			
Liabilities			*Assets*	*Liabilities*			*Assets*
Foreign bank	\$ x	Client A	\$ x	Client A equivalent in NM of	\$ x	American bank	\$ x

owned by the foreign bank to which A has transferred his credit in order to transform it into foreign currency.

The fact that capital exports are not the cause of a deflationary disequilibrium does not restrain banks from efficaciously using stabilising measures related to this kind of operation. In the Swiss case, for example, the obligation to convert national money into foreign currency when Swiss francs are exported, allows the National Bank to partially reabsorb the money issued in connection with the inflow of foreign capital, and contributes to preserving the stability of internal purchasing power.

Interest rate control

In order to provide the system with relative price stability, monetary authorities try to avoid important variations in interest rates or else try to restore equilibrium through their variation when monetary disequilibria are manifest. During periods of inflation, for example, the Central Bank can support a rise in interest rates in the hope of reducing the growth of money by increasing its cost, whereas during periods of recession it can promote a fall in interest rates with the aim of encouraging economic recovery by increasing the quantity of money. A lot has already been said about the efficacy of these interventions and about their social and economic consequences. Leaving out considerations of a social order (also because they are heavily dependent on economic considerations), let us briefly analyse the arguments put forth to justify Central Bank interventions on interest rates.

Let us first observe that, as far as interest rate determination is concerned, the more important the role played by Central Banks the greater is their influence over expectations. 'Because market expectations about future interest rates are diffuse and weakly held, the central bank, though only a small market participant, is able to exert great influence over expected rates of interest – and thus also over current rates' (Dow and Saville 1990: x). Once it has been noted that interest rates are not simply determined by the interplay of saving and investment, but that they depend heavily on monetary market forecasts, it becomes evident both that they are essentially unstable, and that Central Banks can influence them despite the limited amount of their financial transactions. Having said this, it is now necessary to establish what the impact of interest rate intervention can be, with particular reference to the attempt at controlling the quantity of money.

Let us suppose the existence of an inflationary gap between money and output. By encouraging a rise in interest rates, monetary authorities rely on the principle that the demand for money is inversely proportional to the cost of money and, thus, that the increased cost of bank credits will lead to a reduction in the quantity of money demanded by economic agents. In order to assess the validity of this argument it is useful to distinguish between supply of income and demand for money. As far as available income is concerned it is obvious that interest rates cannot modify its amount. An increase in interest rates will probably reduce the demand for loans and create difficulties for debtors, but the income already created will remain unaltered. Since, according to the principle regulating bank deposits, savings are necessarily lent, the increase in interest rates cannot diminish either the quantity of income or the demand financed by it. However, by making debts with the banking system more expensive, the rise in interest rates can discourage entrepreneurs and lead to a decrease in the demand for money. Firms could be pushed into reducing their production, which would entail a reduction in the quantity of money, it is true, but without it being matched by a corresponding decrease in inflation since, besides the contraction in the quantity of money, there would also be an equivalent reduction in current output.

The inflationary situation that seems to justify interest rate intervention is determined by a disequilibrium between money and output. This means that output is 'carried' by a quantity of money greater than the one it was initially associated with. By increasing interest rates, however, it is impossible both to reduce this quantity, and to modify the amount of output. Relative to the inflationary gap existing at the moment of intervention by monetary authorities, the impact of a rise in interest rates is therefore nil. Nevertheless, this measure could prove perfectly up to its task if it contributed to curbing future inflation. Now, as we have seen, the increase in monetary costs can induce firms to reduce production, an effect that would make interest rate intervention doubtful. To fight inflation with recession is absurd, especially considering that production in itself can certainly not be a cause of inflation. This is also true as far as the monetisation of output is concerned. If money were issued only to be associated with produced goods and services, there would be no inflationary gap and no need to intervene in order to reduce the quantity of money.

It is true that money is also issued to allow for the purchase of current output. Yet this emission refers to a process of intermediation between income holders and output sellers which leaves the equilibrium unchanged. The money thus issued by banks simply carries a pre-existent income, without altering the initial relationship between national currency and national output.

Difficulties could arise only if the purchase of output were *definitively* financed by monetary creation. The inflationary creation of money is theoretically possible when the emission of money is meant to finance the *final* purchase of a product; only in this case could the measures intended to restrict the volume of bank credit prove efficacious. However, the reality of facts does not support the thesis imputing the cause of inflation to the activity of banks. In the monetary systems of industrialised countries, interbank control is sufficient to avoid the danger of inflationary emissions.

Within these systems, secondary banks' credit policy is subjected to a budgetary constraint ensuring a substantial equilibrium between money and output, so that Central Bank intervention on interest rates can be meaningful only if it aims at controlling the social distribution of income. Moreover, if we think of the fact that a rise in interest rates makes foreign investment more attractive, thus favouring the inflow of capital, we become aware of how difficult it is to intervene efficaciously on the market by modifying the 'cost of money'.

Having said this, it is necessary to add that interest rate interventions can have a provisory positive effect on the decisions related to the investment of inflationary profit (see Chapter 4). As will be remembered, in the actual monetary system the accumulation of pathological capital (generated by the amortisation of fixed capital) tendentially leads to a fall in the margin of profit and to a consequent increase in the risk of recession due to the necessity to invest inflationary benefits profitably. In the long term the fall of this margin has a determinant impact on the level of employment, and the adoption of apt measures to oppose it would help to limit its negative effects. By increasing the gap between rate of profit and rate of interest, monetary authorities' intervention would make the productive investment of the profit due to fixed capital amortisation attractive again, and would lead to a temporary slow down in the rate of unemployment. Yet, in addition to what has already been said in Chapter 4, it must be noted that the new production would increase the over-accumulation of capital, nullifying the result reached through decreasing interest rates. Hence, the Central Bank would have to intervene again on interest rates in order to widen the margin between the rate of profit and the rate of interest. Its intervention, however, would have a negative effect on capital over-accumulation and the profit margins related to it, thus making a new intervention necessary, and so on in a spiral which would rapidly bring to zero the efficacy of interest rates policy.

Let us conclude by observing that, even according to a more traditional approach, the intervention of the Central Bank over interest rates has no relevant effect on the money supply. 'The conclusion would seem to be that central bank rate is likely to be more or less completely ineffective as an instrument for controlling the rate of growth of broad money' (Dow and Saville 1990: 139).

Minimum reserve requirements

The variation of levies charged on secondary banks by central monetary authorities is a measure which has proven almost useless and which has been generally put aside. If we are discussing it here it is not in order to dispute this matter of fact, but to try to establish to what extent the system of obligatory reserves is compatible with the banking nature of money.

According to present monetary norms, secondary banks must hold part of their deposits with the Central Bank. In Great Britain banks 'have agreed to hold a fixed proportion of their liabilities as a deposit with the Bank of England [whose] purpose is not operational but to provide the Bank with an income' (Dow and Saville 1990: 128), while 'for operational purposes, the banks hold balances at the Bank of England over and above this amount' (1990: 129). The relevance of these liquidity reserves (of which minimum reserves are usually part) lies essentially in the protection of creditors. Besides this all important function (which is necessary to protect the public against the risks inherent to banks' financial activities), it seems that, through the so-called multiplier of credit, minimum reserve requirements can influence the quantity of money determination. It is thus pertinent to ask if the granting of credit must be limited through this or other mechanisms of control (the power to call on secondary banks to make Special Deposits at the Bank of England) intended to restrict the growth in the quantity of money.

Credit multiplier theory states that, on the basis of initial deposits, secondary banks can grant credits according to a decreasing progression whose magnitude depends on the percentage of deposits which have to be recorded with the Central Bank. If we suppose, for example, that the initial deposit is of 1,000 units and that obligatory reserves are equal to 20 per cent, 800 of these 1,000 units can be lent by the bank in which they are deposited; in their turn, if they are deposited with another bank the 800 units give rise to another credit of 640, and so on until the initial deposit is entirely disposed of (that is, until the sum of the units deposited with the Central Bank is equal to 1,000). By aggregating the various induced incomes we reach the sum of 5,000 units and conclude that the credit multiplier is equal to 5.

The theory we have very briefly summarised enjoys an usurped renown founded on the miraculous idea that the repeated loan of the same deposit can lead to its multiplication. The illusion that new credits can be induced from previous credits simply through a book-keeping mechanism results from an analysis which is too superficial. Let us suppose that a bank lends the totality of its deposits to its clients. If those who benefit from the credit simply deposit it with another bank, it would be absurd to claim that the whole income deposited in the banking system is now equal to twice the amount of the initial one. In reality, income remains unchanged and there is no multiplication whatsoever. Things seem to be totally different when the income lent by the bank is spent by those who get the loan and re-deposited by those who earn it through the sale of their services. Effectively, in this case income is doubled, yet the cause of this apparent multiplication is not the mechanism of deposit but the renewed activity of production. In other words, there are now two deposits since the products (goods and services) are also doubled, and, therefore, the incomes generated by the whole economic system. Even in this case there is no multiplication of deposits.

Let us consider separately the two main activities of private banks. As financial intermediaries, secondary banks only transfer to some clients what has been deposited by others. From savers, income is transferred to consumers, and in this operation banks can at most transfer a sum of income equal to the one which is deposited. To protect themselves against the possible insolvency of debtors, banks can limit the amount and validity of their loans, but it is logically impossible for them to lend more than they get as deposits (or that they will get as deposits, if we include advances in our example) (Figure 5.1). Since they can only transfer what they collect, as financial intermediaries banks are not the source of any income multiplier.

If the idea of multiplication still finds wide consent it is because, besides transferring income, banks create money, and because this last function is erroneously mixed up with the former. If by issuing money banks created income, then it would certainly be necessary to limit their activity (or even abolish it, since there are no reasons for letting banks benefit from creating wealth out of nothing). Yet income creation is not a faculty banks can be endowed with, so that restrictions on the emission of money would be meaningless if money were kept separate from income. If money were issued only in order to be associated with current output (and thus define a new income) or to 'carry' a pre-existent income (with which it would be identified), there would be no need to limit banking activity by introducing an arbitrary constraint between deposits and loans.

Given the difficulty of the argument it is opportune to reconsider the relationship between monetary emission and production. Let us start again from the more general case in which a firm pays its workers drawing on its line of credit. Before being activated, the line of credit does not correspond to any deposit and is not part of the quantity of money. Conveyed by the circular use of an acknowledgement of debt spontaneously issued by a secondary bank, the payment of workers gives rise to the following entries in the bank's balance sheet (Table 5.10). The payment ends up with the indebtedness of firm A towards its bank and of the bank towards A's workers. Production is thus both the source of the debit of A and of the credit of W, this being confirmed by the fact that their object is nothing other than the output of production: workers hold the purchasing power

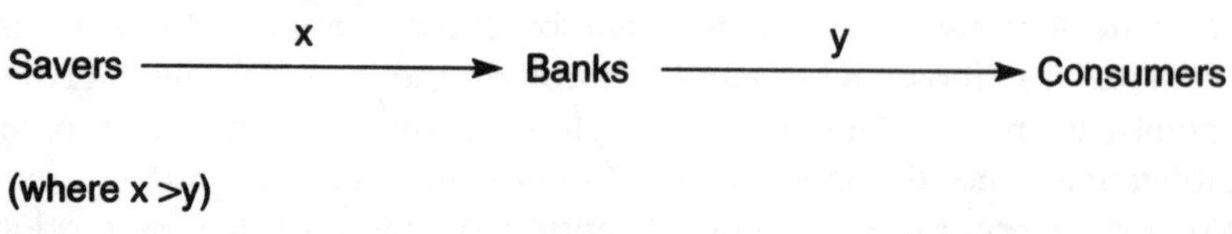

Figure 5.1

Table 5.10

Secondary Bank			
Liabilities			*Assets*
Workers (W)	x	Firm (A)	x

corresponding to the real output temporarily 'deposited' with the bank as the object of the debt incurred by A at the moment wages are paid out on its behalf. In other words, money issued by bank B is associated with production through the payment of wages and the resulting income is deposited in the form of a credit in favour of workers. It is important to observe that the deposit corresponding to W's income does not have its origin in any other previous deposit since the payment of wages does not require the expenditure of any pre-existing income but is carried out through the activation of a line of credit. What is earned by workers is not lost by anyone, thus confirming the fact that productive activity is a source of wealth for the entire economic system.

Credit originated by monetary creation is fundamentally different from ordinary credit. While the latter defines the transfer of a saved income (deposited in the banking system), the former does not entail a transfer but defines the deposit of a new income created by production. If money issued by banks is associated with a new production there is no need to link the monetary creation to already existent deposits since, let us say it again, even though it does not require the presence of any positive income (and, therefore, of any positive deposit), the payment of wages gives rise to a deposit (of income) that entirely covers the debt incurred by the firms on whose behalf banks acknowledge their indebtedness to workers. The conformity of banking emission with the stability of the relationship between money and output is proof that it does not alter the equilibrium of money, whatever the amount of obligatory reserves.

We already know that difficulties and disequilibria arise when the emission takes place without complying with the distinction between money and income, that is, when a newly created money is added to the sum of income without being associated with a new production. The task of monetary authorities would then be that of restructuring the banking system in order to allow for the automatic respect of what we have called the principle of payments, thus securing the only true stability of prices which can effectively be secured: that which derives from the stability of the relationship between money and output.

From what we have seen, the system of interbank control adopted in the highly industrialised countries is up to the task of avoiding secondary banks' activity being a cause of renewed inflationary disequilibria. From this point of view, the greatest dangers come from the measures of monetary policy taken by Central Banks, even if it must be observed that the recent evolution of several techniques of intervention has taken into due consideration the risks of destabilisation inherent in some of these measures. The levy of minimum reserves does not pertain to this category at risk since it does not alter the relationship between money and output. Adopted to safeguard savers' interest, this measure finds its *raison d'être* in the aleatory evolution of our monetary systems, particularly that of our monetary and financial markets. On the other hand, it proves to be useless as an instrument of price stabilisation, for it does not allow for modification of the amount of bank deposits. The growth in secondary bank obligatory reserves does not reduce the amount of their deposits, but that of their explicit loans. This means that part of the deposits will be implicitly lent to firms, which will hold their debt with banks for a longer period of time (since obligatory reserves protract the selling of output) (Table 5.11).

By preventing the explicit loan of y units of income, obligatory deposits with the Central Bank do not allow firm F to obtain the whole amount it owes to the secondary bank, forcing it to pay debit interests until initial income holders, W, decide to spend part y of their deposits (implicitly lent to F, as clearly results from the book-keeping entries recorded in the bank's balance sheet). This situation of protracted indebtedness of the firm has nothing to do with its possibilities of selling the product (which remain unchanged, since the amount of available income is itself unchanged), so that, far from representing an impediment to the inflationary growth in prices, it can eventually lead, if firms decide to transfer to consumers the cost of their indebtedness, to a (non-inflationary) increase in retail prices.

The problem of obligatory reserves must be analysed taking into account the fragility shown in the past by many monetary systems, and the public's desire to safeguard individual and collective interests from possible crises in the credit system. Likewise, measures related to the gold cover of bank notes and to the maintenance of official reserves have to be apprehended

Table 5.11

Secondary Bank

Liabilities			*Assets*
Workers	x	Firm	x
Central bank	y	Bonds (CB)	y
Clients	x – y	Bonds (clients)	x – y
Firm	x – y	Clients	x – y
Workers	x	Firm	y
Central bank	y	Bonds (clients)	x – y
		Bonds (CB)	y

in the same way. Despite appearances to the contrary, central money is issued without regard to the amount of Central Bank reserves, and the value of national currencies has no relationship to the value of the assets accumulated by monetary authorities. It is production, not official reserves, which defines the value of a national currency, and if today it is still necessary to hold large reserves it is because the public is reluctant to give up the material conception of money inherited from the past. However, the whole evolution of the banking system shows that this idea is entirely obsolete, and that money is a purely numerical 'form' whose 'materiality' is represented by the product, its only real 'content'.

Now, the present international monetary system assigns a particular status to some national currencies and allows for the development of speculative capital whose investment exerts unforeseeable destabilising pressures on exchange markets and often requires the massive intervention of monetary authorities. It is at this level that the existence of important official reserves can prove an indispensable instrument in the defence of the stabilisation of money's external value. Official reserves owe their importance to the still defective order of the international monetary system and it is within this context that we have to analyse the measures of external intervention usually adopted by Central Banks.

EXTERNAL MONETARY POLICY

The aim of external monetary policy is essentially that of limiting the variations in exchange rates due to speculative transactions, and whose effect is considered negative for the development of the whole economic system. Exchange rate interventions are usually carried out through the buying and selling of foreign currencies, or through suitable interest rate variations. Let us examine these two possibilities separately.

The buying and selling of foreign exchange

As we shall see in the second part of this work, the constant expansion of Euromarket and speculative transactions have greatly contributed to worsening a situation of instability whose origin goes back beyond the Bretton Woods agreements, but which has acquired the modern characteristic of volatility since the decisions taken on that famous occasion. The internationalisation of the dollar as well as its adoption as money of the world have accelerated the process of destabilisation by creating an ever-increasing gap between 'weak' and 'strong' currencies, but it is since Nixon's decision to suspend convertibility that exchange rate fluctuations have become the rule. In order to limit the instability of their currencies, Central Banks have resorted to buying and selling foreign exchange, initially without any rigorous coordination and then by agreeing upon common interventions better suited (though often insufficient) to influencing market expectations.

The official purchase of foreign currencies is particularly relevant when speculative pressures threaten to modify national currencies' parity, and is part of Central Banks' foreign exchange transactions. Whether it is carried out to increase official reserves, counterbalance national currency appreciation or satisfy secondary banks' demand for liquidity, Central Banks' purchase of foreign exchange always gives rise to a creation of money. Yet, whereas the increase in official reserves takes place through a purchase of foreign currencies on the internal market and corresponds to the monetisation of an external gain (the last example of 'mercantilist' seigniorage), intervention in support of national money's external value has not the same effect since it is carried out on the international monetary market. In the same way as capital flowing in from the rest of the world and invested on the Euromarket does not modify the amount of national currency available within the country, the international purchase of Eurocurrencies has a limited impact on exchange rates and can neither be a cause of inflation nor deflation.

Let us analyse the purchase of foreign exchange carried out by Central Banks in order to increase demand and counterbalance the effect of the rising demand for domestic money exerted on the international market.

Let us consider the case in which the Central Bank of a given country (C) has to intervene to limit the appreciation of its currency relative to the dollar, and let us suppose that the exchange rate between national and American currency is $1 for 1 unit of NM (national money). As shown by the following book-keeping entries, the purchase of dollars carried out directly by the Central Bank on the Euromarket has no influence on the internal monetary situation. The increased demand for dollars causes an exchange rate variation which compensates the variation provoked by the purchase of NM. The effect wears out on the exchange market, without any repercussion for the internal quantity of money, whose amount remains unchanged (Table 5.12). The result would be analogous if the purchase in the Euromarket took place through secondary bank intermediation. Being a simple mediator, secondary banks (SB) would not play any determinant

Table 5.12

CB			
Liabilities			*Assets*
Eurobanks	y NM	Eurobanks	$ y
Eurobanks	$ y	Eurobonds	$ y
Eurobanks	y NM	Eurobonds	$ y

role, thus leaving unaltered the relationship between money and output existing before the intervention on the exchange market (Table 5.13).

The same neutrality is verified when, because of a massive purchase of foreign currencies, the Central Bank intervenes to support its national money's exchange rate by selling part of the previously accumulated foreign currency reserves (Table 5.14). The first entry corresponds to the transfer of monetary claims (equal to y units of national money) to the rest of the world (RW), which becomes the owner of a deposit with the secondary banks of country C. Not even one unit of national money leaves the banking system from which it is issued since the object of the transfer is the claim to the deposit and not money itself. The operation leads to a variation in the exchange rate of NM without causing any inflationary

Table 5.13

SB

Liabilities		*Assets*	
Eurobanks	y NM	Eurobanks	$ y
Eurobanks	$ y	Eurobonds	$ y
Eurobonds (CB)	$ y	CB	y NM
Eurobanks	y NM	CB	y NM

CB

Liabilities		*Assets*	
SB	y NM	Eurobonds (SB)	$ y

Table 5.14

Direct sale

SB

Liabilities		*Assets*	
RW	y NM	Clients	y NM

CB

Liabilities		*Assets*	
Eurobanks	$ y	Eurobanks	y NM

Indirect sale

SB

Liabilities		*Assets*	
RW	y NM	Clients	y NM
CB	y NM	CB	$ y
Eurobanks	$ y	Eurobanks	y NM
Eurobanks	y NM	CB	y NM
RW	y NM	Clients	y NM
Eurobanks	$ y	CB	$ y

CB

Liabilities		*Assets*	
SB	$ y	SB	y NM
SB	y NM	Eurobanks	y NM
SB	$ y	Eurobanks	y NM

change in the internal relationship between money and output. As far as the Central Bank is concerned, whether it takes place directly or through secondary banks' intermediation, its sale of dollars against national money only re-establishes the initial rate of exchange, and must therefore be considered as perfectly neutral from the monetary point of view.

Hence, the buying and selling of foreign exchange on the international market is not the cause of any variation, either inflationary or deflationary, between national money and national output. The only impact of this intervention can be found at the exchange rate level. The sale of foreign currencies determines an excess of supply which, according to the law of supply and demand, leads to a decrease in its external 'price', while the purchase of foreign currencies determines an excess of demand which increases their prices in terms of national money.

The exchange market is a typical example of a market where the prices of the 'objects' that are exchanged are essentially *relative*. Exchange rates are subject to supply and demand, and no 'objective' value intervenes as 'centre of gravity' or as 'equilibrating principle' of their fluctuations. Once transformed into final goods, key-currencies are the object of unilateral exchanges, of supply and demand exerted on the basis of speculative criteria or in the repeated attempt by monetary authorities to stabilise their exchange rate.

Interest rate policy

We have already discussed the way monetary authorities can act on interest rates in the attempt to influence inflows and outflows of capital. In Switzerland, in the early 1970s, the National Bank adopted a system of negative interest rates, together with a whole set of restrictive measures, with the purpose of discouraging the huge inflow of foreign capital and to stop its investment. Other countries have implemented opposite measures in order to attract foreign capital with the aim either of financing public debt or of supporting the exchange rates of their national currencies.

In a system where exchange rates define the relative prices of national currencies, it is certain that every measure capable of modifying the demand for and the supply of these currencies plays a part in the determination of their exchange rates. Interest rates are one of these measures. Due to the working of financial markets, their fluctuation can be affected by Central Banks (for example through a variation in discount rates) with the sole object of devaluating or re-evaluating national currencies

Even in this case, however, the margin for manoeuvre is rather small, both because interest rate policy can have unpleasant internal repercussions, and because transactions taking place on the Euromarket can easily neutralise external pressures, contrasting with the interest of international speculative capital.

Unpredictability of speculative flows is the fundamental cause of erratic fluctuations in exchange rates. Yet, this is not the end of the story; as we shall try to show in the third part of this work, external debt servicing is a further cause of monetary disorder whose repercussions can be particularly evident on the exchange market. Let us conclude this chapter by observing that the origin of international speculative capital cannot be ascribed either to secondary banks' or to Central Banks' behaviour. Once again it is not a matter of stigmatising the actions of one or more economic agents, public or private, but of stressing how some operations are the ineluctable consequence of a system in which money is still erroneously identified with a net asset whose creation is arbitrarily dissociated from the productive process.

Part II

MONEY AND INTERNATIONAL TRANSACTIONS

6

INTERNATIONAL PAYMENTS WITHIN THE GOLD STANDARD AND THE GOLD-EXCHANGE STANDARD

THE SPECIFICITY OF INTERNATIONAL PAYMENTS

From an economy of production to an economy of exchange

The first difference between national and international monetary systems is that the former is concerned with a production economy while the latter is related to a simple economy of exchange. If we take into consideration the whole set of national productions, there is no room left for a hypothetical international output. Multinational production, as the name clearly suggests, takes place in various countries, and not in a true international 'space'. This is confirmed by the fact that a production 'nationality' is not determined by the place where it is carried out, but by the money it is associated with. Petrol extraction in extra-territorial waters is defined on the basis of the money used to cover its costs, and it is therefore part of the national production of the country (or countries) whose money is paid out to the factors of production.

National production is determined monetarily, that is, it is possible to assign each single production to this or that country according to its monetisation. Commodities produced in the USA, for example, are monetised in dollars, and it is precisely this monetary identity which defines their origin. If the same goods and services were monetised in marks, they would be part of German national output despite being materially produced in America. By analogy, the production of Nestlé's Brazilian branch is part of the national output of that country to the extent that its costs correspond to a payment in cruseiros; on the contrary, if Nestlé paid its workers in Swiss francs, the monetisation of the goods and services produced in Brazil would transform them into a Swiss output.

The absence of any extra-national production makes the international economy an economy of exchange, so that the existence of an international purchasing power can only be explained by referring to that created within every single national system. Every national economy has at its disposal a vehicular money, issued by banks, and a product associated with it. Purchasing power is thus accounted for as the result of this association between numerical form (money) and real content (output). Since no specifically international production exists, it is obviously impossible to define a purchasing power of extra-national origin. Even if a true international money existed (and, thus, also a supranational bank capable of issuing it), we would have no product to autonomously fill it with. If we want to go on speaking of international income or purchasing power we have to remember, therefore, that its existence is related to exchange only, which means that it has to be derived from national productions (which are the unique source of income at the planetary level).

Inserted into an exchange economy, international transactions require the intervention of money as simple vehicular intermediary between national outputs which have already been fully monetised in their countries of origin. International money is thus given the task of making the sets of national goods and services reciprocally homogeneous, their internal homogeneity being already provided for by each national currency. The monetisation of international exchanges is a problem linked to the necessity of supplying the world with a common unit of measure capable of collecting national currencies within a unique monetary 'space', which would simultaneously allow for their sovereignty and their homogeneity.

Monetary heterogeneity

The simple observation of facts is enough to clarify the terms of the problem. National currencies are issued by different banking systems and must therefore be considered as fundamentally heterogeneous. Unlike transactions occurring between regions of a country, which do not come up against any monetary (as opposed to financial) difficulty, international payments require the working out of a system that can solve the problem of the heterogeneity of national currencies.

Let us recall the fact that every payment calls for the presence of both a monetary vehicle and a positive income. Within a single monetary area, the monetary vehicle is unique. The Italian lira circulates in the North and in the South of Italy, and both the payments of the North and of the South take place in lira, neither region being forced into onerously obtaining the vehicle necessary to the transfer of its financial resources. In order to settle its debt, a region must find the corresponding income. Yet, having found it, no other problem arises since, in order to provide for its transfer, the regions of every single country have at their disposal a perfectly homogeneous monetary vehicle.

As we know, this homogeneity is assured by the presence of a Central Bank which, as Bank of banks, gathers, in a unique monetary area, the acknowledgements of debt spontaneously issued by secondary banks.

At the international level we are still lacking a Central Bank of Central Banks capable of carrying out the same function carried out by each Central Bank within each single country. In the absence of a common monetary standard, every nation pertains to a different monetary area so that the transfer of income from one country to another can take place only through the vehicular use of one or more national currencies. The difficulty arising in this context is related to the choice of the method allowing for the passage from one national currency to the other. It is true that, initially, exchange rates can be conventionally determined, and that, if the system of payments were monetarily neutral, they would not tend to vary. In reality, however, the system is far from being neutral. Thus, the conversion of currencies through exchange rates is affected by persistent variations that put its validity under discussion.

The solution to the problem of national currencies' heterogeneity calls for the determination of a common standard through which they can be collected in a single numerical 'space'. It is known, however, that a good unit of measurement must be invariable. If the meter varied when the distance it has to measure changes, it could not be considered a good standard of length. Analogously, how is it possible to claim that national currencies are made homogeneous through exchange rates, given that exchange rates vary when (demand for and supply of) currencies vary?

This problem is not new to economics. The determination of prices, the common denominator capable of making physically heterogeneous goods homogeneous, also meets with similar difficulties. Is it possible to measure output by using a *relative* unit of measurement or is it necessary to apply an *absolute* standard? According to neoclassical authors, prices are directly determined through exchange, without it being necessary to worry about the physical heterogeneity of the commodities that are exchanged. By so doing, however, they seem to forget that the unit of measurement has to be *unique*. The relative exchange between two commodities determines *two* standards. If we refer to a famous example, in the exchange between iron and wheat, iron is the standard of wheat and wheat is the standard of iron. From the physical heterogeneity of exchanged commodities we thus move to the heterogeneity of their measures, and relative prices seem to be doomed to total indeterminacy. If to all this we add the fact that exchange depends on the equilibrium between supply and demand and that these two forces are directly influenced by price variations (so that prices take part in the determination of prices), we become aware of how problematic the neoclassical choice is.

Transferred to the monetary level, this choice comes up against the same difficulties. The relative exchange between national currencies does not determine a unique standard, and can therefore not solve the problem of their heterogeneity. Moreover, the very idea of relative exchange is inconsistent with the vehicular nature of bank money. Demand and supply have real goods and services as their object, and not a simple numerical vehicle. To subject money to the law of supply and demand amounts to considering it as a real good, a net asset purchased and sold on the basis of its presumed intrinsic value. Within every single country money is used as an *instrument* or *means* of payment. That is to say that the final object of monetary transactions is not money itself. What the payee gets from the payer is the content of vehicular money and not the vehicle itself, which, as such, has no real value.

By distinguishing between money and money's worth (or between nominal and real money), the classical authors showed that they understood perfectly that money's real content must not be mixed up with the numerical container (money itself). Thus, a payment is effective since it allows its beneficiary to obtain a bank deposit (income), i.e. a drawing right over national output, and not a mere vehicular money.

Internationally, the absence of extra-national production is certainly not sufficient to justify the use of a nominal money both as means *and* final object of payment. On the contrary, the nature of bank money is consistent only with its vehicular use, and requires the content of the payment to be real. As at the national level, payments call for the simultaneous presence of a monetary vehicle and of its real charge, international transactions have to be monetised (an operation requiring the use of a monetary standard common to every country) and financed through the transfer of corresponding real assets. Monetary and financial aspects must be kept rigorously distinct, in order to avoid a simple numerical instrument being assimilated with a real good. In the absence of a true international banking system, international transactions become the privileged place for the confusion between money and income. It is by starting from these two concepts that we intend to investigate the actual system of international payments.

THE GOLD STANDARD

The analysis of the gold standard carried out by Ricardo is particularly relevant for the understanding of the monetary problems related to internal as well as to international circulation. Both the advocates of the quantity theory of money and of the purchasing power parity refer to the works of Ricardo, and it is in his writings that the distinction between nominal and real money introduced by Smith is pushed to its most rigorous and extreme consequences.

In this section we intend to analyse the gold standard in its dual role of system of measurement and system of international payments following the teachings of the 'prince of economists' and opposing the 'circular' vision of international transactions to the traditional model of the automatic re-equilibrium of the balance of payments.

Gold as a standard of measurement of value and money

Let us start from the definition of the gold standard proposed by Arthur Bloomfield. According to the American economist, in the countries which adopted the gold standard

> the national monetary unit was defined in terms of a given quantity of gold; the central bank or treasury stood ready to buy and sell gold at the resulting fixed price in terms of the national currency; gold was freely coined and gold coins formed a significant part of the circulating medium; and gold could be freely exported and imported.
>
> (Bloomfield 1981: 452)

Gold is, first of all, the unit of measurement of commodities. Physically heterogeneous, they are made commensurable through the determination of their value. The task of expressing this value is assigned to gold, whose stability allows the evaluation of the appreciation or depreciation of commodities. As claimed by Ricardo, without an invariable standard of value it would never be possible to establish if the depreciation (appreciation) of a commodity is due to a variation in its value or to one in the standard itself. On the contrary,

> if we had a perfect measure of value, itself being neither liable to increase or diminish in value, we should by its means be able to ascertain the real as well as the proportional variations in other things and should never refer the variation in the commodity measured to the commodity itself by which it was measured.
>
> (Ricardo 1951–5, vol. IV: 399–400)

In its first function, gold is thus considered as the standard of produced goods and services, as the best unit of measurement available in a world where commodities have an intrinsically unstable value. As a real good, gold itself has its own value which, besides being unstable, can only be expressed through the use of a unit of measurement; as a standard, gold somehow avoids its physical determination to acquire that invariability which is the necessary requirement of every unit of measurement.

The 'transcendental' character of the gold standard is definitively confirmed by the fact that money-gold itself is a commodity measured by the standard. Ricardo excludes the fact that bank notes disjointed from real output can have a value whatsoever, and claims that, linked to gold, money can exert its function only if it is itself measured.

> When two commodities vary in relative value, it is impossible with certainty to say, whether the one rises, or the other falls; so that, if we adopted a currency without a standard, there is no degree of depreciation to which it might not be carried.
>
> (Ricardo 1951–5, vol. IV: 62)

The gold standard is given the task of measuring both real goods and money-gold. This means that gold is measured both as a commodity and as a money whereas, as a standard, it is only a means of measurement. To avoid a sterile recurrence *ad infinitum*, the standard of value has to acquire a status which, although allowing it to be made identical to the whole set of real goods and services, does not assimilate it to any of them. Ricardo laid down the foundations for the working out of a purely numerical unit of measurement despite the fact that the use of gold made the elaboration of an a-dimensional conception of money particularly difficult. According to the great economist, money is still identified with a specific commodity (gold), but at the same time it is affected by the need to be measured on the basis of a logically invariable standard. Since 'while the precious metals continue to be the standard of our currency, money must necessarily undergo the same variations in value as those metals' (p. 55), and since 'nothing is so easy to ascertain as a variation of price, nothing so difficult as a variation of value; indeed, without an invariable measure of value, and none such exists, it is impossible to ascertain it with any certainty or precision' (p. 60), the standard cannot be identified with any particular commodity. It is as a unit of measurement of every commodity that the standard becomes their common denominator.

The gold standard also plays this role of common denominator with regard to national currencies. The possible fluctuations of gold notwithstanding, its use as a standard of national currencies makes of it a perfect unit of measurement at the international level. Let us recall how the gold standard is a system in which the determination of exchange rates is extremely simple. Every currency is defined in terms of gold, a precious metal from which it is supposed that it derives its value and with which it is convertible (*de jure* if not *de facto*). Thus, gold is perceived as the common denominator of national currencies, the intermediary thanks to which exchange rates between currencies can always be unequivocally determined.

In *The High Price of Bullion* we read:

> While the currency of different countries consists of the precious metals, or of a paper money which is at all times exchangeable for them; and while the metallic currency is not debased by wearing, or clipping, a comparison of the weight, and degree of fineness of their coins, will enable us to ascertain their par of exchange. Thus the par of exchange between Holland and England is stated to be about eleven florins, because the pure silver contained in eleven florins is equal to the pure silver contained in twenty standard shillings.
>
> (Ricardo 1951–5, vol. III: 70–1)

The homogeneity of national currencies is thus obtained on the basis of their respective contents in precious metals. Their parity is not derived from any process of adjustment, but is determined by the 'objective' relationship between their gold or silver contents. A process of adjustment can take place only if the value of gold varies within any given country. The possibility of arbitrage and of the consequent speculative profits would lead to a variation in the gold content of the country's currency, and to the restoration of parity through an adjustment in exchange rates, which is the reason for their very existence. In other words, in the Ricardian system, exchange rate variations take place in order to restore parity when an excessive increase in the quantity of money modifies the initial gold content of a national currency.

The gold standard and the automatic re-equilibrium of the balance of payments

Referring to the relationship between quantity of money and level of prices proposed by David Hume in 1752, Thornton and Malthus maintain that the persistence of a negative commercial balance or the payment of a subsidy generates, both in the country carrying out the payment and in that benefiting from it, a re-equilibrating mechanism based on gold export and the consequent variations in prices.

According to price-specie-flow theory, the payment of an extraordinary subsidy or of an exceptional commercial deficit (caused, for example, by the necessity to import huge quantities of wheat because of a famine) elicits, first, a change in the par of exchange due to the indebted country's increased demand for foreign currencies, and then a flow of gold into the creditor's country. In its turn, the transfer of gold leads to a reduction in the quantity of money available within the debtor country, and, as a consequence, to a decrease in the price of its commodities, whereas, in the creditor country, the positive inflow of gold provokes an increase in the quantity of money and in prices. Thus, goods and services produced in the exporting country become relatively less expensive than the ones produced in the importing country, and, since international transactions are directly influenced by the level of prices, it is easy to infer that the variations caused by the transfer of gold will allow the first country to increase its commercial exports. The demand for the deficit country's money will tend to grow relative to the creditor country's money, leading to a readjustment in exchange rates that will restore parity to its previous level.

It is important to observe that the mechanism of automatic re-equilibrium of the balance of payments represents the first application of the quantity theory of money and of the theory of purchasing power parity. In contrast to what is claimed by the leading classical authors (Smith, Ricardo and Marx), the advocates of this approach maintain, more or less explicitly, that prices are determined by the relationship between two independent masses: the quantity of money and that of real output. When a mass varies relative to the other, prices change and so does the purchasing power of money, which is defined by the relationship between money and output. Hence, taking for granted the fact that net imports decrease the internal money supply, authors such as Malthus and Thornton infer that commercial deficits bring about a reduction in prices. And, since purchasing power increases when prices decrease, commercial exports grow, causing an increase in the money supply which restores the initial relationship between money and output as well as the purchasing power parity between all the countries taking part in international trade.

Ricardo's point of view

Besides Hume, the origin of the quantity theory of money is often attributed to Ricardo himself. Although he has undoubtedly related the increase in prices to that of the money supply, it must not be forgotten that for him, as well as for the main classical authors, prices are not determined by comparing the mass of goods with that of money. On the contrary, the variation in prices presupposes their pre-determination and shows that their natural level can be modified only by an inflationary emission of bank money. Hence, while in the quantity theory prices are always determined by comparing two independent masses, in the Ricardian theory the two masses coincide and it is only because of a deep disequilibrium of a pathological origin that one can vary relative to the other, thus provoking a variation in prices.

This analysis is corroborated by several passages in Ricardo's works, where the great economist maintains that gold is exported only if it is the most convenient commodity to export and, therefore, only if the price of other commodities undergoes an inflationary increase.

> If in France an ounce of gold were more valuable than in England, and would therefore in France purchase more of any commodity common to both countries, gold would immediately quit England for such purpose, and we should send gold in preference to any thing else, because it would be the cheapest exchangeable commodity in the English market; for if gold be dearer in France than in England, goods must be cheaper; we should not therefore send them from the dear to the cheap market, but, on the contrary, they would come from the cheap to the dear market, and would be exchangeable for our gold.
>
> (Ricardo 1951–5, vol. III: 57)

As clearly stressed by Maria Cristina Marcuzzo and Annalisa Rosselli,

> for Ricardo, the conditions of the internal monetary circulation characterised by a high price of gold and by currency exports are not the

> *effect* of an unfavourable balance of payments, or, which is the same thing by definition, of an export of gold. It is the excessive quantity of money, and the consequent loss of value of the pound on the internal and international markets the *cause* of an unfavourable balance of payments.
>
> (Marcuzzo and Rosselli 1986: 144)

Strictly speaking, the export of gold due to an excess in the quantity of money is neither the effect of a balance of payment deficit, nor its cause. Two arguments lead to this conclusion. Let us first suppose that money-gold is effectively exported. What we have to determine is whether gold is exported as a money or as a commodity. Let us immediately observe that, in the first case, money would be transformed from a mere *instrument* into an *object* of payment. Yet if gold becomes a final good this means that it leaves its monetary form to recover that of a commodity. As a matter of fact, gold permits the payment of international transactions without itself becoming an object of exchange. The common denominator of national currencies, gold is a true world money and, as such, it is neither purchased nor sold, but acts only as an intermediary, a 'vehicle' of real circulation. Given by the importing country in exchange for real goods, gold is not purchased as money by the exporting country. At the most we could claim that money-gold carries an equivalent sum of commodity-gold, and that the payment is effective precisely because it implies the transfer of a commodity (gold) in exchange for commodities (goods and services transferred by the exporting country). The idea implicit in this first answer is therefore that, although they are carried out monetarily, payments must have a real content. After having carried out its vehicular function, money-gold disappears to leave its place to commodity-gold, the real content of the importing country's monetary payment.

If the export of money-gold really took place, it would contribute to maintaining unaltered the equilibrium of the balance of payments. The net import of foreign goods would be immediately balanced by an equivalent export of the precious metal which, besides allowing for the equality of real flows, would also provide for the stability of exchange rates by decreasing the money supply of the country exporting gold.

Yet Ricardo carries his analysis further, claiming that the export of gold never really takes place since the variation in the value of gold (caused, let us recall it, by the excess of circulating money) has a direct consequence on the parity of exchange. If a currency depreciates on the internal market, its gold content decreases, and it is only through an exchange rate adjustment that its parity with the other national currencies can be safeguarded. 'Thus then it appears that the currency of one country can never for any length of time be much more valuable, as far as equal quantities of the precious metals are concerned, than that of another' (Ricardo 1951–5, vol. III: 56).

Let us reconsider monetarist and Ricardian analyses starting from a simple numerical example. Let us suppose the world to be made up of only two countries, A and B, whose national currencies have the same gold content. In equilibrium and giving the internal gold parity of country A, so that 100 units of money *a* have a content of 10 grams of gold, and of country B, 100 units of money *b* = 10 grams of gold, the exchange rate between *a* and *b* is equal to 1 *a* for 1 *b*.

According to the quantity theory of money, a sudden inflationary increase in the money supply of A would cause a rise in internal prices and a variation in the purchasing power parity. Residents of country A would find it profitable to import goods from country B since, given the exchange rate of 1 *a* for 1 *b*, the purchasing power of their currency would be greater in B than in A. However, the money inflow in B would increase the quantity of money in this country, pushing up its internal prices until the purchasing power parity between the two countries is restored.

According to Ricardo's analysis, on the contrary, the inflationary growth in the money supply of country A would create the conditions for the realisation of a speculative profit, a situation which would induce countries A and B to modify the exchange rate between their currencies before the intervention of any mechanism of re-equilibrium of the balance of payments. The increase in the price of money-gold in A would allow residents of country B to get rich simply by exchanging their currency with money *a*, converting it into gold at the rate of 100 *a* for 10 grams of gold, melting the gold and selling it as a commodity. By so doing, they would obtain a quantity of money *a* greater than the initial one, that they would convert into money *b*, thus realising a benefit due only to an operation of arbitrage. In such a situation, country A would have to modify the exchange rate between its currency and money *b*, re-establishing the previous gold parity between the two currencies. Assuming that country A is hit by an inflation of the 10 per cent, the new exchange rate between *a* and *b* would be equal to 1.1 *a* for 1 *b*, and the new gold content of money *a* (110 *a* for 10 grams of gold) would correspond to the price of commodity-gold, which would avoid the danger of realising a speculative profit through arbitrage.

Moreover, the working of the gold standard is even more rigorous since the possible variation in the value of gold calls for monetary authority intervention. Even before any exchange rate adjustment, monetary authorities anticipate the formation of a speculative profit, and safeguard parity by re-absorbing or creating money.

Gold as a vehicular money

In the previous paragraphs we have seen how the export of gold is related to excess money supply, and how it is neutralised by a variation in the par of exchange. What we would like to stress now is that, by proclaiming the logical impossibility of exporting gold, Ricardo provides proof of the constant and necessary equilibrium of the balance of payments and for the essentially vehicular nature of money.

Let us immediately observe that the equilibrium of the balance of payments is always evident if the impossibility to export and import money is verified. Now, it is not only true that for Ricardo the export of gold is never caused by a deficit in the balance of trade, but it is also possible to show that, whether in excess or not, money can never be transformed into an object of export.

If money supply were in excess, gold would become the cheapest commodity, and, therefore, the most advantageous to export. Yet, as we have seen, the decreasing value of gold due to its plethora would lead to a change in parity, thus subtracting it from export. In the absence of an inflationary increase in the quantity of money the conditions laid down by Ricardo for the export of gold would no longer apply, and we would have to conclude that a country can be a net importer of goods and services only if it exports an equivalent net amount of bonds. Thus, consistent with the rigorous equilibrium of the balance of payments, imports would be entirely matched by exports.

Empirical observation seems to contradict Ricardo's theoretical conclusion. Balance of payment disequilibria seem to be the rule, and it is difficult to deny that key-currency countries pay for their net commercial imports by exporting money instead of financial bonds. Yet, as will be confirmed throughout this book, the analysis worked out by Ricardo is far from being surpassed. Being logically impossible, the export of money is denied even when international payments have no real content. The banking nature of money does not allow for its effective transfer outside its country; if, in spite of this, international payments are financed through unilateral flows of money, it is the law discovered by the great Anglo-Portuguese economist that triumphs: if 'facts' do not comply with it, they introduce a disorder which marks the presence of serious anomalies.

Besides having the great merit of having discovered the laws of money despite the difficulties implicit in the gold standard system (mainly due to the risks of mixing up money-gold and commodity-gold), Ricardo also contributed to developing the vehicular conception of money first propounded by Adam Smith. The impossibility of exporting or importing gold shows that money is essentially a 'vehicle', an instrument of payment and not its own object. Money is 'the great wheel of circulation' (Smith 1776/1978: 385) which conveys goods without being itself conveyed. Through the circular flow of money real goods are transferred from one country to another. If, as is claimed by Ricardo, payments are carried out through the transfer of money's worth, the object of the payment is money's real content and not money itself. Hence, the task of money is to convey the real content of reciprocal payments. This means that, used as an international currency, gold circulates allowing for the exchange between goods, services and bonds, the latter being the real content of the payment of net commercial imports.

Summarising, the implications of the logical impossibility of exporting gold lead us to the following representation of the exchange between two countries, A and B (Figure 6.1).

Money-gold circulates from one country to the other as a mere instrument of payment, allowing for the exchange of real goods. The effective payment of B's net commercial imports implies the transfer of an equivalent amount of financial securities. Playing its role of intermediation, money flows back to its point of departure, in a movement that, consistent with the teachings of Adam Smith and David Ricardo, defines it as 'the great wheel of circulation'.

The empirical application of the gold standard

Officially adopted until 1914, the gold standard is still appreciated by several economists, who recognise that it has strongly contributed to a long period of equilibrated growth of the world economy. Now, if it is true that under the gold standard regime monetary stability were maintained, both at the national and international level, without resorting to the constant intervention of Central Banks, it is also true that secondary banks, together with other financial intermediaries, acquired a growing importance and played an incessant work of adjustment within a system only nominally based on gold. As claimed by Ronald Michie, gold rapidly gave way to bank money, whose emission was not essentially linked to the precious metal. The use of book entry money was spreading and in this context the task of providing for the equilibrated working of the system was taken over by secondary banks.

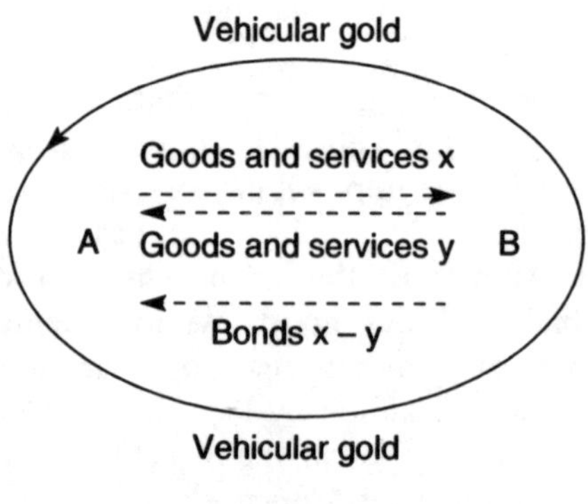

Figure 6.1

> Issues of paper currency, backed only by the authority of the government, were only the most obvious forms of money independent of gold. Of even greater importance were general developments in financial sophistication, especially the growth of commercial banking, that reduced or removed the need for any kind of circulating medium, whether metal or paper. The accumulation of credits and debits within banks, and the manipulation of these through cheques, discounts, advances and other means, became the very foundation of the world's money supply, and left all other forms with increasingly minor tasks in developed economies or significance only in backward countries.
>
> (Michie 1986: 170)

Referring again to the effective use of gold as the basis of money's value, it has to be observed that the enormous growth in bank money made the principle of gold convertibility inoperative.

> In the heyday of the so-called gold standard, paradoxically, it was in fact credit money, rather than gold or silver, which dominated the evolution of the monetary stock and fed the bulk of the monetary requirements of a growing world economy. After 1872, 95 percent of the expansion of world money was derived from bank money, as against 5 percent from silver and gold together.
>
> (Triffin 1968: 54)

Moreover, it must be remembered that, under the gold standard, monetary stability was often aleatory. Observation of statistical data shows that, in its period of greatest development (1850–1913), the gold standard was characterised by strong variations in prices and interest rates.

The importance of gold-money decreased rapidly even at the international level. The development of credit instruments (trade bills and bills of exchange) and techniques fostered its replacement with the pound, which became the national currency most widely used internationally. London became the world's financial capital and the gold standard was transformed *de facto* into a sterling standard.

Yet the system was still anchored to the principle of fixed exchange rates, and was thus exposed to destabilising pressures related to the use of a national money as international standard. This explains the recurrent abandonment of fixed parity and the search for a new monetary order after the political and economic changes following the Great War.

Let us finally recall how, despite Ricardo's efforts to persuade his contemporaries of the circular nature of money, the gold standard was considered a system of fixed exchange rates based on the deflationary re-equilibrium of the balance of payments. It is as such that it was re-introduced between 1925 and 1930. It was Churchill who supported its reinstatement in Great Britain, under the pressure from Bank of England and Treasury experts and against the opinion of Keynes. According to the great English economist, the gold standard would cause a sharp rise in unemployment due to the depression exporting industries would suffer from, because of wage rigidity. The decrease in exported goods prices is limited, in fact, by the possibility of lowering costs, and if wages (which represent an important part of these costs) are downwardly rigid, the reduction will not be sufficient to induce the increase in exports necessary to re-equilibrate the balance of trade. Keynes's forecasts came true and, being unable to bear the high levels of unemployment required by the deflationary policy of the gold standard, Great Britain was forced to abandon the gold standard in a period of crisis. The United States followed the English example in 1934, and little by little the other nations were forced to take analogous decisions.

The abandoning of gold parity was immediately followed by a devaluation of national currencies: thus in 1931, for example, the pound devalued by 30 per cent relative to the dollar (which had not yet abandoned the gold standard), while in 1934 the dollar devalued by 60 per cent relative to gold.

After the collapse of the gold standard, international transactions were settled by entangled systems of payment where exchange rates between national currencies were multiplied and differentiated in repeated attempts to avoid one country from taking advantage of the others by devaluing its currency. Apart from the attempt that gave rise to the tripartite agreement of 1936 between France, England and the United States, the situation of international payments remained chaotic during the whole Great Depression, and countries often resorted to protectionist measures which, the creation of monetary zones notwithstanding, certainly did not promote their economic development. It was only towards the end of the Second World War that 730 delegates, representing 44 members of the United Nations, met at Bretton Woods to lay the foundations of a new system of international payments taking into account the failure of both the gold standard and protectionism.

BRETTON WOODS

At the American meeting held in 1944 participants had to choose between two projects, one propounded by Keynes and the other by Harry Dexter White, director of the Division of Monetary Research of the American Treasury. The confrontation between the two economists was settled in favour of White. It was his plan that was adopted, and it was on the basis of the American proposals that the International Monetary Fund was created. Hence, the orientation that prevailed at Bretton Woods was that of the American Treasury and not that of the British academic and political world. Besides the interest aroused by the confrontation between culturally and politically different positions, it is important to analyse both plans in the light of what happened after Bretton Woods and, in particular, of the instability and uncertainty characterising the present system of international payments.

The Keynes plan

In 1941 Keynes had already pointed out the inefficacy of the previous systems of international payments and put forward new proposals for the creation of an International Clearing Union. These proposals were then further investigated and presented at the Bretton Woods meeting. In the official text of the English delegation, written by Keynes, the accent was immediately placed on the reform's essential aspect: the creation of a true international money, of a currency, therefore, circulating only among countries (and not inside them) and conveying the payment of their commercial and financial transactions.

> We need an instrument of international currency having general acceptability between nations, so that blocked balances and bilateral clearings are unnecessary; that is to say, an instrument of currency used by each nation in its transactions with other nations, operating through whatever national organ, such as a Treasury or a central bank, is most appropriate, private individuals, businesses and banks other than central banks, each continuing to use their own national currency as heretofore.
>
> (Keynes 1973, vol. XXV: 168)

The task of creating this international currency – called 'bancor' by Keynes – was to be given to an international institution (the Clearing Union) which would have played the role of World Bank and would thus have been an intermediary between Central Banks of member countries. As the word chosen by Keynes indicates, the new currency would have had the twofold characteristic of being a bank money defined in terms of gold. Member countries were to agree to use the bancor as the sole means of international payments, and to accept it on the basis of the value corresponding to its gold definition.

> The proposal is to establish a currency union, here designated an *International Clearing Union*, based on international bank money, called (let us say) *bancor*, fixed (but not unalterably) in terms of gold and accepted as the equivalent of gold by the British Commonwealth and the United States and all the other members of the Union for the purpose of settling international balances.
>
> (Keynes 1973, vol. XXV: 170–71)

The bancor is seen, first of all, as the common denominator of national currencies, which keep fulfilling their functions within their reciprocal countries of origin. Keynes was well aware of the necessity of providing the world with a standard for national currencies, a common unit capable of making them homogeneous by establishing their absolute exchange rates. He thus attributes to the bancor the task of both endowing national currencies with a common form, and allowing for their international circulation.

Yet how would the bancor circulate? How would it play its function of international means of circulation with regard to real goods and national currencies? The answer can be found in the following quotation.

> The principal object can be explained in a single sentence: to provide that money earned by selling goods to one country can be spent on purchasing the products of any other country. In jargon, a system of multilateral clearing. In English, a universal currency valid for trade transactions in all the world.
>
> (Keynes 1973, vol. XXV: 270)

The vehicular use of the bancor within a system of multilateral clearing provides for the effective payment of commercial transactions. However, does maintaining that imports have to be paid for by exports mean forcing countries to equilibrate their trade balances? Definitely not, since current trade surplus or deficit is perfectly consistent with multilateral clearing. It is always possible, in fact, to match the difference between imports and exports of real goods and services with a difference of the opposite sign between imports and exports of financial bonds. Keynes's proposals for world monetary reform are not aimed at reducing trade transactions. On the contrary, they provide the monetary framework necessary for their consistent development. One of the fundamental principles for the orderly working of the monetary system states that net purchases of goods and services must be paid for by using money as a *means*, and not as an *object* of payment. Multilateral clearing is conceived, indeed, as a mechanism that, while monetising international transactions, does not allow money to be the real content of any of them. By giving financial securities in exchange for goods and services, the country with a trade imbalance effectively pays for its net commercial imports, the bancor being given the task of conveying compensated exchanges.

The International Clearing Union is a true World Bank with the function of issuing the international currency necessary to convey transactions among the different countries, who are members of the multilateral clearing system. Its role is, first of all, monetary (vehicular). Yet, nothing prevents the International Clearing Union from also carrying out the function of financial intermediary. Although this institution, like any other, cannot create net assets, it can obtain them through the sale of bonds denominated in bancor. By so doing, the International Clearing Union would be able to lend deficit countries the capital necessary to finance their net trade imports. In this case too, the imports of goods and services would be paid for through the selling of financial securities, but the World Bank, intervening as an intermediary, would provide countries with a supplementary *means* for the development of their transactions.

Going back to the monetary role played by the bancor, it is interesting to observe that, conveying compensated real exchanges, it circulates to and from its point of origin in a way similar to that advocated by Ricardo. Issued by the World Bank, the international money flows instantaneously back to it, in a movement allowing for the transfer of its real content from one country to the other. To claim that the bancor conveys real goods amounts to claiming that it is changed into the national currency of the country which obtains it from the International Clearing Union. However, since the bancor is necessarily issued in a circular operation, the national currency is also immediately changed into the international one, so that it is simultaneously offered and demanded in terms of bancor. Since every international transaction submits national currencies to a couple of opposing and equivalent forces, the system proposed by Keynes has the great advantage of assuring exchange rate stability.

Stability, however, does not mean irrevocability. Keynes knew that it is necessary to allow for the re-adjustment of parities when one or more countries are repeatedly confronted with serious problems of financial disequilibrium. The plan supported by the British economist is concerned with two fundamental equilibria: the internal one, related to the general level of prices, and the external one, related to the balance of payments. The invariability of absolute exchange rates depends on these two equilibria. In other words, although exchange rates are essentially stable since they are no longer submitted to speculative market forces, they can periodically be modified in order to avoid permanent trade balance deficits of member countries. A re-adjustment which can be carried out without it being necessary to worry about the internal relationship between supply and demand, whose stability is guaranteed by the fundamental neutrality of the bancor.

The following quotation is fundamental to the understanding of Keynes's project.

> The idea underlying such a Union is simple, namely, to generalise the essential principle of banking as it is exhibited within any closed system. This principle is the necessary equality of credits and debits. If no credits can be removed outside the clearing system, but only transferred within it, the Union can never be in any difficulty as regards the honoring of checks drawn upon it. It can make what advances it wishes to any of its members with the assurance that the proceeds can only be transferred to the clearing account of another

> member. Its sole task is to see to it that its members keep the rules and that the advances made to each of them are prudent and advisable for the Union as a whole.
>
> (Keynes 1973, vol. XXV: 171)

The principle of the necessary equality of credits and debits is that on which the monetary system, whether national or international, must be based. For Keynes money is of a banking nature. All that we need in order to benefit from the correct working of a monetary system is thus reduced to the book-keeping rules related to the recording of monetary transactions. Let us consider the creation of national money by bank B, and let us suppose the client benefiting from this creation to be C. The amount obtained by C is meant to finance a payment, and is thus immediately transferred by B to the economic correspondent of C (A). As a result of the entire operation, C is indebted to B, which, in its turn, owes A an equivalent sum of money. Now, where can we trace back money if not to B? Paid to A on behalf of C, the money issued by the bank defines a credit of A and a debt of C or, in other words, a positive deposit of A and a negative deposit of C. The debt of C is thus covered by A's deposit, and the bank's position is perfectly balanced. Not even a fraction of what has been created by the bank escapes from its circuit, and this simply because money is, by definition, a book-keeping entry of the issuing bank.

A great theorist of bank money, Keynes had already exposed its principles in *The Treatise on Money* (1930/1973) and in *The General Theory* (1936/1973) and it is to these very principles that he refers in order to elaborate his proposals for a world monetary reform. By analogy with what happens at the national level, the World Bank would provide its clients with the currency necessary for international circulation, being certain to recover the money it creates and which, transferred from the importing to the exporting country, defines the deposit of the latter. As claimed by Keynes, the Clearing Union would never be uncovered, since the debt of a country would always be matched by the credit of another country, and, therefore, by its deposit in bancor with the World Bank. This does not mean that a country can import without limits, in the certainty that its net purchases are automatically financed by an equivalent deposit of exporting countries. The equality of credits and debits implies no mechanism of this sort. In order to effectively pay for its net commercial imports, a country must sell bonds of an equal amount, and this sale can certainly not be ensured by the simple monetary intermediation carried out by the International Clearing Union. Hence, whereas monetary equilibrium is always guaranteed by the book-keeping principle we have just been referring to, financial equilibrium requires the World Bank to intervene in its function as financial intermediary. In the same way as, within every single country, the Central Bank allows for interbank clearing, the World Bank intervenes to guarantee the real payment of net commercial imports. Since this payment requires the transfer of bonds to the benefit of net exporters, it is clear, however, that it is not automatically ensured, but is subject to the decisions taken by the various economic agents. Although financial equilibrium can be reached through World Bank intervention, its level is not arbitrarily determined, but depends on the trade relations determined by Clearing Union members.

It must be noted that, consistent with what was still going on at the national level, Keynes attributed a positive value to the bancor on the basis of its gold parity. Members of the United Nations were to be asked to acknowledge this value and accept the bancor 'as if it were gold'. Now, national and international money do not pertain to the same category. National currencies do not effectively derive their value from gold, but from the production of goods and services they are associated with. The bancor, on the contrary, cannot find its value in any international production (since world output is simply the sum of national outputs). Hence, while gold parity is superfluous at the national level, as far as the bancor is concerned it seems necessary to link it with a particular good of indisputable value such as gold. At this point the problem becomes complicated. If countries are bound to accept the bancor according to its gold parity, and if the bancor is created by the World Bank on request of Clearing Union members, how is it possible to simultaneously provide the world with the necessary international liquidity and avoid the emission of money which is not backed by the necessary reserves? To what extent can the equality of debits and credits solve this problem?

If no answer is given to this question, it is impossible to understand the revolutionary significance of Keynes's proposal, which, besides looking utopian, seems to follow the national monetary system's model too mechanically. It is precisely for these reasons, and because it did not give sufficient economic (and political) weight to the American dollar, that the English plan was put aside. More in line with American ambitions, the White plan was accepted and led to the creation of the International Monetary Fund.

The White plan

An official representative of the American government, Harry White proposed the institution of an International Stabilisation Fund aiming at improving the balance of payments of member countries, stabilising exchange rates, favouring trade and financial transactions as well as the utilisation of the funds blocked because of the war and, finally, reducing the restrictive measures and the discriminatory procedures hampering the development of international trade. According to White, in order to attain these objectives it was not necessary to create an international currency. The building up of a limited reserve ($5 billion) made up of gold and foreign currencies provided by the members of the Fund together with a system of fixed exchange rates would have been enough to guarantee that the system functioned well.

As already pointed out by Keynes in 1942, the White plan was not founded on banking principles and was not intended to provide the world with a new means of international circulation. It favoured, instead, the countries with important gold reserves, whose decisions were determinant for the working of the Stabilisation Fund.

> Since the proposed stabilisation Fund is to perform clearing functions for its members, it might seem, at first sight, to have a closer resemblance to the Clearing Union than is the case. In fact the principles underlying it are fundamentally different. For it makes no attempt to use the banking principle and one-way gold convertibility and is in fact not much more than a version of the gold standard, which simply aims at multiplying the effective volume of the gold base. [. . .] The scheme is only helpful to those countries which have a gold reserve already and is only helpful to them in proportion to the amount of such gold reserve.
>
> (Keynes 1973, vol. XXV: 160)

Successively, in his 'Easter holidays' note, Keynes specified that the main shortcoming of White's plan lay in the fact that, unlike the bancor, the unita (White's currency) was not conceived as a true international currency.

> The great majority of the difficulties arise from not making unitas an effective international unit in the sense that bancor is. If the Fund dealt only in terms of unitas, instead of dealing in dozens of different currencies, many of these difficulties would be resolved.
>
> (Keynes 1973, vol. XXV: 258–59)

The aim of White's proposition was to reach monetary stability through increased international cooperation under the aegis of the United States. 'The International Stabilization Fund of the United and Associated Nations is proposed as a permanent institution for international monetary cooperation' (White 1943/1969: 85). Moreover, the International Stabilisation Fund was the coordinating organism whose resources were designed to correct possible balance of payment disequilibria amongst member countries. No great novelty, therefore, either practical or analytical, but an attempt to pragmatically overcome the difficulties caused by the international system of payments. It is within this context that the foundation of the International Monetary Fund has to be assessed.

The International Monetary Fund

The objectives of the International Monetary Fund (IMF) were those that the countries present at Bretton Woods had proclaimed: harmonious development of international trade and monetary stability. Convinced of the unreliability of a system which was, like the gold standard, essentially deflationary, the signatories of the 1944 convention entrusted the IMF with the task of providing the monetary resources necessary to the development of the international economic system. To carry out this task, the Monetary Fund based its activities on four fundamental principles.

According to the first principle, interest rates were adopted on the basis of national currencies' parity, expressed in gold or in dollars with a specific gold content. As a rule, exchange rates were fixed, and their stability ensured through monetary authority interventions on the exchange market. Parities could be modified only in case of extreme necessity (the correction of a fundamental disequilibrium), and subject to member countries' consultation.

The second principle forbade the adoption of exchange control over international transactions, as well as any other discriminatory agreement or monetary practice. A country detaining the currency of another country was bound to convert it at par, in order to allow for the greatest unity and stability of exchange rates.

The third was probably the most important principle. It provided for the right of each member country to buy foreign currencies with its own national currency up to an amount equal to 125 per cent of its quota. Instalments had to be paid for partially in gold (usually 25 per cent), and partially in national currency, so that a purchase of currencies equal to 125 per cent of a country's quota implied an increase in the country's national money held by the Monetary Fund greater than 125 per cent. Drawing rights were automatic only up to the gold quotas of member countries. Beyond this limit specific guarantees were required, as well as the Fund's formal agreement. In each case, the country having recourse to drawing rights promised to give back, within five years, the currency bought or any other currency suitable to the Fund. Passive interest was paid by the country during the whole period of drawing rights utilisation.

The last fundamental principle established at Bretton Woods was that both deficit and surplus countries are responsible for the problems related to international monetary disequilibria. The origin of this principle is analytical. Theory seems to establish a reciprocal relationship between deficit countries' debts and surplus countries' credits. The relationship is so evident as to look like a tautology. If a country exports more than it imports, how is it possible to deny that other countries' imports must necessarily overcome their exports by an equivalent amount? If we consider only two countries, A and B, the exports of A define B's imports and vice versa, so that A's surplus can only coincide with B's deficit. The principle of reciprocal responsibility for monetary disequilibria can thus be easily deduced from this simple empirico-theoretical observation. An observation that still represents the point of departure of traditional monetary analysis, but whose validity, as we shall see, is far from being proved, both statistically and theoretically.

From gold to the dollar

As has already been observed, at the Bretton Woods conference it was decided to abandon the old gold standard system essentially to avoid relying heavily on deflationary policies. The correction of fundamental disequilibria of the balance of payments was (and still is) the main objective of the International Monetary Fund, yet it was decided to replace the re-equilibrating mechanism of the classical authors with a policy revolving around exchange rates ('crawling peg'), drawing rights and international collaboration. However, the passage from the gold standard to a system under the leadership of the IMF did not mark the total abandonment of gold. In this respect, the way in which Keynes justified the position adopted at Bretton Woods before the House of Lords is exemplary.

> There must be *some* price for gold; and so long as gold is used as a monetary reserve it is most advisable that the current rates of exchange and the relative values of gold in different currencies should correspond. The only alternative to this would be the complete demonetisation of gold. I am not aware that anyone has proposed that. For it is only common sense as things are to-day to continue to make use of gold and its prestige as a means of settling international accounts. To demonetise gold would obviously be highly objectionable to the British Commonwealth and to Russia as the main producers, and to the United States and the Western Allies as the main holders of it. Surely no one disputes that? On the other hand, in this country we have already de-throned gold as the fixed standard of value. The plan not merely confirms the de-thronement but approves it by expressly providing that it is the duty of the fund to alter the gold value of any currency if it is shown that this will be serviceable to equilibrium.
>
> (Keynes 1973, vol. XXVI: 18)

The dollar remained convertible into gold (until 1971) and the other currencies maintained a link with the precious metal through the dollar. Gold went on being part of official reserves and being considered as the ideal means for the final settlement of balance of payment deficits. Despite these official functions, gold lost most of its importance, namely at the practical level. By then, the greatest part of international liquidities was made up of drawing rights with the IMF and key-currency reserves (particularly the American dollar). The place of gold as international money was thus taken over by the dollar, and the gold standard system was transformed into what was nominally called the gold exchange standard, but was really a dollar standard; that is a system in which the dollar was the effective point of reference, both practically and theoretically. The growing importance of the dollar is shown in the following table related to the composition of world reserves between 1949 and 1971 (Table 6.1).

With the implementation of the new system agreed upon at Bretton Woods, the dollar acquired a crucial position as means of payment, reserve asset and international standard. Since the dollar was the sole currency convertible into gold (according to a fixed parity), and since all the other currencies were defined relative to the dollar, exchange rates were determined by using the dollar as a standard. Thus, giving the fixed gold parity of the dollar, American monetary authorities could not modify the exchange rate between their currency and those of other countries. A revaluation or a devaluation of the dollar was possible only through a change in the price at which the other countries bought and sold dollars, so that the United States could not apply the mechanism allowing for the balance of payment re-equilibrium through exchange rate fluctuation.

> The dollar is a money's money, a numeraire for foreign exchanges, and cannot be regarded as other currencies. It cannot float, except as other currencies float against it, and its value is the reciprocal of the value of all other currencies, not its price in one.
>
> (Kindleberger and Shonfield 1971: xii)

Table 6.1 Composition of world monetary reserves: 1949–71 (in billions of US dollars)

		1949	*1969*	*1970*	*1971*
I	Gold	33.5	39.1	37.2	39.2
II	Special Drawing Rights	–	–	3.1	6.4
III	Reserves in IMF	1.7	6.7	7.7	6.9
IV	Foreign currencies	10.4	32.4	44.5	77.6
	Dollars	3.2	16.0	23.9	50.7
	Sterling	6.9	9.0	6.6	7.9
	Eurodollars, etc.	0.3	7.4	14.0	19.1
V	Total	45.5	78.2	92.5	130.1
	United States	26.0	17.0	14.5	13.2
	Other countries	19.5	61.2	78.1	116.9

Source: IMF *International Financial Statistics*

On the other hand, the growing use of the dollar was coupled with a persistent deficit in the American balance of payments. The deficit had the consequence of both increasing international liquidity and causing distrust in the dollar stability. Monetary authorities were thus forced to intervene, adopting measures which did not always correspond to those required by the internal economic situation of their countries. The persistent increase in the American deficit was a reason for worry for several economists, who identified in the use of the dollar (or of any other national currency) as international currency the cause of the growing difficulties met by the new system. Confronted with the obvious impossibility of ensuring the gold convertibility of the dollar, Robert Triffin did not hesitate to claim that: 'The basic absurdity of the gold exchange standard is that it makes the *international* monetary system highly dependent on individual countries' decisions about the continued use of one or a few *national* currencies as monetary reserves' (Triffin 1961: 67).

Despite the alarming forecasts of some economists, the dollar went on being used as world money in an increasing number of international transactions, and the American deficit reached levels unimaginable by the participants at the Bretton Woods conference. Besides, not all the experts of international problems regarded the expansion of the American deficit with apprehension.

> While the United States has provided the world with liquid dollar assets in the postwar period by capital outflow and aid exceeding its current account surplus, in most years this excess has not reflected a deficit in a sense representing disequilibrium. The outflow of U.S. capital and aid has filled not one but two needs. First, it has supplied goods and services to the rest of the world. But secondly, to the extent that its loans to foreigners are offset by foreigners putting their own money into liquid dollar assets, the U.S. has not overinvested but has supplied financial intermediary services. The 'deficit' has reflected largely the second process, in which the United States has been lending, mostly at long and intermediate term, and borrowing short.
>
> (Despres *et al.* 1966: 608)

According to the same authors, the use of the dollar was to be considered advantageous even if coupled with a deficit in the American balance of payments. Their opinion seemed to be confirmed by the pattern followed by private markets, where the confidence in the dollar did not suffer despite the scepticism shown by academicians, journalists and government officials.

> Such lack of confidence in the dollar as now exists has been generated by the attitudes of government officials, central bankers, academic economists, and journalists, and reflects their failure to

understand the implications of this intermediary function. Despite some contagion from these sources, the private market retains confidence in the dollar, as increases in private holdings of liquid dollar assets show. Private speculation in gold is simply the result of the known attitudes and actions of government officials and central bankers.

(Despres *et al.* 1966: 608)

However, Kindleberger's opinions were not shared by American officials, worried about the dangerous decrease in gold reserves. Since the 1960s, the United States has shown its intention to reconsider the role played by the dollar at the international level. In particular, three propositions have been put forward: that of replacing gold and dollar with a new international asset, that of increasing the price of gold and, therefore, its value as a reserve asset, and, finally, that of demonetising gold, adopting the dollar as the main international reserve currency. Only the first of these propositions was opposed to the use of the dollar as world money, the second was aimed at making it momentarily less problematic, while the third, by abolishing all links between gold and dollar, sanctioned the supremacy of the American currency. Keynes himself had stressed the necessity to create a world money in order to allow for the effective settlement of international transactions. Is the choice of the dollar compatible with Keynes's insight? Can the dollar be transformed into a world money without deeply modifying its national character?

As noted by Kindleberger and Shonfield, the use of the dollar at the international level implies a transformation of the role played by the United States, from commercial enterprise to Bank of the world. The dollar, in fact, is the American bank money and, as such, it defines the acknowledgement of debt of the American banking system. If the United States represented a commercial enterprise, its promise to pay would force it to transfer part of its real assets to creditor countries. The payment would be effective only if the firm America fulfilled its promise in real (as opposed to monetary) terms. The acknowledgement of debt issued by the United States is the dollar, a currency used internationally as a banking IOU. This means that every American payment is the transfer of a debt that every country accepts as money and which, *de facto*, transforms the United States into Bank of the world.

If the dollar is a world money, the United States is a bank and not a firm as other countries are. The difference between a firm and a bank, of course, is that the liabilities of the former are expected to be paid off at regular intervals, while those of the latter are passed from hand to hand as money, and tend to be permanent in fact, despite being 'demand' in form. To the extent that a country is a bank and not a firm, its balance of payments must be viewed from a different

> perspective, with equilibrium, deficits and surplus measured on a different basis.
>
> (Kindleberger and Shonfield 1971: xiii)

As the American national currency, the dollar is an excellent means of payment within the United States. Then why should it not be accepted also as a means of payment for international transactions? In other words, why should the United States not be allowed to act as Bank of the world, in a context where only the American nation seems capable of providing the necessary requirements of stability and growth? Once it has been clarified that the problem is not of a political nature (so that the analysis could as well be applied to whatever national currency was chosen on the basis of the changing political and economic conditions), it must be asked if it is proper to assume that what is valid at the national level has to be valid also at the international level. Does not the fact that the American banking system acts as Bank of the world transform the dollar into a simple IOU that the United States will never be forced to honour? And if this is true, is it not likewise true that the United States can thus import real resources giving in exchange a promise that will be fulfilled only if the American balance of trade became (and remained) positive?

> It has been said that by financing its deficit through its own creation of international money, the United States obtains a kind of 'free' command over real resources, which can be used to enlarge its purchases of foreign goods, services, and assets (including interest-paying reserves). This benefit is sometimes likened to the gain from 'seigniorage' – the reference being to an earlier period when the state treasury gained the difference between the circulating value of a coin and the cost of bullion and its minting. By running a cumulative deficit in its balance of payments, the United States can create internationally held dollars in a costless fashion and gain an increase in real national expenditure relative to national income.
>
> (Meier 1982: 79)

According to this analysis, the United States would benefit from the privilege of printing money, thus obtaining real goods and services in exchange for simple IOUs issued by its banking system. A privilege that, if confirmed, must be extended to all those countries whose money is accepted as international means of payment, since, let us repeat it, the anomaly is not of a political order, but is related to the system unanimously adopted at Bretton Woods. What the theory should determine is whether it is licit or not to use the dollar (a national currency) as international money, and this irrespective of the advantages or disadvantages of an extra-economic nature deriving from the adoption of the dollar (key-currencies) standard system.

The fact that in the 1960s the United States decided to foster the creation of a new standard of international payments can perhaps be considered as a symptom of the acknowledged weakness of the system, but it gives no proof of its intrinsic inadequacy. As we shall see, the monetary crisis led to the creation of Special Drawing Rights, a new international instrument that would soon be set aside (although not completely abandoned) in order to privilege the American decision to suspend the gold convertibility of the dollar (1971), and to generalise a system based on the use of key national currencies as principal means of international payments. Historical evolution seems therefore to be invalidating more than confirming the analysis first developed by Keynes. Confronted with this situation some economists deemed it their duty to rigorously examine the theoretical aspect of the problem, giving rise to an interesting debate that animated the academic world between the mid-1960s and mid-1970s.

7

INTERNATIONAL LIQUIDITY: PROBLEMS AND ATTEMPTED SOLUTIONS

THE DEBATE RELATING TO THE INTERNATIONAL LIQUIDITY PROBLEM

The analysis of Robert Triffin

Triffin is one of the economists who, referring back to Keynes's teachings, pertinaciously opposes the international use of any national currency. His arguments, expounded since 1960 (the year of publication of *Gold and the Dollar Crisis*), refer essentially to the difficulties necessarily faced by the country whose currency is chosen as international intermediary; difficulties which worsen the liquidity problem and negatively affect the whole international community.

After having analysed the passage from the gold standard to the gold exchange standard, Triffin observes that, since the tragic experiences of the First World War and the subsequent Great Depression, the role played by monetary reserves has drastically changed. The disappearance of gold as a means of monetary circulation, the evolution of national banking systems and erratic private capital flows (which do not play that re-equilibrating function of the balance of payments they were supposed to be capable of carrying out) made it necessary increasingly to resort to monetary reserves as a cover for possible balance of payment deficits. 'Countries must still look today to their own monetary reserves as their first and most important line of defense against temporary deficits in their balance of payments' (Triffin 1961: 33).

In the system of international payments officially implemented after the Bretton Woods conference, not every national currency benefits from the same status. Apart from the dollar, only a few currencies are generally accepted as a means for financing international transactions and are called upon to make up the monetary reserves on which the gold exchange standard regime is based. As Triffin observes, the working of the whole system depends on the decisions taken by those countries that have to provide for international liquidity needs. Monetary reserves can increase only if these countries – and particularly the United States – accept a persistent deficit in their balance of trade and the accumulation of their short-term debt. If this occurs, as shown in the American case, the persistence of an unbalanced situation can only be detrimental to the prestige of the currency chosen as international standard, and the very conditions that should lead to an increase in liquidity reduce it drastically precisely because they cause a generalised crisis of the entire system.

> The gold exchange standard *may*, but *does not necessarily*, help in relieving a shortage of world monetary reserves. It does so only to the extent that the key currency countries are willing to let their net reserve position decline through increases in their short-term monetary liabilities unmatched by corresponding increases in their own gross reserves. If they allow this to happen, however, and to continue indefinitely, they tend to bring about a collapse of the system itself through the gradual weakening of foreigners' confidence in the key currencies.
>
> (Triffin 1971: 67)

As we have already pointed out, the use of the dollar as international liquidity in a system of gold convertibility is a source of serious difficulties. According to Triffin, as dollars held outside the United States increase and American gold reserves decrease, the international monetary system tends to lose its credibility and becomes highly unstable. When convertibility is abandoned and fixed exchange rates are replaced by floating exchange rates, the problem does not radically change. As repeatedly stressed by the Belgian economist, parallel to the accumulation of dollars in the rest of the world the system is also characterised by a continuous expansion of the American trade deficit, so that for the currency universally accepted as international unit of payment there is a corresponding decrease in its capacity to make real payments. Using modern terminology we would say that the United States is the most indebted country in the world precisely because dollars define a promise of the American banking system to pay, a promise that will never be honoured both because it has reached an extraordinarily high level, and because the American trade balance is still far from becoming positive.

The point of view of Jacques Rueff

Particular attention must be devoted to the French economist Jacques Rueff, whose opinions have given rise to heated disputes about the role of the dollar as international currency. Having observed that the international community decided to adopt national currencies convertible into gold as official reserves at the conference of Genoa (1922), Rueff notes that, after the Second World War, 'only the dollar was redeemable into gold. Hence, it is only the American currency that was held in the banks' balance sheet' (Rueff 1980: 302). Now, the dollars the United States uses to pay for its imports can only be deposited with their issuing banks. 'The very day they were obtained, dollars were placed on the New York market, either as bank deposits or in the purchase of Treasury bills. From there they were sent back to their place of origin, which thus recovered the liquidity it had just lost' (1980: 303). In exchange for its exports, the rest of the world obtains an equivalent sum of deposits in dollars which, by definition, are an acknowledgement of debt of the American banking system. In other words, by paying in dollars the United States acquires goods and services in exchange for a mere promise to pay which it will never be asked to honour since the American currency benefits from the particular status of international currency. What Rueff calls the 'deficit without tears' is the consequence of a system allowing for the identification of one or more national currencies with net assets capable of financing international transactions. Being paid with a mere duplicate – since the original is deposited with the American banking system – the commercial partners of the richest country in the world are thus bound to gratuitously give away part of their national resources.

> Everything took place on the monetary plane just as if the [American] deficit had not existed. This is how the gold exchange standard brought about an immense revolution and produced the secret of a deficit without tears, to the countries in possession of a currency benefiting from international prestige allowing them to give without taking, to lend without borrowing, and to get without paying.
>
> (Rueff 1963: 322)

The lack of payment of the American deficit and the duplication of dollars – which, as has already been said, are simultaneously recorded in the American banking system and in that of the creditor country: 'Entering the credit system of the creditor country, but remaining in the debtor country, the claims representing the deficit are thus doubled' (1963: 324) – is also the cause of an equivalent emission of domestic money by the creditor country's banking system. 'The claims transferred for the settlement of the deficit are bought against the creation of money, by the banking system of the creditor country' (1963: 323). The book-keeping entries relative to American net trade imports' payment and to the corresponding creation of national money are shown in Table 7.1. On the basis of the deposit in dollars, the creditor country's banking system creates an equivalent amount of domestic money in favour of the exporter. As we know, this process corresponds to the monetisation of the 'mercantilist' external benefit realised by the net exporting country. If we take into account the fact that in a system based on national sovereignties, transactions carried out by residents

Table 7.1

American banking system				*Banking system of the creditor country*			
Liabilities			Assets	*Liabilities*			Assets
BS of the creditor country	$ x	Importer	$ x	Exporter eq. in national money of	$ x	American banking system	$ x

have an impact on their own country (see Chapter 13), net exports define a benefit that the country obtains under the form of an increase in its official reserves. This increase implies the intervention of the Central Bank which, in exchange, gives secondary banks an equivalent sum of domestic currency. Exporters are thus paid through the creation of money elicited by the annexation of the dollars obtained in exchange for net exports of real goods and services. The transformation of the currencies recorded on the asset side into empty duplicates is therefore linked to the seigniorage exerted by the Central Bank. The whole process sanctions the final transformation into duplicates of the key-currencies used internationally, which, by simple means (or instruments), are transformed into objects of payment.

The duplication of dollars is the necessary consequence of the fact that currencies cannot be subtracted from their national banking system. Being a completely dematerialised object, money is created in a circular movement and is immediately deposited in its issuing bank. Book-keeping entries reflect the circulation of money, and it is impossible for a payment in bank money not to be recorded simultaneously on the assets and on the liabilities side of the bank which carries it out. The sum entered on the bank's debit side shows that it benefits from a deposit made by the client the payment is credited to. If the owner of the new deposit is also indebted to the bank for an equivalent amount, the payment gives rise to a destruction of (real) money, it is true, but this does not mean that money can be taken away from its bank of origin to be deposited elsewhere. If money is not destroyed, it exists as a deposit with its issuing bank, the identity of the deposit holder, whether a national or a foreigner, being irrelevant.

When American external purchases are paid for in dollars, the bank of the foreign exporter holds a deposit with the bank of the American importer. Hence the whole of the American income is deposited with American banks, even though, once foreign creditors are paid, part of this income is owned by banks established outside the United States. Dollars entered as assets in the bank of the foreign exporter are claims on an American deposit, and cannot be used as money except through a duplication of the American currency. Simultaneously present (as deposits) in the United States and abroad, dollars are duplicated, and those paid to net creditors, residents of the rest of the world, acquire an autonomous existence which transforms a simple duplicate into an international unit of payment: the Eurodollar.

Let us consider for a moment what happens in a national banking system. The payment made by client A of a bank B_1 in favour of client C of another bank, B_2, leads to the book-keeping entries shown in Table 7.2. The sum entered on the assets side of B_2's balance sheet refers to the deposit formed in B_1; must we conclude, therefore, that because of A's payment to C the money initially issued by B_1 is duplicated? The answer is founded on the principles ruling a national banking system, which contemplate, in this case, the Central Bank's intervention as clearing house of secondary banks. The interbank debt between B_1 and B_2 is thus transformed into a debt of B_1 and a credit of B_2 to the Central Bank (Table 7.3).

Through this mechanism, the funds available for the purchase of national output are only those deposited by C with bank B_2. Thanks to the Central Bank compensatory intervention, no duplication takes place therefore at the national level.

Internationally, however, there is no extra-national bank capable of acting as a Bank of Central Banks. No monetary compensation is available to avoid the duplication of foreign key-currencies and the consequent expansion of the Euromarket. It is thus confirmed that the solution to the problem of net international payments, financed today by a currency with no real content, will be possible only if it is agreed to accept:

Table 7.2

B_1				*B_2*			
Liabilities			*Assets*	*Liabilities*			*Assets*
B_2	x	A	x	C	x	B_1	x

Table 7.3

B_1				*B_2*			
Liabilities			*Assets*	*Liabilities*			*Assets*
CB	x	A	x	C	x	CB	x

CB			
Liabilities			*Assets*
B_2	x	B_1	x

> (1) the substitution for the monetary system existing in these countries of a system which will not favor or maintain the deficit of countries whose currency is considered as equal to gold by the banks of issue which receive it; and (2) the removal of a situation rendered dangerously vulnerable by the duplication of the edifice of credit built up on the gold stock of countries with a currency which is taken as being equal to gold.
>
> (Rueff 1963: 325)

The common elements of the main theories

Several authors have taken part in the animated debates between advocates and opponents of the gold exchange standard or of the dollar exchange standard, of convertibility or inconvertibility, of fixed or floating exchange rates, of the return to gold or of the creation of an international currency. Now, despite the divergences characterising their analyses, it is possible to find important common elements allowing for their gathering in a unique category which we could call 'traditional'.

Let us consider, for example, the monetarist approach and that of Triffin. Both are based on the idea that, except in case of perfect equilibrium, international transactions modify the quantity of money available within each country. The fundamental principle is that of the equality between debits and credits which, indifferently applied to domestic and foreign currencies, leads Triffin to claim that 'actual changes in money supply may be analyzed into money of internal origin (internal credit monetization by banks) and of external origin (net purchases of external assets by the banking system)' (1966: 214). Both Triffin and the monetarists are thus claiming that external sources can increase internal expenditure through an increase in the quantity of money. National and foreign currencies are assimilated into a unique mass defining the global money supply. Hence, though essentially different, national currencies are considered as elements of one and the same set.

When gold was the common denominator of dollars, francs, pounds, etc., these currencies were made immediately homogeneous by their gold parity. In a way, they were assimilated to gold, and as such they could be gathered into a unique 'mass'. In the absence of this privileged link with gold, it seems possible to overcome national currencies' heterogeneity through their exchange rates. Given the relationship between *a* and *b*, it is not difficult to pass from one currency to the other, so that it seems perfectly proper to establish equality between credits and debits not only within any national banking system, but also among different systems.

Respect for the golden rule of double entry book-keeping is a necessity of all theories investigating the nature of money, either national or international. It is not surprising, therefore, to find it as a pivotal element in the analyses developed following the Bretton Woods conference. The important fact is not the general acknowledgement of this principle of banking theory, but the unanimous belief that its implementation at the international level is perfectly consistent with the nature of the different national currencies. No one doubts that this principle can easily be implemented between two regions of a same country. However, is it also certain that it can be complied with when different countries are concerned, without requiring the working out of a system of payments taking into account the fundamental heterogeneity of national currencies? Experts answer this question in the affirmative, since they start from the hypothesis that, once exchange rates have been determined, the heterogeneity problem is definitively solved. The equality of debits and credits together with national currencies' homogeneity are thus common elements which can be found in the numerous variants of traditional analysis.

Another important common element is related to the currency used as international means of payment, which is usually considered as a net asset in the same way as that which, at the national level, defines a domestic income. The claim according to which exports cause an increase in the quantity of money has to be interpreted in the light of this 'real' definition of international money. This is precisely the interpretation that can be found both in the monetarist analysis of income and in that worked out by the Keynesians. Another proof of the almost unanimous adoption of this principle is given by the general acceptance of the thesis that it is possible to increase the domestic expenditure of individual firms and households 'indifferently from abroad or from internal sources' (Triffin 1966: 216), and by the banking practice of balancing the entry of foreign currencies with the creation of an equivalent amount of domestic currency. If foreign currencies were not considered as income, they could obviously not increase the internal expenditure of a private resident or a firm. On the other hand, by entering the deposits in foreign currencies obtained as payment on their asset side, banks can enter an equivalent sum of national money on their liability side.

Even those who emphasise the role of Bank of the world played by the country whose currency is used as international means of payment do not doubt that, for the receiving countries, foreign key-currencies represent a net asset; a belief that is also confirmed by the fact that foreign key-currencies are part of countries' official reserves and are important factors in the determination of their wealth.

The final proof of the general adoption of this second principle is given by the assimilation of national currencies to the real commodity set. This aspect is particularly evident in the determination of foreign exchange rates. These are defined, in fact, as the 'prices' of currencies and are determined through supply and demand, that is in exactly the same way as prices of real goods are determined. Money market and product market are essentially similar because currencies are considered to be real goods. For a given supply, the increased demand for a currency increases its price (its exchange rate) in the same way as the price of a product goes up when demand for it increases. If currencies were not net assets, they would not be supplied and demanded as if they were final goods, and their price could not be determined by the famous neoclassical law. By accepting the hypothesis of a Walrasian monetary market (in which prices are determined by supply and demand) experts on international money show no hesitation in identifying the national currencies used internationally with assets such as gold and commodities, which define the real wealth of a nation.

A PRACTICAL ATTEMPT AT SOLVING THE INTERNATIONAL LIQUIDITY PROBLEM: THE CREATION OF THE SPECIAL DRAWING RIGHTS

The Rio de Janeiro agreement

In a period in which international reserves were growing less rapidly and their composition was substantially changing (from 1961 to 1972 American gold reserves declined from $18.75 billion to $13.15 billion), the monetary authorities of IMF member countries feared that international liquidity would not be sufficient to satisfy the needs of a growing world economy. In particular it was thought that liquidity shortage could lead countries to adopt trade restrictions and slow down domestic growth. An attempt was thus made to avoid these dangers by creating new international reserves capable of solving a priori the liquidity problem. The decision to resort to the creation of the Special Drawing Rights (SDRs) was taken by member countries in the IMF meeting held in Rio de Janeiro in 1967, and the agreement became effective in July 1969.

According to the official definition, SDRs are 'entries in the IMF ledgers that allow deficit countries to settle part of their payments imbalances with allotments of SDRs' (Meier 1982: 90). Hence, the IMF agreed to grant special credits which the beneficiary country could take advantage of for purchasing the gold and convertible currencies it needed to face its balance of payments needs.

> These special drawing rights, created, as it were, by a stroke of the pen, will be essentially entries in the books of the Fund. [. . .] Their value will derive essentially from the fact that participants will be obliged to accept them when properly transferred and to provide in exchange convertible currency or gold, up to a point where they are holding three times as many special drawing rights as have been allocated to them by the Fund.
>
> (Schweitzer 1967: 11)

An important aspect of the new unit created by the IMF is that it is not based on the pre-existence of any financial reserve. Its emission is a true creation out of nothing which endows the Fund with a faculty that, although supported by Keynes, had been denied it since its foundation. With the adoption of the new system, each member country can claim a specified amount of Special Drawing Rights. The emission of SDRs gives rise to a book-keeping entry showing the debt to the Fund incurred by the country benefiting from their creation and, simultaneously, the debt incurred by the Fund to this same country. Special Drawing Rights are then used to acquire an equivalent amount of key foreign currencies, under the obligation of reconstitution in accordance with principles laid down by the Fund. Since allocation of SDRs depends on the quotas subscribed by each member country, the emission of the Fund is limited, even though countries can always obtain SDRs in exchange for an equivalent amount of key-currencies.

The creation of SDRs was enthusiastically welcomed by some economists, who identified in this operation the first concrete step towards the institution of a new system of international payments based on the use of a world bank money. Others, however, were more sceptical about the effective innovation represented by SDRs, and were not certain about the real status of what was called a 'funny money'.

> Some people like to think of them as money, others as a form of credit. As Dr. Emminger, the former Chairman of the Deputies of the Group of Ten, has aptly put it, they are a sort of zebra which can with equal accuracy be described as a white animal with black stripes or a black animal with white stripes. The material point is not how they are named but what can be done with them.
>
> (Schweitzer 1967: 11)

The opinion of Schweitzer, Managing Director of the IMF, was shared by several experts of the General Counsel, who claimed that Special Drawing Rights were to be considered neither as money nor as a form of credit, but as *sui generis*.

> The characteristics of special drawing rights are not the result of any single approach. They are the distillation of a chemistry – some might say an alchemy – in which many theories and many compromises, economic, legal, and political, went into the alembic. The product cannot be classified according to such familiar categories as 'legal tender', 'money', or 'credit'. Special drawing rights are *sui generis*.
>
> (Gold 1970: 28)

The transformation of Special Drawing Rights into a world money has never taken place. SDRs have been confined to a secondary role and international payments are still carried out through the use of key-currencies. Even at the level of official reserves SDRs had a limited impact: if between 1970 and 1972 9.3 billion SDRs were created, in the same period international dollar reserves grew by 45.5 billion. A quick look at the diagram relative to the composition of reserves between 1974 and 1990 elaborated by the IMF *International Financial Statistics Yearbook* (1993) (Figure 7.1) is enough to see how little importance the role played up to now by the Special Drawing Rights has had. Finally, even though for the first time in monetary history an international reserve was created through a simple book-keeping entry recorded by an international organisation, the introduction of SDRs did not substantially modify the world system of external payments, which went on being based on the principles of the gold exchange standard.

A short theoretical appraisal of SDRs

According to the *Outline of Reform* (IMF 1974) published by the Committee of Twenty in 1974, the Special Drawing Rights were considered as the ideal

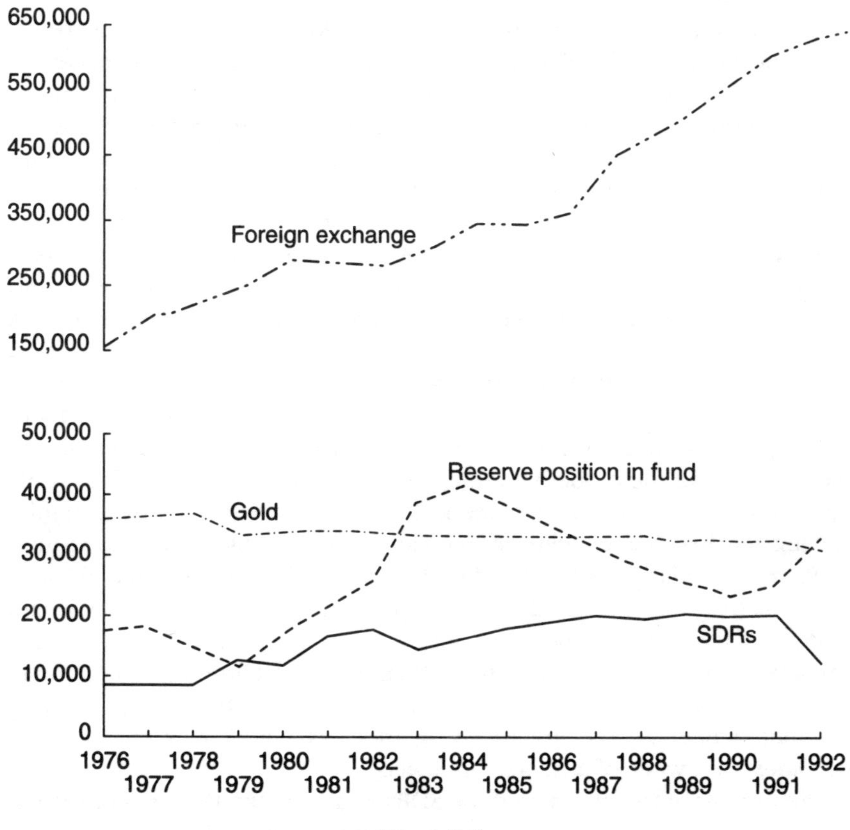

Figure 7.1

substitute for gold and the national currencies then used as main international resources. In particular it was proposed to transform SDRs into the principal reserve asset. Besides playing the role of unit of payment, SDRs were also to become the international unit of account *par excellence*. 'The SDR will become the principal asset and the role of gold and of reserve currencies will be reduced. The SDR will also be the numeraire in terms of which par values will be expressed' (IMF 1974: 20).

As we have seen, SDRs are issued by the International Monetary Fund through a simple book-keeping entry. It is proper, therefore, to ask if SDRs are effectively a first example of international currency and what their economic status is. This question arises because the IMF does not fulfil the requirements for being a true supranational bank. The emission of an international money calls for the existence of such an institution, so that we have to choose between two alternatives: either we maintain that SDRs are a world money, in which case the IMF is effectively – though only implicitly – a supranational bank; or we show that SDRs are not a true international currency, thus confirming that the IMF is not the materialisation of Keynes's International Clearing Union.

The analysis of monetary creation is determinant. Let us first consider the fundamental principle of double entry book-keeping, i.e. the necessary equality of credits and debits. As claimed by Keynes, modern bank money must comply with this principle both nationally and internationally. As far as the domestic monetary system is concerned things work smoothly: newly created money is immediately deposited with the same bank which issues it. It is precisely because money is of a banking origin that it is represented as a bank deposit. The beneficiary of a monetary payment is credited by the bank of his economic correspondent, and this simply implies the substitution between payer and payee as owner of a bank deposit.

By defining money as the great wheel of circulation, Adam Smith had pointed out its vehicular nature perfectly, and this despite the fact that banking activity was still little developed. Today our task is made easier by the workings of the modern banking system, and it is not difficult to verify that money is, first of all, a numerical vehicle circulating between banks. Having reached this conclusion, we can wonder if, like domestic money, SDRs are circularly issued by the IMF. Since they are created through book-keeping entries recorded in the Special Drawing Account, SDRs exist under this form and define a deposit for the countries that accept them in exchange for an equivalent sum of their national currency. The country making use of its drawing rights becomes indebted to the Special Drawing Account, while the country receiving them as payment is credited and becomes the owner of a deposit in SDRs.

We now have to determine if the SDRs issued by the IMF are considered in the same way as national currencies even as far as their intrinsic value is concerned. As is well known, the bank money created within each country has no intrinsic value. The abolition of any real or nominal link between money and gold, and the widespread use of modern data-processing techniques, leaves no room for doubts about the dematerialisation of vehicular money. This does not mean, of course, that money has no value at all, but only that it does not stem from any specific quality of the object used to represent it. In other words, if money has a value it is only because it is associated with current domestic output, of which it represents the 'economic' definition.

The lack of a true international output means that SDRs cannot be endowed with any positive value. Since they cannot be associated with any real production, SDRs are a simple book-keeping entry which, as such, can obviously not possess a specific economic value. To claim the contrary would amount to endorsing the metaphysical assumption of a creation *ex nihilo*. If SDRs had a value, their emission by the IMF would define the creation of a financial asset. The Fund would thus be endowed with the faculty of creating a positive amount of income out of nothing, and this at a ridiculously low cost and without any real production whatsoever. The absurdity of this hypothesis is so obvious that it can be left aside without any further analysis. Now, the SDRs were created with the aim of increasing international financial liquidities and providing for new reserve assets. This means that SDRs were issued as financial assets, exchangeable with national currencies precisely because endowed with a positive purchasing power over monetary assets issued at a domestic level. For example, the exchange between SDRs and American dollars was thought of as an exchange between two equivalent monetary assets so that there were laid down the foundations for the substitution of the final payments made in SDRs with those made in dollars.

As we know, the project to transform SDRs into a world money was rapidly abandoned. Despite this, it still represents the most serious attempt at implementing some of the most significant principles of the Keynes plan. In particular, the analysis outlined here shows how the book-keeping principle of the equality between credits and debits is unfailingly respected by a monetary system analogous to that existing at the national level. Unfortunately, however, the circular aspect of money is only partially complied with. By endowing the IMF with the supernatural faculty of creating a net asset without founding it on any real production, the advocates of a monetary reform based on the emission of SDRs entirely miss the originality of Keynes's proposals. The bancor was conceived as a pure vehicular means whose task was not to finance international transactions, but to convey them from one country to another through the Clearing Union intermediation. The problem Keynes aimed at solving was not the financial one, but the monetary one. From the financial point of view, each country must find the resources necessary to cover its purchases, and this independently of the monetary structure of the system. Imports of goods are thus financed both through commercial exports and the sale of bonds. The task of international money is that of conveying payments which remain, fundamentally, real. Given this vehicular function, extra-national money has to be neutral in regard to national currencies and their relationship with domestic output. This is the result Keynes wanted to reach through the use of the bancor. Now, it is only if it is issued according to the principles of double entry book-keeping and without any intrinsic value that the bancor can play its role without interfering in the relationship between national currencies and domestic output. If, as in the case of SDRs, international money is conceived of as a financial asset, monetary payments add to the real ones and neutrality is replaced by generalised disorder.

By insisting on the vehicular function of money, the classical authors (particularly Smith and Ricardo) and Keynes emphasise the need to distinguish between nominal (vehicular) money and real money (income and capital). The lack of an international production does not put this distinction under discussion; on the contrary, it is precisely on the basis of this distinction that it is possible to understand the nature of international money. Keynes put forth the bancor as nominal world money whose aim is to convey international payments instead of carrying them out in person. Instead, Special Drawing Rights are conceived irrespective of the distinction between nominal and real money. The magic power ascribed to the IMF of creating income independently from production makes it possible to use SDRs as final means of payment for international transactions. They are not considered, therefore, as a mere vehicular instrument, but as a final good, a financial asset pertaining to the category of real goods. Fundamentally similar to real assets, SDRs must comply with the same rules governing their fluctuation. In particular, if IMF regulations did not oppose it explicitly, they could be bought and sold against national currencies, thus giving rise to movements of revaluation and devaluation that would seriously threaten exchange rate stability.

In conclusion, the analysis of SDRs and of the way they are issued by the IMF shows that they are already an embryonic form of international money since their circulation respects the identity between credits and debits. Their status of reserve assets, however, prevents them from playing a purely vehicular role. Moreover, it must also be observed that the use of SDRs, initially limited to the purchase of national currencies, has never been generalised, and that the IMF has only very partially acted as an international bank.

THE DOLLAR EXCHANGE STANDARD

The dollar has been playing the role of international money since the end of the Second World War, at first as the sole currency effectively convertible into gold and then as the main international reserve asset. Whether the passage from the gold exchange standard to the dollar exchange standard was caused by the decision of August 1971 to suspend convertibility or not is a moot point. What is certain is that gold no longer played an essential role and that the United States was nevertheless bound to give up gold in exchange for dollars offered by foreign monetary authorities at the price of $35 per ounce. And since the other currencies were convertible into dollars and the dollar used as unit of account and means of payment, American monetary authorities were technically unable to modify the dollar exchange rate. The United States suffered a loss of its gold reserves, which, between 1957 and 1968, decreased from $23 to $11 billion, and an increase in its balance of payments deficit. As we have already observed, the international monetary system was thus in the absurd situation of being allowed to increase its liquidity only by increasing a disequilibrium which, by weakening confidence in the dollar and making exchange rates unstable, ended up by worsening the very problem of international liquidity. In this chapter we shall examine the validity of this analysis with regard to the monetary crisis that led to the suspension of convertibility, and we shall try to show how one of the most important consequences of the dollar standard, the birth and expansion of the Eurodollar market, is directly linked to the system of international payments chosen at Bretton Woods.

The phenomenon of Eurocurrencies

Eurocurrencies are currencies of any country held on deposit outside their home markets and used as a source of short- or medium-term finance. Dollars deposited with non-American banks define the amount of Eurodollars accumulated in the world since the American currency has been used as a reserve asset.

The mechanism leading to the creation of Eurodollars is simple: when a foreign bank becomes the owner of an American deposit in dollars, the claim on this deposit acquires a proper autonomy and can be invested in the offshore circuit of Eurobanks. The operations that can activate this mechanism are related to the use of the dollar as international reserve currency. It was when the American currency was given this particular status that the premise for its deposit in foreign banks' assets was laid down. Hence, among the most important reasons for the formation of Eurodollars we find the deficit of the American trade balance as well as all the transactions allowing foreign countries to increase their official dollar reserves independently of their trade surplus (as, for example, in the case of royalties or unrequited aid).

After having been created through key-currencies' primary deposits, the Eurocurrency market has developed thanks to repeated lending and today we distinguish three main areas of trading:

1 Eurocurrency short-term market, where banks offer each other short-term credits (with maturities ranging from overnight to twelve months);
2 Euro-credit market, where loan facilities are usually offered by a number of syndicated banks to private firms or governments for periods ranging from five to ten years;
3 Eurobond market, where generally unsecured bonds issued by a variety of institutions (firms, banks, international organisations, companies) are offered by international syndicates of banks to private and institutional investors.

The articulation of primary and secondary deposits makes it difficult to establish the real statistical dimension of the Eurocurrency market, also because the deposits (in dollars or in other key-currencies) held abroad by foreign residents are not taken into account (as stateless money they are not counted statistically). By way of example, let us note that at the end of 1992 Eurocommercial papers and Euronote placements by banks located within the Bank for International Settlement (BIS) reporting area amounted to $176.8 billion, the stock of international bond financing was $1,687.2 billion, of net international bank lending $3,660 billion, and of interbank positions in foreign currencies $4,651.3 billion.

Eurocurrencies as the result of net commercial exports

The phenomenon of Eurodollar formation is of a particular theoretical interest. It cannot be doubted, in fact, that the deposits in dollars held by foreign banks stem from a deposit which was initially formed in the United States. By crediting a foreign bank, the American bank is still the bank in which the dollars are deposited. What is transferred abroad is not dollars, but the claim on the deposit in dollars formed in the American bank. It is on the basis of this claim that the foreign bank grants credits in Eurodollars, so that we witness an effective duplication of the dollars, which are simultaneously deposited in the United States and lent on the Eurocurrency market. As is claimed by Jacques Rueff, the dollars that foreign banks are credited with are re-invested

> on the market of the debtor country. Thus everything happens as if these currencies had never been exported in the first place. Entering the credit system of the creditor country, but remaining in the debtor country, the claims representing the deficit are thus doubled.
>
> (Rueff 1963: 324)

The phenomenon of duplication is not confined to the system of international payments worked out at Bretton Woods and known as the gold exchange standard. The convertibility of the dollar into gold is not directly responsible for a state of affairs which finds its *raison d'être* in the fact that the dollar is universally considered as a net asset within and outside the American border. This leads to a series of book-keeping entries which, although respecting the monetary nature of the dollar (which defines a deposit with its issuing banking system), allow foreign banks to finance new loans in Eurodollars despite the fact that they are simple duplicates of the dollars deposited in the United States. Hence, the determining factor of this process is not the convertibility of the dollar, but the status internationally ascribed to the American currency and the way in which international transactions in dollars are recorded as book-keeping entries.

Let us briefly recall the example analysed in the section on Jacques Rueff (p. 151). The payment of net commercial imports by any country whose domestic currency is internationally accepted as reserve asset, is recorded as in Table 7.4. Importing country A pays by crediting exporting country B with x units of national money (NM), which remain entirely deposited in A's banking system (and which define A's acknowledgement of debt). The duplication denounced by Rueff consists in the fact that the same amount is simultaneously deposited in its country of origin and entered on the asset side of the exporting country's balance sheet (that is, on the asset side of its Central Bank). Instead of a monetary flow from A to B, which would imply a reduction in the quantity of money available in A and an increase in that available in B, we observe a multiplication of the initial deposit, whose duplicate is invested by B's Central Bank on the Eurocurrency market.

It is important to recall here how the phenomenon of duplication is related to that of seigniorage. Foreign currencies earned by the exporting country are transferred to its Central Bank, which increases its official reserves of valuable currencies by financing the operation through domestic money creation. Once purchased by the Central Bank, foreign currencies are invested on the Euromarket, thus provoking an equivalent increase in the international speculative capital. In those countries where financial legislation allows it, key-currencies obtained through net commercial exports can be purchased by the public, for example by private firms for liquidity reasons, thus giving rise to reserves of a private nature. In this case the purchase is not financed by a mere monetary creation, but by the income spent by the purchaser. However, the transformation of a

Table 7.4

Banking system of the importing country (A)				*Banking system of the exporting country (B)*			
Liabilities			*Assets*	*Liabilities*			*Assets*
BS of the exporting country	x MA	Importer	x MA	Exporter (eq. in MB of x MA)	y MB	BS of the importing country	x MA

promise to pay into a final good, which is the object of the reserves formed in the country, has a negative repercussion at the international level. Even in this case, in fact, foreign currencies accumulated as reserves are not kept inactive, and their investment on the Euromarket is the unmistakable sign of a growth in the global amount of Eurocurrencies.

At this stage of the analysis it is perhaps necessary to ask if the mechanism leading to Eurocurrency creation does not extend also to the exporting country currencies, so that the duplication would concern both surplus and deficit key-currency countries.

The birth of Eurocurrencies and their relationship with trade and financial transactions among key-currency countries

Since hard currencies are considered as final goods, the net sale of real goods and services is not necessarily matched by an equivalent purchase of bonds from the deficit country. Instead of flowing back to their country of origin, foreign currencies earned by country B, a net commercial exporter, are purchased by B's Central Bank and lent on the Euromarket.

This result can also be reached when the purchase of Eurobonds is financed by a net export of securities to a key-currency country. Let us suppose that the internal financing of the external sale of domestic bonds is obtained through the sale of foreign currencies to residents who invest them on the Euromarket. Country B thus balances the sale of bonds to A with an equivalent purchase of Eurobonds, while exporters of bonds are paid with the income saved by those who invest on the Euromarket (Table 7.5). Internal equilibrium is perfectly complied with, in accordance with the rule requiring the daily coverage of credits granted by secondary banks. The purchase of foreign currencies, however, instead of financing commercial imports, nourishes international speculative capital. Even though it does not define an increase in the country's official reserves, the purchase of Eurobonds carried out on behalf of B's residents increases the mass of

Table 7.5

Banking system of country B

Liabilities			*Assets*
Initial IH	x MB	Firms (output)	x MB
Sellers of bonds	y MB	Banking system of the rest of the world	z FC
Eurobanks	z FC	Residents (IH)	y MB
Initial IH	x – y MB	Firms (output)	x MB
Sellers of bonds	y MB		

Eurocurrencies and leads to a worsening of the monetary instability due to the present structure of international payments.

An example of this mechanism of duplication connected to capital flows is given by the Euroyen formation. As is known, Japan's trade balance has been positive for a long time. The formation of Euroyen can therefore not be explained by the payment of Japan's net commercial imports. Now, trade surpluses make Japan a net capital exporter. If the country of the rising sun traded only with weak-currency countries, it would lend them the precise amount, in yen, of its net sales of goods and services. Its purchases of bonds would be perfectly matched by its commercial sales, and the yen would all flow back to their point of origin. Because of the existence of other strong-currency countries, however, parts of Japan's sales are paid for in foreign currencies (for example in dollars). It is thus possible that Japan invests yen in the purchase of bonds of country B, and that these yen are then invested on the Euromarket by B's residents, who pay for their commercial imports from Japan in dollars. The Japanese currency spent on purchasing bonds undergoes a process of duplication leading to the formation of offshore deposits in yen which are not matched by a destruction of other Eurocurrencies. Hence, on the one hand the payment of American net commercial imports from Japan in dollars leads to an increase in the dollar reserves of the Japanese Central Bank (and, thus, to an increase in the Eurodollars invested on the Euromarket) while, on the other hand, the investment in yen carried out by Japanese residents through the purchase of American bonds leads to a duplication of the Japanese currency, simultaneously entered as a deposit in its national banking system and as an asset in the American banking system (Table 7.6). If the dollars earned by Japan through its net commercial exports were not added to the official reserves of its Central Bank, the purchase of American bonds by Japanese residents would lead to a compensation between the secondary banks of the two countries, and we would witness a reduction in the amount of Eurocurrencies which originated from the payment of the American trade deficit. The existence of monetary sovereignty, however, has as a consequence the fact that it is the country itself that benefits from its residents' net commercial exports. Entered on the asset side of the Japanese Central Bank, the dollars paid by the United States are invested on the Euromarket and thus escape compensation with the yen entered as a net asset in the American banking system. The duplication of dollars and yen can be explained by referring to the distinction between nation and residents. It is Japan as a nation that benefits from the net inflow of dollars corresponding to the Japanese trade surplus, whereas the net payment in yen in favour of the United States is carried out by the residents. It is because the nation is not identical to the sum of its residents (see Part III of this work) that Euroyen are created in addition to Eurodollars. In conclusion we can thus claim that, considered within the actual system of

Table 7.6

American banking system (ABS)			
Liabilities			*Assets*
IH	$ x	Output	$ x
JBS	$ y	Importers	$ y
IH	$ x – y	Output	$ x
JBS	$ y		
Sellers of bonds	$ y	JBS	v yen
Eurobanks	v yen	IH	$ y

Japanese banking system (JBS)			
Liabilities			*Assets*
IH	z yen	Output	z yen
Eurobanks	$ y	ABS	$ y
Exporters	v yen	Revolving fund	v yen
IH	z yen	Output	z – v yen
		Revolving fund	v yen
ABS	v yen	IH	v yen

international payments, trade surpluses and deficits of strong-currency countries are concomitant causes for the rapid growth of the mass of Eurocurrencies.

The purchase of Eurocurrencies by residents of a strong-currency country leads to a variation in their composition

Let us suppose that residents of country A choose to invest part of their income in purchasing Eurocurrencies and lending them on the Euromarket. As is well known, these transactions are carried out on a fiduciary basis. Banks simply purchase and lend foreign currencies on behalf of their clients, who take on the entire risks of the operation. Residents who invest part of their savings in Eurocurrencies become the new holders of equivalent Eurodeposits; there is therefore a simple substitution between old and new owners of Eurobonds, which can modify the Eurocurrency composition but which does not alter its total amount. Let us suppose, for example, that German residents R_1 invest marks on the Eurodollar market. The Eurobank implied in this transaction becomes the owner of a deposit in marks with the bank of R_1 (Table 7.7). The first entry of Table 7.7 refers to the initial investment in Eurodollars carried out by the Central Bank of a given country C_w; the second to the loan in dollars carried out on behalf of German residents. As a result of the second operation, dollars are replaced by marks on the Eurobank's asset side, with a consequent modification in the composition of Eurocurrencies. If other German residents, R_2, took over R_1's investment there would be a simple alternation of those who lend their monetary assets to the Eurobank. If successive investments on the Euromarket were carried out by residents of another country, for example Japan, yen would take the place of Euromarks and their lending would again modify the Eurocurrency composition (Table 7.8). In the same way

Table 7.7

	Liabilities		Assets	
		Eurobank		
(1)	Central Bank of C_W	\$ x		\$ x
(2)	Clients	\$ x	German Bank of R_1	y marks

Table 7.8

	Liabilities		Assets	
		Eurobank		
(1)	Central Bank of C_W	\$ x		\$ x
(2)	Clients	\$ x	German Bank of R_1 (or R_2)	y marks
(3)	Clients	y marks	Japanese secondary bank	z yen

as in (2) the dollars are replaced by an equivalent amount of marks (where \$x = y marks), in (3) yen take the place of marks (y marks = z yen). Dollars and marks are spent by those who borrow them and are replaced by the yen the Japanese bank credits the Eurobank with, on behalf of its clients.

A change in the composition of Eurocurrencies can also be caused by an intervention of Eurobanks on the foreign exchange market. Upon request, Eurobanks can change the denomination of their credits by substituting part of their Eurocurrencies with other hard currencies on the foreign exchange market. If the owners of a deposit in Eurodollars decided to transform it into Euroyen, the Eurobank concerned with this transaction would carry it out by offering dollars in exchange for yen.

Strictly speaking, Eurocurrencies are a phenomenon linked to the balance of payments. Their formation requires the use of one or more national currencies as final unit of international payment. In order to have a creation of Eurocurrencies it is therefore necessary for a country to earn foreign currency through the sale of goods, services and bonds, and this can certainly not derive either from the purchase of the Eurocurrencies already present on the market or from exchange market operations.

Another important consequence of the Eurocurrency market can be found in the strict solidarity existing between a domestic currency and its foreign duplicate. For example, an excess demand for Eurodollars on the international market leads to a revaluation of their exchange rate, and therefore also of that of the dollars, while their excess supply leads to a joint devaluation of dollars and Eurodollars. This simple observation shows how exchange rate stability, particularly that of the dollar, depends heavily on Euromarket fluctuations. Speculative movements characterising this market have unpredictable effects, so that even what is considered as one of its main advantages, i.e. the fact of increasing the international circulation of capital, is seriously threatened by the risk inherent in the exchange rate instability deriving from this very circulation.

It is also useful to recall that, unlike what happens within each single country, where banks are watched over by a national monetary authority, offshore transactions take place without undergoing any superior external control. This has contributed to the intensifying of interbank collaboration, it is certain. Yet, given the peculiar Eurocurrency market structure, interbank agreements are inadequate to cope with the risk due to the intrinsic unpredictability of international speculative movements. None of the proposals for the creation of a supranational Bank have yet been concretised, maybe because this would also lead to a substantial change in the present system of international payments. If the Bank of International Settlements (BIS) (or any other international institution) were given the task of acting as Central Bank of national Banks, the dollar exchange standard system would leave its place to a structure similar to that proposed by Keynes in his plan for the creation of an International Clearing Union and the Eurocurrency market expansion would come to an end for lack of new funds.

Before analysing this possibility, let us conclude this chapter by referring to the path effectively followed internationally after the monetary crises of the 1960s.

The end of convertibility

The 1960s were characterised by a series of monetary crises involving all the major economic powers. Pounds and French francs on the one hand, marks and Canadian dollars on the other, were subject to opposite pressures leading to a devaluation of the former and a revaluation of the latter without any serious measure of international collaboration being adopted to contrast speculative flows from one currency to the other. The failure of the major countries of the world to coordinate their monetary and fiscal policies and to agree on a common intervention policy put the system of fixed exchange rates under pressure. The lack of coordination in a system where the dollar, the international reserve asset, unit of account and means of payment, was convertible into gold brought about the decision to suspend gold sales to the private market and to work out a mechanism which allowed the official price of gold to be maintained at $35 per ounce. As stressed by Gerald Meier, the implementation of this measure sanctioned the passage from the gold exchange standard to the dollar standard whose origins can be traced back to the decisions taken at Bretton Woods.

> With this action, the world's monetary authorities had taken a major step towards the demonetization of gold. The result of this decision could be interpreted as putting the world de facto on an international dollar standard, since it was obvious that the United States could also at any time refuse to convert dollars into gold for official holders of dollars. The action of the Gold Pool also left ambiguous the future role of gold and made its price uncertain.
>
> (Meier 1982: 89)

Despite all these efforts, the outflow of dollars from the United States went on, particularly to Germany, the United Kingdom, France and Italy, and the American balance of payment deficit continued to worsen. The situation became so worrying as to induce the Joint Economic Committee to suggest measures allowing for the fluctuation of the dollar relative to the other currencies and for the determination of an exchange rate more in conformity with the international economic reality of the day. Although the experts all agreed about over-evaluation of the dollar, they proposed different remedies for it, ranging from key-currency revaluation, to Federal Reserve intervention on foreign exchange, to the abandonment of gold convertibility. During August 1971 the situation worsened: capital outflow from the United States reached its highest level, gold reserves decreased at a high speed and the American trade balance deficit grew together with the unwillingness of foreign countries to accumulate dollars. The decision to officially suspend convertibility of the dollar into gold was taken by President Nixon on 15 August, and represents the first important attempt at stopping the international pressure exerted on the American currency without consulting the IMF or asking for its authorisation. This led the major European countries to close their exchange markets, seeking to find a common response to the American initiative. Unfortunately, no agreement was reached and the world had to accept the official passage to the 'reign of the dollar'.

8

THE INTERNATIONAL PAYMENTS PROBLEM AND THE BALANCE OF PAYMENTS

THE BALANCE OF PAYMENTS AND ITS AUTOMATIC RE-EQUILIBRIUM

The definition of the balance of payments officially adopted by the International Monetary Fund is the following:

> The balance of payments is a statistical statement for a given period showing (a) transactions in goods, services, and income between an economy and the rest of the world; (b) changes of ownership and other changes in that economy's monetary gold, special drawing rights (SDRs), and claims on and liabilities to the rest of the world; and (c) unrequited transfers and counterpart entries that are needed to balance, in the accounting sense, any entries for the foregoing transactions and changes which are not mutually offsetting.
>
> (IMF 1977: 1)

Thus, the balance of payments collects the book-keeping entries corresponding to commercial transactions and capital flows taking place between a given country and the rest of the world. The criterion chosen by the IMF for identifying the transactions concerning the balance of payments is that of residence.

> The balance-of-payments accounts identify foreign operations on the basis of residence of the transactor, foreign liabilities are therefore those owed to non-residents. Residence (as opposed to currency, ownership, nationality or another basis) was chosen as the criterion for distinguishing foreign from domestic because it provides a clear rule for identifying those transactors whose main economic interest lies within an economy.
>
> (WB, IMF, BIS, OECD 1988: 17)

Traditionally, the balance of payments is divided into a current account, a capital account and a foreign exchange balance (recording the variations in the Central Bank official reserves). The current account balance is made up by the balance of trade (imports and exports of goods), the balance of invisible items (imports and exports of services as well as of earned and capital income), and the balance of unrequited transfers (financial flows with no real counterpart). Trade balance and invisible items form the balance of goods and services. Exports and imports of financial assets are recorded in the balance of capital, whereas the difference between current account and capital flows is balanced through a variation in the foreign exchange account (Figure 8.1).

Considering that the variations in official reserves correspond to the monetary balance of current account transactions and capital movements, the balance of payments is clearly always in equilibrium. On the other hand, the balance of current account transactions is necessarily equivalent (albeit of the opposite sign) to that of capital and foreign exchange flows, since every current account surplus defines an increase in the loans granted abroad (import of bonds) and/or an increase in official reserves, whereas every deficit is financed through an export of bonds (import of capital) and/or a decrease in foreign currency reserves. The necessary equilibrium of the balance of payments derives from the inclusion of clearing balances in the

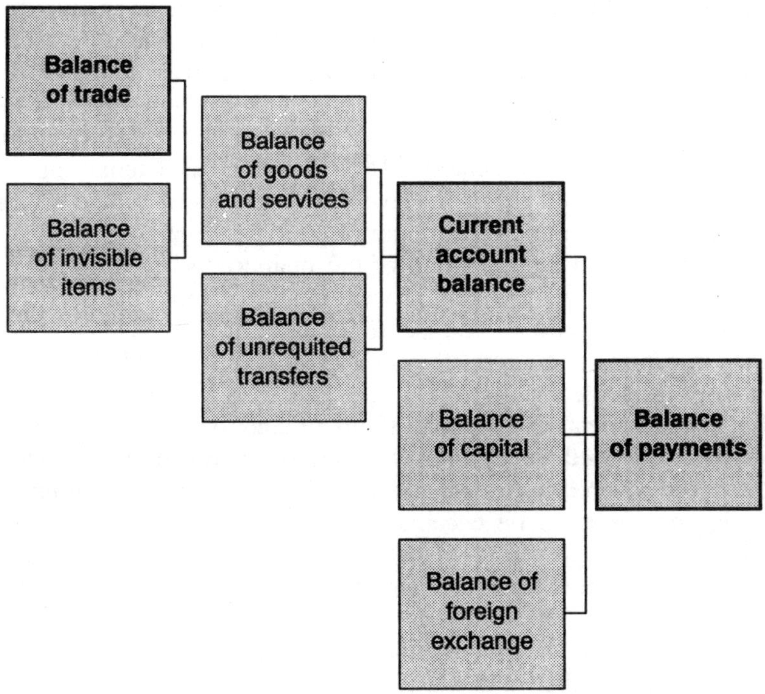

Figure 8.1

overall account of foreign economic transactions. On the contrary, clearing balances are usually excluded from the definition of trade and capital balance. Hence, a positive deficit between imports and exports of goods leads to a deficit of the trade balance, while a net import of capital defines a surplus of the capital balance and, therefore, an increase in foreign debt.

The expression 'balance of payments disequilibrium' refers to the offsetting balance of current account, capital flows and 'errors and omissions' (an item also accounting for the phenomenon of capital flight). When this offsetting balance is positive, foreign currency inflows are greater than outflows and we speak of a balance of payments surplus; otherwise monetary outlays exceed inputs and we speak of a balance of payments deficit. Deficits are financed either through a net export of bonds, an equivalent decrease in official gold and foreign exchange reserves, or a combination of these measures which, in their turn, can give rise to a more or less automatic mechanism of re-equilibrium of the balance of payments. Let us examine briefly the two best-known examples of this mechanism.

The gold and foreign exchange flow

Particularly during the period when international payments were organised on the basis of the gold standard or the gold exchange standard, the financing of external deficit implied the transfer of an equivalent sum of gold or foreign currencies to creditor countries. Both gold coverage of foreign deficit, and decrease in official foreign exchange reserves, seemed to guarantee a twofold re-equilibrating effect. In fact, besides offsetting external deficit, they also seemed able to determine an internal monetary situation which, by modifying the exports/imports ratio, would establish the conditions for a future equilibrium of the balance of payments. Referring to a mechanical interpretation of the quantity theory of money, the advocates of this re-equilibrating process maintained that the decrease in reserves would provoke a decrease in domestic prices, thus favouring an increase in exports and a reduction in imports which would eliminate the very causes of the deficit.

The abandonment of the gold standard and of the gold exchange standard has confined the 'classical' solution to a marginal role (deficits are almost never covered by a decrease in official reserves) whose effect is generally considered to be exceptionally positive. The reduction in the quantity of money provoked by decreasing reserves is seen as a deflationary measure which leads to a growth in unemployment only partially compensated for by the new opportunities given to export industries. Moreover, it is widely thought that the decrease in price of exported goods could well not be sufficient to adequately increase foreign demand, which would make this measure only partially effective at the external level while detrimental at the domestic level.

Though the analysis of bank money develops along different paths, it brings us to the same negative conclusions concerning the hypothetical re-equilibrating effect of payment in gold or foreign exchange. Official reserves are not part of the quantity of money monetising national output, and their reduction cannot have, therefore, a deflationary impact within the deficit country. Given that in the present system of national and international payments the increase in official reserves is linked to the creation of central money (see Chapters 5 and 7), we can at most claim that, if Central Banks provided the foreign currencies necessary for the payment of the deficit, the decrease in reserves would cancel out the increase in prices due to seigniorage. Nothing allows us to claim, however, that the new prices would make it possible for the country to balance its commercial flows. Let us start with commercial equilibrium, and let us suppose that a successive deficit leads to a decrease in foreign exchange reserves. Since official reserves can only be positively formed through a trade balance surplus, our initial situation of equilibrium is characterised by domestic prices which are higher than those corresponding to the periods of trade surplus. The passage from equilibrium to deficit implies a further increase in prices, with a consequent decrease in foreign demand. Independently of the reasons causing it, this increase in prices has to be added to that due to the seigniorage exerted by the Central Bank when official reserves are made up. The reduction in foreign exchange reserves thus leads to a reduction in prices relative to the level determined by the Central Bank intervention, without re-establishing the initial situation of equilibrium. In other words, the effect of the payment is not that of abolishing the causes of the deficit. The decrease in prices is linked to that of external incomes, but this does not modify the internal conditions which, by provoking an increase in these same prices, caused the deficit in the first place. No mechanism of automatic re-equilibrium of the balance of payments is therefore elicited by the assumed coverage of the deficit through a transfer of gold or foreign exchange.

It is important to note, nevertheless, that the system based on the gold coverage of the deficit benefits from a determining advantage with respect to that in which the payment takes place through a transfer of foreign exchange. The content of the payment in gold is the precious metal itself, whereas, as we have repeatedly stressed, that of foreign currencies is a simple promise. By giving gold in exchange for goods and services, the importing country hands over a real good and re-establishes equilibrium in real terms. By giving up foreign exchange, instead, it gets goods and services in exchange for an IOU whose object is the promise to pay itself. The payment is empty, and disequilibrium definitively confirmed by the duplication leading to Eurocurrency creation.

The suppression of the gold standard and fixed exchange rates removed the obligation to resort to official reserves in order to face balance of payment problems, and the 'classical' re-equilibrating mechanism was replaced by that based on exchange rate variation.

Exchange rate fluctuations

After the American government decision to suspend convertibility, the system of international payments converted to floating exchange rates. As is known, more articulate methods ranging from the determination of intervention margins, through gliding parities, to temporary floats were preferred to free fluctuation. However, as far as the automatic balance of payments re-equilibrium is concerned, the only mechanism we have to analyse is that of free floating. As claimed by Richard Cooper, exchange rates allow for the re-absorption of external imbalances only if they are determined on the basis of the free working of market forces.

> Prospective imbalances in payments would exercise upward or downward pressures on a given country's exchange rate in the market, and any excess demand for foreign exchange would automatically be eliminated by a movement in the exchange rate, much as is the case with equity prices on the commodity exchanges today. Balance-of-payments deficits or surpluses would never be observed.
>
> (Cooper 1987: 123)

Being defined as the relative price of a currency with regard to others, the exchange rate is influenced by all those factors which modify the relationship between its supply and demand. Let us consider the factors concerning international transactions, leaving aside those, purely speculative, operating on the Euromarket. External purchases are carried out by residents in national money and define a demand for foreign exchange. Reciprocally, external sales entail a demand for domestic money in terms of foreign currencies. Hence, commercial imports, unilateral transfers and capital exports (imports of bonds) define a demand for foreign exchange, while commercial and financial exports (capital imports) determine its offer. When the balance of payments is in equilibrium, demand and supply cancel out and the exchange rate remains stable. On the contrary, in the case of a balance of payments deficit (surplus), foreign exchange demand (supply) would be greater than supply (demand), thus provoking a devaluation (revaluation) of domestic money. What we now have to ask is whether or not the exchange rate variation has the twofold effect of offsetting the balance of payments disequilibrium and creating the premises for global transactions to recover their initial level.

Let us consider first the mechanism which should allow for the constant equilibrium of the balance of payments. According to the neoclassical scheme of relative price determination, supply and demand adjust through price variation until they reach a level allowing for their equality and for the selling of the entire production. Let us suppose that, for a given price, agent *a* offers 10 units of its commodity, but that only 8 units are demanded by his economic correspondent. Excess supply will then lead to a decrease in price which, in its turn, will elicit an increase in demand, reducing the initial discrepancy. Through successive adjustments a price of equilibrium is reached, at which agent *a* is able to sell all his commodities. By analogy with what happens on the domestic market for goods and services, a variation in the price of foreign exchange seems able to reduce an excess demand (balance of payments deficit), thus re-establishing the level of equilibrium of transactions even before it effectively manifests itself. As the adjustment of relative prices takes place, through bargaining, before exchange really occurs, exchange rate fluctuation works *ex ante*, through an adjustment between virtual or desired magnitudes which makes exchanges converge towards their point of equilibrium. However, unlike exchanges taking place on the domestic market for products, decisions referring to imports and imports are taken independently from one another, and there is no reason to believe that market forces necessarily work towards balancing them. What has to be asked is not whether exchange rate variation allows for the elimination of balance of payments problems, but if these problems lead (*ex post*) to a variation in exchange rate and if this variation is capable of creating the conditions for avoiding the recurrence of disequilibrium in time.

Let us suppose for a moment that the balance of payments deficit of a given country leads to the devaluation of its currency. According to the supporters of free exchange rate fluctuation, this would lead to a decrease in export prices for goods and a consequent increase in foreign demand which would allow the country to solve the difficulties inherent in the previous scarcity of international liquidity. Yet, economists are unanimous in observing that this process of re-equilibrium is subjected to what is theoretically defined as the elasticity of exports with regard to exchange rate variations. Thus, in order for the value of what is earned through exports to increase it is necessary that the rate of increase in exports be greater than that in exchange rate. Devaluation can lead to a growth of exports, but also reduces the quantity of foreign exchange obtained per unit of exported goods, and it is only if this reduction is more than balanced by the increase in exports that exchange rate variation is capable of reducing the gap between supply of and demand for foreign currency. If to these considerations we add the fact that exchange rate fluctuation is often determined by monetary authority intervention, whose decisions rarely correspond with those required by the market, it is obvious that it is not possible to regard exchange rate variation as a mechanism for the automatic re-equilibrium of the balance of payments, either *ex ante* or *ex post*.

We still have to establish if, in the hypothetical case of free floating, a balance of payments disequilibrium leads to a variation in exchange rates or if the necessary coverage of the deficit is already consistent with monetary neutrality. Before examining this argument, however, it is necessary to clarify its terms, and in order to do this it is useful to further analyse (below) the monetarist approach to the balance of payments (point 2) so as to introduce the distinction (p. 185) between monetary and financial balance (point 3).

THE MONETARIST ANALYSIS OF THE BALANCE OF PAYMENTS AND THE HOMOGENEITY POSTULATE

According to the analysis propounded by monetarists, variations in international transactions recorded in the balance of payments affect the quantity of money available in each exchanging country and lead to the re-equilibrating intervention of monetary authorities, who have the task of neutralising any possible domestic gap between supply of and demand for money. In short, the central idea is that monetary flows of international origin modify the domestic money supply and must therefore be offset by taking into account the demand for money exerted by economic agents. Since for the monetarists money supply is a stock, equilibrium of monetary flows related to the balance of payments seems possible thanks to a series of adjustments to the variables determining the demand for money. As is claimed by Johnson, the balance of payments is a phenomenon defining a disequilibrium of the money market, which is supposed to bring about its own corrective mechanism 'summarisable in the theory of real balance effects' so that 'balance-of-payments policies should accordingly be analysed in terms of their impacts on money flows within this self-corrective framework' (Johnson 1974: 262).

According to the advocates of the quantity theory of money, the determining factor for balance of payments equilibrium is the demand for money. Measures of monetary policy intended to preserve this equilibrium have therefore to take into account the possible gap between domestic supply of and demand for money as well as the fact that an increase or a decrease in reserves is the direct consequence of the adjustment between these two forces. An increase in the demand for money which is not balanced by an equivalent increase in domestic money supply thus gives rise to a growth in exports and, as a consequence, to foreign exchange reserves. On the contrary, a decrease in the demand for money leads, through a reduction in exports, to a contraction in reserves. In the quantity of money theory, monetary equilibrium should be attained by taking into consideration both the domestic supply of and demand for money, and the influence exerted on these factors by international transactions; that is, by the balance of payments situation.

> Since the demand for money is a demand for a stock and not a flow, variation of the supply of money relative to the demand for it associated with deficit or surplus must work towards an equilibrium between money demand and money supply with a corresponding equilibration of the balance of payments.
>
> (Johnson 1974: 153)

Since the balance of payments is defined as 'the difference between the value of the country's output (its national income) and its total expenditure' (1974: 55), it follows that exports increase national income whereas imports decrease it. Monetary expenditures between countries are thus seen as a transfer of income analogous to that taking place between regions of the same monetary area, so that the total amount of available income is given by the following equation:

(1) total income = national income + (exports – imports)

The validity of equation (1) must be examined, first of all, in the light of the specific socio-economic status with which national currencies of the various countries are entrusted. The currency exchange standard system is based on the use of a limited number of key-currencies as international liquidity. Only these reserve currencies (together with the Special Drawing Rights) are considered as effective means of international payment. We are thus faced with an asymmetry between strong and weak currencies whose repercussions on the assumed possibility of adding up domestic and foreign income cannot be ignored. Let us analyse them by distinguishing between balance of payment deficit and surplus.

The monetary effects of the payment of a trade deficit

Let us start from a situation in which imports of goods and services are greater than exports. Whether the deficit is incurred by a strong-currency or by a weak-currency country, it is proper to assume that it is initially paid for in domestic money. Facts show, however, that only reserve currency countries are given the chance to cover their deficit by transferring an equivalent sum of national money. The other countries are bound to find the currencies necessary for the covering of their deficit on the financial market. We could thus be tempted to conclude that the payment of net imports modifies the domestic money supply only when a country is given the possibility to pay its debt by getting indebted (it must be remembered, in fact, that, by definition, money is the acknowledgement of debt of its issuing bank and, as an extension, of the whole banking system of which the issuing bank is a part).

When the deficit is paid for by a weak-currency country, which cannot pay by transferring its domestic currency, only two alternatives are offered it: either to decrease its official reserves or get hold of foreign currencies by selling bonds on the international market. In both cases domestic money supply does not decrease and equation (1) cannot apply.

On the contrary, the result seems to comply with the monetarist equation when payment is made by a strong-currency country. Is it not true, indeed, that the transfer of domestic currency to creditor countries leads to a decrease in the quantity of money (and income) available within the deficit country? To answer yes would mean to erroneously mix up money with a real asset. As we know, money cannot leave the banking system from which it has been issued to be transferred (except as an empty duplicate) to another banking system. By analogy, the income created in a given country can only be spent in that country (also on behalf of residents of other countries, of course). Hence, its 'transfer' abroad corresponds to the conveyance of bonds certifying its deposit with the banks entrusted with monetising national production.

Let us record in the balance sheets of debtor (A) and creditor (B) countries' banks the book-keeping entries relative to the payment of A's trade deficit (Table 8.1). The first entry refers to the monetisation of country A's domestic production, and defines the amount of available income deposited in favour of income holders (IH). Production is thus the source of an income, equal to x units of national money (MA), entirely deposited with A's banking system (BSA). The payment of net imports, second entry, takes place on behalf of income holders (importers) and implies the partial transfer to B of the deposits initially owned by IH. This does not mean, however, that a sum of national income leaves A's banking system to be deposited in that of B. By crediting B's banks with a sum of y MA, the banking system of the deficit country simply transfers a claim that makes B the owner of a deposit with it. The amount of income available within country A (third entry) is therefore unchanged: the trade deficit's payment in national currency does not alter the domestic relationship between money and output.

Table 8.1

Banking system of A			
Liabilities			*Assets*
IH	x MA	Output	x MA
Banking system of B	y MA	Importers	y MA
IH	x − y MA	Output	x MA
Banking system of B	y MA		

Banking system of B			
Liabilities			*Assets*
Exporters	z MB	Banking system of A	y MA

It is thus definitively proved that the relationship between international payments and money supply assumed by equation (1) is totally groundless in the case of a balance of payments deficit. As claimed by Johnson, if monetary authorities of the deficit country decided to purchase bonds with the domestic currency they got from net importers, the quantity of money would recover its initial level and equation (1) would be reduced to equation (2):

(2) national income = national output

> The cash balances of residents are being replenished by open market purchases of securities by the monetary or foreign exchange authority. [. . .] In this case, the money supply in domestic circulation is being maintained by credit creation, so that the excess payments over receipts by residents could continue indefinitely without generating any corrective process.
>
> (Johnson 1974: 50–1)

Yet the reader should be aware of how, in this context, the maintenance of money supply is subject to the behaviour of monetary authorities. Equation (2) is thus verified only in one of the two cases suggested by the monetarists: 'a balance-of-payments deficit implies *either* dishoarding by residents, *or* credit creation by the monetary authorities' (1974: 51).

Recent analysis diverges from the monetarist approach to the balance of payments since it proves the absolute impossibility of establishing a causal link whatsoever between net imports (trade deficit) and the decrease in domestic money. Does this negative conclusion also apply when a country benefits from a payment in reserve currencies?

Money supply and the payment of a trade surplus

Is it not true that, on the basis of foreign exchange entered on the asset side of its balance sheet, the banking system of a surplus country creates an equivalent amount of national currency defining an increase in the domestic money supply? According to what is claimed by Rueff, it is through a monetary creation within its banking system that the creditor country gets hold of the foreign currencies obtained in exchange for its net commercial exports. By referring to our usual book-keeping scheme, the inflow of foreign exchange corresponding to the trade surplus and their purchase through money creation can be represented as in Table 8.2. Entry (1) defines the monetisation of the exporting country's national production. Among the produced goods we also find those that are exported, whose net amount (z NM) defines part of the debt incurred by exporting firms to secondary banks. The payment in foreign exchange made by the rest of the world which corresponds to our country's net commercial exports leads to

Table 8.2

Secondary Banks			
Liabilities			*Assets*
(1) IH	x NM	Output	x NM
(2) Exporters	z NM	Foreign exchange	y
(3) IH	x NM	Output	x – z NM
		Forign exchange	y
(4) Foreign exchange	y	Central Bank	z NM
(5) IH	x NM	Output	x – z NM
		Central Bank	z NM

Central Bank			
Liabilities			*Assets*
(4) Secondary banks	z MN	Foreign exchange	y

an equivalent creation of domestic money in favour of the exporting firms (second entry), whose debt is thus decreased by z units. Firms have a product equal to x – z units of NM (corresponding to their banking debt), while income holders always have at their disposal a credit equal to x NM (third entry). At this point, the emission of domestic money that secondary banks carry out on the basis of the foreign exchange recorded on the asset side of their balance sheets is definitively confirmed by the surplus country's Central Bank, which incorporates the foreign currencies into the country's official reserves by transferring an equivalent amount of central money to secondary banks. This operation (fourth entry) sanctions the increase in the quantity of money, whose global amount, equal to x units of NM, exceeds by z units that of the domestic output still available (fifth entry).

If the payment of net commercial exports is carried out in foreign currencies, we observe an increase in the domestic money supply similar to that assumed by the monetarist equation. But what if the surplus country were paid in its own national currency? Let us suppose that the United States is successful in modifying its trade balance, thus becoming a net commercial exporter. Would the payment in dollars of its net commercial flow lead to an increase in the quantity of money available within the country? It is easier to understand the answer by observing the book-keeping entries corresponding to this hypothetical case (Table 8.3). Once again, the first entry gives us the measure of national output, while the second refers to the payment in dollars of the American net commercial exports. Following the entry of dollars on the asset side of the balance sheet, exporting firms are credited in domestic money. The decrease in American available output, therefore, does not correspond to any reduction in the credit American income holders benefit from (third entry). The gap

Table 8.3

American Banking System

	Liabilities		*Assets*	
(1)	Income holders	\$ x	Domestic output	\$ x
(2)	Exporting firms	\$ y	Rest of the world	\$ y
(3)	Income holders	\$ x	Domestic output	\$ x – y
			Rest of the world	\$ y

between money (\$x) and output (\$ x – y) defines the monetisation of an external gain realised by the country and which, though confirming equation (1), shows its inadequacy as an instrument of monetary analysis.

The monetarist equation is unable to distinguish between the operations which, in the present system of international payments, lead to a change in the domestic relationship between money and output, and those which, if carried out, would necessarily lead to a pathological variation of that relationship. It is useful to remember that the internal monetisation of foreign exchange by the surplus country's Central Bank is needed in order to avoid a deflationary gap. The foreign demand the exporting country benefits from, provokes an increase in its domestic prices that must be counterbalanced by an equivalent growth of the money supply. The Central Bank emission eliminates the potential gap between (macroeconomic) prices and available income. As we have stressed in Chapter 5, it is an emission that sanctions the mercantilist character of the gain in foreign currencies, and defines an operation of seigniorage. Because of monetary sovereignty, it is the nation that benefits from the net inflow of foreign exchange, and the fact that the nation balances the increase in its official reserves through a creation of money in favour of its exporting residents proves that foreign currencies are effectively obtained gratuitously by the country. The gain realised by exporters (who give up goods and services in exchange for national money) must be added to that of their own country which, by exerting the right to print money, becomes the owner of the key-currencies transferred to it by the rest of the world. Being a net exporter, our country benefits from a transfer of foreign currencies and, through an equivalent emission of domestic currency, participates in maintaining the internal equilibrium between money and output. Moreover, it must not be forgotten that the creation carried out by the Central Bank on behalf of its country is not cumulative in time. Once created (through external gain monetisation), money remains available in the system, where it makes up a fund which can be re-utilised any time that, thanks to renewed net exports, the country's official foreign exchange reserves increase. The use of this fund, whose reconstitution is automatic and is the result of book-keeping entries concerning Central and secondary banks, avoids an inflationary increase in the money supply, thus preserving a stable relationship between domestic output and national money.

The equation proposed by the quantity theory of money, on the contrary, establishes a direct relationship between foreign currency inflows and growth in money supply. Yet if foreign exchange were directly added to domestic currency in order to determine the total amount of the money supply, the payment of net commercial exports would necessarily lead to an inflationary increase in the quantity of money, with the consequent anomalous variation of the relationship money/output. Now, this theoretical vision is not confirmed by facts. The principal reason for the analytical deficiency of the monetarist approach is the paradigmatic acceptance of national currencies' homogeneity, an assumption which is not supported by facts. Indeed, equation (1) can be written only if the currencies obtained in exchange for net commercial exports can be amalgamated to domestic income. In other words, external income can be added to (or deduced from) internal income only if foreign and national currencies are homogeneous units of measurement.

Let us consider the transactions taking place within a unique monetary zone. No one doubts that their results can be aggregated without it being necessary to raise the problem of their common unit of account. The very fact that they are carried out in national money is sufficient proof of their fundamental homogeneity. A payment in dollars carried out in New York can immediately be compared with any other payment in dollars carried out in the United States for the simple reason that the dollars issued by the American banking system are perfectly inter-exchangeable. Yet, it must be kept in mind that this characteristic, common to national currencies, is not guaranteed a priori. On the contrary, it is the result of interbank clearing carried out by each single country's Central Bank. Monetary homogeneity is made possible by the existence of a national banking system, which requires the presence of a Central Bank capable of gathering the various secondary banks in a common area. Without any such institution, every private bank would issue a currency totally heterogeneous with regard to the others, and it would no longer be possible to speak either of a national monetary system, or monetary sovereignty.

Likewise, at the international level currencies can only be considered homogeneous if they are inserted into a structure making them mutually exchangeable. This task should be assigned to a true international Bank. Since we do not yet enjoy the existence of any supranational Bank, we can only verify how the heterogeneity of national currencies is hopelessly opposed to the equation propounded by monetarist analysis.

The reader will not fail to observe that this conclusion is confirmed by the analysis of exchange rate determination. Let us simply remember here that exchange rates between national currencies can logically be determined only by referring to their *absolute* exchange. Relative exchange rates can therefore be derived only from absolute exchange rates. The attempt at determining them directly, through the exchange of currencies on the money market, is bound to fail, since each relative exchange is a bipolar operation. The exchange between dollars and pesos, for instance, determines two units of account, dollars and pesos, which are as heterogeneous as the exchanged currencies. Homogeneity is obtained by means of a common standard and, as we have tried to show, this result can be reached only if it is money that is made to play the role of unit of account. The solution to monetary heterogeneity requires the intervention of a supranational Bank that is given the task of issuing a currency which, through absolute exchange, acts as a catalyst with regard to national currencies. It is only if the model proposed at the European level (the creation of a European Central Bank as European Clearing Union, see Part III) were adopted internationally that national currencies would be integrated in a unique monetary area that would guarantee their homogeneity.

Let us observe also that, were the monetary reform to be applied, the monetarist homogeneity postulate would acquire the validity it still lacks, and, contemporaneously, equation (1) would have to be re-interpreted by taking into account the purely vehicular nature of supranational money.

To sum up, we can state that it is not possible to ascribe any particular heuristic meaning to the monetarist equation, whose theorem of existence is based on an assumption, the postulate of monetary homogeneity, which is openly contradicted both theoretically and empirically.

THE NECESSARY DISTINCTION BETWEEN MONETARY AND FINANCIAL BALANCE

Balance of payments equilibrium: an inexplicable result

Being worked out from the statistical survey of data referring to real and financial flows, the balance of payments is subjected to a whole series of errors due to the difficulties inherent in data collection. It is certainly not a mystery that many of them are not very reliable, and it is likewise well known that often financial transactions carried out by multinational firms escape statistical coverage. Nevertheless, despite these shortcomings, capital net flows should not differ too much from current account imbalances. A quick glance at the data recently published by the IMF in its *Report on the Measurement of International Capital Flows* (1992) shows, however, that the discrepancy between real and financial flows of the seven most industrialised countries is inexplicably high (Figure 8.2). Even taking into account errors and omissions which, as far as major industrial countries are concerned, cannot be exorbitant, discrepancies brought out by the experts of the Working Party are so large that they can certainly not be entirely

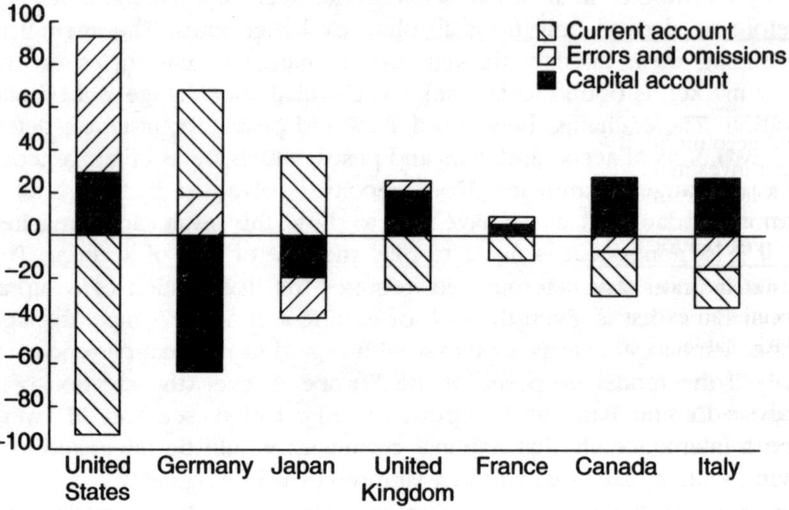

Source: *Balance of Payments Statistic Year book*, 1991

Figure 8.2 Balance of payments accounts of major countries, 1990 (in billions of US dollars)

ascribed to them. On the other hand, unless we introduce new elements of analysis, traditional theory is unable to explain the source of this anomaly and 'ascertain each country's true capital (and current) account position and, therefore, how much saving the country has been providing to, or absorbing from, the rest of the world' (IMF 1992: 1).

Another difficulty arises concerning financial flows. As recognised by the authors of the IMF *Report on Capital Flows*: 'In the absence of errors and omissions, this discrepancy should be zero because the sum of inflows in the world should equal the sum of outflows. However, the discrepancy has fluctuated over the last decade, and it amounted to $66 billion in 1989' (1992: 1). Even in this case, errors and omissions can only partially account for these discrepancies. After adjustment of the statistical data at their disposal, IMF experts have been able to provide us with the following table on the global discrepancies between global capital inflows and outflows (Table 8.4). It is immediately clear that there are substantial gaps, and it is likewise evident that the equality between negative and positive capital flows is not respected, either globally or at the disaggregated level. On this subject it must be observed that 'consideration of only the statistical discrepancies in a component total would hide an important part of the problem because errors in inflows or outflows could be larger than the recorded discrepancy' (1992: 2).

Although everybody seems to agree in claiming that the problem is getting worse and that statistical coverage is not up to the task of explaining

Table 8.4 Global capital account discrepancies, after adjustment, 1986–89 (in billions of US dollars)[1]

	1986	*1987*	*1988*	*1989*	*1986–89 average*
Capital account, total	3.0	8.4	31.7	25.5	17.0
Direct investment	3.3	–9.9	–13.6	1.3	–4.7
Portfolio investment	7.1	11.2	–5.6	40.0	13.2
Other capital	–9.1	7.6	51.0	–18.4	7.8
Reserves/LCFAR[2]	1.7	–0.5	–	2.4	0.9

1 No sign indicates an excess of recorded inflows over outflows; a negative sign indicates an excess of outflows.
2 LCFAR: liabilities constituting foreign authorities' reserves.

it, analysis does not seem to be adequate and, too often, instead of looking for the fundamental causes of the anomaly, experts fool themselves by believing that it can be dealt with simply by improving statistical techniques. Yet discrepancies as important as those pointed out by Working Party members can only be partially imputed to technical shortcomings. On the contrary, these gaps have to be seriously investigated as symptomatic manifestations of a congenital disorder of our monetary system. The theory is thus asked to give a satisfactory explanation of a phenomenon whose gravity can neither be concealed nor mystified. The introduction of a precise distinction between monetary and financial balance has to be inserted in this context.

Monetary and financial equilibrium

As we have repeatedly stressed, the distinction between money and income is essential to enable us to understand the functions played by the banking system. Monetary and financial intermediations must not be mixed up if inflation and deflation of a pathological origin (their only true origin) are to be avoided. As a simple instrument, money is a purely numerical vehicle with no intrinsic value, and it is as such that it is issued by the banking system. Its immediate association with production gives vehicular money a real content which, precisely because of its association with money, takes the form of income: a financial deposit with the issuing bank.

Now, the distinction between money and income finds another field of application at the international level. Even at this level we are confronted with the necessity of providing the system with a means of payment, that is, of a vehicle allowing for the reciprocal exchange of real goods of different kinds (for example commodities and financial bonds) among countries. Every international transaction is therefore defined by a means of exchange (which, as a simple instrument of circulation, pertains to the category of vehicular money) and by its real content.

Let us consider the net commercial imports of any country whatsoever C_w. Because of the dual nature, monetary and financial, of each transaction, C_w has to find both the income to finance its trade deficit, and the monetary instrument necessary for carrying out the payment. If we suppose that it obtains the income required for its payment by selling bonds, country C_w is subject to an increase in its external debt (or a decrease in its external credit) equal to its financial balance deficit. The offsetting balance of the country's financial account shows therefore the evolution of its credit position with the rest of the world.

As any single economic agent, a country can grant or raise loans by purchasing or selling bonds. These transactions are obviously subject to the criteria of reliability and profitability applied by banks, whose intervention as financial intermediaries is determinant for the growth of international trade. Thus, equilibrium of the financial balance is not a necessary condition for the sound working of the system. On the contrary, it is easily realised how its disequilibrium can be extremely useful both to poor countries, whose development requires substantial financial investment, and to industrialised countries, whose capital is looking for profitable and risk-free opportunities of investment. However, it is precisely at this level that major difficulties arise. If financial balance deficit is given a negative meaning it is not essentially because of the indebtedness involved in it, but because it is difficult to see how indebted countries could solve their monetary problems and attract new foreign investment.

The financial problem goes, therefore, with the monetary one. Let us go back to country C_w's trade deficit. Besides selling bonds to obtain the income financing its net commercial purchases, C_w must find the vehicle necessary to convey the whole of its buying and selling transactions. If C_w is given the privilege of using its national currency as international vehicle, the real payment (in bonds) of the deficit takes place smoothly. Since the same amount of money is defined in a circular movement conveying bonds from C_w to the rest of the world and commodities from the rest of the world to C_w, the country's monetary balance is in perfect equilibrium (Figure 8.3).

Things get more complicated when country C_w has to convey its payments using another country's currency. In this case conditions are created for a possible monetary balance disequilibrium. Being forced to obtain the vehicular money onerously (by borrowing or purchasing it), C_w is the victim of a fundamentally unjust situation which, as we shall try to prove in the third part of this work, by forcing it to service its external debt both financially and monetarily, deprives it of part of its internal resources.

Since it is a simple numerical intermediary, vehicular money should never become an object of trade. It should intervene in each transaction defining a circular movement, to and from its point of origin. As a consequence, no one country should ever be confronted with a disequilibrium of its monetary balance. Every disequilibrium of this balance is

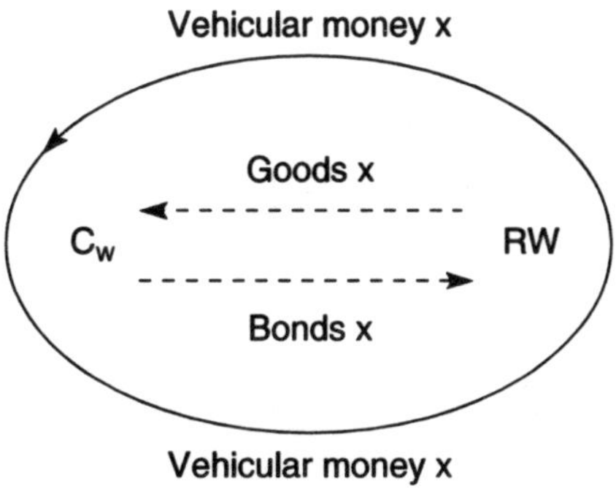

Figure 8.3

thus the unmistakable sign of an anomaly whose repercussions make the situation facing weak-currency countries particularly difficult.

The criterion of demarcation between financial and monetary balance is rigorously established by the nature of bank money. What remains to be done is to apply it with the same rigour in order to avoid international payments being carried out according to an asymmetrical scheme harmful to both weak currency countries (which must pay in financial and monetary terms), and strong currency countries (which do not pay either financially, since they transfer their own acknowledgement of debt in exchange for goods, nor monetarily, since the currency transferred to the rest of the world remains entirely deposited in their banking system). In a world where producing and financing activities of all countries are becoming more and more interdependent and where the crisis of some is bound to negatively affect the others, equilibrated economic revival cannot leave aside a reform of international payments allowing countries to get rid of their problems which are of a purely monetary (vehicular) order. In the same way as, within each country, no resident has to worry about the vehicular side of his payments (since his only worry is that of getting the income required to finance them), at the international level each country should be allowed to freely benefit from the monetary vehicle of its payments (whose content can only be real and represents the only justifiable cost). It is only when the importance of the distinction between monetary (vehicular) and financial (real) aspects of international transactions are understood that it will be possible to work out a book-keeping system capable of providing for the constant equilibrium of the monetary balance, thus definitively avoiding currencies being subjected to market forces and speculative movements altering their exchange rates.

9

THE EXCHANGE RATES PROBLEM

THE FIXED EXCHANGE RATE SYSTEM

From the beginning of the First World War, the international monetary system was organised along the lines of the gold standard, and exchange rates among national currencies could only vary within the restricted limits of the gold points. The gold standard was a system founded on gold parity, so that currencies were all defined in terms of gold and convertible into the precious metal at a fixed rate. They were exchangeable through gold, and their relationship was kept constant thanks to monetary authorities' commitment to buying and selling gold at a price fixed on the basis of currencies' gold content.

The gold standard was supposed to guarantee an equilibrated development of international transactions through an automatic mechanism capable of reducing prices in deficit countries, while simultaneously increasing them in surplus countries. The flow of gold among countries, together with the variation in gold reserves and money supply, were the steps which should have brought forth the automatic re-equilibrium of the system. It is well known, however, that this theory does not sufficiently take into account the effects of a deflationary income and employment policy, and that it assumes a flexibility of prices and interest rates which is not verified by facts. Moreover, if we consider that the currency traditionally used as a means of final payment was not gold, but the British pound, we are led to conclude that the gold standard, and the system of fixed exchange rates related to it, worked effectively only because of an exceptional series of favourable circumstances, which no longer existed after the Great War. If we bear in mind that the expansion of international trade was linked to a reduction in reserves or a squeeze in exporting goods' prices, we become aware of the minimal effect the gold standard and its automatic re-equilibrium mechanisms had on the removal of trade barriers – a situation which regularly presented itself after the war and after the signature of the Bretton Woods agreements. Referring to the system of fixed exchange rates based on the gold convertibility of the dollar, Milton Friedman wrote:

> Yet these two methods – drawing on reserves and forcing down prices – are the only two methods available under our present international payment arrangements, which involve fixed exchange rates between the U.S. dollar and other currencies. Little wonder that we have so far made such disappointing progress toward the reduction of trade barriers, that our practice has differed so much from our preaching.
>
> (Friedman 1963: 453)

It is also true, however, that not every country was in the situation described by Friedman, and that the United States (and, before 1914, United Kingdom) could increase their imports without having to decrease their gold reserves. The particular status of international currency the dollar was endowed with, allowed (and still allows) the United States to import real goods and services in exchange for monetary units created by the American banking system. From this point of view, the gold exchange standard system offered the USA the possibility of purchasing and postponing payment *sine die* (since the dollar is a simple promise to pay of the American banking system). On the other hand, the dollar was officially convertible into gold, so that the increase in international liquidity due to the growing quantity of dollars available outside the US, was accompanied by an increasing fear that foreign holders of dollars could ask for their gold conversion, thus exposing to risk the American gold reserves as well as the entire international economic system. Under these conditions, the maintenance of a fixed exchange rates regime implied an elevated degree of risk, and introduced a rigidity into the system that slowed down the expansion of international transactions. It is not surprising, therefore, that the monetary crisis of the 1960s forced the US to suspend convertibility of the dollar into gold, a decision that marked the end of the Bretton Woods attempt to provide the world with a system of fixed exchange rates.

Yet a fixed exchange rates regime is not necessarily bound to the adoption of a gold system. In the last section of this chapter we shall try to show how it is possible to introduce fixed exchange rates even when starting from a situation in which money is totally dematerialised. For the time being, let us simply observe that fixed exchange rates offer numerous and obvious advantages, among which are stability and certainty in international trade and investment. Of course, these advantages are effectively real only on condition that fixed exchange rates are inherent to the system of international payments, and not a mere artifice adopted in order to protect a highly unstable currency. For example, the fixed exchange rates introduced by the Mexican government on several occasions to avoid the continuous devaluation of the peso in terms of the dollar, certainly do not represent a suitable solution to the crisis of international payments. Far from fighting the causes of the peso's instability, they erect a barrier bound to collapse with the increasing external pressure put on the Mexican currency. On the contrary, if fixed exchange rates were a consequence of the international monetary system, the peso would remain stable without there being any need for the Mexican monetary authorities to introduce a rigid control over exchange rates or to intervene on the monetary market in support of their national currency.

In conclusion, experts seem to agree that, although fixed exchange rates are to be theoretically preferred to flexible exchange rates, their enforcement necessarily implies (given today's monetary structure) the adoption of a system incompatible with the requirements of an expanding economy. The gold model can no longer be proposed today, either in the lax gold exchange standard form or in the rigid gold standard form. At present, currencies have no link with gold: they are no longer convertible into it, and they do not derive any legal value from it. To restore a system similar to that existing before 1971 would be anachronistic and damaging. As for the decision to give up the advantages of fixed exchange rates, it depends on the possibility of enjoying a fixed parity among currencies of different countries without being forced to adopt a regime of gold convertibility.

Fixed exchange rates are incompatible with a system of payments using a national currency as final 'object' of payment

Considered as a net asset, the currency used internationally benefits from the same economic status as any other asset and becomes the object of transactions that modify its price on the basis of the law of supply and demand. The stability of money's price is therefore subject to the stability of all the transactions involving its intervention as means of payment, reserve of value and object of speculation.

Let us analyse the case in which the British pound is used as international currency. Each country pays and is paid in pounds, which accumulate in net exporting countries' reserves. In order for these payments to take place, England must provide the rest of the world with the necessary amount of pounds. If this is obtained through the payment of net English imports of goods and services, its effect on the pound's exchange rate is nil, since the demand for foreign exchange exerted by British importers is perfectly balanced by their infinitely elastic supply. The entry of foreign currencies on the asset side of net exporting countries' balance sheets entails an emission of national currency by the Central Bank that, instantaneously matching supply and demand, prevents the payment of net commercial exports from having a positive effect on the external value of domestic money. Exporters are credited by the banking system of their country with an amount of national money equivalent to that of the pounds entered as assets on the Central Bank's balance sheet. The Central Bank increases its official reserves through an emission of domestic currency corresponding to the monetisation of the country's external (commercial) gain. Hence, what the national currency exporters are credited with is not purchased on the financial market, but is created on the basis of the pounds, which, as a net asset, are comparable to any other real product of the same value. Whatever the amount of pounds is, the exporting country's banking system is always in a position to satisfy the external demand for domestic currency. This means that the supply of national money adjusts, perfectly and instantaneously, to the demand exerted by foreign importers, so that the payment (in pounds) of British net commercial imports has no effect on exchange rates.

The same conclusion applies when pounds are made internationally available through a net purchase of foreign bonds. Although in this case foreign Central Banks do not monetise any external gain (since the inflow of pounds obtained through the sale of bonds does not define a net increase in official reserves), the demand for foreign currencies does not alter their exchange rates. While the pounds entered as assets on the countries' balance sheets increase the demand for domestic currencies, they are also subjected to an increased demand exerted in terms of these currencies. Transformed into Europound, the British currency is invested on the Euromarket on behalf of the residents of the countries it was initially transferred to. The demand for domestic currencies is thus balanced by an equivalent demand for pounds, whose exchange rate remains unchanged.

Things are radically different when we consider the effects deriving from the successive speculative buying and selling of foreign exchange. On the Euromarket, pounds become a mere object of exchange whose price mainly depends on expectations as to speculative earnings related to its trade. In such a context, the pound's exchange rate varies erratically, creating destabilising imbalances between its officially desired value and its market value.

Table 9.1

Secondary banking system of the exporting country			
Liabilities			*Assets*
Exporter eq. in NM of	£ x	British banking system	£ x
Central banking system	£ x	Central banking system eq. in NM of	£ x

Central banking system of the exporting country			
Liabilities			*Assets*
Secondary banking system eq. in NM of	£ x		£ x

In a fixed exchange rate regime, the difference between these two values is the cause for further speculative earnings, deriving from the possibility of arbitrage, and it is bound to create a situation of instability leading to the forced abandonment of fixed exchange rates (and the consequent modification of parities), or into the development of a parallel market, entirely separate with respect to the official one.

The condition for the existence of a fixed exchange rate system is thus linked to the nature of the currency used internationally. Exchange rate stability must not be the occasional result of a set of favourable circumstances neutralising destabilising forces, but the intrinsic effect of a system in which currencies are no longer subjected to supply and demand. Exchange rates would no longer fluctuate because of speculative transactions on currencies only if the currency used internationally were no longer assimilated with a net asset. The presupposition necessary for the adoption of a fixed exchange rate regime is thus the purely vehicular use of international money.

During the gold standard system and the first years of the gold exchange standard, the international currency used as final object of payment was a national currency (initially the pound and, later on, the dollar) whose value was considered as positive notwithstanding the logical impossibility (due to the banking nature of money) of exporting the slightest fraction of national income. Not surprisingly, therefore, the two systems were increasingly subject to destabilising pressures that led to their being discarded in favour of a regime allowing for exchange rate fluctuation.

THE FLOATING EXCHANGE RATE SYSTEM

Apart from the inter-war period, when the gold standard was discarded by most industrialised countries, the fixed exchange rate regime remained the model of the international monetary system until 1971. For example, the United States switched to floating exchange rates between 1862 and 1879, between 1917 and 1925 and between 1933 and 1934; Great Britain used them from 1918 to 1925 and from 1931 to 1939, and Canada did the same between the First and the Second World War, and from 1950 to 1962. However, none of these countries gave up fixed exchange rates definitively before the American decision to suspend convertibility of the dollar into gold.

The abandonment of convertibility marks the beginning of a system in which exchange rates are allowed to float within limits that vary in compliance with the choice of monetary authorities and with the unpredictable behaviour of the market. According to the most drastic doctrine, of which Milton Friedman is the champion, exchange rates should be left free to float, without any external intervention that could distort the natural working of the market. According to monetarist theory, the high elasticity of exchange rates does not necessarily imply their instability, which, on the contrary, would be the consequence of inherently structural disequilibria, and would thus essentially depend on development policies (particularly those of a monetary and fiscal order).

Introduced with the explicit intent of guaranteeing economic policy independence, by isolating countries from the negative effects of balance of payment problems, the floating exchange rate system was soon shown to be unfit for its task. Structural differences among economies are inconsistent with a system which, through the rapid variation in exchange rates, tends to accelerate inflationary pressures in weak currency countries, and to subject key-currencies to continuous re-evaluations. As clearly stated by Henry Wallich, a former Governor of the Federal Reserve System, the system tends to polarise the world into two groups whose interests are increasingly bound to diverge.

> Vicious circles seem to have developed in which exchange rate depreciation feeds inflation and accelerating inflation, in turn, feeds back upon the exchange rate. Countries with appreciating currencies have found themselves caught up in virtuous circles, with cheaper imports reducing inflation and reduced inflation further strengthening the currency. These vicious and virtuous circles have threatened to polarize the world into countries with strong and weak currencies which has come uncomfortably close to splitting the world into strong and weak countries
>
> (Wallich 1979: 3)

Traditionally, the central point of the problem related to the use of floating exchange rates is represented by their supposed inflationary character. The argument proposed is the following. By applying the method of the free fluctuation of exchange rates to the case of a balance of payment deficit, it can first be observed that it leads to a devaluation of the deficit country's currency. In its turn, devaluation causes an increase in exports and a decrease in imports which elicits a growth in internal aggregate demand, thus satisfying the conditions for demand-induced inflation. But this is not all: besides discouraging demand for foreign output, the increase in imported good prices (due to domestic currency's devaluation) pushes the production costs of domestic firms up, thus provoking an inflationary growth in prices (cost-push inflation). Moreover, the increased cost of living induces a decrease in real wages and an intensification of trade unionist requests, which can lead to an upward movement of wages and, therefore, to a further inflationary increase in domestic prices. On the other hand, the appreciation of the surplus country's currency does not entail an equivalent reduction in prices, both because there is a clear wage rigidity (downward), and because firms prefer to match the reduction in costs (due to the decreasing price of imports) with an increase in profits rather than with a decrease in the price of produced output. On the whole, we would observe a growth in the general level of prices whose main cause seems effectively to be the free fluctuation of exchange rates.

Other objections have been raised against the free market determination of currency exchange rates. One of them refers to the inefficacy of exchange rate fluctuation as a measure to fight balance of payment disequilibria when they are due to structural causes or to an important capital outflow. If a country's exports were to decrease for reasons different from those inherent to prices, monetary devaluation would not effectively help re-equilibrate the balance of payments; analogously, if disequilibrium were due to capital outflow, devaluation would make it worse (weakening of the currency and uncertainty being among the determinant factors of capital outflow) rather than alleviating it.

Another criticism is related to the speculative nature which seems to characterise the floating exchange rate system. If the internationalisation of the capital market and the constant expansion of the Euromarket have certainly favoured the development of international speculative investments, it is also true that speculation has found a fruitful field of application thanks to the uncertainty created by exchange rate fluctuations. Besides feeding speculative transactions, exchange rate market instability makes them more erratic, since, by tending to promote speculation, exchange rate fluctuations are also influenced by it. Created as an instrument to be used to fight balance of payment disequilibria, floating exchange rates are therefore subject to variations that have nothing to do with the working of the real economy, and this can seriously penalise those countries which need the most help in achieving a relative stability to their currencies.

Here we reach another critical element put forward against the adoption of a free system of floating exchange rates. If, on the one hand, it is acknowledged (as is done by the advocates of free floating) that monetary instability can be caused by a structural instability of the economic system, on the other hand it is stressed that underdeveloped countries are not in a position to protect their currencies from variations caused by factors external to their economic structure (such as, for example, international speculation and official exchange rate interventions). The attempt to stabilise exchange rates by pegging national currencies of underdeveloped countries to a key-currency is also disputable, since variations in the latter would have repercussions on the former by modifying their exchange rates (with the currencies of the rest of the world) independently of their economic transactions. It must also be observed that the price paid by less developed countries is made more onerous by monetary instability, which discourages foreign investment and hinders regional integration.

Another difficulty due to monetary instability is represented by the huge external debt accumulated by these countries. As analysis carried out in Chapters 13 and 14 shows, the present structure of international payments is such that indebted countries' currencies are subject to a destabilising pressure every time they are able to service their external debt (in interest and principal). Moreover, the continuous deterioration of the terms of trade forces these countries to export an increasing quantity of real domestic output (whose price falls relative to the price of imported goods and services) in order to pay for an increasingly high sum of interest (whose amount grows proportionally with the devaluation of their national currencies).

It must be reaffirmed that the solution to this dramatic state of affairs cannot consist in maintaining arbitrarily fixed exchange rates for underdeveloped countries. As already observed, monetary authority interventions cannot neutralise the forces determining the actual instability of exchange rate markets. If a solution exists, it has to be found in the investigation of the causes for the destabilising working of these forces. This means that the exchange rate system adopted internationally is not the ultimate cause of monetary disequilibria, but its more or less faithful detector. In other words, the variation of exchange rates in a regime of free floating appears to be the effect more than the cause of monetary and structural disequilibria. The criticisms worked out relative to the floating exchange rate system must therefore be addressed to the system of international payments as a whole, since it is at this level that the anomalies highlighted by the fluctuations in exchange rates are focused.

As far as the historical aspect of the problem is concerned, an argument which is examined in Chapter 10, let us simply observe here that the system based on free floating has never been effectively adopted. Since 1971 there have been repeated attempts to determine feasible and defensible limits of fluctuation; a problem that clashes with the great difficulty of finding a unit of reference. The years following the general acceptance of floating exchange rates have been characterised by the choice of a national currency as international standard. However, the international use of the dollar has made it the object of strong destabilising pressures, caused by speculation and linked to its role of payment and reserve currency. Monetary authorities have thus been forced to intervene on the exchange rate market, trying to compensate, more or less efficaciously, for the unpredictable variations in financial agents' behaviour. Moreover, the intertwining of the roles ascribed to the dollar as domestic and international currency has led to dangerous interactions between the monetary policies adopted nationally (for example in order to guarantee the internal stability of prices) and those required at the international level. Several meetings among economic and political experts of the leading industrialised countries testify to this state of affairs and to the difficulties related to international monetary collaboration. Before analysing some of the proposals put forth (and occasionally adopted) to modify the structure of international payments, it is useful to further examine the problem of exchange rate determination in a regime of floating exchange rates.

The determination of exchange rates in relation to national outputs

Traditionally, the theoretical determination of floating exchange rates can be traced back to the principle of purchasing power parity and to the balance of payment approach. In both cases, exchange rates are thought of as relative equilibrium prices among domestic products of different countries. Let us analyse them successively.

Purchasing power parity

As we already know, according to the purchasing power parity (PPP) postulate, exchange rates would be determined so as to allow national currencies to exert the same purchasing power within every single country. The exchange rate between two currencies is thus determined by the relationship existing between the level of domestic prices of the two countries involved. In case of a sudden variation of equilibrium (caused, for example, by a decrease in prices taking place in one of the two countries) the possibility of an international arbitrage on products would provoke an automatic adjustment in the balance of payments that would restore the initial rate of exchange.

Also according to its advocates, the theory of PPP, whether in its 'absolute' or 'relative' form, has a limited validity, since it is capable of accounting for exchange rate determination only in relation to variations in the general level of monetary prices. Variations in relative prices do not allow for the application of PPP, which is strictly dependent on the most orthodox version of the quantity theory of money. The other conditions for its implementation are extremely restrictive: that products are homogeneous, international markets perfectly competitive and integrated, and that there are no transport costs are unlikely assumptions reducing considerably the significance of an approach which, on top of all this, does not grasp the particular nature of bank money and arbitrarily assimilates money with a net asset.

In this respect it has to be noted that the theory of PPP is based on the monetarist assumption of monetary homogeneity (see Chapter 8). In a world with a unique currency, this hypothesis would be verified, and it could be maintained that free circulation of capital and goods lays the foundations for the establishment of a unique world market, and, therefore, for the final realisation of purchasing power parity. Now, reality is far from validating the monetarist postulate. In the present key-currency standard, national currencies are essentially heterogeneous, and are bound to remain so until the institution of an international Bank capable of conveying them in a common monetary zone. The creation of a true international monetary system (as opposed to the actual non-system) is of a significance that still escapes monetarist analysis. The passage to monetary homogeneity neither implies the abolition of national currencies, nor the setting up of a unique market. As we shall see later on (Chapter 12), bank money allows for a solution which is entirely consistent with safeguarding the monetary (and political) sovereignty of every single country, and with the free adoption of differentiated economic policies. Founded on the vehicular nature of money, the future international system will not be confronted with the false problem of the fair and uniform distribution of international liquidity. Precisely because international money will no longer be erroneously identified with a net asset the assumption of PPP will thus become plausible. It is certain, in fact, that if it depended, as implicitly claimed by its advocates, on the possibility that 'A newly acquired stock of money would diffuse itself over all countries until money has diffused itself so equally that prices had risen in the same ratio in all countries, so that the alteration of price would be for all practical purposes ineffective' (Mill 1893: 194–5), the purchasing power parity would remain a mere chimaera.

Criticised from different points of view, the PPP theory is today only partially accepted, mainly as an instrument of analysis for short-term adjustments. Yet even the most elaborate techniques of exchange rate determination cannot always do without it, and it frequently happens that PPP theory is more or less explicitly re-introduced to make up for the gaps in its more sophisticated step-sisters.

The balance of payment approach

According to this approach, exchange rates are essentially determined by supply of and demand for money. The functions of supply and demand are derived from the transactions entered in the balance of payments, and refer to commercial and financial external flows. The demand curve corresponds to the request for money exerted by importers (of goods, services and bonds), while the supply curve represents the money offered by exporters. On the whole, the determination of exchange rates by means of money's supply and demand is analogous to the neoclassical determination of domestic prices: as an increase in the demand for a given commodity leads to a growth in its price of equilibrium, an increase in the imports of a given country leads to a rise in price of foreign currencies, that is, to a devaluation of its national currency.

Usually criticised because it does not take into account the monetary flows inherent to the inclusion of foreign exchange in the financial portfolio of international investors, this approach is particularly unsatisfactory since it does not respect the fundamental distinction between commodities and money. Forgetting that money is of a banking nature, the supporters of the balance of payment approach do not realise that, except in the particular case of the effective servicing of external debt (see Part III), commercial and financial transactions can never be the cause of a net demand for money among countries, and cannot, therefore, modify the par of exchange.

A key-currency country, which is a net importer of goods and services, exerts a demand for foreign currencies that puts a strain on its domestic currency. This is true, but it is also true that, simultaneously, the elasticity of money supply in the exporting country is such as to immediately neutralise the effect of external demand, thus avoiding every variation in the initial level of exchange rates. On the other hand, as far as countries whose currency is not given the status of international unit of payment are concerned, the demand for foreign exchange related to the payment of imports is necessarily matched by a demand for domestic currencies exerted by key-currency countries in their purchase of goods, services and bonds. Since they cannot pay for their purchases using their own national money, less developed countries are forced to obtain the foreign exchange necessary for their international payments, exporting commodities and financial securities: a transaction defining a demand for their domestic money equal to the demand for foreign exchange defined by their commercial imports. Demand and supply balance out, which makes it impossible to impute exchange rate fluctuations to real flows.

The assets approach

Unlike what happens in the balance of payment approach, in the assets approach the supply of and demand for money are not derived from real transactions, but from financial activities carried out internationally. The monetary as well as the portfolio models assume that 'the international financial market is highly integrated and characterised by an almost perfect mobility of capitals' (Fiorentini 1990: 44). However, whereas for the advocates of the monetary approach exchange rates are determined by financial flows concerning money only, according to the experts of the portfolio approach their determination cannot ignore the supply of and demand for bonds (imperfect substitutes for money).

Behind the various models typifying these two categories of approaches we find the idea that exchange rate variations must be ascribed to a disequilibrium between supply of and demand for money (whether it is meant in its strict or broad meaning). The direction and range of these variations depends on the assumptions of each model. In the monetary approach, for example, the flexibility or rigidity of prices leads to opposite results as far as the relationship between exchange and interest rate is concerned, while in the portfolio models the initial variation in exchange rates can generate the phenomenon of overshooting.

In order to briefly illustrate some characteristics of the best-known models, let us analyse the case in which money supply is suddenly increased. In the hypothesis of flexible prices and from the monetary approach point of view, the increase in the quantity of money is matched by an equivalent increase in spending. The increased demand for goods and services leads to a growth in domestic prices which, in its turn, modifies the ratio between exports and imports and provokes, through the mechanisms of the balance of payments automatic adjustment, an equivalent deterioration in exchange rates. Finally, the new monetary equilibrium re-establishes the *real* exchange rate at its previous level, in compliance with the principles of a purchasing power parity whose validity is taken for granted both in the short and long run. The same result is obtained when the initial increase concerns the rate of interest, since it is assumed that this increase reduces the demand for money, creating a positive gap between the quantity of money effectively supplied and that desired by the public.

Even in the fixed price model the increase in money supply leads to an exchange rate deterioration, but this time the adjustment between supply of and demand for money takes place through the mechanism of interest rates. The increase in the quantity of money, it is claimed, causes a reduction in interest rates and a consequent outflow of capital leading to an exchange rate devaluation. As in the previous case, the variations in exchange rates are bound to be re-absorbed at the real level, although this time the hypothesis of purchasing power parity is retained only relative to the long term.

In both analyses expectations play an important role, being in a position to hinder restoration of the initial equilibrium if monetary authorities' intervention is not up to the task of providing for the necessary coherence in the pursuit of a stable and predictable monetary policy (even though both theories assume monetary policies to be tendentially neutral). Let us also observe that, while in the monetarist approach (flexible prices) interest rate reflects expectations on inflation, in the 'Keynesian' approach (fixed prices) expectations can lead to exchange rate overshooting. In the case of monetary expansion, for example, exchange rate depreciation in the short term could be greater than required by the new long-term equilibrium, which would lead to a further adjustment in exchange rates obtained through its (relative) appreciation.

Let us now consider the portfolio models. More complex than the monetary models, they take into account both monetary and financial flows, and they consider current account to play a role in the determination of long-term exchange rates. Financial activities are made dependent on interest rates (foreign and domestic), exchange rate expectations, and wealth. An increase in the quantity of money gives rise to a series of adjustments whose importance is derived from that of these variables. A decrease in domestic interest rates leads to a reduction in exchange rates whose magnitude is determined by the increase in the demand for foreign exchange. In its turn, the exchange rate depreciation encourages the rest of the world to increase its imports, provoking an accumulation of foreign securities and a current account surplus which leads to a revaluation in exchange rates, whose entity depends on numerous factors, among which expectations and the degree of substitutability of national and foreign financial bonds stand out.

To conclude with this quick survey of the assets-approach models, let us note that in the portfolio analyses, in contrast to what happens in the monetarist and Keynesian models, monetary policy can permanently modify real exchange rates, and cannot therefore be considered *neutral*, either in the short or long term.

Now the critical observations put forward against the balance of payment approach can be extended to the assets approach. The mechanisms postulated by the theories we have just been describing are based on the idea that currencies can be exchanged as if they were goods, and that exchange rates are the expression of their prices. Yet, how can a simple numerical vehicle be supplied and demanded as such? If money had an intrinsic value, it would be a commodity; and a commodity can certainly be supplied and demanded. However, the dematerialisation of bank money is a matter of fact. Money is not a commodity, but the numerical (and, therefore, a-dimensional) form of the output it is associated with and which it must convey.

Let us very briefly recall the example of the cloakroom tickets. What would be the sense in maintaining that cloakroom tickets are freely supplied and offered on the market and that their price is determined by their exchange rate with other commodities? Can the cloakroom ticket associated with a coat have a price corresponding to a pair of shoes or to any other product substantially different from the one defining its real content? If it is illogical to transform the cloakroom ticket into an autonomous object which can be freely bought and sold, it is likewise illogical to consider money as an object whose value can be determined independently from the product of which it is the numerical form. Like the cloakroom ticket, money as such has neither value nor price. Its purchasing power is nothing other than a drawing right over the product it is momentarily associated with. Hence, in the same way that before the coat's deposit and after its withdrawal the ticket is only a numerical token which nobody dreams of demanding in exchange for real goods, money exists as a net asset only in so far as it is identified with the output it conveys.

At the international level, the inconsistency implied in the buying and selling of money is even more evident. It should not be forgotten, in fact, that money exists only within the banking system from which it is issued. Payments carried out by country A make country B the owner of a deposit in A's banks, money A flowing instantaneously from and to its point of origin (Figure 9.1). Money transfers bank deposits (BD) from A to B, and is immediately re-absorbed by the banking system of country A. Thus, to

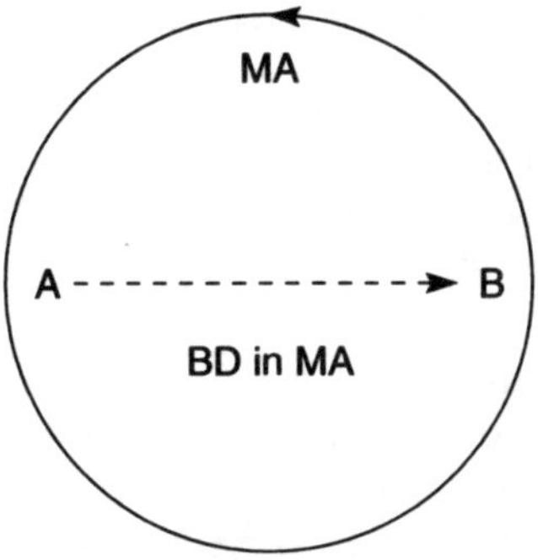

Figure 9.1

maintain that bank deposits earned by B increase the quantity of money within this country amounts to mixing up form and content, vehicular money and real output. Bank deposits pertain to the category of (monetary) bonds and, as such, they are subjected to supply and demand, and their interest rate is determined through the interaction of these two forces. The mistake to be avoided is that of believing that the purchase of foreign monetary claims (bank deposits) can modify the exchange rate between national currencies. In reality, when country B demands bank deposits from A, country A demands goods (or bonds) from B, and the two demands balance, leaving exchange rates unchanged.

If, despite this fundamental neutrality, exchange rates vary so worryingly, it is because the present system transforms national currencies into objects of exchange. As we have already seen, money A enters the banking system of B only by way of its duplication. Thus, what is added to B's quantity of money is not A's money, but its duplicate. Successively, money A's duplicate is invested on the Euromarket, where its price is determined, relative to other currencies, by supply and demand. But, then, how is it possible to claim that exchange rates significantly reflect the ratio among the prices of real outputs? Being essentially speculative, the Euromarket introduces a high degree of uncertainty into the determination of exchange rates, and makes the whole international monetary system fundamentally unstable.

In order to solve the problem of exchange rates it is therefore necessary to refer to the modern conception of bank money by working out a system which breaks with the archaic tradition of identifying money with a commodity and determining its external price through the relative exchange of monetary assets.

FIXED AND FLOATING EXCHANGE RATES AS RELATIVE EXCHANGE RATES

What we would like to show in this section is that the regime of fixed exchange rates adopted after Bretton Woods, and the regime of floating exchange rates, are particular cases of a system which, to resurrect a term cherished by neoclassical theory, we could define as a system of relative exchange rates.

What is meant by 'relative exchange' is well known to every economist. If we refer to the commodity market, for example, the exchange between two commodities, *a* and *b*, is said to be relative since the price it determines allows us to express the value of each commodity relative to the other (with which it is exchanged). It is an exchange between distinct objects whose value (price) can only be determined precisely on the basis of their exchange. Even though they exist separately, *a* and *b* have no proper value. It is because the two commodities are distinct that their exchange is relative, as is the price it defines. Making use of a spatial representation, we could say that relative exchange implies the reciprocal displacement of two (or more) objects occupying different points in space. The result of the operation is to commute the terms of the exchange, so that commodity *a* replaces *b*'s position and vice versa. In terms of supply and demand we would say that commodity *a* is demanded by an agent (the one owning commodity *b*) and supplied by another (the owner of *a*), and that it is through the interaction of these two forces that exchange can effectively take place and relative prices be determined.

If we now pass from the exchange between commodities to monetary exchange, we immediately note that its relative character is due to the fact that currencies are considered as goods. Either nationally or internationally, domestic currencies are identified with net assets, so that both the exchange between commodities and money, and exchanges between currencies, seem to pertain to the category of relative exchanges.

Let us consider exchanges between national currencies. On the exchange market, currencies are supplied and demanded as are commodities on the product market. Analogously, relative prices or exchange rates result from a process where one currency takes the place of another. 'Exchange rate is the price expressed in the form of a relationship between two monetary units of a foreign credit on demand' (Byé 1965: 111). The determination of exchange rates through the free interplay of market forces is perfectly consistent with the 'relative' definition of monetary exchange. The system of floating exchange rates is the most suitable for the theory of relative exchanges since, besides considering currencies as net assets, it relies only on supply and demand for the price determination of these particular real goods.

On the other hand, however, the regime of fixed exchange rates also seems to belong to the category of relative exchanges. The gold definition of currencies and their convertibility into the precious metal make of them net assets *par excellence*, so that their exchange seems to possess all the necessary requirements to be defined as relative. This is the way monetary exchanges were conceived of during the periods of fixed exchange rates implementation, even though, from a purely theoretical point of view, it is possible to maintain that fixed exchange rates and relative exchanges are not necessarily the two faces of the same coin. In particular, if the gold standard were applied according to the rigorous logic of the Ricardian scheme, currencies would never be exchanged as distinct objects, since their rigid gold definition would make them fundamentally equal (the exchange between dollars and Swiss francs, for example, would amount to an exchange between equivalent quantities of gold). Besides, within trade equilibrium we would witness a compensation among currencies with the same gold content and different denomination, while outside trade equilibrium transactions would be directly financed in gold, and if we could still speak of relative exchange we would have to refer to that of gold and commodities and not to that among currencies. In reality, however, the fixed exchange rate regime never took on the rigorous form of the classical gold standard. First the pound and then the dollar were used as world standards and accepted as final objects of payment in the same way as the gold they represented. Countries did not hesitate in introducing these currencies into their official reserves, thus confirming their assimilation to net assets. In other words, under the fixed exchange rate regimes of the gold standard and gold exchange standard, currencies were already supplied and demanded as final goods and their prices subject to market adjustments.

Considered from the point of view of its effective application, the fixed exchange rate system can thus be compared to that of floating exchange rates, at least with regard to the 'material' character granted to national currencies, and particularly to those internationally used as standards. In both systems currencies are considered as real goods and made dependent on supply and demand, and in this sense it is possible to claim that, in both systems, exchange rates are defined in relative terms.

FROM THE SYSTEM OF RELATIVE EXCHANGE RATES TO THAT OF ABSOLUTE EXCHANGE RATES

Until now, exchange rates have been analysed on the basis of the presumed 'intrinsic' value of money, so that, independently of any possible link between money and gold, each transaction implies the reciprocal exchange between monetary assets. In the actual system of payments, where currencies are all bank monies and their value is not derived either from gold or any other precious metal, exchange rates are considered as the relative price at which currencies are exchanged. Moreover, since currencies are not only exchanged among themselves (as happens in speculative transactions), but are also used as a means of payment for the purchase of goods, services and bonds, relative exchange takes place also between money and output, and leads to their reciprocal substitution in the assets of the negotiating parties.

Besides this 'traditional' approach to money, dogmatically seen as a net asset, it is possible to propose another approach closer to the spirit of the classical authors and Keynes. If we consider the Ricardian theory of the gold standard in the light of Keynes's analysis, we soon realise that money plays a purely circular role, similar to that already stressed by Adam Smith. In the ideal gold standard, trade transactions are never paid in money. The exporting country, for example, is effectively paid only when the importing country gives it a quantity of gold equivalent to its commercial exports. Money is only a simple intermediary, without any intrinsic value and is incapable of defining a final payment. This was clearly stated by Bernard Schmitt:

> Every international payment carried out in a bank money with a legal gold content is a *wave-like* process, the creditor country obtaining first a mere promise for gold; the payment becomes effective at the instant money is given back, in exchange for its real content, to the debtor country. Since the payment does not consider vehicular money as a final good, it is defined in a circular flow of money between the buying and the selling country, the terms of every international exchange being necessarily *real*.
>
> (Schmitt 1988: 44)

According to this analysis, money as such is not a net asset, but a mere promise to pay which plays its role through a circular flow whose aim is to carry out the exchange of real goods. International payments are all real, and currencies, with no proper value, are no longer the object of a self-contained demand.

Let us consider the case of a Mexican export to the United States. According to the present regime of relative exchange rates, it defines a demand for pesos and results in an exchange between a sum of Mexican goods and an equivalent sum of American currency. According to the system advocated by Keynes, on the contrary, the dollars are simultaneously supplied and demanded by Mexico, since the importing country's effective payment takes place through the transfer of an equivalent sum of American bonds (real goods in every respect) which entails the flowing back of the dollars to their point of origin. Being a simple promise to pay, the American money thus leaves its place to real goods: the sole effective object of payment.

In this circular flow the dollars are supplied and demanded by both countries and the entire process is entirely neutral with regard to the value of their national currencies. In other words, exchange rates are fixed not because they are thus maintained through the onerous intervention of monetary authorities, but because they are no longer subject to the destabilising pressures of supply and demand. Thus, exchange rate stability is no longer dependent either on the behaviour of single economic agents or on the economic policies followed by the different countries, but is due to the choice of a system in which money is a simple means of circulation fundamentally distinct from the set of real goods (which it can be identified with, without being a constitutive element).

Now, if money is used in a circular flow having the issuing banking system as its point of departure and arrival, this means that, in the exporting process we are analysing as well as in all other international transactions, it is exchanged with itself through the currency of another country. In the case of Mexico, the American dollars are changed into pesos, at the moment Mexican goods are purchased, to be again changed into dollars, at the moment (the same) American bonds are transferred as final payment. In a system where money is vehicular and payments are all real (though they take place with the intermediation of money), trade imports are covered by equivalent exports of goods and services (when the balance of trade is equilibrated) or bonds (in the case of a trade deficit). Having no value as such, money leaves its place to real goods, and in its circular flow defines what Bernard Schmitt has called an *absolute exchange*, that is, an exchange whose two terms are money itself. From dollars to dollars through pesos, this is what absolute exchange of the American currency implies. Hence it is clear that dollars cannot be demanded without being simultaneously offered (and, reciprocally, offered without being demanded) by the same country (Mexico, and, reciprocally, the United States). It is thus confirmed that the system of absolute exchange rates is intrinsically a system of fixed exchange rates.

The choice of a system of international payments allowing for exchange rate stability does not imply the restoration of the gold standard. On the contrary, fixed exchange rates are perfectly compatible with the general use of bank money, on condition that it is not arbitrarily assimilated with a final good. A system respecting the vehicular nature of money is perfectly suitable for providing the stability classical authors believed to be fundamentally linked to gold definition and convertibility. On the other hand, by preventing the international accumulation of foreign exchange (let us recall that Eurocurrencies exist because national currencies are supposed to have an intrinsic value and are thus accumulated abroad), the system of absolute exchange rates is a barrier against the expansion of those speculative transactions that even the partisans of floating exchange rates reckon an important cause of monetary disorder. The internal causes of disorder would still be present, it is true, but if they persisted despite the contribution to expansion that international stability would provide for, nothing would prevent an international meeting from modifying the level of absolute exchange rates. Finally, the new system would guarantee an unheard stability of exchange rates, while allowing for their re-alignment if one or more economically disadvantaged countries were to face persistent financial difficulties.

As we have said, the principle of absolute exchange rates is related to a conception of money going back to the analyses of the great classical authors and then taken over and further developed by Keynes. In his project for the institution of an International Clearing Union, the famous English economist stressed the banking origin of money and the vehicular nature deriving from it. Since it must comply with the rules of double entry book-keeping, bank money can only be used in a circular flow which makes it instantaneously move back to its point of origin (the issuing bank). Starting from this fundamental observation, Keynes worked out a plan for the reform of the international monetary system whose implementation would have replaced *de facto* the relative exchange rate system with that of absolute exchange rates.

Too innovative to be entirely understood and accepted, the Keynes plan was put aside, and the participants at the Bretton Woods conference preferred to adopt what seemed to be the result of a good compromise between theoretical and political realities. However, the plan elaborated by White and supported by the American authorities did not take into serious consideration any of the important novelties present in Keynes's proposal. Thus, the American currency was granted a special status officially sanctioning its character of final good. The dollar was endowed with an extra-territorial value only apparently justified by its link with gold. As became evident after the official suspension of convertibility, the value internationally acknowledged to the dollar was (and still is) the consequence of its a priori identification with a net asset. As such, the American money became not only the 'final' means of payment of international transactions and the essential component of official reserves, but also the object of intense international speculation. Traded daily on exchange markets, the dollar was subjected to a series of destabilising pressures that made it necessary to abandon the fixed exchange rate regime. This shows how exchange rate stability is inconsistent with the system of relative exchange rates which formed the basis for the structuring of international economics before and after Bretton Woods.

10

TOWARDS A NEW SOLUTION TO THE CRISIS OF INTERNATIONAL PAYMENTS?

In this chapter we shall briefly trace back the path followed by the system of international payments, through some of the crises that have characterised it, the solutions successively proposed and the modifications effectively implemented. (Let us note that, in the short analysis proposed here, we have left out important events such as the European attempt at working out a more stable monetary system than the international one, and the external debt crisis, to whose study Part III of this work is already devoted).

THE JAMAICA AGREEMENT AND ITS CONSEQUENCES

The American decision to suspend convertibility of the dollar into gold decreed the end of the regime of fixed exchange rates adopted at Bretton Woods, and the international monetary system was confronted with the problem of determining new monetary parities and their margin of fluctuation. After an initial period of confusion, the Group of Ten met at the Smithsonian Institution in Washington in December 1971 and, besides establishing new parities for the greatest world currencies, they fixed at 2.25 per cent the margins of exchange rate fluctuations (above and below the new central rates) and decided to increase the price of gold, taking it to $38 per ounce and thus sanctioning an 8.57 per cent devaluation of the American currency.

The settlement reached in Washington and known as the Smithsonian Agreement did not succeed in solving the problems related to the increasing instability of the international monetary system caused by dollar inconvertibility, and was abandoned after only 14 months. In the meantime, the countries of the European Economic Community agreed to reduce by half the margin of fluctuation of their currencies, giving birth to the famous 'snake in the tunnel'.

The entire international system was rocked by successive crises that undermined its stability, caused especially by the growing pressure exerted on the main foreign currencies by the dollar. Central Banks had to frequently intervene to sustain the dollar exchange rate, and the situation became so critical as to induce European Community members to close their foreign exchange markets for two weeks, and to let their currencies float jointly against the dollar (with the sole exception of Italy, whose currency was to float alone).

Despite the general malaise and the flourishing of initiatives that were thought to allow a country (or a group of countries) to protect itself against the recurrent monetary crisis, the IMF was able to maintain a strategic importance and to play a determinant role as a financial and monetary intermediary. As stated in a study elaborated by IMF experts in 1972, the situation was rapidly deteriorating and the impelling necessity for a monetary reform was clearly felt by most IMF members. On the basis of this preliminary work, the IMF's Board of Governors decided to establish a Committee of Twenty (from the number of representatives of member countries appointing an Executive Director of the Fund) charged to work out the measures required for a reform of the international monetary system. Among the proposals put forward by this Committee in 1974 were those aimed at strengthening the role of the International Monetary Fund, which was given the task of 'encouraging the growth of world trade and employment, promoting economic development, and helping to avoid both inflation and deflation' (IMF 1974: 7), those devoted to the exchange rate problem (favouring the adoption of adjustable par values, without excluding, in particular cases, the use of free floating exchange rates), and those aiming at transforming Special Drawing Rights into the principal reserve asset. It is also noteworthy that the idea of convertibility was not completely abandoned, since it was thought that it could play an important function in the settlement of imbalances.

> The main features of the international monetary reform will include:
> (a) An effective and symmetrical adjustment process, including better functioning of the exchange rate mechanism, with the exchange rate regime based on stable but adjustable par values and with floating rates recognized as providing a useful technique in particular situations;
> (b) cooperation in dealing with disequilibrating capital flows;
> (c) the introduction of an appropriate form of convertibility for the settlement of imbalances, with symmetrical obligations on all countries;
> (d) better international management of global liquidity, with the SDR becoming the principal reserve asset and the role of gold and of reserve currencies being reduced;
> (e) consistency between arrangements for adjustment, convertibility, and global liquidity; and

(f) the promotion of the net flow of real resources to developing countries.

(IMF 1974: 7)

According to the Committee of Twenty, the IMF was not to play a function of coordination among countries, which would be left free to choose their monetary destiny. On the contrary, its task was to be that of pointing out and promoting the changes required for the equilibrated development of international transactions, without leaving out possible interventions aimed at correcting situations of persistent instability as well as the possibility of exerting a control over the monetary policies followed by countries in great difficulties. Moreover, changes in par values would be introduced only subject to the authorisation of the Fund, which would also be able to prevent member countries from controlling capital flows in order to influence the quotation of their national currencies.

A particular relevance was bestowed on the monetary problems of developing countries, with the aim of exonerating them from controls over commercial and financial flows (trade exports and capital imports), thus encouraging them to adopt economic and monetary policies capable of promoting foreign investment. To increase LDCs' inflow of real resources it was also suggested that they should be granted financial support under the form of Special Drawing Rights allocations and that the IMF should adopt a new form of long-term financing of their balance of payment deficits

Following the proposals put forth by the Committee of Twenty and given the necessity to modify the IMF's articles as a result of the evolution undergone by the whole system of international payments, a meeting was convened in Jamaica in 1976. The Jamaica agreement, which gave rise to the second amendment to the IMF's articles approved in 1978, only partially took into account the suggestions contained in the final report and in the *Outline of Reform* (IMF 1974) worked out by the Committee of Twenty. Besides legalising the floating exchange rate system, it was decided that the IMF would have to watch over exchange rate agreements, increase the quotas of member countries, and sell one-sixth of its gold reserves creating, with the receipts of this sale, a trust fund to assist underdeveloped countries.

The exiguity of the proposals that emerged from the 1976 IMF meeting in Jamaica was stressed by several economists who, though agreeing with the decision to introduce a regime of managed floating exchange rates and create the conditions for the coordination of Central Banks interventions, did not fail to observe that the reform was far from having substantially modified the system of international payments previously agreed at Bretton Woods. In particular, without giving up the use of one or more national currencies as international standard and reserve asset, the intent to transform Special Drawing Rights into the world's principal reserve asset was bound to remain a dead end. 'The alleged objective of making the SDR the "principal reserve asset" is shown to be a sham by the absence of any attempt to reduce the role of foreign-exchange reserves' (Machlup 1976: 34). On the other hand, the Jamaica agreement provided no restraint to the uncontrolled development of speculative transactions and Euromarkets, and did not modify the situation of unjustified privilege bestowed on the countries whose money was considered as a reserve currency. Thus, the dollar went on playing a predominant role in the system of international payments, increasing uncertainty on foreign exchange markets and keeping the United States in an anomalous situation with regard to other countries.

Finally, changes introduced following the agreement signed in Jamaica only sanctioned what was already a matter of fact, the passage towards floating exchange rates and the irrevocable demonetisation of gold, re-evaluating the role of the International Monetary Fund and promoting interbanking cooperation at a central level.

FROM THE REIGN OF THE DOLLAR TO THAT OF THE KEY-CURRENCIES?

Officially sanctioned at Bretton Woods, the international dominion of the dollar went on unopposed until the mid-1970s, when the United States FED and the Central Banks of several other countries started including currencies such as the mark, yen and Swiss franc in their official reserves. The reasons for this must be looked for in the increased instability of the American currency, the persistent fluctuation of exchange rates, and the inability to endow the system with a true international reserve asset. The attempt, suggested by the Committee of Twenty and only partially taken over by the Jamaica agreement, to transform SDRs into the predominant international reserve asset remained unfruitful, and, in order to limit the risks related to exchange rate variations, countries could only differentiate the composition of their reserve. As for the United States, the policies followed since 1978 (like the taking up of loans in marks and Swiss francs by the American Treasury, the selling of SDRs, and the use of the IMF's facilities) have led the country to the same kind of diversification of official reserves as that of other industrialised countries, without substantially modifying its role of supplier of dollars on the Euromarket.

The rapid increase in Eurodollars, linked to the protracted American trade deficit, explains why, though decreasing in percentage (Table 10.1), dollar reserves have been growing year after year. The main key-currency countries, though diversifying their reserves, have been accumulating substantial amounts of Eurodollars, and the same has been done by petrol-producing countries. The relative decline of the American currency has therefore to be seen within a system in which this currency is still the principal one used internationally (Table 10.2). Made possible by

Table 10.1 Share of national currencies in total identified official holdings of foreign exchange, end of year 1983–92 (percentages)

	1983	*1984*	*1985*	*1986*	*1987*	*1988*	*1989*	*1990*	*1991*	*1992*	*Memorandum ECUs treated separately 1992*
All countries											
US dollar	71.1	69.9	64.8	67.0	67.8	64.6	60.2	57.5	58.4	64.4	55.3
Pound sterling	2.5	2.9	3.0	2.5	2.4	2.7	2.7	3.4	3.6	3.2	3.1
Deutschmark	11.7	12.6	15.1	14.6	14.4	15.6	19.0	18.6	16.5	13.0	12.5
French franc	0.8	0.8	0.9	0.8	0.8	1.0	1.4	2.3	2.8	2.5	2.4
Swiss franc	2.3	2.0	2.3	2.0	1.9	1.9	1.5	1.4	1.4	1.3	1.3
Netherlands guilder	0.8	0.7	1.0	1.1	1.2	1.1	1.1	1.1	1.1	0.7	0.7
Japanese yen	4.9	5.8	8.0	7.8	7.5	7.7	7.7	8.8	9.4	8.1	7.8
Unspecified currencies	6.0	5.4	4.9	4.1	3.9	5.4	6.5	6.9	6.9	6.8	16.9

Source: IMF *Annual Report* 1993

Table 10.2 Currency composition of official holdings of foreign exchange, end of year 1986–92 (in millions of SDRs)

	1986	*1987*	*1988*	*1989*	*1990*	*1991*	*1992*
US dollar	187.168	225.867	243.094	254.220	271.110	286.140	324.104
Pound sterling	7.572	8.792	11.144	12.341	17.363	19.372	18.304
Deutschmark	43.466	53.296	63.880	87.364	95.997	89.389	73.346
French franc	2.398	2.987	4.204	6.570	12.016	15.172	14.354
Swiss franc	6.031	7.173	7.918	6.911	7.355	7.412	7.621
Netherlands guilder	3.282	4.554	5.305	5.083	5.606	5.798	3.881
Japanese yen	23.418	27.769	31.525	35.564	45.615	50.891	45.634
European Currency Unit	40.720	57.241	51.257	51.621	52.113	56.159	60.614

Source: IMF *Annual Report* 1993

diversification, the passage to a new multi-monetary system is being hindered by the reluctance of the leading key-currency countries to become the 'bankers of the world'. Germany, Switzerland and Japan do not seem to be willing to subject their currencies to the continuous pressures that their increased use as reserve currencies would not fail to generate. As has been shown by the American experience, the currency chosen to play the role of international standard escapes the control of its issuing country, thus becoming the source of destabilising fluctuations in exchange rates. To safeguard the external and internal stability of their national currencies, reserve currency countries prefer to avoid switching from the dollar standard to a multi-currency standard. On the other hand, because of the relative exiguity of these countries' financial markets and of the difficulties of the free circulation of their capital, the use of the dollar remains comparatively more flexible and the American currency is still preferred as international standard. As observed by Henry Wallich:

> Countries holding dollars as reserves have rarely found it necessary to engage in negotiation or even consultation with the United States when they needed to invest or mobilize funds or intervene in exchange markets to buy or sell dollars. The natural breadth of U.S. financial markets has been assisted in achieving this result by special investment facilities offered by the U.S. Treasury through non-marketable issues of U.S. Government obligations. This has resulted in a very flexible use of the U.S. dollar by foreign monetary authorities.
>
> (Wallich 1979: 7–8)

It is true that Germany, France, Japan, Switzerland and Great Britain already benefit from the privilege of paying part of their net purchases of goods, services and bonds by issuing their own national currency; to which extent they contribute to the increase of the Euromarket, transforming their domestic currencies into international reserve assets. Yet it is also true that Japan (and Germany until reunification) has a highly positive trade balance, so that the internationalisation of its currency would lead to a whole series of disequilibria – at the internal level of fiscal and monetary policy, and at the level of foreign exchange rates – that could rapidly undermine it.

The position adopted by Germany, Switzerland and Japan, as well as their numerous official interventions in support of the dollar, is not surprising. Besides the negative aspects related to the internationalisation of their currencies, these countries' experts have also observed that the adoption of a multi-currency system would make the stabilising intervention on exchange rate markets particularly problematic. Moreover, they claim, difficulties related to the determination of the optimum composition of a country's official reserves and of the proportion of key-currencies due to each country would increase instability in the entire system, making it necessary to adopt more complex and onerous stabilising measures. Hence the suggestion not to abandon the system centred on the dollar, unless it could be replaced by a system where the role of money of the world is entrusted to an international unit such as the Special Drawing Rights issued by the International Monetary Fund.

Before analysing the proposals for the creation of a true world money, let us briefly note that the refusal of a multi-currency system at the international level is matched by its acceptance at the European Community level. The European Monetary System (EMS) is based on the coordinated and multilateral intervention of member country Central Banks. In the intentions of the advocates of this system (see Chapter 11), European domestic currencies should soon leave their place to a unique currency (ECU) bound to become the sole European monetary standard. Even in this case, therefore, there seems to be no doubt about the superiority of a one-currency system and about the necessity to create a supranational Central Bank with responsibility for issuing it.

TOWARDS THE CREATION OF A WORLD CENTRAL BANK?

By refusing the project propounded by Keynes, participants at the Bretton Woods conference did not support the creation of a supranational institution functioning as Bank of the world, being content with the generalisation of the status acquired by the dollar as international reserve currency. With the following decision to suspend convertibility of the American currency into gold and pass from (relatively) fixed to (relatively) floating exchange rates, the dollar's supremacy was internationally confirmed, even though its increasing instability persuaded the Committee of Twenty to propose its gradual substitution with the Special Drawing Rights issued by the IMF. Despite the increase in SDRs (in absolute terms) observation shows, however, that this proposal was substantially put aside, in favour of an eminently pragmatic approach based on the international use of one or more national currencies.

As will be remembered, the internationalisation of domestic currencies has been openly criticised by economists like Keynes, Rueff and Triffin, who have not hesitated in denouncing its inconsistency with the banking nature of money. Even though this analysis has continuously been confirmed by facts, the idea of organising international payments on the basis of the (circular) use of an international vehicular money has not been accepted, mainly because the majority of economists have never stopped identifying money with a real asset. The idea of creating a World Central Bank has to be seen in this context, that is, by distinguishing between the proposals advocating a radical reform of the system of international payments, and those aiming at a simple centralisation of the functions played by the United States and by the few countries whose currencies are given the status of reserve currencies. Among the first proposals we find those of Keynes and, more recently, those of Bernard Schmitt; among the latter of a particular significance are those (propounded, for example, by the Committee of Twenty and by the Group of Twenty-four – from the number of ministers, representing as many underdeveloped countries, meeting in Belgrade in 1979) aiming at investing the IMF with increasing responsibilities and transforming SDRs into the main reserve currency.

Among the countries favouring monetary reform, an important role is played by LDCs, for whom the disorder and uncertainty of the actual system of payments are significant causes of their difficulties in external debt servicing. Their proposals are often radically opposed to the dollar standard and are aimed at organising a new structure of international payments revolving around the creation of a supranational currency and a World Central Bank.

Although many different proposals have been launched, what is common to all of them is the willingness to shape the international monetary system by following the schemes already existing at the national level, that is, by creating a Central Bank allowed to operate as Bank of banks and issuing a single currency. Apart from the plans worked out by Keynes and Schmitt (based on a conception of bank money which, taking over and elaborating the classical distinction between nominal and real money, stresses its eminently circular and vehicular nature) most proposals endorse the creation, by the Central World Bank, of an international currency endowed with a positive and stable purchasing power. 'The case for a world central bank is similar to the case for a central banking system within a nation – to provide a uniform and universally acceptable currency with a stable purchasing power, and to exercise systematic control over the total supply of currency reserves' (Heldring 1979: 60). According to the partisans of a substantial reform of the present system of international payments, the new money should work both as a reserve currency, and as a means of financing interbanking deficits (among Central Banks). Moreover, and this is an important point of divergence from the actual system, access to the international currency would be precluded to residents and private banks, and Central Banks could not use it to intervene on exchange markets.

This last indication is particularly relevant, since it suggests the idea that national currencies must not be subject to buying and selling, and, therefore, that their nature is not that of being final goods. Observation shows that currencies are today assimilated to real goods, and that, as such, they are supplied and demanded on the exchange market. Yet facts also show that international speculation and consequent exchange rate instability are the unavoidable result of this 'materialistic' conception of money. The creation of a system in which international currency is prevented from buying and selling domestic currencies seems therefore to be a first step towards doing away with these practices and finally acknowledging the peculiarity of money.

Coming back to the aspects which usually characterise the proposals for the creation of an international banking system, we have to note that the new world money is defined relative to a basket of national currencies, so that its value varies according to the chosen basket composition and to the effective market exchange rate. The avowed aim of the identification of world money with a basket of national currencies is that of reaching greater monetary stability. This increased stability would then make the new money more attractive than the dollar, thus accelerating the substitution of the American currency as reserve currency. To reach this goal more quickly it has been suggested that a substitution account administered by the new World Central Bank be created. By progressively substituting traditional reserve currencies for the new world currency and thanks to the World Central Bank's emissions we would thus achieve a generalised reform of the system of international payments, and the final replacement of the dollar standard with a true supranational standard.

It must not be forgotten, however, that the basket stability is directly linked to that of the national currencies of which it is made up. Thus, the money-basket neither enjoys a status independent from that of its components, nor a value of its own. Logically, this means that the choice between today's key-currencies and the future world money leads to an almost unlimited number of combinations starting from domestic currencies. The money-basket does not really represent a new money and its stability is the mathematical result of an operation (weighted average) that adds nothing to what is already present in its factors. The substitution of the dollar would sanction the passage from the key-currency standard to a multi-currency standard more than to the international-currency standard.

Despite the advantages that the abolition of the key-currency standard would seem to provide, none of the proposals put forward has been accepted up to now. Among the reasons for the reiterated negative opinion expressed by the competent international monetary authorities there seems to be the fear that the reform could undermine national sovereignty. In answer to this, the partisans of a new monetary order observe that national sovereignty is already seriously threatened by a highly unstable system of payments.

> And yet, national monetary authorities are far from free to act independently, and the cost of maintaining the illusion of sovereignty has been a high one. The existing system certainly does not shelter nations from the international consequences of ill-considered domestic economic policies, nor does it protect nations with sounder domestic policies from the effects of the instabilities created by the improvident.
>
> (Heldring 1979: 62)

According to the advocates of this approach, the greater stability of the new system and the gradual passage from the dollar to the world currency should reduce fears of a possible limitation in sovereignty.

Let us make clear, first of all, that the loss of national sovereignty is a possibility linked to the abolition of domestic currencies, and not to the creation of an international money. It is only if national currencies are replaced with an international standard, as the European Community intends to do, that conditions for the abolition of national sovereignties are created. Hesitations in reforming the system of international payments are not concerned with the disappearance of nations, but with the negative repercussions that the measures adopted by the World Central Bank could have over countries' internal monetary systems.

Without underestimating the fear that some countries could have of losing their supremacy at an international level, let us try to understand the deeply felt reasons that seem to justify the caution and scepticism with which proposals for world monetary reform are received.

Let us start by observing that if the world money is identified with a net asset, its creation becomes a very delicate operation. The eventuality of its over-emission is perceived as a cause of inflationary disequilibria, while it is not clear how the criteria for its distribution among countries can be univocally determined. If money were considered as a simple numerical vehicle and its emission complied with this a-dimensional definition, these problems would not even arise; the World Central Bank would act as an intermediary and international transactions would finally be settled in real terms. Things change when money itself is considered as a real good. Its emission is no longer a neutral operation, and the country benefiting from it obtains a drawing right over other countries' internal resources. The need to control monetary creation thus derives from the dangers related to the possible failure to pay back the loans granted by the World Central Bank. Once the dogma according to which money is created already endowed with a positive intrinsic value has been accepted, it becomes extremely difficult (if not impossible) to avoid these dangers. The problem laid down by those who oppose monetary reform is that of determining what has to be done to prevent the World Central Bank from becoming a source of disequilibria which are greater than those produced by the present system. The answers provided by the advocates of a substantial reform of international payments have not so far convinced monetary authorities, who, with the sole exception of the EC, have pragmatically tried to re-absorb persistent disequilibria without fundamentally modifying the actual system. Besides, the European attempt at working out a monetary union differs substantially from that propounded by the partisans of an international monetary reform, since it is centred both on the emission of a European currency, and on its introduction within the national monetary circuits.

Finally, although the proposals referring to a global restructuring of the system of international payments are being given less attention today (1994) by monetary authorities, we can still maintain, with Frederick Heldring, that

> the strongest argument in favour of the creation of a world central bank is that no alternative has worked well. Each succeeding system has tended to generate instabilities in the world economy. Unless international unity can be created in money matters, the probability of continued instability will remain high.
>
> (1979: 63)

THE PRAGMATIC APPROACH

Since 1971 international transactions have taken place within a system of managed floating based on the principle (which was effectively applied only after 1985) of coordinated intervention by monetary authorities of the different IMF member countries. The function of control and planning was essentially ascribed to the International Monetary Fund which, through a series of subjective (countries' *desiderata*) and objective (data referring to the monetary and economic situation) indicators, was to choose the intervention best suited to face monetary instability. Variations in reserves, and, therefore, in the balance of payments, were, and still are, the principal element in monetary stability.

Various kinds of interventions are proposed to counter a persistent situation of disequilibrium (countries being forbidden to resort to variations in exchange rates in order to avoid balance of payment re-adjustments or to obtain illicit trade benefits). Among them, exchange market interventions remain of fundamental importance and countries are unanimous today in considering essential the commitment to coordinate an intervention policy to avoid, or at least limit, the disorderly fluctuations of their currencies.

As we know, international speculative flows must be included among the causes of these fluctuations; speculative flows which are themselves influenced by such factors as the variation in interest rates taking place in each country and the risk related to the devaluation several national currencies are exposed to. Problems are extremely intricate and solutions complex, if not openly contradictory. Let us take, for example, the case of the United States. For years its trade balance has been negative and its public deficit increasing. To counter the first disequilibrium it is useful to avoid the re-evaluation of the dollar (and both the Federal Reserve and the main Central Banks intervene to this effect). On the other hand, to provide for the growing amount of public debt, fiscal authorities are bound to issue treasury bonds whose sale is obviously influenced by their profitability. Yet high interest rates attract foreign investment which, though it contributes to financing the American public deficit, pushes the price of the dollar upward, thus worsening the balance of payment situation. The conditions needed to fight external disequilibrium are inconsistent with those required to oppose internal imbalance and the United States finds itself in the uncomfortable position of having to choose a solution that can never be the right one.

In reality, with the present system of international payments we witness an interweaving of problems related both to internal and external monetary stability. The measures of monetary policy implemented to fight internal disequilibria have repercussions at the international level and, vice versa, interventions aiming at safeguarding international stability affect the delicate national equilibria. The struggle against inflation has been fought, for example, by increasing interest rates so as to make access to credit more difficult and thus restrain demand; but the increase in interest rates makes domestic currency attractive and can lead to its appreciation on exchange markets. According to traditional theory, however, the need to intervene on this market by increasing national currency supply is essentially inflationary, which makes this operation inconsistent with the first one.

It is difficult to see clearly through the meandering measures and countermeasures which, until the beginning of the 1980s, were adopted in a more or less disorderly fashion, thus causing generalised uncertainty. To put an end to the growing instability, members of the Group of Seven (the United States, Japan, Germany, France, Great Britain, Canada and Italy) met, first in New York (Plaza Meeting, 1985), and then in Tokyo (Economic Summit Meeting, 1986) and Paris (Louvre Meeting, 1987), to work out a common intervention policy. The first objective was that of encouraging a further depreciation of the dollar to reach a parity re-alignment among the main currencies; in Tokyo and Paris the monetary and fiscal measures of internal policy necessary to stabilise exchange rates were then established. The most important of these agreements is concerned with the expansion of surplus countries' domestic demand. Japan and Germany were asked to stimulate national demand through an adequate fiscal (reduction in taxes) and monetary policy in order to restrain commercial exports and thus give the United States the opportunity of reducing its balance of payment deficit.

Harmonisation and collaboration are the elements on which all recent attempts to stabilise a system dependent on the measures adopted internationally as well as nationally are based; internal policies become, therefore, an essential instrument in the fight against external imbalances. Besides, it should not be forgotten that, efficient as they may be, interventions by fiscal and monetary authorities, have no permanent effects and must be continuously repeated and adapted to an erratic and changing situation. According to several experts, a long-lasting improvement could be obtained only if intervention policies were backed by structural changes. Yet apart from the difficulty of these changes, doubts have been cast on their efficacy, both from a practical and a theoretical point of view, because of the simple observation that, far from calling for a reduction in industrialised countries' exports, the economic development of the entire world depends on their continued increase. If international disequilibria could effectively be safeguarded against only by limiting commercial exports, we would be faced with a much more difficult situation than the one usually foreseen. The increasingly underdeveloped countries would not only be confronted with international monetary disorder, but also with the compelling necessity, derived from the attempt to oppose this disorder, to restict their imports, thus reducing their exiguous hopes of economic development.

The objectives that the international monetary system has repeatedly laid down are fundamentally inconsistent: the need to oppose protectionism to safeguard free trade is confronted with the attempt to force some countries to intervene in a *dirigiste* (though indirect) way on domestic production, while Third World countries are asked to develop domestic output without being given the chance to increase substantially their imports of consumption and investment goods. According to logic, on the contrary, industrialised and underdeveloped countries should be allowed to export and to import almost without restrictions. Why should highly industrialised countries not invest in foreign bonds, and less industrialised countries not accelerate their development process by importing goods and services? The answer is contingent: because of the high risk of foreign investment, it is of little interest to invest capital in countries which cannot even service their external debt and whose currency is constantly subject to devaluation and inflation. But then the circle closes, and it becomes obvious that the real difficulty is represented by the monetary instability characterising the present system of international payments. It is because of monetary disorder that development becomes extremely uncertain, and not vice versa. If payments took place within a perfectly neutral monetary structure, it would no longer be necessary to resort to the absurd principle of trade equilibrium in order to counterbalance the opposing destabilising pressures of the system.

The main shortcoming of the pragmatic approach is that of giving up fundamental analysis, considering the actual system as a natural product whose distortions are due only to economic agents' behaviour, and, therefore, to the deficiency of international collaboration. To take the neutrality of the international monetary apparatus for granted is a serious mistake, and it is likewise mistaken to assume that, as the simple reflection of real transactions, monetary flows never have negative 'autonomous' consequences.

Eurocurrencies, international speculative movements and monetary crisis

The best example of the autonomy attained by money in the present system is given by international speculative capital. As we have seen, foreign payments made by countries whose currencies are accepted as net assets are the source of Eurocurrencies, that is, of a growing mass of 'stateless' capital whose only aim is to be profitably invested. The erratic movements of this speculative capital are customary events, so that the coordination of international monetary policies has to give them a place as prominent as aleatory.

There should be no doubts about the autonomy enjoyed by this capital with regard to real production. Since their birth, Eurocurrencies have represented a mass of money with no link with production whatsoever, for they are issued through a series of book-keeping entries leading to the duplication of an equivalent sum of national currencies. Eurodollars deposited offshore, for example, are mere duplicates of American dollars and unlike them – which, issued by the American banking system and associated with that country's real production, define part of the American national income – represent no real wealth. On the other hand, it is also certain that the speculative movements of this international capital have no direct relationship to the evolution of real economy. Unfortunately this does not mean that speculation has no repercussion at the productive level. As shown by the Great Crisis of the 1930s, the existence of a strong speculative component can generate a series of highly destabilising processes for the whole economic system, and this is proof that monetary and productive aspects can never be dissociated in a dichotomous perception of reality that has always been symptomatic of a fundamental incapacity to understand it.

The pathological increase in the quantity of money, both national (see Chapter 3) and international (Eurocurrencies), leads to a growth of speculative capital that confirms the lack of integration between real and monetary sectors. On Stock Exchange markets, for example, shares become the object of speculative transactions so that their price has very little to do with their intrinsic value, which is linked to production.

The 'black Monday' crisis of 1987 is emblematic in this respect, even though the system was partially able to control the situation, avoiding the transformation of the Stock Market crash into a generalised breakdown of the entire economy. On the whole, the present monetary system is intrinsically unstable because money is made an object of trade and speculation. Further proof of this is given by the recent (1992–93) crisis within the European monetary system. The attempt to implement a fixed exchange rate system at the European level has been no more successful than that propounded at Bretton Woods. After a period of relative stability, during which the gaps between monetary and real exchange rates got worse in several countries, pressure on exchange rates became so strong as to force countries such as Italy and Great Britain to abandon the EMS fluctuation margins. Devaluations of the lira and pound were followed rapidly by those of other European currencies, thus determining a climate of uncertainty in which speculative movements have been added to fluctuations caused by real factors. Finally, monetary authorities have once again been forced to accept the fact that it is fundamentally impossible to guarantee the stability of a system in which currencies must play the twofold and contradictory role of means and object of payment. Being simultaneously subject to market forces and to the requirements of internal economic policy, the currencies of EC member countries cannot be maintained within the restricted limits of fluctuation determined by the EMS, unless they are prepared to pay such a high price that it could lead to the near collapse of national economies (France, for example, in an attempt to give the franc the same status as the mark, has been forced to adopt an onerous intervention policy on exchange and interest rate markets).

Part III

TOWARDS THE CREATION OF A SUPRANATIONAL MONEY

11

THE PROBLEM OF EUROPEAN MONETARY UNIFICATION

FROM THE WERNER PLAN TO THE EUROPEAN MONETARY SYSTEM AND FROM THE DELORS PLAN TO THE TREATY OF MAASTRICHT

The monetary snake

Monetary crises preceding and following the American decision to officially suspend convertibility of the dollar for gold, as well as the destabilising effects of the growing mass of Eurodollars and the continuous pressure exerted by the American money over European currencies, led to a whole series of devaluations and to the decision to close down foreign exchange markets for a week (4 March 1971). The situation was serious and called for the rapid adoption of measures which could permit the common fluctuation of European currencies against the dollar, and for control over inter-community fluctuations. It was therefore essential for Europe to work out a common monetary policy to deal with the 'dollar empire'. On 24 April 1972 the European agreement on the restricted fluctuation of the exchange rates, known as the 'European monetary snake', came into effect. Countries accepting the exchange rate agreement were committed to maintaining inter-community exchange rate fluctuations within a band of 2.25 per cent relative to indirect parities.

According to the agreement signed in Basel by the Central Banks of the six countries then members of the EC, the European fluctuation band was half that established internationally by the Smithsonian agreement of 1971 between each currency and the dollar. As we have said, the aim of this agreement was to provide the greatest possible stability for EC currencies. Yet results were not up to expectations, mainly because of the decisions taken by some European countries, by the United States and by other countries as to dollar fluctuations. From the 'snake in the tunnel' we thus passed to the 'snake outside the tunnel' without achieving either a high degree of stability or reaching a good level of cooperation among the different monetary zones the EC was subdivided into. Countries which were already members of the EC or were considering adhesion took part discontinuously in the exchange rate mechanism, and between 1972 and 1979 parities were often re-aligned, until the snake was absorbed into the European Monetary System (13 March 1979).

The Werner Report

Signed during a period in which the international monetary system seemed capable of guaranteeing exchange rate stability, the Treaty of Rome (1957) did not provide any precise suggestion as to monetary cooperation, and it was only when disequilibria started becoming serious that EC countries felt the need to achieve greater stability of inter-community exchange rates and closer coordination of their monetary and economic policies. Despite the common aim, however, two distinct lines of thought soon emerged on the priority that should be given to the different phases leading to monetary unification. According to some experts, economic policy harmonisation remains the unavoidable premise of monetary integration, whereas according to others it is monetary unification which is the unavoidable presupposition for economic integration.

> Advocates of progressive European economic and political integration have held out the hope that the EMS could pave the way towards a European exchange-rate and monetary union which, in turn, should strengthen the political cohesion of the European Community. Central banks and monetary officials from European treasuries, on the other hand, have tended to exhibit a somewhat more sceptical and reserved attitude and generally profess the view that monetary mechanisms – seen in isolation – might not be very efficient in promoting the European unification process.
>
> (Dudler 1984: 228)

Supported particularly by the Germans and Dutch, the second point of view considers monetary unification as the crowning of a harmonisation and integration process which should lead member countries to similar economic and structural levels. The approach advocated by Belgium, France and Luxembourg, on the contrary, puts a particular emphasis on monetary unification, considered to be the most appropriate means of achieving greater economic integration.

The history of the EMS is marked by the continuous contraposition of these two theses and by the constant search for compromise. The plan worked out in 1968 by Pierre Werner, Prime Minister of Luxembourg, represents an attempt to mediate between these two opposing points of view by proposing the parallel carrying out of monetary integration and economic policy convergence. In order to achieve monetary unification,

Werner suggested it was necessary to gradually reduce the margins of fluctuation in exchange rates and to harmonise the various instruments of monetary policy, while as far as economic policies were concerned, he suggested a whole series of reforms aimed at achieving uniformity with regard to fiscal policies, capital markets and the financing of public deficits. One of the principal aims of the project was to create a European Monetary Fund with the task of providing the instruments for inter-community financial aid and managing EC foreign exchange reserves.

The final objectives of the three stages proposed by the Werner plan were monetary unification and the introduction of a single European currency (either explicitly or implicitly, through the total and irreversible convertibility of currencies, the elimination of margins of fluctuation in exchange rates and the irrevocable fixing of parity rates). Hence, although it was an ambitious project bound to raise dissatisfaction among all those who saw in the single currency the end of national sovereignty, the Werner plan had the advantage of proposing monetary unification as a progressive movement of integration, both monetary and economic, and not as a radical reform attempting to immediately replace national currencies with a European single currency. According to Werner, monetary integration could be achieved thanks to a fixed exchange rate system and through perfect currency substitutability. These seemed to be the fundamental requirements for the creation of a European monetary zone, while the effective introduction of a single currency was considered to be an optional step of political and psychological interest.

Despite being accepted by the European Council, the Werner plan was never implemented, both because of the economic and structural disparities existing among EC countries, and because of the worsening of the international monetary crisis. Nevertheless the Werner proposals remain a milestone on the road towards European integration and, as we shall see in the plan proposed by Jacques Delors, still represent the official opinion of a consistent part of the EC as regards monetary unification.

The European Monetary System (EMS)

The foundations for the elaboration and adoption of a European monetary system were laid down in Bremen, in July 1978, following the decision of the European Council to set up a zone of monetary stability in Europe. On that occasion it was decided that the EMS was to develop along three simultaneous guidelines, aiming at improving the exchange rate mechanism (ERM), creating the European Monetary Fund and working out borrowing facilities in favour of less developed economies. Let us analyse successively these three main objectives.

The European exchange rate mechanism

Implemented in 1978, the exchange rate mechanism is a relevant element of a strategy aimed at creating a zone of monetary stability which would favour the harmonious development of EC countries. Briefly, it is the result of a compromise reached in Bremen between the proposals advocated respectively by France and Germany. The main divergence between these two models lay in the role to be played by the European currency unit (ECU). According to France, the ECU, defined as a basket of European currencies, should represent the European unit of account and the unit of reference for the determination of both the EMS fluctuation band and the necessity for exchange market intervention by EC countries. On the contrary, according to Germany, the ECU was to be used only to determine a grid of bilateral rates and the system would work in the same way as in the monetary snake model, confining the ECU to a marginal role of a simple unit of account.

Enforcement of the French system would imply that responsibility for intervention would pertain to the country whose currency fluctuates the most, taking into account the fact that the margin of fluctuation of each currency in bilateral terms would be proportionate to its weight in the basket, and that variation in bilateral rates relative to the deviating currency would entail the 'revision of all central exchange rates relative to the ECU, and the redistribution of all currencies' weights' (Masera 1987: 65). On the other hand, the German scheme emphasises the need for a bilateral determination of a grid of parities and intervention margins, thus introducing asymmetry in the sharing of responsibility for intervention since the burden is essentially put on the currencies reaching the lower boundary of the fluctuation range. In other words, the system linked to the ECU allows for greater symmetry, since responsibility for intervention is 'defined in relation to the average of European currencies and to be called forth, for a specific currency, as soon as the maximum authorized deviation between the central rate and the market value of the ECU in terms of that currency was reached' (Van Ypersele and Koeune 1985: 48). In this way the burden of adjustment is also put on those countries whose currencies reach the highest margin of fluctuation with regard to the central rate in ECUs. Those who support the principle of bilateral intervention margins maintain that the alleged symmetry of the ECU model implies more frequent and onerous interventions for weak currency countries, since, because of the preponderant weight of strong currencies in the ECU basket, their variation determines that of weak currencies. In reality, what they fear most is that all the weak currencies together could carry enough weight to provoke the fluctuation of a strong currency, pushing it to the edge of the intervention threshold and forcing monetary authorities to intervene by issuing domestic money to the detriment of internal price stability.

According to the compromise adopted by the European Council in Brussels (December 1978), the ECU is used as unit of account and indicator of divergence, whereas parities and intervention thresholds are determined on a bilateral basis, and interventions on foreign exchange markets are made compulsory according to the same rules previously in force under the monetary snake. The divergence threshold, calculated by referring to the ECU, is thus a simple indicator of the degree of deviation from parity and of the opportunity to intervene in a diversified way before intervention on foreign exchange markets becomes unavoidable. Bilateral fluctuation margins were fixed at 2.25 per cent (with the exception of the Italian lira, which was allowed to fluctuate within a wider 6 per cent band), and the divergence threshold at 75 per cent of the bilateral margin agreed for each currency and weighted according to its importance.

As noted, the indicator of divergence is calculated on the basis of the ECU exchange rate. More precisely, the divergence threshold of a currency is determined by referring to the maximum spread between its central rate in ECUs and its market rate. Since each currency is part of the basket, the maximum spread varies according to the currency's weight: the greater its weight, the less its maximum spread. The divergence threshold depends, then, on the relationship between the premium on the ECU market rate and the maximum spread of divergence.

The importance given to the European exchange rate mechanism shows how monetary stability is considered to be a fundamental requirement for the balanced development of industry and trade, and how exchange rates are seen as an essential means towards reaching this end. On the other hand, disparities existing among Community members call for the periodic realignment of parity, in the expectation of greater coordination of economic policies to allow for monetary integration. Besides, it must not be forgotten that since 1979 several important realignments have also partly been caused by the destabilising pressures exerted by the dollar. Periods of relative monetary stability coincide, in fact, with a strong appreciation of the dollar and the consequent depreciation of the mark, while with the devaluation of the American currency there is an increased degree of instability.

As a matter of fact, the EMS revolves around the German Bundesbank. 'The system has become increasingly dominated by the role of the German Bundesbank, whose policy has determined the general strategy of economic policy in the other member states' (Britton and Mayes 1992: 10). The mark is the European currency which can most easily be substituted internationally, and it is the Bundesbank which can best influence the determination of exchange rates between European and major foreign currencies. Monetary authorities of the other member countries thus intervene to guarantee the stability of their currencies in relation to the mark. A weakening dollar, for example, leads to an appreciation of the mark and to an increase of tension within the EMS. This also shows how much the system is put under pressure by the unbalancing effects of international speculation, which often causes structural and real changes which are inappropriate to a situation of increasing discrepancies among Community members. As Rainer Masera, former Head of the Research Department of the Banca d'Italia, says: 'In the presence of potentially destabilising financial flows, the convergence of fundamental variables no longer seems sufficient to guarantee exchange rate stability, which can be realised only in the presence of a reinforced process of monetary policy coordination' (Masera 1987: 157). Finally, the calculation of the divergence thresholds itself cannot ignore the evolution of the main foreign currencies, so that the entire system is in a delicate position of virtual instability which makes it particularly vulnerable.

The European Monetary Cooperation Fund (EMCF) and the financial support mechanisms

As with the European exchange rate mechanism, the discussion about the mechanisms of financial assistance revealed a deep rift between the advocates of a major reform and those who wanted only a slight modification of the system existing before the Bremen summit. In this case too, agreements reached in Brussels were closer to the minimalist position, reserving a secondary role for the European monetary unit. The proposal to allow for the creation of ECUs against deposits of national currencies was put aside, while it was decided to strengthen the borrowing facilities already existing within the monetary snake. Very briefly, they can be summed up as follows: first, very short-term financing facility (VSTF), i.e. interbank credits (among Central Banks) obtained through the sale of Community currencies in exchange for credit in EMCF accounts in ECUs. In this context the creation of ECU accounts against transfer of Central Bank reserves in gold and dollars (up to the maximum limit of 20 per cent per each) is also envisaged. However, the use of ECUs is not particularly encouraged since 'a creditor Central Bank is not forced to accept a payment in ECUs of more than 50 per cent of its credit' (Masera 1987: 76). Second, short- and medium-term financial support (STFS and MTFS), which is financial help granted without conditions to each Community country whose balance of payments suffers momentarily from a deficit (STFS), and to those countries whose deficit is linked to serious economic difficulties (MTFS). In this last case, the financial support is usually limited to 50 per cent of the maximum quota and subject to the country adopting measures in favour of a return to equilibrium.

As far as the creation of a European Monetary Fund (proposed at Bremen and which should have taken place in the two years following the meeting) is concerned, we can simply observe that its realisation depends on a more radical reform of the European Monetary System. The problem of the EMF is strictly related to that of the ECU, and it is to this that we shall now turn our attention. Yet, before doing so, let us finally observe that at Bremen it was also decided to support less prosperous economies, since such a policy was considered essential for the success of the European zone of monetary stability. It was thus claimed that progressive monetary integration required the creation of a series of supranational fiscal instruments to compensate for the gradual loss of financial and monetary autonomy and to guarantee an equilibrated solution to national balance of payments problems. This project has only rarely and partially been put into practice, and very little progress has been made towards the adoption of measures in favour of less developed economies.

The Delors plan

The task of proposing a plan for the realisation of economic and monetary union (EMU) was given to a committee of European central bankers under the chairmanship of Jacques Delors. The project was presented in April 1989 and suggests that EMU be reached through a process involving three stages, ranging from the limited fluctuation of European currencies to the introduction of a single European currency.

The first stage envisaged by the Delors committee is the natural continuation of the measures previously adopted by the Community, particularly those relating to the total liberalisation of inter-European capital flows. Officially in force since the summit of Madrid (summer 1989), these agreements concern the coordination of economic and monetary policies, the reinforcement of the committee of European central bankers, and the application to all European currencies of the same margins of fluctuation adopted within the EMU: +2.25 per cent relative to the ECU. 'During this stage, all Community currencies should be limited to a fluctuation of 2.25 per cent against their target or "central rate" against each other ERM currency and the ecu' (Emerson and Huhne 1991: 17).

As for the second stage, agreed upon by all member States except Great Britain, it was planned that it should begin on 1 January 1994 but 'would only start to operate after the treaty committing member states to EMU had been signed' (Emerson and Huhne 1991: 17). It should entail the gradual narrowing of the margins of fluctuation, the creation of a European system of Central Banks called the European Central Bank, the institution of a fund for exchange market interventions, and the progressive transfer of decision-making powers as regards monetary and fiscal matters to a common institution.

> Stage 2 [. . .] would involve the progressive narrowing of the bands of fluctuation for each currency, and any change in their target value

> would only occur in the most exceptional circumstances. The fledgeling institutions which would run a monetary union would begin to operate.
>
> (Emerson and Huhne 1991: 17)

Let us note, that the European Central Bank has been conceived as a federal structure endowed with a high level of independence with respect to member States, and to those institutions whose main function is the search for price stability within the Community area.

Finally, stage three, whose implementation should be re-examined no later than in 1997, involves the passage to an irrevocable system of fixed exchange rates and the subsequent substitution of domestic currencies for a single European currency whose emission would be entrusted to the European Central Bank.

> Stage 3 would involve irrevocable locking of exchange rates without any margin of fluctuation. At this point, the Euro-fed or European Central Bank would take charge of monetary policy, including the setting of interest rates. This system of truly fixed exchange rates would subsequently give way to the use of the ecu as the single currency of the whole Community.
>
> (Emerson and Huhne 1991: 17)

Although it represented the official point of view of the Community, the Delors plan was not unanimously accepted. The UK, for example, expressed continuing doubts about the project to replace national currencies with a single European currency, and went so far as to propose an alternative project based on the principle of the free circulation within each country of the twelve domestic currencies of the Community and of a thirteenth currency called the hard ECU. Managed by a European monetary fund and freely convertible into each currency of the Community, the hard ECU could not have been devalued and would have become, so it was claimed, the most influential and desirable European currency. The superiority of the new currency would then have led to its gradually substituting national currencies and to the implementation of a single currency regime. 'Eventually, this system could develop into one of fixed exchange rates, or the "hard ecu" could become a substitute for national currencies "if governments and peoples so choose" as Prime Minister John Major has said' (p. 185). The British proposal is thus one of the projects which sees the single European currency as the point of arrival of a process based on the constant interaction of market forces and on the use of the ECU as a parallel currency (whose analysis is developed on p. 248). Unlike the proposal of the Delors committee, the British plan does not involve the creation of the ECU as a single currency immediately replacing all others, but as an alternative currency whose destiny would be determined by free competition. If it were able to prove superior to national currencies, the hard ECU would effectively become the currency of Europe 'by substitution' and not 'by creation'. However, as noted by Pierre Villiaz, the hard ECU proposed by the British government would not be a true currency, but a financial product, an asset whose emission would not have any congenital relationship with the needs of monetisation of European production. 'Hence, the British become the champions of the hard ECU. Yet nobody in the City believes that such a formula can herald a true currency. It is only one of the countless forms that financial products can take on' (Villiaz 1991: 8).

The Maastricht Treaty

The plan worked out by the Delors committee was taken over by the European Council during its meeting at Maastricht in December 1991 and represents the essential part of a new treaty replacing all the previous Community agreements, from the Treaty of Rome to the Single European Act. The purposes set out in the Maastricht Treaty are both political and economic and include the construction of a new Europe and the introduction of a single currency. As far as economic integration is concerned, monetary union is made to play a central role, and, as in the Werner and Delors plans, it is intended to take place in three stages.

In stage one, which ended 31 December 1993, member countries have started to adopt all the measures required for the implementation of a single market and for achieving price stability and sound public finances, the main purpose of this first stage being to provide the lasting economic convergence needed to reach economic and monetary union.

Beginning on 1 January 1994, stage two involves the establishment of a transitional institution, the European Monetary Institute (EMI), which will take over the tasks of the European Monetary Cooperation Fund and lead to the creation of the European Central Bank (ECB). According to article 109 D of the Treaty, the EMI will strengthen cooperation between European Central Banks as well as the coordination of monetary policies, monitor the functioning of the EMS, facilitate the use of the ECU, prepare the instruments needed for carrying out a single monetary policy and for operations to be undertaken by national Central Banks in the framework of the European System of Central Banks, and supervise the technical preparation of ECU bank notes. The EMI will also report to the Council, at the end of stage two, on whether a majority of member countries fulfil the necessary conditions for entering the third stage of economic and monetary union. Then, if the conditions for the adoption of a single currency are complied with by the majority of member States the Council will, not later than 31 December 1996 and acting on a qualified majority, fix the date for the beginning of stage three. If these conditions are not fulfilled by the majority of countries, the third stage will start on 1 January 1999, the question of a majority being no longer relevant. Fulfilment by member countries of the required degree of sustainable convergence will be judged according to the following criteria:

> – the achievement of a high degree of price stability; this will be apparent from a rate of inflation which is close to that of at most the three best performing Member States in terms of price stability;
> – the sustainability of the government financial position; this will be apparent from having achieved budgetary positions without a government deficit that is excessive as determined in accordance with Article 104 B paragraph 6;
> – the observance of the normal fluctuation margins provided for by the Exchange Rate Mechanism of the European Monetary System, for at least two years, without devaluing against any other Member State currency;
> – the durability of convergence achieved by the Member State and of its participation in the Exchange Rate Mechanism of the European Monetary System being reflected in the long-term interest rate levels.
>
> (Treaty of Maastricht: Article 109 F)

These convergence criteria are then further specified in a final Protocol, where it is stated that the rate of inflation shall not exceed that of the three best performing member countries by more than 1.5 percentage points, while the rate of interest will be contained within 2 percentage points with respect to that of the three best performing countries.

In stage three the European Central Bank will be definitively established, and the process leading to the introduction of a single currency will reach its final phase with the irrevocable fixing of exchange rates,

> At the starting date of the third stage, the Council shall, acting with the unanimity of the Member States without a derogation, on a proposal from the Commission and after consulting the ECB, adopt the conversion rates at which their currencies will be irrevocably fixed and at which irrevocably fixed rate the ECU shall be substituted for these currencies, and the ECU will become a currency in its own right. This measure shall by itself not modify the external value of the ECU. The Council shall, acting according to the same procedure, also take the other measures necessary for the rapid introduction of the ECU as the single currency of those Member States.
>
> (Treaty of Maastricht: Article 109 H, point 4)

As in the case of the previous agreements reached by the Community member countries, the Maastricht Treaty is the result of a compromise between a monetary centred and an economic centred point of view. The final product has not escaped criticism, and derogations have become necessary to avoid failure. Uncertainty over timing and the participants of stage three has reduced the credibility of the process of monetary union, and the results of Dutch and French referendums, as well as the UK refusal of collective acceptance of stage three, have not contributed to improve general feelings about the feasibility of European unification. A further blow to the Maastricht project has been caused by the recent crisis (autumn 1992) of the European Monetary System which led to major devaluations and, *de facto*, to the suspension of the European exchange rate mechanism.

From this short summary of the various projects concerning the setting up of the European Monetary System and its evolution towards economic and monetary union it appears that the whole problem is characterised, on the one hand, by the possibility of transforming the Europe of the Twelve into a single monetary zone by adopting a system of fixed and irrevocable exchange rates, and, on the other hand, by the role that the ECU will play in the transitional and final stages of the process of unification. While the analysis of the ECU is developed in the second section of this chapter, it is useful to end this section with some critical notes about the possibility of creating a homogeneous monetary area by fixing exchange rates between national currencies.

Fixed and irrevocable exchange rates do not allow for the creation of a single monetary zone

As we have seen, it is widely believed that European monetary union can be achieved through free convertibility of national currencies and fixed exchange rates. 'The third stage shall be completed only after the definitive fixation of parities: the ecu becomes the Community currency when the mark, franc . . . are linked by fixed and irreversible exchange rates' (Villiaz 1991: 7). The restriction and the successive abolition of the margins of fluctuation within the EMS are thus considered necessary steps towards the creation of a homogeneous monetary area similar to the one existing among the different regions of a single country.

Now, the perfect homogeneity of the currency issued by secondary (or regional) banks is due to the presence of a Central Bank. The whole of secondary money is transformed into central money, and this allows for private banks operating on the same national territory to be grouped in a single monetary area. Hence, money created by a secondary bank SB_1 can be exchanged with that issued by any other secondary bank since, thanks to the Central Bank, any secondary currency can instantaneously be changed into another. Currencies issued within a single monetary area are perfect substitutes, so that it is always possible to pass from one to the other through an operation of 'absolute' exchange. As we already know, absolute exchange differs from relative exchange in that, unlike the latter, it does not take place between separate objects, but between a single object and its monetary form. In our case, the money issued by SB_1 is changed into that issued by any other secondary bank whatsoever, SB_w, since the emission of SB_w substitutes the preceding emission of SB_1. In practice, an absolute exchange takes place every time the Central Bank intervenes to guarantee the equilibrated carrying out of interbank clearing.

In every project presented so far, the creation of a European Central Bank is seen as the final step of the process after the achievement of exchange rate stability. Even in the Maastricht Treaty, the ECB shall operate as a true Central Bank only after this objective has been entirely fulfilled.

> As soon as the Executive Board has been appointed, the ESCB and the ECB are established and shall prepare for their full operation as described in this Treaty and the Statute of the ESCB. The full exercise of their powers will start from the first day of the third stage [when the value of the ECU shall be irrevocably fixed, Article 109 E].
>
> (Article 109 H)

The absence of an ECB, however, does not allow for the implementation of a system of absolute exchange rates so that, even with fixed exchange rates and perfect convertibility, European currencies would remain substantially heterogeneous and their exchange pertain to the category of relative transactions. The exchange between pounds and marks, for example, would amount to a trade in between two separate objects, and not to the metamorphosis of one currency into the other (Figure 11.1). In the exchange represented in Figure 11.1, pounds take the place of marks and marks of pounds without either of the two currencies disappearing into the other. Within a single monetary area, on the contrary, exchange between currencies issued by two different banks implies the destruction of one and the creation of the other. Literally speaking, one currency is changed into the other; it abandons one form to acquire another, equivalent to the first.

To illustrate the difference between absolute and relative exchange rates, let us analyse 'in parallel' the various stages of an inter-regional and an international payment.

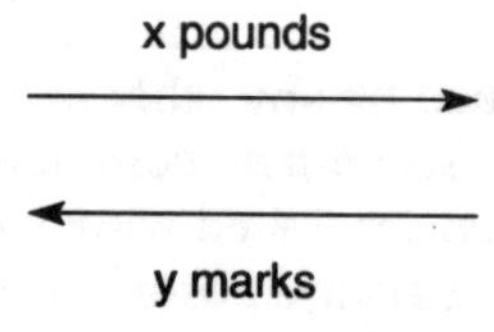

Figure 11.1

Payment between regions of a single monetary zone

The client of a regional bank, SB_1, pays the client of another regional bank SB_2.

The payment makes SB_2 a creditor to SB_1 and a debtor to the client benefiting from it (Table 11.1).

Table 11.1

SB_1

Liabilities		*Assets*	
SB_2	x	Client 1	x

SB_2

Liabilities		*Assets*	
Client 2	x	SB_1	x

Money SB_1 corresponding to the deposit of client 1 is destroyed and instantaneously substituted for an equivalent sum of money SB_2 issued to client 2.

The whole operation is carried out through the intermediation of the Central Bank and interbank clearing gives rise to a transfer of bonds by SB_1 and to a monetary emission of SB_2 'compensating' for the destruction operated by SB_1 (Table 11.3).

Payment between sovereign countries in the absence of a Bank of Central Banks

The client of a bank of country A pays the client of a bank of country B.

The operation leads to the banking system of country A being indebted to that of country B (Table 11.2).

Table 11.2

BS(A)

Liabilities		*Assets*	
BS(B)	x MA	Client	x MA

BS(B)

Liabilities		*Assets*	
Client equivalent in MB of	x MA	BS(A)	x MA

Money entered as an asset in the banking system of B does not disappear to leave its place to an equivalent amount of money B, but remains deposited in its country of origin. The exchange between money A and money B is therefore a (relative) exchange between two amounts of money whose autonomy is that of their issuing banking system.

The absence of a supranational Central Bank does not allow for the transformation of one currency into the other by means of international clearing.

Table 11.3

SB_1

Liabilities		*Assets*	
CB	x	Client	x
Bonds	x	CB	x

SB_2

Liabilities		*Assets*	
Client	x	CB	x
CB	x	Bonds	x

CB

Liabilities		*Assets*	
SB_2	x	SB_1	x
SB_1	x	SB_2	x

According to the projects worked out by Pierre Werner, Jacques Delors and their collaborators, homogenisation of national currencies would be achieved through fixed exchange rates and perfect convertibility: 'monetary union can mean one of two things: either it can mean the irrevocable fixing of exchange rates for all time, or it can mean the replacement of national currencies with one single European currency' (Emerson and Huhne 1991: 18). Apart from the fact that a situation of fixed and irrevocable exchange rates would lead to the gradual substitution of national currencies for the strongest of them, it is important to stress that the fulfilment of these conditions does not involve the grouping of the various national monetary systems within a homogeneous monetary area. It must also be observed that even the introduction of a single currency which is different from those of the Community countries cannot be achieved just by making their monetary systems perfectly uniform. Besides the harmonisation of monetary policies, creation of a common monetary area is possible only on condition that a Central Bank of Central Banks capable of acting as a European Clearing Union is established. In the absence of a European Central Bank thus conceived, national currencies are bound to remain heterogeneous since, even if they are part of a system of fixed and irrevocable exchange rates, they do not benefit from that mechanism of interbank clearing which distinguishes a regime of absolute exchange rates.

At this point it seems opportune to ask whether monetary homogeneity could not be achieved through the abolition of national currencies and the adoption of the ECU as single European currency. Let us point out the fundamental elements of the answer by critically assessing the different proposals for the use of the ECU as an instrument towards monetary union.

EUROPEAN MONETARY UNION AND THE ECU

Official and private ECU

The official ECU

According to the European Council resolution of 5 December 1978, the creation of a zone of monetary stability in Europe was to be achieved through the establishment of a European Monetary System (EMS) centred on the use of a European Currency Unit (ECU) as:

1 the denominator (*numéraire*) for the exchange rate mechanism;
2 the basis for detecting divergences between Community currencies;
3 the denominator for operations in the intervention and credit mechanism;
4 a means of settlement between monetary authorities of the European Community.

At the beginning the value and composition of the ECU was defined by referring to the structure of the European unit of account (EUA), that is, on the basis of a basket composed of EC currencies. As will be remembered, however, the attempt to define the central rates of European currencies and their margins of fluctuation in terms of the ECU was abandoned in favour of a traditional 'snake' system where central rates and margins of intervention are determined bilaterally. In this system of bilateral adjustment the ECU plays no relevant role so that, from a technical point of view, 'the EMS could work just as easily without the ECU' (Masera 1987: 231). André Louw, a staff member of the Commission of the European Communities, thus seems fully justified in claiming that plans for the official use of the ECU as a reserve asset and a means of settlement 'have not been fulfilled: the institutional stage has not been implemented and the role of the ECU in the present stage of the EMS remains below par' (Louw 1988: 92).

In the text of the Brussels Resolution it can also be read that:

> To serve as a means of settlement, an initial supply of ECUs will be provided by FECOM [the European Monetary Co-operation Fund] against the deposit of 20 per cent of gold and 20 per cent of dollar reserves currently held by central banks. This operation will take the form of specified, revolving swap arrangements. By periodical review and by an appropriate procedure it will be ensured that each central bank will maintain a deposit of at least 20 per cent of these reserves with FECOM.
>
> (Fraser 1987: 338)

The initial supply of official ECUs is thus determined as the counterpart of 20 per cent of gold and 20 per cent of dollar reserves held by Central Banks of countries participating in the EMS. The ECU reserve creation is carried out through swaps, renewed every three months, in which Central Banks switch part of their reserve assets for an equivalent credit in ECUs with the EMCF. When reciprocal credits fall due, EMCF and Central Banks set out the changes made necessary by fluctuations both in the price of gold and dollars, and in the amount and composition of countries' official reserves.

> Each quarterly renewal gives an opportunity to adjust the *volume* of the reserves transferred (to take account of possible changes in central banks' holdings of reserves) and to adjust the *value* of the ECU issue (to take account of variations in the market prices of the assets transferred).
>
> (Van Ypersele and Koeune 1985: 100)

It is immediately evident that the official ECU has a very precarious existence, totally cut off from the monetary reality of member countries. Moreover, if we add that the management of the assets deposited with the EMCF is carried out by the depositing Central Banks (on which the revenue on these assets accrues), we realise that the creation of ECUs is a purely formal operation which does not substantially modify the nature of the EMS. In short 'the official ECU is simply a new name for part of the central banks' gold and dollar reserves' (Allen 1986: 5).

Irrespective of their gold and foreign exchange reserves, Central Banks issue national money on the sole basis of double entry book-keeping. In other words, domestic currencies are not just a reflected image of Central Banks' official reserves. In each country, money has its *raison d'être* in its association with the world of national production, irrespective of official reserves.

If we now consider the emission of ECUs by the EMCF, we notice that, unlike national currencies, 'ECUs are only the reflection of the deposited reserves' (Masera 1987: 77). Thus, the official ECU exists only as a new denomination of the EMCF's reserves, and not as a new, additional money.

> The official ECU's low profile is highlighted even more when compared to a regular national currency. The latter is there to stay; a central bank controls the volume in circulation and it is legal tender for all possible uses. As for the ECU, its permanence is not firmly secured, the ECU's volume is uncontrolled, and it is no legal tender except for a few limited uses.
>
> (Louw 1988: 95)

By playing a passive function in the emission of official ECUs and having no discretionary power over its gold and dollar assets, the EMCF has not been successful in providing the Community with a true European currency. This is confirmed by the fact that, besides representing a new name for the EMCF's reserves in gold and dollars, the official ECU is the name for the basket of European currencies. Every transaction carried out in ECUs affects the price of all the currencies in the basket and represents an exchange rate risk for creditor and debtor Central Banks. 'Thus the creditor and debtor central banks incur the risk, in the value in national currency of their ECU-denominated claims and debts, of suffering from actions taken by other monetary authorities' (Van Ypersele and Koeune 1985: 59).

Hence, despite being officially used as a reserve and as a very short-term financing facility, the European unit plays an extremely limited role, since strong-currency countries prefer to carry out their interventions in Euro-currencies or in foreign exchange rather than in official ECUs. As claimed by Rainer Masera, the former 'entail simultaneous opposite effects on the domestic monetary base of both the country which causes the intervention and the country whose currency is being used' (Masera 1988: 130), while in the second case 'it is only on the initiating central bank that monetary base repercussions of interventions fall' (1988: 131). What Masera calls 'symmetric monetary-base interventions' are thus opposed by Central Banks of strong-currency countries which, in order to maintain control of their domestic monetary policy, prefer to implement a system encouraging asymmetric monetary-base interventions.

The private ECU

The analysis concerning the use of the private ECU seems to be completely different. Since the EMS has been implemented, transactions expressed in terms of ECUs have registered spectacular growth. The use of the ECU on the international monetary and financial markets has rapidly increased, particularly in periods of relative stability in European exchange rates, and what was initially a simple unit of account seems today to have acquired the status of a true foreign currency.

Among the principal reasons for this expansion we can enumerate the greater stability offered by the basket compared with the fluctuations of many of the currencies of which it is composed, the engagements taken on by the countries participating in the European exchange rate mechanism, and the fact that interventions carried out in private ECUs, unlike those in official ECUs, entail asymmetric monetary-base effects.

If the rapid development of the ECU market is partially explained by rational portfolio strategy, uncertainty as to exchange rates and domestic interest rates plays a role which is difficult to assess. Monetary instability within the Community simultaneously encourages and discourages investment in ECUs, since a smaller fluctuation with regard to strong currencies is often coupled with a reduction in the rate of return. The ECU has established itself as a satisfactory portfolio choice for investors of countries participating in the European exchange rate mechanism since 'the ready-made basket provides for a reduction in transactions costs compared with transacting individually tailored currency cocktails' (Masera 1988: 136).

The reduction in costs due to the private use of the ECU has contributed to a remarkable expansion in international banking transactions and to the working out of a compensation mechanism which considerably eases the use of the ECU as a means of settlement and of exchange risk management (since March 1988 the mechanism of compensation created in 1982 in the context of the Mutual ECU Settlement Agreement, MESA, has both a netting function, based on the SWIFT system, and a settlement function, under the aegis of the BIS). Firms holding ECU accounts and banks granting credits and issuing deposit certificates in ECUs are thus steadily increasing in number. Big banks within and outside the Community lend in ECUs, issue ECU bonds and operate on the ECU exchange market. According to BIS statistical coverage, for example, total gross bank credit in private ECUs has grown from \$6.2 billion in 1986 to \$35.6 billion in 1991, while during the same period the gross internal and international emission of ECU bonds has passed from \$7 billion to \$61.2 billion (treasury bonds and short-term notes included).

Derived from a basket of national currencies, the ECU is considered by Community countries as any other foreign currency, and it is subjected to the same juridical prescriptions regulating its use and circulation. It is a foreign currency 'built' on the basis of the weighted average of the European currencies adhering to the EMS and whose existence is neither linked to a particular national monetary system, nor to a true monetary system of the European Community. It is therefore proper to ask, as we have done for the official ECU, if the private ECU really exists as a currency or whether it is only the name given to a set of currencies of which it is merely a representative agent. To answer this question it is sufficient to analyse the emission of private ECUs. Within the EMS, any secondary bank can 'issue' the European currency simply by expressing in ECUs its debt towards the owners of a deposit in domestic or foreign money. Hence, for example, on the basis of a deposit in dollars a bank can credit its client in ECUs and successively, if requested, transfer it to any other economic agent. The value of the ECUs issued as counterpart of the deposited dollars, corresponds to that of the basket, and it is in the twelve national currencies making it up that the issuing bank incurs its debt. This means that 'in order to have an ecu the basket of European currencies must effectively be built up, by purchasing or borrowing any of them' (Villiaz 1991: 4). Thus, the private ECU is simply a basket of European currencies which are given a new denomination and whose value remains pegged to that of the currencies which make it up. 'We can represent the private ecu as a basket of currencies wrapped in a band. The content of the basket defines the value of the product while the band gives it a specific name. Wrapped, the basket is quoted by banks under the heading ecu' (1991: 4–5). The emission of private ECUs is thus reduced to a change of name, a 'baptism' of the basket which does not substantially modify the monetary system of the twelve EC countries.

Investing in ECUs means, in reality, opting for a portfolio of European currencies whose value is determined by the weighted sum of these currencies. Hence, although it is certain that the ECU can be advantageously used by the residents of those countries whose currency is subject to important fluctuations, it is also true that the ECU's greater stability is matched by a decreased rate of return. Finally, financial transactions carried out in ECUs do not substantially differ from those which could be carried out in terms of some other basket of national currencies (let us remember here that in the 1960s bonds were already issued in terms of the European Unit of Account, EUA, representing the currencies of the seventeen member countries of the European Payments Union, while from 1973 to 1979 it was the EURCO, a basket of the nine currencies of the EC which were used as unit of reference). Since it simply provides for the nominal definition of the European basket, the emission of ECUs by secondary banks is a mere exercise of terminological conversion: the ECU exists as a name and as a unit of account, but not as a genuine European currency. 'The ECU will not be a new currency as long as it is only a name affixed to ancient objects, a denomination with no proper object' (Schmitt 1988: 154).

Let us finally observe that the market value of the private ECU can diverge from its theoretical value, i.e. from the value of the basket which it nominally defines. In particular circumstances, such as the decision taken by the Spanish monetary authority to adhere to the EMS without immediately integrating the peseta into the official ECU, or the supply of ECUs provided by Central Banks, the market quotation tends to fall, whereas in the presence of important emissions of ECU bonds, such as those carried out by the Italian and French Treasury, it tends to rise. Interventions by Central Banks and decisions of member countries as to their participation in the exchange rate mechanism can therefore generate a margin of profit between market and official quotation of the ECU, thus creating the premises for an activity of arbitrage which, although it has not reached high levels, remains a symptom of the instability related to the creation of a purely nominal financial asset. 'For bankers, the ecu is only one out of many financial instruments. Despite its prestige in the eye of clients, general managers could thus decide to promote other products whose definition seems less problematic' (Villiaz 1991: 6).

The proposals for integration between the official and private ECU

Unanimity as to the future of the European currency is far from being a reality. Advocates and opponents of the project for monetary union do not miss any opportunity to stress its merits and its deficiencies, while the solutions adopted so far have contributed very little to making the ECU into a true currency. As we have seen, the growth of the ECU's private market has not been matched by a corresponding development of the official market, and at the moment it is extremely difficult to forecast what the future of the EMS will be.

Now, according to some European experts, the ECU can be established as a full money only if is used, in a complementary way, both at official and private levels. As stated by Rainer Masera, if this were the case

> ECU market intervention, invoicing and pricing in ECU, holding reserves in ECUs would represent the tripartite facets of a unique process leading to the establishment of the ECU as a full *money* in both the official and private sectors, in respect of its properties as a medium of exchange, unit of account and store of value.
>
> (Masera 1988: 142)

But how could the official and private circuits of the ECU be effectively integrated? Let us briefly analyse the three possible solutions suggested by Masera.

The first and most radical solution aims at endowing the European Monetary Cooperation Fund (EMCF) with 'the power to open accounts in official ECUs with private institutions, and in particular with commercial banks' (Masera 1987: 235). The EMCF would thus become the Central Bank of all private banks opening an account with it. The European unit of account would thus be effectively created as a money and economic unification would be achieved through the monetisation in ECUs of the different European productions. The official ECU would become the private currency of the Community, and the foundations would be created for the gradual and definitive substitution of the national currencies of member countries for the ECU.

It should be remembered, however, that the creation of official ECUs does not correspond to a true monetary emission. Official ECUs have no autonomy with respect to the gold and dollars deposited with the EMCF and of which they simply represent the new European denomination. For the ECU to effectively exist as a money it is therefore necessary that it be issued by the EMCF (or by the European Central Bank) according to the same principles regulating the monetary emission within each country. It is only if it were decided to allow secondary banks of all EC countries to issue ECUs and if the ECB were assigned the role of Central Bank of United Europe that the conditions for the passage to the generalised use of the ECU as single European currency would be laid down. This is obviously the most revolutionary project, both from the economic and the institutional point of views, and its acceptance does not seem to be likely in the near future. The financially strongest countries of the Community are not ready to sacrifice their monetary autonomy on the altar of an integration which, through the generalised use of a single currency, would lead to a substantial change in the present national sovereignty and to the creation of the United States of Europe.

The second solution faces the problem in an alternative way, attempting to associate the private ECU to the official one allowing 'central banks to deposit private ECUs with the EMCF' (Masera 1987: 236). However, this attempt does not seem very promising since the increased use of the ECU as inter-European means of payment would still be subjected to bilateral agreements between monetary authorities, with the risk, therefore, of the majority of transactions still being financed and carried out by strong currencies, not to mention the fact that the private ECU does not yet exist as an autonomous currency, and that, if it did exist as such, its use would lead to the loss of monetary sovereignty by EC member countries.

The last proposal, worked out by Masera and based on a scheme originally suggested by Kenen, relies 'on the idea of linking the private and the official markets through the intermediary of a clearing house, recognized as an "other holder" of official ECUs' (Masera 1988: 144). In this model, transactions take place according to a triangular scheme where vertices are represented by a Central Bank, a private bank, and the clearing house. If it wants to get private ECUs, the Central Bank transfers an equivalent amount of official ECUs to the secondary bank which, in its turn, transfers them to the clearing house. Thus, the Central Bank incurs a debt in official ECUs and is credited in private ECUs, while the secondary bank balances its debt in private ECUs (to the Central Bank) with an equivalent credit in official ECUs (with the clearing house). As far as the clearing house is concerned, it owns a deposit in official ECUs with the EMCF and carries a debt, in the same official ECUs, to the secondary bank. Hence, through this mechanism it seems possible to integrate official and private circuits without resorting to monetary creation and without imposing on EC countries any adjustment implying a symmetric monetary-base effect.

The advantages of this proposal are related to the asymmetry which would characterise monetary interventions carried out in private ECUs (which are dealt with in the same way as foreign currencies by member and non-member countries), as well as to the possibility of implementing it without resorting to any institutional change. The BIS already operates as a 'third holder' of ECUs and as a final clearing institution of the ECU clearing house system MESA, so that the plan proposed by Masera could be applied to this structure. It must be emphasised, however, that instead of promoting the use of the official ECU as a means of payment for inter-European transactions, this solution propounds the use of a mechanism allowing for the official ECU to be replaced by the private ECU. The creation of official ECUs would be limited to the present swap arrangements, and the evolution of the system towards greater monetary integration would essentially depend on the possibility of transforming the private ECU into an autonomous Currency of the European Community.

The ECU as a parallel currency

Being convinced that the transition from national currencies to the European money must take place gradually and consistently within free market laws, several economists have proposed the introduction of the ECU as a parallel currency, that is, as a money which would initially be put into circulation in parallel with national currencies. The central idea is that free competition between the ECU and the European currencies would lead to the gradual replacement of domestic currencies and to the creation of a single European monetary area. It would be up to the public to decide about the future of the ECU, and to eventually sanction its adoption as a single currency.

A priori the role of parallel money can be played by any of the twelve national currencies of the Community or by a supranational currency, the ECU, issued by Central Banks in exchange for domestic currencies. Let us analyse these two alternatives separately.

The 'parallel' use of one or more national currencies

The proposals concerning the use of a particular national currency as a parallel money, and those suggesting a system of free competition among the twelve domestic currencies of the Community, are all based on the idea that monetary union can result from a gradual renovation worked out by market forces more than from monetary authority intervention. According to this 'liberal' approach, the process of monetary unification would lead to the choice of the best national currency as European money and to the creation of a single monetary system for Europe. As emphasised by several authors, however, the gradual substitution of their domestic currencies would lead to a decrease in the monetary autonomy of member countries, empowering only one of them to officially supply the Community with a single European currency. This would be the cause of tensions, and lead to a dramatic devaluation of the fixed capital of weak currency countries which would provoke a rapid and unacceptable increase in unemployment.

As other economists have suggested, another obstacle would be represented by the fact that, by replacing all other national currencies, the predominant one would curtail their monopolistic profit known as seigniorage. Countries whose currency would be gradually abandoned would lose part of their monetary sovereignty and, with it, the power of issuing money with a profit. As we have already pointed out, the concept of seigniorage is related to the feudal right of the sovereign to print money and to the idea that modern bank money is issued already endowed with a positive intrinsic value. This 'substantial' conception of money is based on the idea that bank emission is a process analogous to real production, so that issuing money is not essentially different from producing goods. Yet if we consider that the cost of production of bank money is insignificant as compared to the value which is created, we immediately realise that, if it were effectively created as a net asset, banks would benefit from the unbelievable privilege of getting rich through a process of spontaneous generation. According to Pascal Salin, a leading supporter of this approach, 'money production is profitable to the extent that money – at least in its scriptural form – is sold at a price greater than its production cost. The difference between cost of production and selling price is called seigniorage and represents a banking profit' (Salin 1979: 22).

The absurdity of this claim should be obvious: if banks could get rich simply by creating money, their power would be practically unlimited. They would be able to create something out of nothing (a privilege metaphysically ascribed only to God), without mentioning the fact that they would go on exerting this faculty irrespective of Lavoisier's principle of the conservation of matter and energy. In reality, however, the absurdity of a financial asset creation seems to be missed by the majority of economists, who persist in neglecting the distinction between money and income. And yet great experts in monetary theory such as Smith, Ricardo and Keynes repeatedly stressed the importance of this distinction. Today the structure of the monetary system is such as to immediately reveal the fundamental immateriality of bank money, so it is difficult to understand how it is still possible to support the idea of a spontaneous generation of income.

However, even if EC countries were able to cope with the difficulties inherent in the divergences existing among their monetary and financial policies, there would still be a major impediment to the use of a national currency as parallel money, represented by the gradual relinquishment of monetary sovereignty by all those countries whose currency was not considered by residents as their first choice. If the banks of a given country could have free access to the currency issued by another country and use it in order to monetise national production, we would witness its progressive transformation into a mere region of the second. What determines the nationality of a production is the money used to convey it. British production is such because it is monetised in pounds; if it were monetised in marks it would become a German production from the Great Britain region. Hence, if it were possible to allow for the free monetisation of the Community's output, we would observe the progressive economic transformation of eleven countries into as many regions of the twelfth. There is no need to stress that the loss of monetary autonomy by eleven member countries would also have political repercussions, and would arouse far greater opposition than that related to the project of introducing the ECU as a single European currency.

Confronted with these difficulties and in order to avoid the direct passage from the EMS to monetary unification, some experts have suggested the use of a supranational currency as the parallel money to replace the national currencies of the twelve EC countries through the free interplay of the market forces. Let us briefly analyse the elements common to the various projects successively propounded by groups of economists (the All Saints' Day Manifesto 1975), Community experts (Optica I and Optica II Reports 1975, 1976), governments (the British project for a hard ECU of 1991), and single economists (Magnifico, Vaubel).

The creation of the ECU as a supranational parallel money

The plan for using the ECU as a supranational parallel money is another example of one of the projects of monetary reform based on the gradual substitution of national currencies. At the beginning it would be a matter of adding to the currencies of the twelve EC countries a European currency endowed with a constant purchasing power, that is, of 'putting into circulation a common currency indexed on a commodity basket and whose rate of conversion into national currencies would be adjustable with regard to their purchasing power' (Prissert 1976: 385), or with a stable external value. In the first case the stability of the ECU's purchasing power would be guaranteed by its being indexed relative to a basket of commodities and by the fluctuation of its exchange rate, and its value would be expressed in terms of a basket of national currencies that would vary according to the variation of their respective purchasing powers. In the second case the ECU basket is modified every time one of the currencies is devalued.

Being endowed with a stable purchasing power or a stable external value, the ECU should become particularly attractive, encouraging economic agents to use it instead of their domestic currency. Within each European country the Central Bank would thus be asked to issue ECUs in exchange for the national currency, in a process that would progressively lead to the transformation of the ECU into the sole currency of the Community.

Besides the difficulties that such a process could be faced with, ranging from the excessively quick disappearance of national currencies suggested by Fratianni and Peeters (1978), to the perpetuation of a system of double monetary circulation aired by Claassen, Krul and Salin (1978), to the fact that the stability of the ECU's purchasing power would be achieved only through the constant intervention of monetary authorities, who would have to sacrifice part of their fiscal resources to this purpose ('in particular, each country would guarantee [. . .] a payment equal to the amount of national currency in the basket times the domestic rate of inflation' (Peeters, de Grauwe and Vaubel 1978: 48)), it must be observed that the ECU issued by the Central Banks of EC countries could not be considered as a single European currency. ECUs created by the Bundesbank, for example, would only be marks re-baptised with the name of the Community's unit of account. In the same way, ECUs issued by the Banca d'Italia would be ECU-lira, those issued by the Banque de France ECU-francs, and so on. As clearly stated by Friboulet and Soichot (1976), the heterogeneity of national currencies would be shared by the ECUs created within the twelve monetary systems of the Community, thus depriving Europe of a single currency and nullifying the efforts for the creation of a currency with a stable purchasing power.

Hence, the ECUs issued by the various Central Banks would only be new denominations of the old national units which they would gradually replace. However, as the new French francs were no less exposed to inflationary disequilibria than the old francs, the ECUs would only be as stable as the domestic currencies of their issuing countries.

The national emission of ECUs would lead to the creation of a single European currency only if the system could benefit from the existence of a European Central Bank acting as final clearing institution of a European Multilateral Clearing Union. It would therefore be through the emission of a supranational currency that the ECB would guarantee the perfect homogeneity of the ECUs created nationally by transforming them into equivalent units of European money.

In the projects of the 1970s (the All Saints' Day Manifesto, Optica I and II, Magnifico, Vaubel, etc.) as well as in those of the 1980s (Kloten, Kyriazis, Louw, etc.), the introduction of a supranational parallel money is seen as problematic, mainly because of the presumed existence of an issue premium or seigniorage. In particular, if a supranational institution were entrusted with the emission of ECUs, the different member countries would suffer from a reduction in their seigniorage to the extent that their national currencies were replaced by the new European money. According to these authors, a solution could be found by working out a system allowing for the equitable redistribution to national Central Banks of the emission profits earned by the ECB. 'This emission benefit obtained on the ECU could be transferred to national Central Banks, for instance, *au prorata* of the quantity of their currency in the ECU' (Kyriazis 1987: 317).

As we have already observed, the belief that the emission of money defines a creation of wealth is not supported by facts. A simple numerical vehicle, bank money is issued according to double entry book-keeping with the aim of monetising real output. To claim that money itself is being produced amounts to mixing it up with the material object (paper, electrical impulse) used to represent it. Even worse is to maintain that, although produced at an irrelevant cost, money can instantaneously be endowed with a positive value equivalent to its numerical denomination before being associated with real production. It is true instead that, were it not associated with money, real output could not be expressed numerically and could thus never define its real content (value). Being the creation of a numerical vehicle, the emission of ECUs cannot be the source of any profit, and it is totally useless to worry about the redistribution of what is defined as a fiscal drag to the benefit of the issuing bank. If the ECU became the EC's currency, its 'value' would not derive from its emission by the ECB but from its association with the production of the Community, a production which, precisely because it would be defined in terms of a single currency, would be specifically European.

To sum up, either the ECU is created in each single country to substitute national currencies, in which case the whole process merely amounts to a nominal change of denominations; or it is issued according to a scheme analogous to that adopted nationally (that is, by transforming the Central Banks into secondary banks of the ECB), in which case the monetary sovereignty of the twelve Community countries is gradually reduced and a European supranational monetary area effectively created. In this second case, the introduction of the ECU as a parallel currency resembles the passage from fixed exchange rates to a single currency. It is thus opportune to critically assess the essential elements of the proposals for a straight realisation of European monetary unification.

The ECU as a single currency

According to numerous projects recently worked out, and particularly to the plan proposed by the Delors Commission and taken over by the Maastricht Treaty, the creation of a single currency must be seen as the last stage of monetary unification which, through exchange rate stability and free convertibility, should allow for the implementation of a new European monetary order capable of promoting the rapid and equilibrated development of EC countries. According to other experts, on the contrary, the progressive evolution of the EMS towards monetary homogeneity is not very likely to be possible in the short or even medium term, which makes them support the idea of a quick adoption of a unified monetary system, with the ECU replacing domestic currencies and acting as a single European currency. The introduction of the ECU can therefore be seen either as the last or the first stage of a project aiming at transforming the Community's Central Banks into regional banks of a single monetary system. The various alternatives share the idea that a single currency would reduce the costs of converting one EC currency into another, thus fostering inter-Community exchanges and achieving a monetary stability that would eliminate exchange rate risks within the Community and limit them considerably outside. Another common element is the fact that both points of view consider the creation of a European Central Bank as the necessary condition for the emission of the ECU as single European currency. The ECB is thus to become the central institution of a European system of Central Banks gathering the monetary authorities of member countries and working, like the American FED, on a federal basis.

Even if all the twelve EC countries decided to change the denomination of their domestic currencies and called them ECU, this would not be sufficient to make the ECU into a single European currency. Each country would issue its own ECUs in the same way as today it issues pounds, francs, marks and so on; the twelve monetary systems would maintain their specific characteristics as well as their autonomy, and the ECUs issued by each of them would remain fundamentally heterogeneous despite sharing a common denomination. The passage to a single currency involves the working of the ECB as a Bank of Central Banks, i.e. as an institution under whose aegis the twelve monetary systems of the Community are gathered and transformed into as many elements of a single system. It is only in this case that ECUs issued in Great Britain would not differ from those issued in France, Italy or Germany, thus becoming perfect substitutes allowing for the common monetary definition of European production.

According to several authors, the main objective of the Community should be to implement as soon as possible the measures needed to use the ECU within each single country in the same way as domestic currencies are. Given its stability and its global yield, the ECU is already demanded by public and private investors. What should be done, therefore, is to widen its range of application by generalising its domestic use so as to promote its progressive substitution for national currencies. The aim of the whole process is that of providing Europe with the same monetary consistency and stability national economies benefit from, thus achieving the perfect homogeneity of capital flows and prices. 'An internal market can efficaciously allocate its resources and be the center of a macro-economic coherence, qualitatively distinct from international adjustments, only under the aegis of a single currency' (Aglietta 1989: 150).

Whether the way towards monetary unification passes through the establishment of a common market and the mobilisation of official ECUs, or through the internalisation of the ECU into the economic systems of EC countries, the project is still far from being unanimously accepted. Key-currency countries, for example, fear that monetary unification could disrupt their domestic policies of internal stability, and some experts are worried by the fact that it would lead to the loss of national sovereignty. As far as domestic monetary autonomy is concerned it is certain that integration would seriously limit, or even abolish, it. Likewise, it is also certain that under monetary unification countries would no longer get indebted to one another since they would become regions of a single monetary area. Besides the debt incurred by its residents, the debt of a region as such is a groundless concept. On the other hand, what distinguishes regions from nations from the economic point of view is the fact that each country has its own currency whereas regions are an integral part of a single monetary system. The single European currency would transform EC countries into as many regions subjected to the decisions of monetary policy taken at a supranational level. The EMCF would become a real European Central Bank and the actual Central Banks its regional branches.

In this context the problem of national sovereignty can obviously not be avoided. In particular, it must be understood whether the loss of monetary sovereignty entails, at least partially, the loss of political sovereignty. At a first glance the answer seems to be yes. All the examples of Confederations of States are proof of this. Although it is difficult to believe that Europe could be an exception, this does not mean that new associative formulae cannot be found, which are capable of granting EC countries a higher degree of political independence. What seems certain, however, is that the political and economic conditions for such an integration will not be fulfilled in the short term. Meanwhile, the disparities in the situations characterising EC countries are such as to make unification highly unlikely.

It is also important to point out that, besides the loss of national sovereignties, the abolition of domestic currencies would create many more difficulties than it would solve. More specifically, the monetisation in ECUs of national productions would extend to the fixed capital of the twelve countries, suddenly eliminating the protective measures allowing for the survival of many relatively uncompetitive industries at the European level. Placed on the same monetary level as those of the most industrialised countries, the production systems of less developed countries would immediately depreciate, so that several firms would have to close down while a major part of investment would be diverted towards more competitive 'regions'. The use of the ECU as a single currency within each country would place the fixed capital of less industrialised countries in a monetary framework where wages and prices were higher and interest and profit rates tended to line up with those of the most competitive markets. Hence, besides being devalued, the fixed capital of these countries would also suffer from the increased cost of amortisation without being able to attract new investment because of the decrease in interest (and profit) rates. A dramatic increase in unemployment would thus be the price that the majority of EC countries would have to pay in order to adhere to a monetary area sanctioning the creation of the United States of Europe.

Let us observe also that, according to the advocates of a single European currency, monetary integration would take place, more or less gradually, through the increasing use of the ECU as a means of domestic payments. The production of ECUs as financial assets and their circulation, both official and private, are therefore the fundamental principles of a process that would lead to monetary unification, and that could even be accelerated if the emission of money could also be carried out by every single resident. 'A true monetary integration favourable to European citizens can be rapidly achieved on condition that competition in the production of money is extended, either by creating a parallel and stable currency, available without limitations, or by recurring to the private creation of money' (Salin 1979: book cover).

It is not necessary to insist on the inconsistency of a thesis according to which not only banks, but also every single economic agent has the faculty of creating income (and therefore wealth) by means of a simple book-keeping entry, that is, independent of any real activity of production. As was already well known to classical economists, income does not result from spontaneous generation, but from a working activity whose cost is undoubtedly positive. This means that if the value of money were determined by its effective cost of production, it would have nothing to do with the income it is entrusted to measure. Being the result of a book-keeping entry, money as such has no proper value; it is a simple numerical standard whose function is essentially a vehicular one. In other words, money is a numerical container and real output is its content; it is the unity of form (money) and content (real output) which defines income, and not the hypothetical faculty of banks to create wealth.

Money defines real production both numerically and nominally. For example, the value of every commodity produced in Great Britain is expressed in terms of pounds, that is in numerical units issued by the British banking system on the basis of which it can be distinguished economically from the same commodity produced in Italy and defined in lira. If Italian banks were allowed to issue pounds, the Italian product associated with pounds would become British and it would no longer be possible to distinguish the two countries economically, which would, therefore, be transformed into two regions of the same monetary and economic area. An analogous argument would apply if the banks of EC countries were allowed to issue ECUs. The present European nations would become the regions of a new country, a Confederation of European States resulting from the substitution of the old national currencies by the ECU.

While waiting for European nations to be culturally and politically ready for this important change, it is necessary to wonder what the near future of the ECU will be. Its partial utilisation as a parallel money would not be meaningful, since it would transform part of the various national productions into a common European production, surreptitiously introducing an economic and political union to which many countries are still opposed. The possibility of adopting the ECU as a means of payment among EC countries and entrusting the European Central Bank alone with the task of monetising inter-European transactions remains open. Before analysing the proposals concerning this last project, let us end this chapter with a few words on the attempt at introducing the ECU as the single currency of the best performing countries of the Community.

The ECU as a single currency of the leading European countries

One of the latest proposals for monetary unification was that presented by Holland in October 1991. Realising that the present level of development of the twelve EC countries is still too disparate to allow for the generalised introduction of a single European currency, Dutch experts put forward the idea of a gradual process involving initially the key-currency countries, and successively expanding to the others as disequilibria causing their monetary instability was reduced. Hence, they suggested that the European Community be regionalised, allowing the most homogeneous countries to adopt the ECU without worrying about the negative repercussions that monetary unification would have if it were immediately extended to all member countries.

As we have seen, the loss of monetary sovereignty and the reduction in the standard of living are unacceptable consequences of all those projects that aim at introducing a single currency within the twelve EC countries. It is not surprising, therefore, to find that the Delors plan has been partially modified and that it has been suggested that progress towards monetary unification should take place step by step. The decision taken at Maastricht to introduce the ECU as a single currency at the latest by the end of the century is bound to apply only to the countries that are successful in respecting the conditions of economic and monetary convergence established by the leading European countries.

> If by the end of 1997 the date for the beginning of the third stage has not been set, the third stage will start on 1 January 1999. Before 1 July 1998, the Council [. . .] shall, acting by a qualified majority, [. . .] confirm which Member States fulfill the necessary conditions for the adoption of a single currency.
>
> (Maastricht Treaty: Article 109 F, point 4)

The fact that a single currency could be adopted whether or not there is a majority of countries qualifying for monetary unification does not mean that by the year 2000 all Community countries will be part of a new monetary area, but that the most stable countries will progressively be able to replace their national currencies with the ECU. However, it remains true that, despite successive regionalisation, the passage from national currencies to a single money would probably worsen real disequilibria among European countries. For example, the development and levels of competitivity of productive capital of countries such as Great Britain, France, Holland and Germany are still too different, so that monetary unification would very likely lead to the closing down of a large number of firms (mainly British and French) and to a substantial increase in unemployment.

The caution with which several countries still consider the proposals for the passage to a single European currency is thus entirely justified. According to an alternative approach, this does not mean that the project for European unification will be abandoned altogether, but that it must be integrated in a wider process in which the ECU is initially given the task of 'homogenising' national currencies without replacing them. In this context, the ECU has to be perceived as a single currency of politically and monetarily sovereign nations, as a means of payment among EC countries and between them and the rest of the world, and not as a domestic vehicular instrument. The adoption of the ECU as an external currency would not entail any of the disadvantages linked to a hasty monetary unification and would allow for inter-European payments to be inserted into a monetary order which would not fail to have positive domestic repercussions.

We still have to clarify the principles and modalities according to which the ECU can be made to work as a supranational currency for the European Community. Let us analyse the main elements of this proposal by referring to modern monetary theory.

12

MONETARY HOMOGENEITY AND MONETARY SOVEREIGNTY: TWO COMPATIBLE OBJECTIVES

THE ECU AS A SINGLE EXTRA-NATIONAL CURRENCY

Robert Triffin is one of the authors who has most coherently denounced the inconsistencies of the present system of international payments, emphasising the fact that the huge increase in international reserves, essentially caused by the use of the dollar as international currency, is the source of great instability in exchange rate markets. In contrast to the non-system adopted at Bretton Woods, Triffin urges Europe to use the ECU as a means of payment in inter-Community transactions. According to the plan proposed by the Belgian economist, the European unit of account should thus become the external currency of each of the twelve EC countries, a currency which would be used to finance both the payments among member countries, and between them and the rest of the world.

> The merging of national currencies into a single Community currency (now dubbed ECU), envisaged for the ultimate stage of full *Economic and Monetary Union* in several summit conferences of the EC heads of state and government, is certainly not for tomorrow. But the use of the ECU as an alternative to Euro-currencies might progress in a spectacular way within the course of 1984.
>
> (Triffin 1984: 54)

The new inter-European currency should be issued by a single Central Bank, called by Triffin 'European Reserve Fund', in exchange for an equivalent deposit in gold and foreign currencies by each member country. Analogous to the mechanism for the emission of official ECUs by the EMCF, Triffin's scheme suffers from the same shortcomings described in the section on the official ECU (p. 241). In particular, the emission of ECUs in exchange for gold and foreign currencies would merely correspond to the re-naming of part of the official reserves held by EC countries. According to this point of view, the ECU would be issued endowed with a positive value and could therefore be handed over only in exchange for an equivalent deposit. Being carried out on the basis of gold and foreign exchange deposits, the distribution of ECUs would take place in compliance with an 'objective' criterion so as to avoid abuses, injustice and inflationary disequilibria.

Modern monetary analysis shows, however, that bank money is created as an asset-liability and that there are no limits to its emission except the need for monetising real production. As a pure vehicle of real output, bank money does not require the use, either direct or indirect, of any reserve of value: double entry book-keeping is sufficient to allow for its creation by banks and for its association with production. What is true at the national level is even more true when the emission of money is carried out by a supranational Bank. If the creation of a net asset by a national bank amounted to a spontaneous generation, the emission by the European Central Bank of ECUs endowed with a positive intrinsic value would correspond to a totally groundless miracle, since it could not even be erroneously referred to any inter-European production whatsoever.

It would be more correct to maintain that the ECU should not be issued as the counterpart of gold and foreign exchange reserves, but as their new European denomination. In this case, however, even if the inter-European currency were not endorsed with any positive intrinsic value, the ECU would be reduced to a simple label putting a new name on the official reserves of the Community. The European currency would only be a new name for the reserves deposited with the ECB so that the payments in ECUs of inter-European and international transactions would be purely nominal: albeit under the name of ECU, payments would go on being carried out in key-currencies.

Having reached this point we could get the impression of being caught in a trap. Metaphysical considerations notwithstanding, the ECU cannot be created as a net asset; however, if it is issued as a simple name for gold and foreign currencies its very existence as a European money is definitively jeopardised. Besides, if we maintained that the ECU issued by the ECB did not have any value, either proper or derived from the official reserves of EC countries, we would have to explain how such a currency could act as a means of payment.

Once again it is the theory of bank money which shows us the way out of the dilemma. Within a country money is a simple numerical vehicle, and it is as such that it is issued by the national banking system. Likewise, it is as a vehicular form that the ECU should be issued by the inter-European banking system. Since it would be mistaken to mix up form and content, vehicle and load, there is no reason to expect that money be transformed from an instrument or means into the object of the payment. Hence, the true problem at the European level is to establish a mechanism through which inter-Community vehicular money is invested with a positive value which it conveys from one country to another.

The ECU as a vehicular money

The argument being of importance, let us insist on the fact that the currency issued by the European Central Bank must essentially play a vehicular role, so that every payment carried out in ECUs will have a real content which is not derived from a hypothetical capacity of creation of the ECB. In other words, the ECB will only provide the numerical instrument needed to monetise inter-European transactions. The ECU will not replace the real payment, but facilitate its execution by lending it a monetary form.

In order to be final, a payment must guarantee the payee the ownership of a final good (commodity or financial bond). In a gold standard regime, whether they take place within a situation of balanced trade (in which case exports pay for imports), or of trade deficit or surplus (immediately covered by an equivalent transfer of the precious metal), all international payments are real. Though preserving the monetary character of the system, the passage to bank money must comply with this requirement. To do so it is enough that international money be conceived as a vehicle with no intrinsic value and whose existence does not exceed its own function. At the European level this means that the ECU will have to exist only as a book-keeping entry in the ECB and for a period of time not exceeding that required for its use as an inter-European monetary instrument.

To clarify the meaning of the vehicular conception of the European money it is useful to resort to an example. Let us suppose the Italian trade balance to be positive with regard to Great Britain. According to our scheme, English importers pay their Italian creditors in pounds, but the operation is taken over by the Bank of England which, instead of crediting the Bank of Italy in pounds, asks the ECB to carry out the payment in ECUs. From a book-keeping point of view, transactions are entered as in Table 12.1. As is shown by book-keeping entries of Table 12.1, British importers and Italian exporters pay with and are paid in their national currencies while between the two countries the transaction is carried out in ECUs. On the Bank of England's request, the ECB credits the Bank of Italy with a sum of ECUs created *ex novo*, and whose counterpart is the debt simultaneously incurred by the Bank of England. Since they are a simple numerical vehicle, it is normal that ECUs are gratuitously supplied to the country which needs them in order to monetise its inter-European transactions. On the other hand, however, it would be mistaken to believe that the transfer of a simple numerical form could amount to a final payment. Such a payment requires the transfer of a real asset, that is, of what is effectively conveyed by vehicular money. Going back to our example it is easy to show that this requirement is entirely fulfilled when the trade balances of the two countries are even. In this case the payment of British exports takes place in the same way as that of Italian exports so that, at the end, the Central Banks of the two countries are credited and debited with the same amount

Table 12.1

British secondary banks

Liabilities		*Assets*	
Bank of England	£ x	Importers	£ x

Bank of England

Liabilities		*Assets*	
European Central Bank eq. in ECUs of £ x	(y ECUs)	Secondary banks	£ x

European Central Bank

Liabilities		*Assets*	
Bank of Italy	y ECUs	Bank of England	y ECUs

Italian secondary banks

Liabilities		*Assets*	
Exporters	z lira	Bank of Italy	z lira

Bank of Italy

Liabilities		*Assets*	
Secondary banks eq. in lira of y ECUs	(z lira)	European Central Bank	ECUs

of ECUs. Book-keeping entries between the ECB and the two Central Banks cancel out, and the final result is an exchange between equivalent sums of national commodities. British exports are thus paid for by Italian exports, and vice versa. Yet, being carried out through the intermediation of money, the exchange cannot be reduced to barter (Table 12.2). Within the two countries commercial transactions give rise to the following entries (Table 12.3). British exporters are paid in pounds, out of the income paid by British importers. Likewise, the payment of Italian exporters is finally carried out by Italian importers, whose income is merely advanced by the Bank of Italy.

It is essential to note that the inter-European vehicle can neither be bought nor sold by EC countries. Thus, the monetisation in ECUs of their commercial transactions leaves unaltered the exchange rate between each

Table 12.2

European Central Bank

Liabilities		*Assets*	
Bank of Italy	y ECUs	Bank of England	y ECUs
Bank of England	y ECUs	Bank of Italy	y ECUs

Table 12.3

Great Britain

Secondary banks

Liabilities		*Assets*	
Bank of England	£ x	Importers	£ x
Exporters	£ x	Bank of England	£ x

Bank of England

Liabilities		*Assets*	
European Central Bank eq. in ECUs of £ x	(y ECUs)	Secondary banks	£ x
Secondary banks	£ x	European Central Bank	y ECUs

Italy

Secondary banks

Liabilities		*Assets*	
Exporters	z lira	Bank of Italy	z lira
Bank of Italy	z lira	Importers	z lira

Bank of Italy

Liabilities		*Assets*	
Secondary banks eq. in lira of y ECUs	(z lira)	European Central Bank	y ECUs
European Central Bank	y ECUs	Secondary banks	z lira

domestic currency and the ECU as well as that among national currencies themselves. In terms of ECUs, and thus also in terms of lira, the pound is simultaneously offered, for the purchase of Italian goods, and demanded, for the purchase of British goods. In the same way lira are equally supplied and demanded in terms of a European currency whose rate of exchange remains unchanged precisely because it is used as a simple intermediary. All this is perfectly consistent with the vehicular nature of bank money, whether of a national or international origin. The intermediation of the ECB between Great Britain and Italy allows for the vehicular use of pounds and lira, whose exchange rate pertains thus to the category of absolute exchange rates.

Let us resume the main lines of the argument. Like any other bank money, the ECU will be issued as a means and not as an object of payment. As a consequence, the system based on the use of the ECU as an inter-European currency will achieve monetary stability only if it respects the vehicular nature of both the European currency and the various domestic currencies. In our example, pounds and lira must be used in a circular movement respecting their mutual exchange rate as well as that with the ECU. This condition is certainly complied with when each currency, through the ECU, is simultaneously supplied and demanded for the same amount. In each country the domestic currency demands a sum of y ECUs (outflow) and is simultaneously supplied (inflow) in exchange for an equivalent sum of ECUs (Figure 12.1). Pounds (lira) are transformed into ECUs to be re-transformed into pounds (lira) in an operation which (see Chapter 7) defines an absolute exchange (Figure 12.2). Hence, the ECU plays the role of a catalyst for inter-European transactions and becomes the common denominator of domestic currencies. It is through the ECU that national currencies are grouped into a single 'space of measure' defining the European monetary zone. The European Central Bank is thus created as a European Clearing Union whose essential role is to homogenise national currencies by monetising, in ECUs, inter-European transactions.

It is easy to verify that Italian exports imply a demand for ECUs in terms of pounds and, through the ECUs, an equivalent demand for lira, while British exports define, again through the ECU, an equivalent demand for pounds in terms of lira. The lira exchanged against ECUs (pounds) flow back in the purchase carried out by the holders of pounds and, reciprocally, the pounds exchanged against ECUs (lira) are spent in the Italian purchase of British goods. The result is an exchange in which the European currency intervenes only as an intermediary. The two terms of the exchange are real: British goods on the one hand and Italian goods on the other. The contents

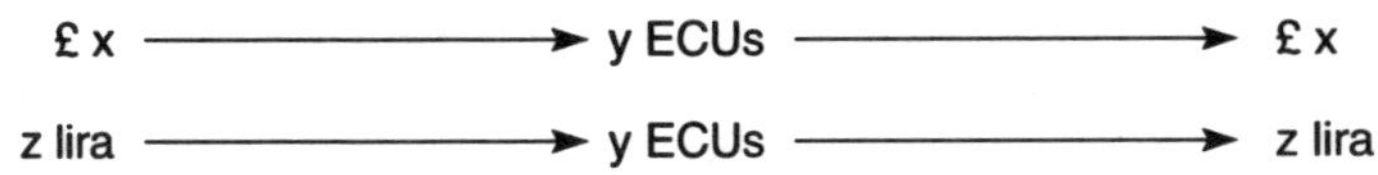

Figure 12.1

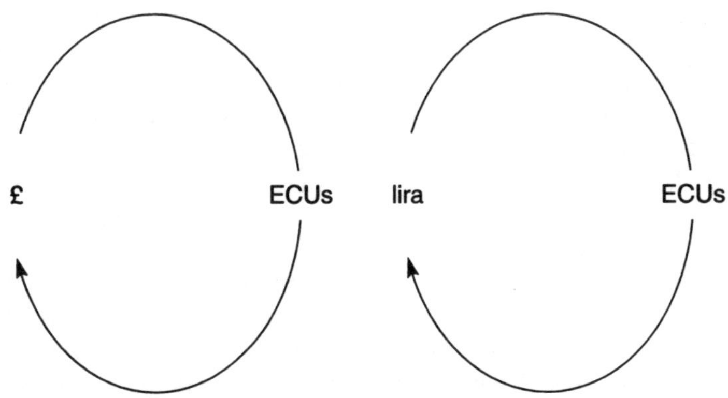

Figure 12.2

of the payments carried out by means of the ECU are also real: Italian goods pay for British goods and vice versa. Thus, the ECU does not nourish any payment; its intervention is purely vehicular and comes to an end at the precise instant the reciprocal transactions of the two countries have taken place.

The ECU and the payment of trade deficits

Referring to our previous example, let us suppose Great Britain to be a net importer of Italian goods. In this case we get the impression that the debt of the Bank of England to the ECB is bound to last in time (at least until the British trade balance with Italy becomes positive). Now, this first impression does not properly take into account the fact that under no circumstances can the ECU be considered either as a final or an intermediary good. Our attention shall therefore be pointed to the object conveyed by the European monetary vehicle.

To pay for the goods purchased in Italy, the British importer spends part of his income. This part of the British domestic income seems thus to be the content of the payment carried out by the ECB on behalf of the Bank of England. Through the intermediation of the ECU, the Italian economy (represented by its banking system) would hold a deposit with British banks confirming the exchange between Italian goods and British bonds. However, we have not yet finished the analysis. The claim on a deposit defines the debt of the issuing bank, and in our example this means that if Great Britain simply transferred its monetary bonds to Italy, its payment would remain a mere promise.

This result is supported by another argument. If, as has been shown, inter-European transactions require the use of a purely vehicular money, and if the payments carried out with it are effective only on condition that it conveys real goods, then the content of the payments in ECUs cannot be a national currency which, as such, is a mere acknowledgement of debt of the bank that issues it. Moreover, if domestic currencies were the content of inter-European payments, there would be no reason to create the ECU as a European currency: national currencies would do the job perfectly.

Now, if domestic currencies cannot be the object of inter-European payments, how can a country's trade deficit be cleared? In our example Great Britain imports Italian goods and services by borrowing ECUs from the European Central Bank. For the payment to be effective the ECUs paid to Italy must convey a real asset in exchange for British net commercial imports. The easiest solution is obtained by transferring to Italy an equivalent sum of non-monetary bonds. The selling of securities and shares, either public or private, would thus compensate the purchase of commodities, and the whole operation would lead to the mutual exchange of real goods. Let us represent the vehicular circuits of ECUs concerning financial and commercial flows (Figure 12.3). As shown in Figure 12.3, the ECU is supplied to the exporting country as a vehicular instrument and it is used to convey commodities and bonds. Having fulfilled its task, the European money flows back to its point of origin, the ECB, where it is immediately destroyed. Hence, the ECU is never the object of the payment, but the mere container of a payment which must be real (that is, which has to give rise to a transfer of goods, services or bonds).

The fact that exports are finally paid for by the exporting country is thus confirmed also in the case of a net commercial deficit. To clarify this

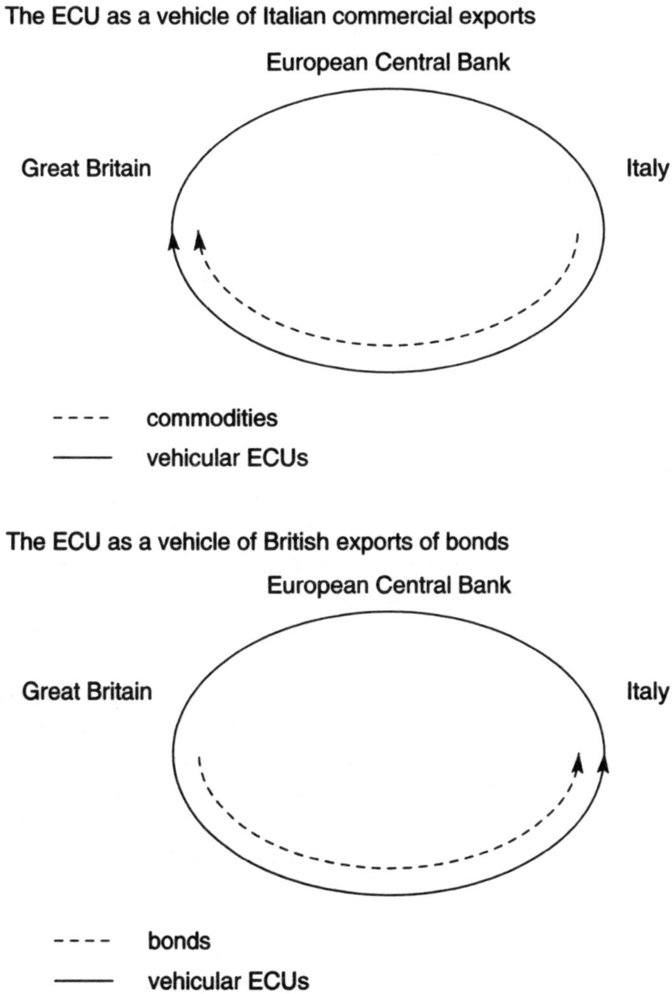

Figure 12.3

apparently absurd proposition, let us refer to what happens within each single country.

It is unanimously recognised that, given two economic agents with a personal income equal to x, each one of them can purchase goods and services for a sum of x + y only if the other is willing to lend him part of his own income. Since income is a drawing right over current output, the net purchase of one agent implies the expenditure of an equivalent part of the other agent's income. Hence, it is the income of the seller which pays for the net purchases of the buyer who, in exchange, gives up bonds of the same value. The deficit agent finances his net purchases by transferring claims on future incomes against the right to benefit from a present income.

Transposed at the international level, this principle establishes our proposition: it is the exporting country which supplies the income required for the payment of its net commercial exports. Its external income being insufficient, the deficit country can finance its net purchases only by borrowing from the exporting country. It is with the income obtained from the exporting country that the deficit country finances its net imports, whose real payment entails the transfer of an equivalent amount in bonds.

In our example, the book-keeping situation at the ECB would be as shown in Table 12.4. As in Table 12.2, the same amount of ECUs is simultaneously supplied and demanded, both in terms of pounds and of lira. Its circulation defines two absolute exchanges, for pounds and lira, which guarantee a perfect stability of exchange rates. Any national currency is supplied or demanded without being reciprocally demanded or supplied in a circular movement that leaves no room for confusion between means and object of payment. In other words, it is through the circulation of the ECU that inter-European transactions are monetised, and it is because they are monetised that money cannot be the real content of their payment. Since the nature of bank money is essentially vehicular, payments cannot convey to the payee a mere numerical instrument. As means and end must be kept separate, money cannot be simultaneously considered as the means and the object of monetary payments. It is not surprising, therefore, that once having monetised inter-European transactions the ECU disappears, leaving exchange rates totally unaffected. What is true for the ECU is also true for the domestic currencies implied in the transactions. Pounds and lira are used in a circular movement which takes them back unchanged to their point of origin (their respective national monetary systems). Finally, since they are used as monetary vehicles, ECUs, pounds and lira elicit perfectly balanced book-keeping entries. Let us first verify it for the trade deficit country (Table 12.5). In Great Britain, exporters of bonds are paid by crediting them with the income paid by the importers of goods; an operation that leaves the initial relationship between domestic money and domestic output unaltered. Since goods and services have not yet been exported, domestic output is still the same, and the income spent by importers

Table 12.4

European Central Bank	
Liabilities	*Assets*
Bank of Italy (commercial movements) y ECUs	Bank of England (commercial movements) y ECUs
Bank of England (capital movements) y ECUs	Bank of Italy (capital movements) y ECUs

Table 12.5

Great Britain

Secondary banks			
Liabilities		*Assets*	
Bank of England	£ x	Importers of goods	£ x
Exporters of bonds	£ x	Bank of England	£ x

Bank of England			
Liabilities		*Assets*	
European Central Bank (commerical movements)	y ECUs	Secondary banks	£ x
Secondary banks	£ x	European Central Bank (capital movements)	y ECUs

and transferred to the sellers of bonds is still entirely available for its purchase.

As far as the trade surplus country is concerned, the problem is slightly more complex since, as we have verified in the first part of this work, the final purchase of real output implies the destruction of the income which defines it. If the payment of net commercial exports were carried out in the same way as that of the net exports of bonds, the situation would be like that shown in Table 12.6. In Italy, the trade surplus country of our example, exporters of goods and services are paid by the importers of bonds; a transaction which implies the destruction of an income equivalent to the value of the exported goods and services. The reduction in income is matched by a corresponding decrease in the domestic output still available in Italy, and this seems enough to achieve perfect internal equilibrium. If we consider the whole process from another point of view, however, we become aware of the fact that the destruction of income linked to the payment of net commercial exports leads to a deflationary decrease in the purchasing power available within the country.

Table 12.6

Italy

Secondary banks			
Liabilities			*Assets*
Exporters of goods	z lira	Bank of Italy	z lira
Bank of Italy	z lira	Importers of bonds	z lira

Bank of Italy			
Liabilities			*Assets*
Secondary banks	z lira	European Central Bank (commercial movements)	y ECUs
European Central Bank (capital movements)	y ECUs	Secondary banks	z lira

Because of its net commercial exports Italy benefits from an external gain equivalent to the amount it lends to Great Britain through the purchase of bonds. It is with this Italian income that Great Britain pays for its net commercial imports. Thus, not only the purchase of British bonds, but also the payment of commercial exports, must not imply any loss of national income for Italy. If this were not the case, Italy would pay for its net exports twice, a first time by transferring to Great Britain its external income and a second time by destroying an equivalent sum of its domestic income. To avoid an unjustified loss of national income, the Bank of Italy must intervene by taking on the payment of Italian exporters. Bearing in mind that an emission of this kind by the Central Bank has no cumulative effect, it is useful to recall that the intervention of the Bank of Italy is needed in order to avoid the rise of a deflationary gap between domestic output and available income. Net exporters are thus paid through a monetary emission only when the Central Bank's revolving fund is first created (or increased), so that every successive net commercial export not exceeding this fund leaves the domestic price level unaltered.

Let us consider the case in which exporters are not paid through the monetisation of an external gain (Table 12.7). Output available within the country after the payment of exporting firms would be x units, an amount equal to that of the income deposited by income holders (IH) with their secondary banks. Now, a difficulty arises because, albeit being equal to x units, domestic output would have a price of x + y. The export of y units of goods would in fact lead to an increase in income and, therefore, in the price at which they would be sold. If we add the income of an external origin, y units, to that formed within the country, x + y, we obtain a total income of x + 2y units for a product x + y units. The price of x + y units of goods would thus be equal to x + 2y, whereas that of the output still available once exports have been accounted for, x units, would be x + y

Table 12.7

Banking system of the exporting country			
Liabilities			*Assets*
IH	x + y	Output	x + y
Exporting firms	y	Importers of bonds	y
IH	x	Output (price x + y)	x

units. Hence, if net exporters were credited with the income paid by the importers of bonds, the income globally available within the country would only be equal to x units, which would be inadequate for the final purchase of domestic production.

As is shown in Table 12.8, this difficulty can be disposed of through the creation of a special revolving fund by the Central Bank. The first entry refers to the monetisation of domestic output and defines the creation of a corresponding income. Entry (2) is concerned with the payment of net commercial exports carried out by secondary banks and by the European Central Bank (an operation entered on the Central Bank's balance sheet). Exporters are paid through the creation (or the re-activation) of a revolving fund by the Central Bank. Importers of foreign bonds are paid by secondary banks as shown in entry (3), while entries (4) and (5) define, respectively, the transfer to the State of the income paid by the importers, and the payment of an equivalent sum of ECUs to the ECB. Hence, the State benefits from a gain in domestic money corresponding to the country's balance of trade surplus. Entry (6) describes the situation after international transactions have taken place. Income holders and the State have at their disposal a total income of x + y units of domestic money, a sum which is both necessary and sufficient for the final purchase of the output deposited with the country's firms. The expenditure of this income, represented in (7) and (8), enables IH and the State to transform it into real goods, and leads to the reconstitution of the revolving fund used to pay net commercial exporting firms (9); a fund whose further re-activation would be possible only if the Central Bank entered a new inflow of ECUs corresponding to a trade surplus.

The export of bonds defines a domestic saving. If the income thus saved were paid to commercial exporters it would be destroyed and the whole country could not benefit from it. This loss is avoided by the intervention of the Central Bank, which issues the amount of domestic money needed for the payment of net commercial exports. This payment is carried out on the country's behalf, which is why the Central Bank becomes the owner of

Table 12.8

Secondary banks of the exporting country

Liabilities			*Assets*
(1) IH	x + y	Output	x + y
(2) Exporting firms	y	Central Bank	y
IH	x + y	Output	x
		Central Bank	y
(3) Central Bank	y	Importers of bonds	y
(6) IH	x	Output (price x + y)	x
(7) Firms	y	Central Bank	y
(8) Firms	x	IH	x
(9) Firms	y	Central Bank	y

Central Bank

Liabilities			*Assets*
(2) Secondary banks		European Central Bank equivalent in ECUs of y NM (z ECUs)	
		Revolving fund	y
(4) State	y	Secondary banks	y
(5) European Central Bank	z ECUs		
(6) State	y	Revolving fund	y
(7) Secondary banks	y	State	y
Secondary banks	y	Revolving fund	y

the income spent by the importers of foreign bonds. Transferred to the State, the income saved by the trade surplus country is still entirely available and can thus be used, jointly with the income owned by IH, for the purchase of x units of output at the price of x + y units of domestic money.

Given the importance and the difficulty of the argument, let us reconsider the book-keeping entries inherent to the Central Bank of the trade surplus country by referring to our British–Italian example and by distinguishing between an external department, where flows referring to international transactions are recorded in ECUs, and an internal department, acting both as an intermediary between secondary banks and external department, and as the country's agency with respect to the internalisation of external gains (Table 12.9). Being a net commercial exporter, Italy is credited by the ECB with a sum of y ECUs. The external department of the Bank of Italy enters a credit in ECUs and a debit to the internal department, which balances its new asset (entered as the equivalent in lira of y ECUs) with a debit in favour of the secondary banks entrusted with the final payment of exporting firms. Unlike what happens when commercial exports are matched by equivalent commercial imports, it is the Central Bank which is entrusted with the

Table 12.9

Bank of Italy

Internal department

Liabilities			*Assets*
Secondary banks	z lira	External dep.	z lira
State	z lira	Secondary banks	z lira
External dep.	z lira	Secondary banks	z lira
State	z lira	Secondary banks	z lira

External department

Liabilities			*Assets*
Internal dep.	y ECUs	European Central Bank	y ECUs
European Central Bank	y ECUs	Internal dep.	y ECUs

payment of the trade surplus. Since the Bank of Italy carries out this payment on behalf of the country, the inflow of lira corresponding to the disbursement of the Italian residents importing British bonds is immediately transferred to the State (Treasury). Simultaneously, the external department of the Bank of Italy releases the ECUs needed for the payment of the Italian import of bonds. The accounts of the external department of the Bank of Italy are thus perfectly balanced, since the inflow of ECUs relative to the trade surplus is matched by an equivalent outflow relative to the import of bonds. The internal department also balances its accounts, even though not all its entries are cleared. The Treasury (State) holds a deposit of z lira equivalent to the Italian income saved by the importers of British bonds. Resulting from the monetisation in lira of the external income (in ECUs) earned by Italy through its net commercial exports, this sum is needed to bring the total available income of the country to the same level as the price of domestic products: x + z lira.

From what we have been analysing so far it follows that all inter-European transactions would be conveyed by the ECU in accordance with the principles of monetary neutrality that must characterise the working of the European Central Bank as a monetary intermediary. However, the example used to illustrate this has the disadvantage of taking into account only bilateral transactions. The fact that Great Britain can pay for its net commercial purchases from Italy only through an equivalent net sale of bonds could lead to the wrong belief that each country must necessarily balance its transactions with regard to every one of its European partners, in order to guarantee the correct working of the system. To clear any possible doubt concerning the multilateral nature of the clearing carried out by the ECB it is therefore opportune to consider an example in which transactions take place among several countries without there being any bilateral equilibrium in their balance of payments.

THE WORKING OF THE NEW EUROPEAN MONETARY SYSTEM

A numerical example of multilateral clearing

Let us consider a set of hypothetical transactions among four countries of the European Community, France, Great Britain, Portugal and Germany, and let us suppose that they take place according to the following scheme (where real flows are expressed in million of ECUs) (Figure 12.4). Let us suppose also that the exchange rates among the domestic currencies of these four countries are fixed as follows: 1 ECU = 1 mark; 1 ECU = £0.4; 1 ECU = 3 francs; 1 ECU = 100 escudos. Within each country commercial

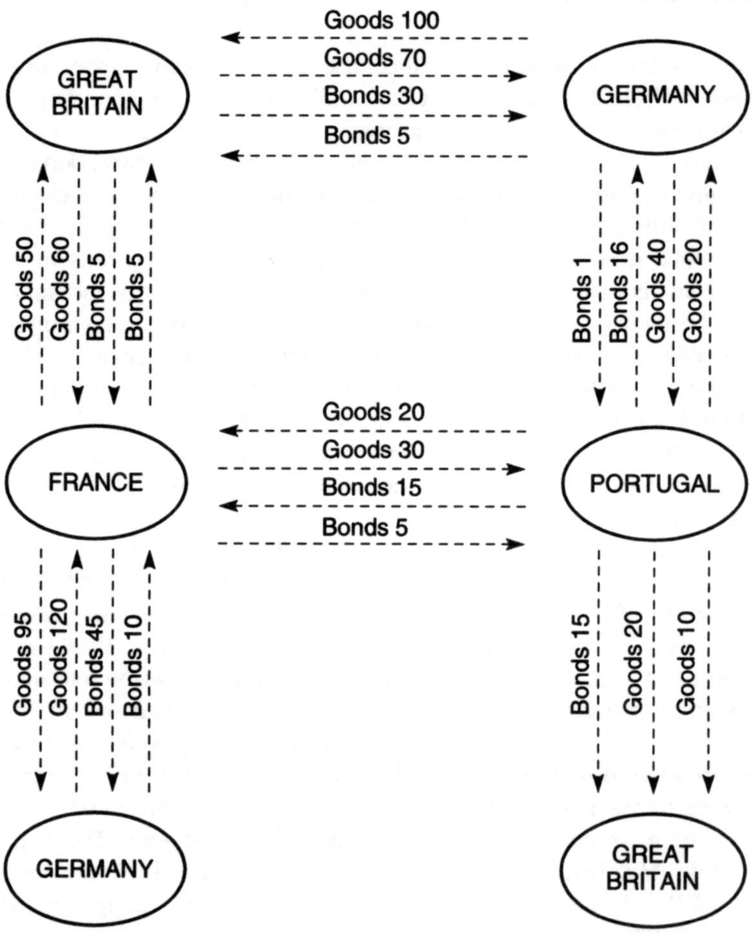

Figure 12.4

transactions and capital flows give rise to book-keeping entries as shown in Table 12.10. Being a net commercial importer, Great Britain covers its deficit through a net sale of bonds. Yet Great Britain balances its accounts only globally, and not country by country. Relative to Germany, it enters a commercial deficit of 30 million ECUs, only partially covered by its net sale of bonds to German residents (25 million ECUs). Great Britain obtains the gain needed to cover its deficit thanks to its net commercial exports to France (10 million ECUs). The remaining 5 million ECUs are then used, together with those relative to the British trade surplus with Portugal, to finance British net investment in Portugal (15 million ECUs).

Like Great Britain, France balances its foreign accounts by covering its trade deficit through a net sale of bonds. In this case also, the adjustment does not take place bilaterally, country by country, but on the whole set of commercial and financial transactions. France's trade deficit with Great Britain (10 million ECUs) is matched by the net sale of bonds to Germany (35 million ECUs), a sale that covers also the French net purchase of German goods. As for its transactions with Portugal, France has a trade surplus of 10 million ECUs with which it can finance its investment in that country (Table 12.11).

Among the four countries taken into account, Portugal has the main trade deficit (40 million ECUs) and, as a consequence, the greatest sale of bonds. Again, trade deficit and financial surplus do not balance bilaterally. Portugal's deficit with Germany (20 million ECUs) is thus covered only partially by its net sale of bonds to German residents (15 million ECUs). The rest comes from the net investment carried out by Great Britain and France (25 million ECUs), which finances the German, British and French net commercial purchases made by Portugal (Table 12.12).

Table 12.10

Great Britain

Internal department of the Bank of England (in millions)		*External department of the Bank of England (in millions)*	
Liabilities	*Assets*	*Liabilities*	*Assets*
Exporters of goods £60 m	External department £60 m	Internal department 150 m ECUs	ECB (comm. flows) 150 m ECUs
External department £64 m	Importers of goods £64 m	ECB (comm. flows) 160 m ECUs	Internal department 160 m ECUs
Exporters of bonds £10 m	External department £10 m	Internal department 25 m ECUs	ECB (capital flows) 25 m ECUs
External department £6 m	Importers of bonds £6m	ECB (capital flows) 15 m ECUs	Internal department 15 m ECUs

Table 12.11

France

Internal department of the Bank of France (in millions) Liabilities	Assets	*External department of the Bank of France (in millions)* Liabilities	Assets
Exporters of goods 525 m francs	External department 525 m francs	Internal department 175 m ECUs	ECB (comm. flows) 175 m ECUs
External department 600 m francs	Importers of goods 600 m francs	ECB (comm. flows) 200 m ECUs	Internal department 200 m ECUs
Exporters of bonds 165 m francs	External department 165 m francs	Internal department 55 m ECUs	ECB (capital flows) 55 m ECUs
External department 90 m francs	Importers of bonds 90 m francs	ECB (capital flows) 30 m ECUs	Internal department 30 m ECUs

Table 12.12

Portugal

Internal department of the Bank of Portugal Liabilities	Assets	*External department of the Bank of Portugal (in millions)* Liabilities	Assets
Exporters of goods 5 billion ES	External department 5 billion ES	Internal department 50 m ECUs	ECB (comm. flows) 50 m ECUs
External department 9 billion ES	Importers of goods 9 billion ES	ECB (comm. flows) 90 m ECUs	Internal department 90 m ECUs
Exporters of bonds 4.6 billion ES	External department 4.6 billion ES	Internal department 46 m ECUs	ECB (capital flows) 46 m ECUs
External department 0.6 billion ES	Importers of bonds 0.6 billion ES	ECB (capital flows) 6 m ECUs	Internal department 6 m ECUs

The German case differs from the previous ones in that Germany is the only country whose global trade balance is in excess. Germany is thus also, in our example, the only country whose purchases of foreign bonds are greater than its sales of domestic securities. The German trade surplus (75 million ECUs) is invested in Portugal (15 million ECUs), in Great Britain (25 million ECUs) and in France (35 million ECUs). It is therefore logical that the Bundesbank monetises in marks the external income earned by Germany, allowing the Treasury to obtain a gain in domestic money equal to the amount saved by the net importers of foreign bonds (Table 12.13).

Entries at the European Central Bank are as shown in Table 12.14. The money issued by the ECB plays a purely vehicular role. Thanks to its intermediation, each country balances its balance of payments multilaterally, no transaction being financed through a simple monetary creation. Hence, the effective payment of inter-European transactions is made up of real goods (commodities and bonds) conveyed by the ECU. This means that the European currency is never subjected to excesses of supply or demand that could modify its exchange rate. In every transaction the ECU is simultaneously supplied and demanded for the same amount precisely

Table 12.13

Germany

Internal department of the Bank of Germany (in millions)	
Liabilities	*Assets*
Exporters of goods 260 m marks	External department 260 m marks
External department 185 m marks	Importers of goods 185 m marks
Exporters of bonds 16 m marks	External department 16 m marks
External department 91 m marks	Importers of bonds 91 m marks
State 75 m marks	Importers of bonds 75 m marks
External department 75 m marks	Secondary banks 75 m marks
State 75 m marks	Secondary banks 75 m marks

External department of the Bank of Germany (in millions)	
Liabilities	*Assets*
Internal department 260 m ECUs	ECB (comm. flows) 260 m ECUs
ECB (comm. flows) 185 m ECUs	Internal department 185 m ECUs
Internal department 16 m ECUs	ECB (capital flows) 16 m ECUs
ECB (capital flows) 91 m ECUs	Internal department 91 m ECUs

Table 12.14

European Central Bank
(in millions)

Liabilities			*Assets*
Bank of England (commercial movements)	160 m ECUs	Bank of England (commercial movements)	160 m ECUs
Bank of England (capital movements)	15 m ECUs	Bank of England (capital movements)	15 m ECUs
Banque de France (commercial movements)	200 m ECUs	Banque de France (commercial movements)	200 m ECUs
Banque de France (capital movements)	30 m ECUs	Banque de France (capital movements)	30 m ECUs
Banco de Portugal (commercial movements)	90 m ECUs	Banco de Portugal (commercial movements)	90 m ECUs
Banco de Portugal (capital movements)	6 m ECUs	Banco de Portugal (capital movements)	6 m ECUs
Bundesbank (commercial movements)	185 m ECUs	Bundesbank (commercial movements)	185 m ECUs
Bundesbank (capital movements)	91 m ECUs	Bundesbank (capital movements)	91 m ECUs

because it is used only as a vehicle, as a means (or instrument) of payment, and not as the object (or content) of this very payment.

The solution proposed here is based on the distinction between national monetary circuits and the inter-European monetary circuit, where internal circulation is totally carried out by domestic currencies while the ECU circulates only among the twelve countries of the Community and not within them. Two important results are thus reached: on the one hand monetary sovereignty of member countries is guaranteed by the use of their respective national currencies as sole domestic money, on the other hand every inter-European transaction is carried out by means of an acknowledgement of debt (the ECU) issued by a supranational institution (the European Central Bank) which is logically not an element of the set of European purchasers. As we know, the use of a national currency as a means of international payment is contradictory, since each domestic currency is, by definition, the acknowledgement of debt of the monetary system which issues it. For instance, imports paid in marks are not paid at all because, outside national monetary borders, marks define the IOU of Germany. With the institution of the ECB and the emission of the ECU it will be possible to create in Europe a supranational monetary system allowing for the vehicular use of an extra-national currency.

Basically it is a matter of creating at the European level a monetary system similar to those existing within each EC country. In other words it is a matter of providing European countries with a common currency enjoying the same status as the domestic currencies issued by the national monetary systems. In the same way as national currencies are never issued by the set of domestic purchasers, the European money must be issued by a Bank which does not pertain to the set of national banks (either private or Central). Moreover, the ECB must play the same role of clearing union within Europe that national Central Banks play within each single country. As is shown in our example, this means that the ECB must guarantee the instantaneous compensation of the monetary balances deriving from the inter-European transactions carried out by the Central Banks of the twelve EC countries. Through this clearing mechanism the ECB makes national European currencies homogeneous in the same way as the domestic currencies issued by the secondary banks of each single country are made homogeneous by national Central Banks.

If we analyse further the system of inter-European payments we soon become aware of the fact that transactions are financed by a purchasing power generated by real production. The ECB's intermediation allows for the transfer to deficit countries of the income saved by creditor countries, thus avoiding the risk that even the smallest percentage of commercial imports be financed by a mere nominal money. Hence, not only is no domestic currency used as final object of payment, but not even the ECU is endowed with this privilege. The European currency has a purely vehicular character and, as such, it monetises only reciprocal purchases (sales). This means, as we have seen, that net commercial purchases of a given country are financed by equivalent sales of bonds. If a trade deficit is financed through the sale of European bonds priced in ECUs, the operation is carried out through the intermediation of the financial department of the ECB and defines a purchase of bonds by the residents of the European countries. Net commercial purchases of a deficit country are thus partially financed by the income lent by residents (of this same country or of other countries) through the purchase of ECU bonds. In the same way as at the national level the purchase of a bond corresponds to the lending of present income in exchange for future income; at inter-European level the credit in ECUs operated by the financial department of the ECB defines the purchase of a right to a future income by all those who decide to invest their capital into ECU bonds. No miraculous purchasing power is thus created by the ECB, whose twofold role, monetary and financial, is carried out in accordance with the vehicular nature of money.

According to this scheme, exchanges all take place among real goods and, therefore, according to the logic of the gold standard system where trade deficits are cleared through the transfer of an equivalent amount of gold. The result obtained here is substantially similar to that advocated by the supporters of the gold standard but, unlike what happens in the classical system, it is reached through a set of monetary relationships.

Relative to barter the use of money undoubtedly represents progress, yet to benefit from a true monetary system it is necessary to avoid both the mistake made by classical authors of identifying money with a commodity (thus reducing monetary transactions to barter), and that of considering vehicular money as the final object of monetary payments. The solution sketched here is based on a conception of bank money that stresses its vehicular character and which, as is confirmed throughout this book, allows for the working out of a new approach to international monetary problems.

From what we have seen so far, shall we perhaps deduce that there is no room for the private use of the ECU, that it cannot circulate as a bank note or serve for the emission of cheques or credit cards?

The ECU as a private currency

According to the treaty agreed upon at Maastricht (December 1991), the ECB will be given the task of providing European residents with ECU bank notes. There are no reasons to oppose the money used to convey inter-European transactions being partly represented under the form of bank notes, and being so used by Community residents as a means of payment for their purchases of goods and services. For example, German tourists will be entitled to spend ECU bank notes in Italy without there being grounds to worry about a modification of the relationship between lira and Italian domestic output or between marks and German national output.

Like the book-entry ECUs described above, ECU bank notes have a value only in so far as they take the place of domestic currencies. Moreover, if they are used to represent book-keeping entries in the ECB, they cannot be considered as an autonomous currency and have to be inserted in the mechanism of extra-national payments centred on the European Central Bank. In the words of Bernard Schmitt, 'ECU-cheques and ECU bank notes are not autonomous but derived currencies since the Bank of Europe will be able to issue the correspondent ECUs only to the profit of member countries involved in scriptural and fiduciary payments' (Schmitt 1988: 163).

Besides this 'international' use of ECU bank notes, it is also conceivable that they will be demanded in order to replace domestic currencies and used as a store of value. It is not a matter of replacing national currencies with a single European currency: domestic production will still be monetised in domestic money and each country will go on enjoying its monetary sovereignty. Yet, savers will be given the possibility of transforming part of their income into ECUs. ECU bank notes will not be added to national currencies, but will become their substitutes, their European replica. Finally, it would be a transformation with no consequences since ECU bank notes will inherit the purchasing power of the domestic currencies which they substitute.

Let us suppose that income holders of a given country decide to hold part of their income in the form of ECUs. The secondary banks of that country will ask the Central Bank for ECU bank notes in exchange for an equivalent sum of domestic currency. In its turn, the external department of the Central Bank will obtain the required bank notes from the ECB, giving in exchange a credit on domestic money. At this point, two scenarios are possible. The owners of ECU bank notes could decide either to spend or to invest them at the European (or extra-European) level. In the first case, ECU bank notes would be transformed into domestic currency and, following the opposite path, flow back to their point of origin: the ECB. The entries corresponding to the first transformation would cancel out and the whole national output would be purchased through the expenditure of domestic income alone. In the second case, ECU bank notes would be spent on the purchase of European (or extra-European) bonds, and this would amount to the external loan of a part of the domestic income. This second scenario is related to the possibility of the ECB playing a role of financial intermediation in addition to its main role of monetary intermediation. Let us briefly analyse this role.

A possible evolution of the role played by the European Central Bank: financial intermediation

Having established that the ECB will issue only a purely vehicular money, it is perfectly possible that, besides monetising inter-European transactions, the European Bank will also be asked to finance extra-national investment through the sale of ECU bonds. Countries needing funds the most would thus be able to get them from the ECB without getting indebted to their richer partners.

Let us suppose that German residents decided to place part of their income with the ECB. Their purchase of ECU bonds would make the financial department of the ECB the owner of a German income which it could transfer, by investing it, to any other EC country, such as Greece for example. By selling bonds, Greece would thus be able to find the income necessary for the financing of new imports. Besides its exports of domestic bonds to EC countries, Greece could therefore make use of the ECB's financial intermediation in order to pay for the import of foreign goods and services.

The ECB's intervention on the financial market would contribute to its further expansion at the international level, providing less developed countries with further access to foreign saving. In our example, Germany would participate, both directly and indirectly, in investments on Greek territory; directly, as far as it is a net importer of bonds from Greece; indirectly, as far as German residents purchase ECU bonds. And since this investment would profit both those who make them, and those who benefit from them, there can be no doubt about the usefulness of the role of financial intermediation which Europeans could entrust to their Central Bank.

Let us clarify a possible misunderstanding. We have claimed that, by selling ECU bonds, the ECB would obtain a German income that it would lend to Greece and that Greece would spend to finance new commercial imports. This does not mean, however, that the investment of the European Bank would be carried out in marks, or that the payment of Greek imports would be conveyed by the German currency. As with any other extra-national transaction, the financial intermediation of the ECB also requires the vehicular intervention of the ECU. Greece would thus benefit from an investment in ECUs, and it is with this money that it would pay for all its imports, both those financed through the sale of domestic bonds to Germany, and those made possible by the ECB's intervention. It remains true that the content of the ECUs lent to Greece and spent in Germany would be part of the German income. Yet this is precisely the real meaning of the vehicular use of the European currency, whose content can only be defined by the real goods (commodities and bonds) exchanged by EC countries.

In conclusion, residents of member countries can be allowed to hold ECU bank notes and ECU bonds without any risk of altering the essence of the plan proposed above. On the contrary, the market for ECU bonds would reinforce the entire system by allowing the ECB to address savings towards less developed countries without directly involving single savers. The purchase of ECU bonds by residents of EC (or extra-European) countries would provide the ECB with private capital that it could invest according to criteria collectively agreed upon and thus conceived so as to favour less rich countries and simultaneously guarantee the reimbursement of the loan granted by each single saver.

13

THE EXTERNAL DEBT PROBLEM

For years the problem of external debt has being worrying the public and troubling economists, bankers and politicians. More important still, its consequences for the populations of indebted countries continue to worsen. Being forced to restrict imports in the desperate attempt to realise a trade surplus which would allow them to earn the income needed to service their debt, Third World countries (among which several European countries should also be included) impose heavy sacrifices on their residents and raise a crippling mortgage on their future development. In this respect, let us simply observe how in these countries the growth in gross domestic investment is usually negative, while the growth in gross domestic output is only slightly positive. Hence, for example, the average annual growth in Mexico, Brazil, Nigeria and Portugal GDP between 1980 and 1991 was 1.2 per cent, 2.5 per cent, 1.9 per cent and 2.9 per cent respectively, while the average annual growth in their gross domestic investment was 1.9 per cent, 0.1 per cent, 8.1 per cent and 2.6 per cent (World Bank, *World Development Report 1993*).

Now, if all these sacrifices were to allow indebted countries to reduce their external debt, a case could easily be made for their necessary acceptance. However, even if we accept the maxim according to which the end justifies the means, the observation of facts shows how the efforts of these countries are in vain because of a mysterious and wicked mechanism that maintains external debt at its previous level every time that it is positively serviced. The thesis of the structural inadequacy of the present system of international payments thus finds a new confirmation in this context. As is acknowledged by Bahram Nowzad, Chief Editor of the IMF:

> Along with others, the IMF perhaps underestimated the severity and obduracy of the unprecedented debt crisis. A problem that had been so many years in the making, and that had been allowed to reach unsustainable dimensions, could not easily be dealt with (even in the

medium term) with instruments designed to cope with 'normal' balance of payments difficulties.

(Nowzad 1990: 13)

The 'severity' and 'obduracy' of the debt crisis both debtor and creditor countries are suffering can be understood only by having recourse to an analysis emphasising the monetary difficulties of external debt servicing. Once again it is a matter of verifying whether the present system of international payments complies with the banking nature of money and with its vehicular definition. After a short introduction devoted to the distinction between international (inter-national) and inter-regional indebtedness, we shall analyse the way external debt is defined and accounted for on the basis of the statistical data entered in the balance of payments. We should thus be able to ascertain, starting from the official statistics published by the World Bank, how the effective debt of Third World countries is far greater than that statistically justifiable. The difference is the pathological and absurd result of an asymmetry characterising today's external debt servicing and whose consequence is the fact that indebted countries have to service their external debt (both principal *and* interest) twice in order to see it decrease once.

SPECIFICITY, DEFINITION AND MEASUREMENT OF INTERNATIONAL DEBT

The distinction between international and inter-regional debt

According to some economists, international debt would differ from inter-regional debt only for technical reasons, since the financial instruments available for the settlement of internal debts are more flexible than those used for the servicing of external debts. In particular it is maintained (Goodhart 1975) that the settlement of inter-regional current account deficits is not a source of serious difficulties since financial claims issued in different regions of the same currency area benefit from a high degree of substitution. On the contrary, though they fundamentally pertain to the same category, international deficits are seen as more problematic because of the lower degree of substitution of financial claims issued in different countries.

The assumption of a strong analogy between internal and external debts is related to the monetary homogeneity postulate enunciated since the time of the classical authors and recently taken over by the monetarists. In fact, if the world were a single currency area, the indebtedness between countries would not differ substantially from the indebtedness between residents of the same country. In both cases the monetary (vehicular) aspect would cause no problem and debtors would only have to worry about finding the financial means required for the settlement of their debts. In the absence of an international Central Bank, however, it is not possible to ascribe an axiomatic status to the monetarist postulate. Domestic currencies remain fundamentally heterogeneous and the concept of foreign debt acquires a meaning totally irreducible to that of inter-regional debt.

Let us proceed in an orderly way and analyse first the concept of internal debt. Let us suppose that resident *a* of a given region gets indebted to another resident, *b*, of the same monetary area. If *a* obtains goods from *b* in exchange for non-monetary claims, the situation can be represented as in Figure 13.1. Being residents of a single country, *a* and *b* carry out their exchange in national money (NM), whose vehicular function is well characterised by the circular movement which takes it back to its point of origin. Hence, through the use of money (means of exchange) resident *a* buys goods through selling bonds, a transaction by which *b* (or any other resident) lends him the income needed to finance his net purchase of commercial goods.

Having borrowed from *b*, resident *a* will remain indebted until he buys back his financial claims from *b*. If we want to speak of an inter-regional debt we have to refer to the debt incurred by *a* with respect to *b*, and not to a hypothetical indebtedness of the region of resident *a* towards the region of resident *b*. Apart from the debts incurred by residents no true inter-regional debt can be accounted for. The meaning of this expression is therefore a metaphorical one, as is confirmed by the fact that regions as such do not build up official reserves to face their internal debts. This does not mean, of course, that it is not useful to express the relationships between regions in terms of commercial and financial flows or that we shall not pay attention to the level of indebtedness among residents of different regions. What we want to stress here is simply the fact that, within a single country, no region as such is ever indebted towards any other, the debts

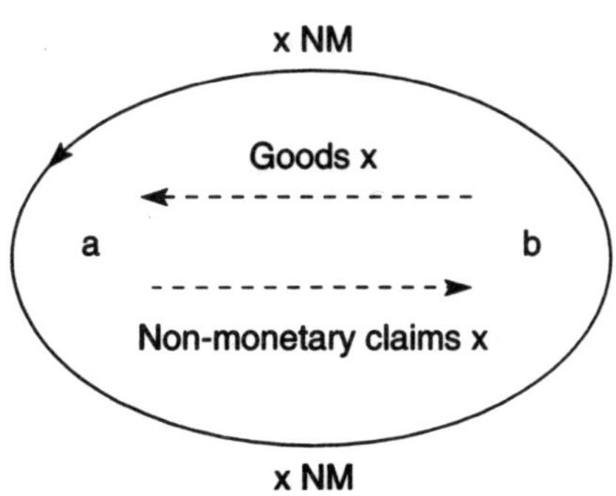

Figure 13.1

incurred by regional institutions being part of those incurred by the set of residents (of which regional institutions are constitutive elements).

The previous conclusion is confirmed when the debt between residents is serviced. Having found the income required for the payment of interest and principal, resident *a* transfers it to his creditor, *b*, through the vehicular use of national money (NM) (Figure 13.2). The payment from *a* to *b* amounts to the transfer of a bank deposit, in exchange for which *b* gives back to *a* the non-monetary claims defining his debt. No monetary difficulty arises in this transaction, and regions are implicated only in so far as they represent the place of residence of *a* and *b*. In the same way as the debt of *a* did not elicit that of his region, debt servicing requires only a financial transfer from *a* to *b*.

Let us now turn to the formation and servicing of international debts.

The first, obvious, observation is that even in this case the debt is incurred by the residents of a given country, A, with regard to the residents of other countries, B. At a first approach, a country's foreign debt can thus be defined as the sum of the external debts incurred by its residents. On the basis of this definition, international debts are formed according to a scheme analogous to that which can be applied at the inter-regional level (Figure 13.3). In our example, residents of country A are net importers of goods from country B, to which they give non-monetary claims of an equivalent amount in exchange. The trade deficit of A is thus covered by the loan granted by the residents of B (through their purchase of bonds issued by A). The currency used as means of payment can indifferently be that of A, that of B, or both that of A and that of B. In every case it flows back to its starting point following a circuit which confirms its vehicular nature (if both currencies are used, country A gives back to B x units of money B in exchange for an equivalent sum of money A, and vice versa).

To speak of a country's debt seems therefore as ambiguous as to speak of an inter-regional debt. Only residents could be indebted, and not the

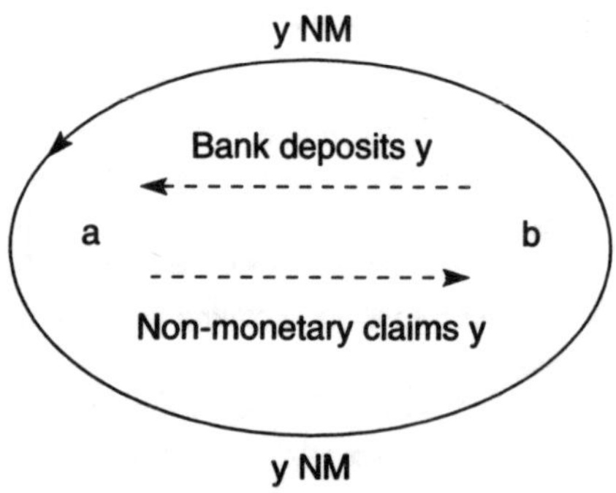

Figure 13.2

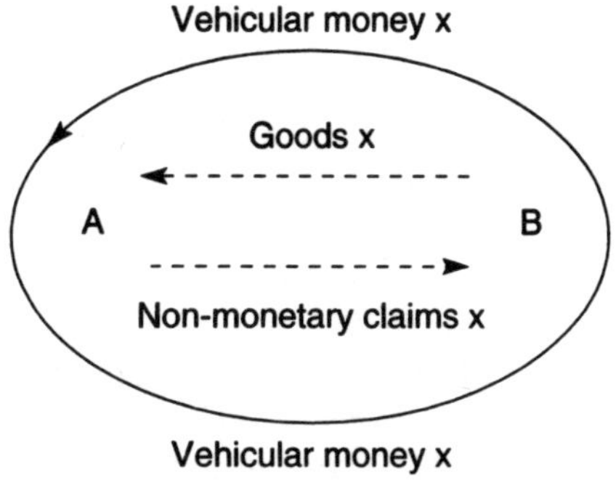

Figure 13.3

country as such, whose debt would merely reflect that of its residents. Yet, a doubt arises as to the presumed 'neutrality' of foreign debt as soon as we start to think about the concept of nation. In particular it is important to ask whether the nation can be identified with the sum of its residents or whether it represents their set (which cannot be reduced to the sum of its elements). In other words, it is essential to know whether the nation has an 'economic' existence and, if so, what its implications for the external debt problem are.

As we know, money is the determinant element. It is thanks to money that physical products (goods and services) can be transformed into commodities and can thus become the object of economic research, and it is thanks to money that output is measured, redistributed and exchanged. Money, by definition, is an acknowledgement of debt of its issuing bank. This means that, with respect to the rest of the world, domestic money defines the acknowledgement of debt of the whole national banking system and, therefore, of the entire country. If countries did not possess a national currency, none of them would benefit from monetary and political sovereignty. The world would be a single country divided into regions. The presence of different currencies shows that each country is sovereign and that nations cannot be reduced to the sum of their populations.

This conclusion is emphasised by the analysis of external debt servicing. Let us refer to our example and suppose that residents of country A (net commercial importer in period p_0) service their debt starting from period p_1. To carry out their payment they have to find an adequate income in domestic money. Yet besides the financial aspect of this payment, country A is faced with its monetary aspect. If country A were part of a single monetary area, debt servicing would amount to the simple transfer to B of the income saved by the residents who incurred it. Using a single currency, A and B would be the elements of a single set and there would be no need to speak of their specific indebtedness (apart from that of their residents) or of their monetary sovereignty. In the present situation, however, it is not enough that indebted residents transfer part of their income to their creditors for external debt servicing to be positive. The payment of the country has in fact to be added to that of its population, since it is the country that must take care of its monetary component.

If our international monetary system were consistent with the vehicular nature of money, the intervention of the nation would take place without modifying either the ratio between national currencies or that between each domestic currency and domestic output. The nation would act as a simple intermediary between residents and non-residents and we would never have to add its indebtedness to that of its residents (that is, of all the economic agents operating on its territory, including the State). The nation would play a decisive and original role respectful of monetary sovereignty.

Unfortunately the present system of international payments does not take sufficiently into account the facts, and this leads to an asymmetry which, besides confirming the existence of nations as such, is the source of a serious monetary disequilibrium. The difficulty arises when foreign debt is serviced. Two cases are possible according to whether or not the country can use its domestic currency as an international means of payment. In the first case A transfers to B a sum of national money in exchange for part of the claims corresponding to the debt of its population (Figure 13.4). Being used as a vehicle, the domestic currency of country A flows back to its banking system after having transferred to B a sum of bank deposits equivalent to the foreign debt securities recovered by A. Although the payment is similar to the servicing of an internal debt described in Figure 13.2, its consequences are substantially different. Unlike what happens in the case of inter-regional settlements, the bank deposit transferred to country B is expressed in monetary units of country A. Moreover, it has to be remembered that domestic income can never really abandon the

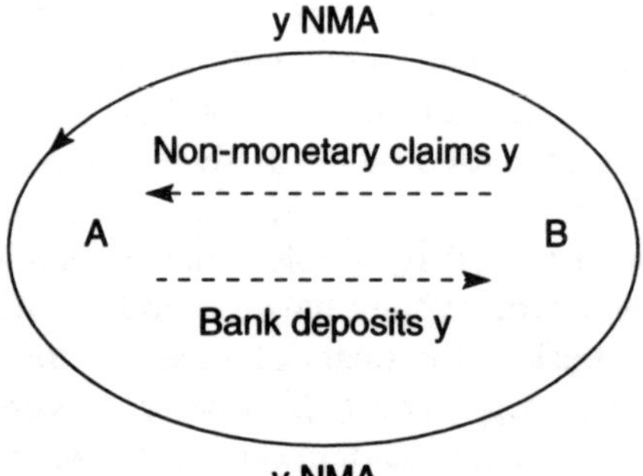

Figure 13.4

banking system from which it originates and in which it exists as a bank deposit. This means that the bank deposits of A are only apparently transferred to B. In reality they are still entirely available within the banking system of A, which transfers a mere duplicate to B. Thus, since money is an acknowledgement of debt, the sum of money entered on the asset side of B's banking system represents an IOU of A. Hence, despite the payment carried out by the population, who give up part of their income, the country as a whole is indebted in so far as it transfers domestic money (its acknowledgement of debt) to the creditor country.

The fact that this debt is of no consequence for country A since this country is given the privilege of *paying by getting indebted* (i.e. of settling its debts in domestic currency), does not reduce the gravity of the situation. On the contrary, as the analysis developed in the second part of this work has shown, payments carried out in foreign currencies increase the instability of monetary markets, which are continuously inflated by new inflows of Eurocurrencies. At this point it has to be added that, by allowing only a few countries to transform their money into a reserve currency, the system introduces, besides the asymmetry between reciprocal payments and debt servicing, the asymmetry between 'strong'- and 'weak'-currency countries.

If country A pertains to this second category, the servicing of the debt incurred by its residents implies the intervention of the whole nation (represented by the Central Bank), whose consequent indebtedness is not only nominal, as is the case for reserve currency countries, but entails a loss of internal resources which seriously hampers a process of development already heavily hindered by such phenomena as capital flight and real terms of trade deterioration. Let us proceed step by step, showing first how the concept of nation also applies when foreign debt servicing is carried out by weak-currency countries (Figure 13.5). Since it cannot convey the payment of its residents with its domestic currency, country A (its Central

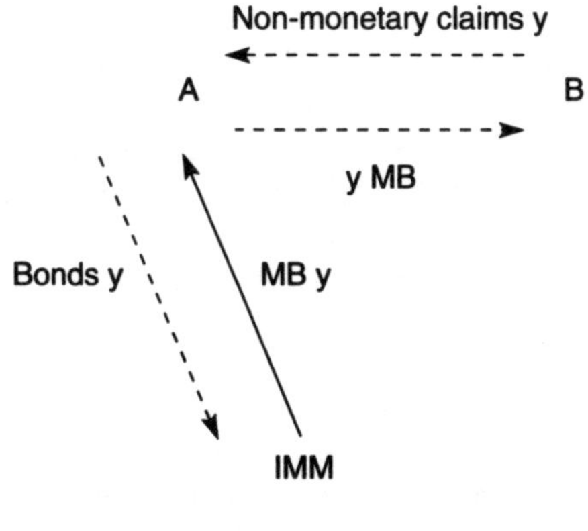

Figure 13.5

Bank) is forced to find a key-currency (MB) on the international monetary market, IMM (as in Figure 13.5) or to decrease its official reserves of foreign exchange. In both cases the country itself is concerned with external debt servicing. Hence, the servicing of external debt carried out by residents leads to the debt (or to the decrease in foreign credits if the payment is conveyed through a reduction in official reserves) of the whole nation, whose transfer of claims to the rest of the world is added to the income transferred by its residents.

As this short introductory analysis shows, international debt differs from inter-regional debt mainly because of the lack of monetary homogeneity. The present structure of payments is incapable of entrusting the nation with a role of intermediation allowing international transactions to be considered as essentially similar to inter-regional exchanges. In this context, foreign debt servicing introduces an anomaly not to be found in normal payment processes, and which does not fail to have severe repercussions both on the definition of external debt and on its calculation.

The twofold definition of external debt

According to the definition officially adopted by the main international institutions, external debt corresponds to the debt incurred by the residents of a given country to residents of the rest of the world. 'Gross external debt is the amount, at any given time, of disbursed and outstanding contractual liabilities of residents of a country to non-residents to repay principal, with or without interest, or to pay interest, with or without principal' (WB, IMF, BIS and OECD 1988: 19). The criterion of demarcation between internal and external debts is therefore that of residence. According to the same official sources 'the residents of any economy comprise the general government, individuals, private nonprofit bodies serving individuals, and enterprises, all defined in terms of their relationship to the territory of that economy' (1988: 21).

Yet to this first definition of international debt we must add that related to the concept of nation or country. Thus, external debt becomes the debt incurred by a country to the rest of the world.

As we have already observed, these two definitions should concern the same phenomenon, so that the debt of the nation should logically never add to that of its residents. If this were the case, international debt would only be concerned with problems of a financial order, and in this respect particular attention should be given to the degree of substitution of claims issued in the different countries. The difficulty related to external debt servicing would thus amount to the creation of the conditions allowing indebted residents (mainly private and State-owned firms) to find the financial resources required to settle their foreign obligations. From this point of view foreign debt would not differ from internal debt. If they possessed the required income, indebted agents, of a single country or of different countries, could clear their debt position by a simple transfer to their creditors.

However, a serious problem arises because of the presence of different national currencies and the absence of an international Bank capable of grouping them within a single monetary area. A problem which is made even worse by the fact that a few national monies are used as reserve currencies. The debt of a strong-currency country acquires a meaning entirely different from that of a weak-currency country, and it is no longer possible to reduce the definition of external debt to the relationship between residents and non-residents. Even though it originates from the transactions carried out by residents, external debt thus acquires a particular international character.

The transformation of the debt of the nation from a simple reflection of that of its residents to an autonomous entity looming over the whole country is related to external debt servicing. The modalities of this payment lay emphasis on the asymmetry characterising the present international monetary system.

The absurdity of the conclusion to which we are led by the analysis of external debt servicing is such as to require further investigation. Let us first show that official statistics do not account for substantial discrepancies between the effective total amount of external debt and the quantity of debt which can logically be justified according to foreign engagements and transactions. Even though it is not formal proof of the double servicing of external debts (residents + nations), this first observation is no doubt the symptom of a serious anomaly which, if confirmed by facts, can no longer be ignored if the debt crisis is to be finally solved.

The statistical analysis of external debt

According to the definition adopted internationally, the total amount of a country's external debt is determined by taking into account the contracts for public and private loans, at short, medium and long term. Statistical data referring to external debt are collected both in the indebted countries, for example through the Debtor Reporting System worked out by the World Bank, and by international institutions such as the IMF, BIS, OECD and WB.

The official approach to external debt calculation is illustrated by the World Bank figure concerning the composition of external debt (Figure 13.6).

As is openly admitted by international experts, the calculation of the debt from financial data must be consistent with that based on economic data. In other words, there must be a perfect agreement between the results obtained from contractual survey and those concerning commercial and financial flows among countries. Hence, the deficit of the balance of goods

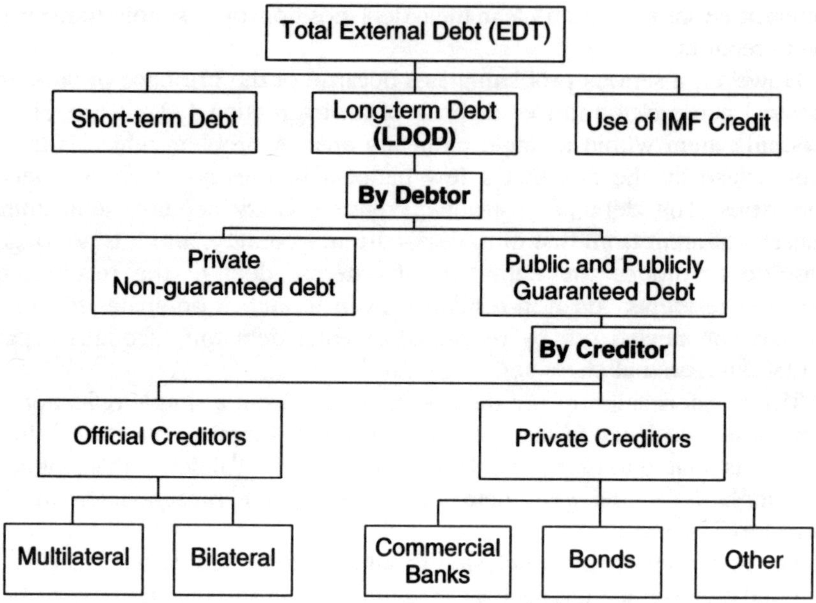

Figure 13.6

and services is the source of an external debt which must find its match in the data referring to the evolution of the global debt. The same applies to the amount of interest payable, the non-payment of which is also the cause of an increase in debt.

In general, referring to the different categories that make up the balance of payments, we can say that the increase in a country's external debt is justified in so far as its current account deficit and/or the increase in its official reserves are not matched by direct foreign investment or by the reduction in debt due to measures of international aid. It is certain, in fact, that a country's debt increases if its gains from commercial exports of goods and services, capital yields, unrequited official and private transfers, are insufficient to cover its expenditures (due to commercial imports, interest payments, increases in official reserve and unilateral transfers). On the other hand, the inflow of foreign exchange corresponding to direct foreign investment reduces the debt, while direct investment abroad increases it. Taking advantage of direct foreign investment, the country benefits from an inflow of foreign exchange similar to that deriving from net commercial exports which allows it to relieve the burden of indebtedness.

From the five examples given here and elaborated from the official data of the World Bank published in the *World Debt Tables* 1989–90, 1990–91, 1991–92 and 1992–93 and referring to five of the most indebted countries observed over a period of ten years, it appears that – except in the emblematic case of India – there is an important discrepancy between the effective amount of their external debts and that which can be logically accounted for. Without rushing to conclusions, it must be noted that this repeated gap cannot be attributed only to errors and omissions of a statistical nature. Apart from the inaccuracy and defectiveness characterising endemically statistical coverage in several indebted countries, it is reasonable to claim that these discrepancies are symptomatic of a pathological anomaly related to external debt servicing which, as we shall prove in the next chapter, leads to the re-indebtedness of the countries that are able to honour their engagements. Let us note that, since global data are calculated at the end of every period of reference, in order to determine the statistical increase in debt and official reserves between 1981–91 we have taken into account the situation as at the beginning of 1981, so that our data refer to the statistical survey of 1980. As far as direct foreign investment and current account deficits (or surpluses) are concerned, the initial year of reference is 1981. Following tradition, a + sign stands for an increase and a – sign for a decrease, while figures are expressed in millions of US dollars (Table 13.1).

In the case of Mexico the total increase in debt from 1980 to 1991 ($57,913 million) is only partially explained by its current account deficit ($36,146 million) and by the increase in its official reserves ($13,877 million), since Mexico has benefited from a debt stock reduction and an inflow of direct foreign investment equal to $35,396 million. Globally, statistical data can only account for an increase in debt of $14,627 million, the $43,286 million remaining being the mark of an unjustifiable discrepancy calling for further investigation into the nature of the international system of payments. Statistical coverage of the Brazilian situation leads to the same conclusion (Table 13.2).

The case of India differs from that of the majority of LDCs since its total

Table 13.1 Mexico

	1980	*1991*	*Total*
(1) Total debt	57,378	115,291	
(2) Total variation in debt			+ 57,913
(3) Current account balance			– 36,146
(4) Direct foreign investment			+ 22,258
(5) Total reserves	4,175	18,052	
(6) Total variation in reserves			+ 13,877
(7) Debt stock reduction (excl. of debt equity swaps)			13,138
(8) Justifiable variation in debt – (3) – (4) + (6) – (7)			+ 14,627
(9) Unjustifiable variation in debt (2) – (8)			+ 43,286

Table 13.2 Brazil

	1980	*1991*	*Total*
(1) Total debt	70,975	117,350	
(2) Total variation in debt			+ 46,375
(3) Current account balance			– 41,846
(4) Direct foreign investment			+ 17,028
(5) Total reserves	6,875	8,749	
(6) Total variation in reserves			+ 1,874
(7) Debt stock reduction (excl. of debt equity swaps)			10,737
(8) Justifiable variation in debt – (3) – (4) + (6) – (7)			+ 15,955
(9) Unjustifiable variation in debt (2) – (8)			+ 30,420

increase in debt ($51,060 million) is almost entirely explained by the data referring to its global external transactions (trade deficit + direct foreign investment – variation in reserves = $47,526 million). As we shall see in the following chapter, this does not mean that statistical coverage of India's data is more reliable than that of Mexico or Brazil but that, unlike these countries, India has never positively serviced its external debt and has thus been able to avoid the pathological process of re-indebtedness related to it (Table 13.3).

The case of Portugal, one of the most indebted European countries, is similar to that of Mexico and Brazil. Given the considerable increase in official reserves ($12,376 million), the total variation in debt ($18,839 million) can partially be explained despite the fact that direct foreign investment is greater than the Portuguese trade deficit. However, the discrepancy between the global and the justifiable variation in Portugal's external debt is still $8,605 million, a far too important amount to be attributed to errors and omissions (Table 13.4).

Table 13.3 India

	1980	*1991*	*Total*
(1) Total debt	20,582	71,642	
(2) Total variation in debt			+ 51,060
(3) Current account balance			– 53,276
(4) Direct foreign investment			+ 1,442
(5) Total reserves	11,924	7,616	
(6) Total variation in reserves			– 4,308
(7) Debt stock reduction (excl. of debt equity swaps)			–
(8) Justifiable variation in debt – (3) – (4) + (6) – (7)			+ 47,526
(9) Unjustifiable variation in debt (2) – (8)			+ 3,534

Table 13.4 Portugal

	1980	*1991*	*Total*
(1) Total debt	9,729	28,568	
(2) Total variation in debt			+ 18,839
(3) Current account balance			– 7,150
(4) Direct foreign investment			+ 9,292
(5) Total reserves	13,863	26,239	
(6) Total variation in reserves			+ 12,376
(7) Debt stock reduction (excl. of debt equity swaps)			–
(8) Justifiable variation in debt – (3) – (4) + (6) – (7)			+ 10,234
(9) Unjustifiable variation in debt (2) – (8)			+ 8,605

Table 13.5 Nigeria

	1980	*1991*	*Total*
(1) Total debt	8,934	34,436	
(2) Total variation in debt			+ 25,502
(3) Current account balance			– 7,877
(4) Direct foreign investment			+ 6,064
(5) Total reserves	10,640	4,678	
(6) Total variation in reserves			–5,962
(7) Debt stock reduction (excl. of debt equity swaps)			1,162
(8) Justifiable variation in debt – (3) – (4) + (6) – (7)			– 5,311
(9) Unjustifiable variation in debt (2) – (8)			+ 30,813

In our last example we examined the case of Nigeria, another heavily indebted country whose total debt can only partially be explained by the flows relating to current account deficit, direct foreign investment and variations in official reserves. In particular, because of the decrease in its reserves and the relatively small trade deficit, Nigeria should have benefited from a reduction in its foreign debt of $5,311 million; which means that, since the effective increase has been of $25,502 million, its external debt has unjustifiably increased by $30,813 million (Table 13.5).

THE FORMAL ANOMALY IMPLICIT IN EXTERNAL DEBT SERVICING

In this section we shall analyse the monetary and real flows characterising international transactions, showing how monetary equilibrium is fulfilled by all of them except one: external debt servicing. The origin of this anomaly is the pathology related to the use of a few national currencies as international standards of payment. External debt servicing would take place in the full respect of monetary neutrality only if no country were allowed to pay for its net commercial imports with an IOU issued by its own banking system. In the key-currencies standard regime, this does not occur and the asymmetry of payments leads to the re-indebtedness of debtor countries, which are forced to service their foreign debt *twice*.

Monetary neutrality is complied with in the majority of international transactions

Let us divide the world into two sets of countries, one made up of countries whose currency is accepted as a unit of payment and the other made up of countries whose currency is not acknowledged as an international standard. Let us call the first set S and the second W. What has to be established is whether the use of the money of set S as a means of payment between the two sets is consistent with the vehicular nature of bank money.

Let us analyse the simplest case first, where S's and W's trade balances are even (Figure 13.7). As shown in Figure 13.7, the money of set S (MS) is used as a vehicle, in a circular movement allowing for the balanced exchange of goods and services between S and W.

Even though the money used is that of S, set W suffers no discrimination: neither S nor W derive any benefit (or loss) from the vehicular use of MS. Besides, the transaction could be carried out equally well with money W, which proves that the whole operation is perfectly symmetrical.

The same symmetry is found when the exchange occurs between goods and financial claims. If we suppose that weak currency countries (set W) are net importers of goods and services, and that they finance their trade deficit through an equivalent export of non-monetary claims (bonds or shares), transactions would take place according to the scheme shown in

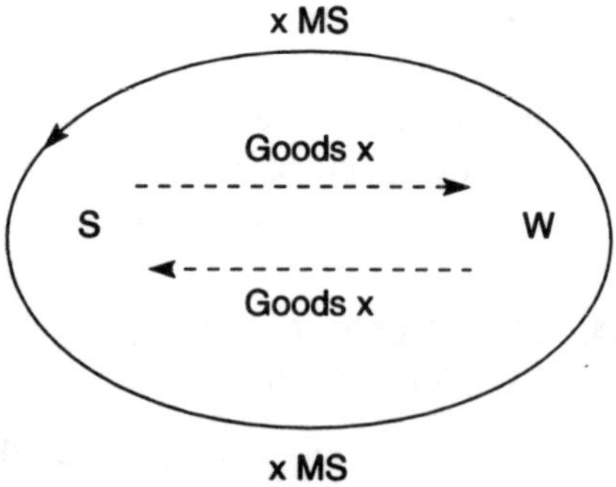

Figure 13.7

Figure 13.8. Money S plays a vehicular role even in this case, and could therefore be replaced by any other currency that would be used in the same way.

Finally, in the two cases analysed so far and in all those that can be derived from them, exchange takes place between real goods (bonds being the purest form of 'real goods'), and money is a simple intermediary. Monetary neutrality is guaranteed by the circular use of money, and the symmetry of the two sets by the reciprocity of the transactions and by the potential substitutability of currencies S and W.

The payment of net commercial imports of set S

In the previous examples, sets W and S paid for their commercial imports through the export of goods, services or non-monetary claims. Payments were all real and neither the currency of S nor that of W was subjected to a net demand in terms of the other. In particular, money S was simultaneously supplied and demanded by importers and exporters of S and, reciprocally, demanded and supplied by importers and exporters of W.

Let us now analyse what happens when S finances its net purchases of goods and services through the transfer of an equivalent amount of monetary claims. Since it benefits from the fact of having at its disposal a reserve currency, set S pays set W by crediting it with its own domestic money (Figure 13.9). Because of its banking nature, money S is however immediately re-deposited in the banking system of set S. Hence, through the instantaneous circulation of money S, set W obtains from set S a sum of bank deposits in exchange for an equivalent amount of exported goods and services (Figure 13.10). Once again the flowing to and fro of money S defines its vehicular use and, therefore, its substantial neutrality. Offered by importers of set S and by exporters of set W, it is simultaneously demanded by exporters of set S and by importers of set W.

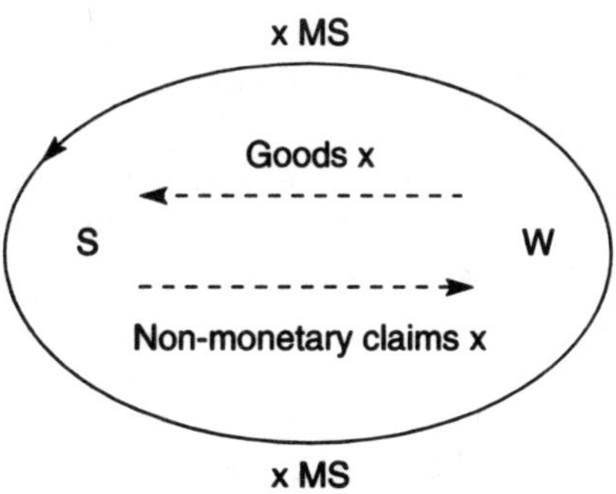

Figure 13.8

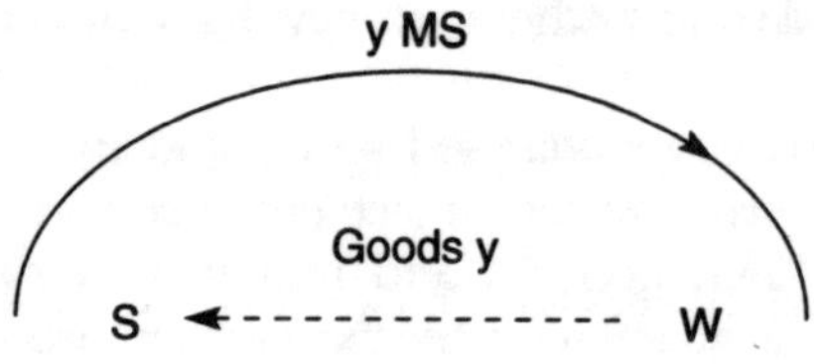

Figure 13.9

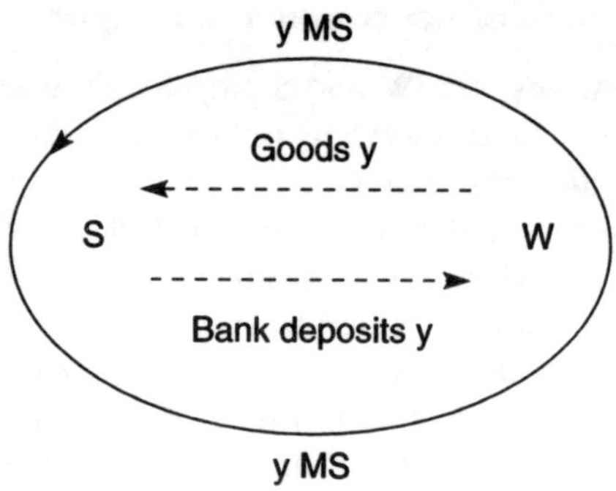

Figure 13.10

However, despite respecting the circular nature of money, this payment does not comply with the principle of symmetry that we observed in the previous examples. While countries of set W can import goods and services only by giving other real goods (goods, services or non-monetary claims) in exchange, countries of set S can cover their trade deficit by transferring simple bank deposits (monetary claims). The symmetry would be respected only if S's net commercial purchases were financed through the transfer of non-monetary claims. It is only in this case, in fact, that all the transactions would define exchanges among real goods. Although it would monetise every transaction, money would not finance any of them and payments would all be perfectly balanced.

Since it does not comply with the principle of symmetry, the system of international payments based on the key-currencies standard puts the countries of set S and of set W in a strongly differentiated situation as regard to the debt problem. The difference appears from the moment in which external debt is formed. Since they must finance their net commercial purchases by exporting financial securities, weak-currency countries cannot avoid incurring a debt to the rest of the world, while strong-currency countries enjoy the privilege of paying for their imports only in monetary terms. Besides the obvious iniquity of treatment, this asymmetry entails other serious consequences for countries W as soon as they start servicing their external debt. Before analysing them, let us show that external debt servicing would not be the source of any monetary anomaly if it were carried out consistently with the principle of symmetry.

External debt servicing according to formal logic

Let us suppose that the international system of payments works to allow the perfect symmetry of transactions and that countries W find the resources needed for the servicing of their debt in their trade surplus. In such a context, net commercial imports of countries S would give rise to the payments shown in Figure 13.11. It is enough to compare this scheme with that referring to the period (p_0) in which the debt of set W was formed (Figure 13.8) to become aware of how debt servicing can easily take place without creating imbalances of a monetary order. By transferring the financial claims obtained in exchange for its net commercial exports of p_1, set W recovers part of the claims corresponding to the debt incurred in p_0, whose amount decreases from x + i (interest) to (x + i) – y units (Figure 13.12). The reciprocal exchange of financial claims between S and W takes place through the circular use of a vehicular money (VM) which can be that of one set or the other. If it is carried out according to this scheme, external debt servicing pertains to the category of monetarily neutral exchanges. Logically, payment must be made by the indebted countries. Yet, in order to comply with this obvious requirement, set W only has to get hold of the necessary financial resources without having to worry about the monetary aspect of the payment.

The same conclusion is reached when the service of the debt incurred in p_0 forces set W to incur another equivalent debt in p_1. If we suppose that W has no commercial surplus in p_1, external debt servicing is charged to export earnings, which leaves imports partially uncovered. Imports can

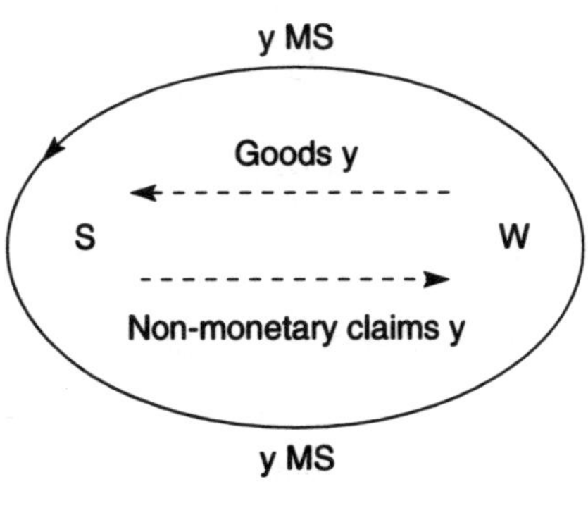

Figure 13.11

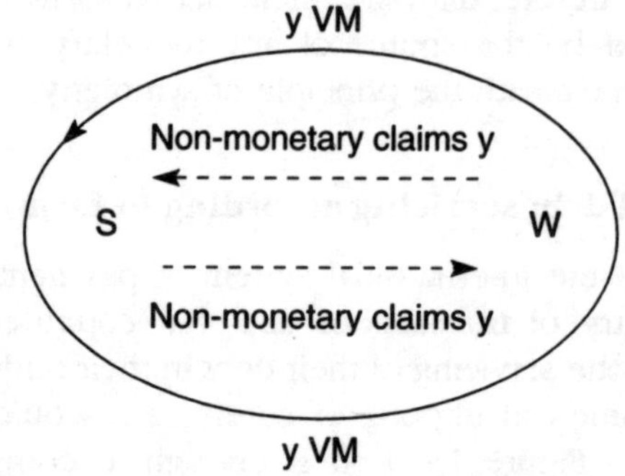

Figure 13.12

thus be totally financed only through a net sale of new non-monetary claims, so that set W cancels part of its previous external debt by exchanging goods and services against securities and incurs a new debt by exchanging securities against goods and services (Figure 13.13).

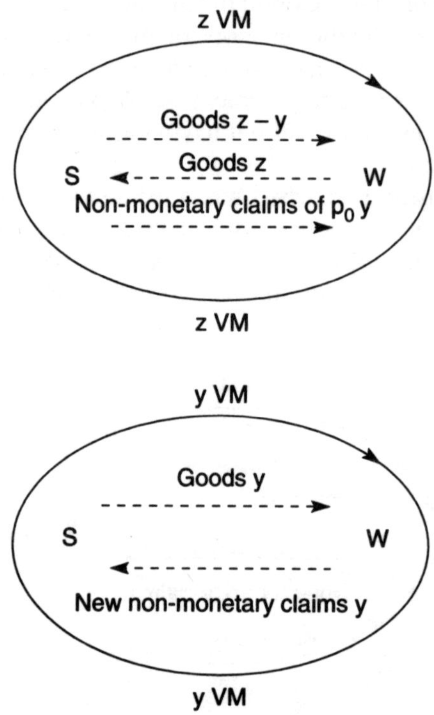

Figure 13.13

Irrespective of whether or not set W has a trade surplus, external debt servicing is positive as long as W gives up commodities or non-monetary claims to S. Moreover, this transaction is monetarily balanced if the currency acting as a means of payment is circularly used as a simple vehicle. Both these conditions are satisfied in the examples we have just been analysing since both external debt formation and external debt servicing involve W and S in a symmetrical way. However, things change when, as in the present system of international payments, the distinction between monetary and financial aspects is no longer strictly complied with, that is, when the monetary vehicle itself becomes an object of exchange.

The anomaly of external debt servicing sanctions its asymmetrical character

The asymmetry pointed out above (p. 295) referred to the payment of net commercial imports. While strong-currency countries simply transfer money deposited within their own banking systems in exchange for their net foreign purchases, weak-currency countries must transfer non-monetary claims. Hence, whereas countries W get indebted by financing their trade deficit of p_0 through the transfer of non-monetary claims, the net commercial imports of countries S in p_1 do not give rise to an analogous transfer of non-monetary claims in favour of W.

This asymmetry lies heavily on weak-currency countries, particularly when they service their external debt, since they have to buy the vehicular money required for the transfer to S of the bank deposits obtained through the sale of commodities or non-monetary claims. The fact is that, having to use money S as a means of payment, countries W must pay for it. Thus, besides having to transfer the deposits earned in its transactions with S, set W is forced to purchase an equivalent amount of money S (MS) (Figure 13.14). As shown in Figure 13.14, countries W suffer from a double loss; that of the bank deposits needed to service the debt to S, and, which is totally illogical, that of an equivalent sum of money S. External debt servicing is thus doubled, set W being forced to carry it out both financially and monetarily.

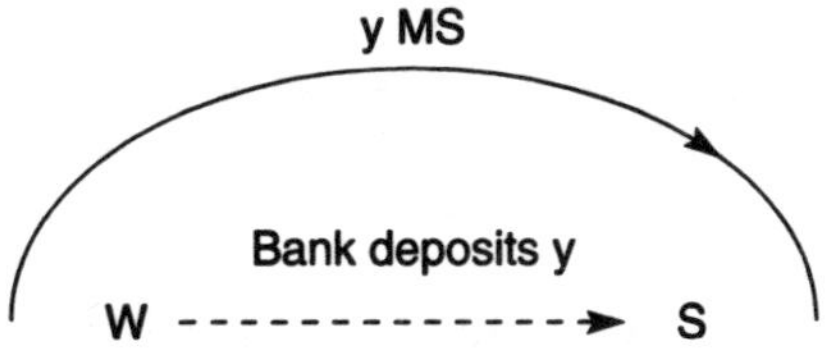

Figure 13.14

If W were supplied with the monetary vehicle gratuitously, external debt servicing would correspond to a single payment. This condition would be complied with automatically if the system conformed to the principle of monetary symmetry. Only in this case would the reciprocal transfer of non-monetary claims between W and S allow for the purely vehicular use of money S. The monetary circuit defined by external debt servicing would provide the strictest guarantee that money would no longer be transformed into an object of exchange.

What distinguishes logical from pathological external debt servicing is thus the fact that the first implies an exchange between non-monetary claims, whereas the second defines a unilateral transfer of bank deposits from W to S. Now, while reciprocity avoids the monetary problem, unilaterality exacerbates it. What should be a simple vehicular money becomes a precious good indebted countries can get hold of only by sacrificing part of their domestic resources. External debt servicing becomes the source of an anomaly whose consequences are particularly negative for developing countries and are, as we shall see, of no benefit to industrialised countries.

The anomaly of external debt servicing as a general phenomenon concerning both weak- and strong-currency countries

Let us refer to the distinction between reciprocal payments and unilateral transfers and show how countries are all subjected to the anomaly inherent in external debt servicing. The key principle is that of monetary neutrality and can be formulated as follows.

> Vehicular money is provided gratuitously in every reciprocal payment between W and S, that is, on condition that countries S transfer goods, services or securities to countries W to the same extent that they benefit from a transfer of goods, services or securities from W.

Following this principle it is not difficult to show that external debt servicing corresponds to a unilateral transfer to the benefit of the creditor country, whose cost is positive both for the indebted population and for their country.

Let us first consider the external debt servicing carried out by any country whatsoever of set W, W_w. In order to service its external debt, W_w must get hold of an equivalent external income. Now, whether W_w finds the foreign currencies needed for its payment by selling goods, services or non-monetary claims, the operation entails a bilateral exchange between W_w and the rest of the world (Figure 13.15). The transfer of goods and/or non-monetary claims carried out by W_w is matched by a reciprocal transfer of bank deposits from the rest of the world. The transaction is perfectly balanced and money entirely neutral.

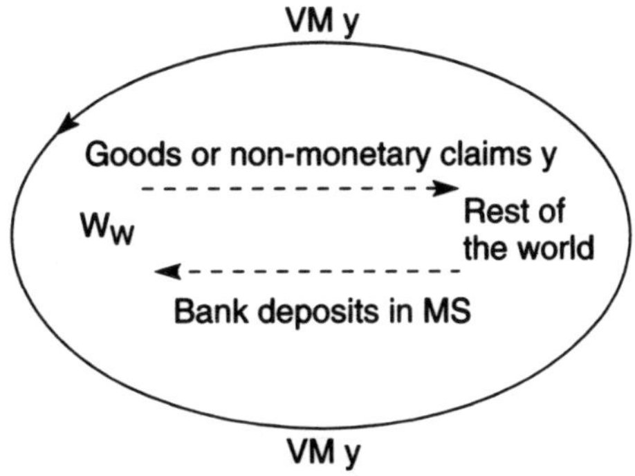

Figure 13.15

Things change when country W_w services the debt previously incurred to a country whatsoever of set S, S_w. In addition to the payment in domestic currency of the residents who carry the debt, country W_w must sacrifice the external income obtained in exchange for its net export of goods and services. Hence, the double payment of external debt consists in the fact that in order to transfer y units of bank deposits in money S (MS), W_w is forced to obtain at a cost the vehicular money that the unilaterality of the transaction does not allow it to obtain in a circular way (Figure 13.16).

Despite appearances to the contrary, an analogous result is reached when external debt servicing is carried out by a strong-currency country. Although the consequences of the double payment are substantially different in the two sets of countries, S and W, it is certain that the servicing of external debt entails the unilateral transfer of bank deposits to the benefit of the creditor country, C_c, even when it is carried out by a country S_w (Figure 13.17). Money S_w is used in a vehicular way since, being issued by S_w's banking system, it can only flow back to it instantaneously. However, the unilaterality of the transfer of bank deposits implied by the flowing back of MS_w is sufficient to prove the double payment of external debt. Even though the debt is entirely paid for by S_w's residents, the whole

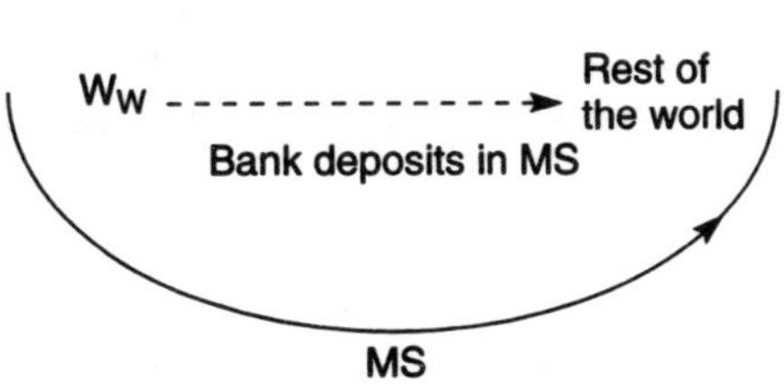

Figure 13.16

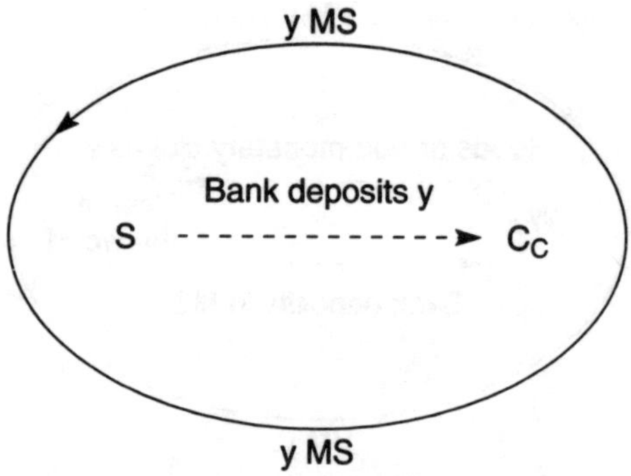

Figure 13.17

country finds itself indebted to the extent that it transfers to C_c part of its bank deposits. It is certain that the owners of a bank deposit have a credit towards the bank in which the deposit is held. By analogy, as owner of a deposit with S_w's banking system country C_c is a creditor to S_w. Moreover, if we take into account the fact that bank deposits never leave country S_w and that their transfer to C_c refers to a mere duplicate (see Chapter 7), we soon realise that S_w is still formally indebted towards C_c even though its residents have positively serviced their debt (although it is a simple duplicate, as soon as it is transferred to C_c, S_w's domestic money corresponds to the acknowledgement of debt of S_w's whole banking system and, therefore, of the very country represented by this banking system).

The source of the asymmetry distinguishing external debt servicing from any other international payment is the unilateral transfer carried out by the indebted country. If the servicing of foreign debts implied the reciprocal exchange of equivalent real assets, the whole operation would take the form of a clearing and money would be involved only in a circular way, thus allowing countries to act as simple intermediaries, so that their payment would not be added to that of their residents.

At this point it is perhaps useful to clarify the terms of a possible misunderstanding. What we have described as a unilateral transfer could no longer appear to be one if we took into consideration the return of the certificates of indebtedness by the creditor country (Figure 13.18).

By putting together Figures 13.17 and 13.18 we get the impression that

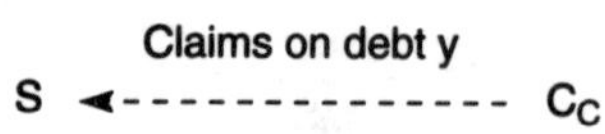

Figure 13.18

everything takes place according to logic and that payments are perfectly balanced. The reciprocal transfer of bank deposits and debt certificates would do away with the presumed asymmetry and transform external debt servicing into a monetarily equilibrated payment. Unfortunately, reality is less generous: it is the reciprocal transfer which is presumed and not the asymmetry hitting external debt servicing. The debt certificates returned by C_c cannot be considered as real goods since, the debt having been paid, they no longer have any value. The cancellation of the debt does not allow S_w to obtain any real good, commodity or security, from the creditor country, whose transfer can therefore not balance that carried out by S_w to its benefit.

Having established that the anomaly declares itself every time a country services its external debt, we must now analyse the impact of the double payment on the countries of sets S and W. We shall thus verify that the asymmetry between strong and weak currency countries is only partially and momentarily apt to neutralise the negative effects of external debt servicing.

14

THE CONSEQUENCES OF EXTERNAL DEBT SERVICING

Carried out jointly by residents and their countries, external debt servicing leads to the re-indebtedness of the debt servicing country, whether it be a strong- or weak-currency country. However, this negative result becomes a concrete issue only when the indebted country manages to achieve a trade surplus. It is only in this case, in fact, that the debt can effectively be paid by the nation, since it is only in this case that the country earns an income of external origin. In every other case, the payment is postponed and so are its negative effects. Besides, because of their privileged status, strong-currency countries can postpone their payment *sine die* or balance the anomaly of external debt servicing with that relative to the very formation of their foreign debt.

Let us distinguish the analysis of external debt servicing according to whether it is carried out by strong- or weak-currency countries, while examining its consequences according to whether the debt is paid for through net commercial exports or through net exports of non-monetary claims.

THE CONSEQUENCES OF EXTERNAL DEBT SERVICING FOR WEAK-CURRENCY COUNTRIES

The servicing of foreign debt is a twofold operation concerning the payment carried out by the indebted residents and their country. Hence, the anomaly inherent in external debt servicing consists in the fact that it is carried out by the country and *additionally* by its population. The first observation is that the country cannot be reduced to the sum of its residents. The economic existence of the nation is proved both by its monetary sovereignty and by the fact that trade surplus countries benefit from a gain of an external origin. Money is what gives a proper content to the economic concept of a nation. No one doubts that national money exists and that, as an acknowledgement of debt of the issuing banking system, it defines an IOU of the country itself. However, because of the existence of the nation as the *set* of its residents, the debt incurred by the latter necessarily involves the former. As such, this does not entail any pathological consequence. In the absence of a single world money, monetary sovereignty requires the intervention of nations in international transactions. Thus, the problem is not that of determining whether or not the country must intervene in the external debt servicing carried out by its residents, but whether or not its payment is added to theirs.

According to logic, the two payments should not be added to one another. In an orderly system of international payments, external debt servicing would be carried out by the country on behalf of its residents. By acting as an intermediary between internal debtors and foreign creditors, the country would guarantee the conversion of domestic income into an equivalent external income without any additional cost to its residents. External debt servicing would thus entail the payment of creditors by the country and the payment of the country by the indebted residents (Figure 14.1). The domestic income (in national money, NM) paid by the indebted residents would be transferred to their country in exchange for the foreign income (in foreign money, FM) that it pays to the rest of the world. The debt incurred by the population being of an international (inter-national) nature, it is normal that their country takes it on; yet to the extent that it takes on the burden of external debt servicing it must be compensated for in domestic money.

The question that must be asked, therefore, is whether under the present system of international payments the servicing of external debt carried out by the country replaces that of its residents or whether the two payments are in addition to each other. To answer this, it is enough to observe that no country earns the domestic income spent by its residents in their external debt servicing. We are thus led to the conclusion that under the present monetary system external debt servicing entails a double payment, which deprives the indebted country of both an external and a domestic income (Figure 14.2). In order for external debt to be effectively paid it is

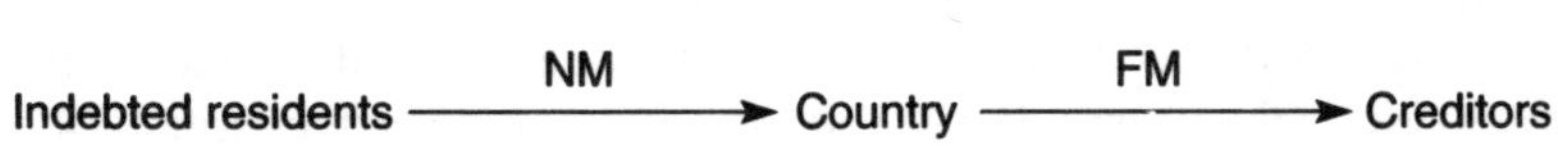

Figure 14.1

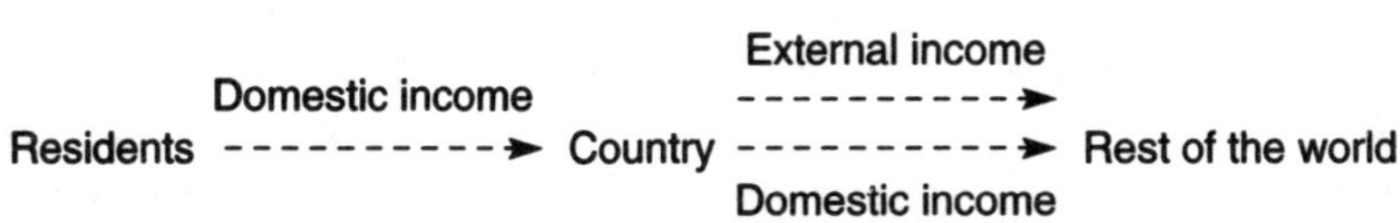

Figure 14.2

therefore necessary that residents save part of their domestic income and, additionally, that the country earns an income of external origin. This last condition is fulfilled if the indebted country achieves a trade surplus equal to or greater than the amount it has to pay, in interest and principal, to the creditor countries. Let us start our analysis by studying this case.

The case of net commercial exports

To illustrate the whole set of possibilities inherent in this case it is necessary to consider two extreme situations: that in which the external debt servicing carried out by the residents of W_w corresponds to the amount of the country's net trade surplus, and that in which it corresponds only to a fraction of its external gain.

The case in which the payment of external debt equals the country's net trade surplus

Let us give further proof of the pathological servicing of external debt by distinguishing between two possible methods of payment adopted by countries of set W.

First possibility

Let us first recall that external debt servicing is carried out, simultaneously, by country and residents, and that, while residents pay in domestic money, countries of set W are forced to pay in a strong currency, MS. According to the first method, the payment of the residents is immediately converted into MS through the purchase of a sum of foreign currency equivalent to that obtained in exchange for net commercial exports.

Let us start from the trade surplus of any country whatsoever of set W, W_w, whose residents pay for their foreign debt in a strong currency, MS (Figure 14.3). The unilateral transfer of bank deposits in money S by W_w's residents can take place only if they spend part of their domestic income on the purchase of a sum of money S equivalent to that earned by their country (represented by the Central Bank) through its net commercial exports.

The duplication of external debt servicing is proved if it is possible to show that, even in this case, the purchase of MS implies an equivalent positive cost for the indebted country. This could be done by referring to the principle of reciprocity introduced in Chapter 13 (p. 300). Since the transfer of the bank deposits in MS is unilateral, it is certain, in fact, that W_w cannot find the vehicular money needed for the servicing of its external debt for free. However, having assumed that the country does not suffer from any direct loss of domestic income, the cost of the purchase of MS does not give rise to a new debt to the rest of the world. In which sense is

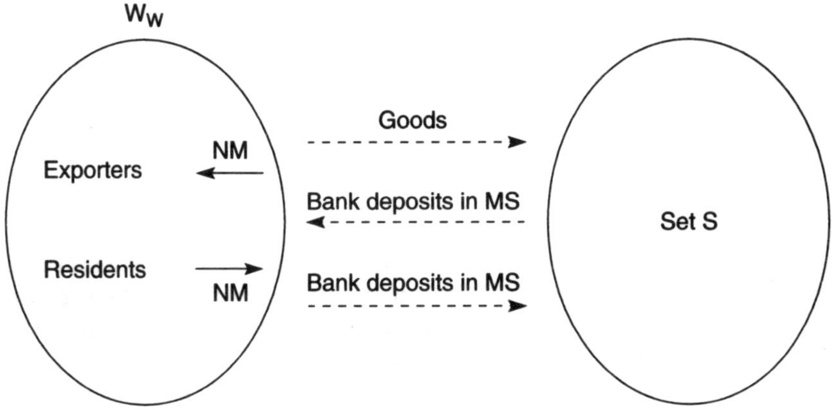

Figure 14.3

it therefore possible to speak of a second payment of the debt? The answer is straightforward: the compulsory purchase of MS defines a net demand that leads to the devaluation of country W_w's national currency.

Let us first consider the effect of net commercial exports on exchange rates. The selling of goods and services to countries S defines a demand for money W_w in terms of money S. It must thus be established whether this net demand leads to an increase in the exchange rate of MW_w with regard to MS. If this were the case, commercial exports would cause a revaluation of W_w's money which would balance the devaluation due to external debt servicing. Globally, the weak currency would be equally supplied and demanded and its exchange rate would not vary. External debt servicing would be a perfectly equilibrated transaction and the asymmetry inherent in it would have no negative repercussion for W_w. In reality, the demand for money W_w exerted by money S has no effect on their exchange rate. The fact is that, as we are taught by the neoclassical theory of supply and demand, a net demand gives rise to an increase in prices only on condition that supply is not infinitely elastic. On the contrary, if supply adjusts immediately and totally to the increase in demand, prices are bound to remain stable. In the case that we are examining, the net demand for money W_w is always matched by a new and equivalent supply since the entry of foreign currencies corresponding to net commercial exports leads to an equivalent creation of domestic money to the benefit of the exporting agents (Table 14.1). The demand for money W_w is thus satisfied by a supply which instantaneously adjusts to it. Hence, since the gap between supply and demand is immediately filled by the creation carried out by the banking system of country W_w, the payment of the trade surplus does not provoke any variation in the exchange rate of the two currencies, MS and MW_w.

Table 14.1

Banking system of W_w	
Liabilities	*Assets*
Exporting firms equiv. in MW_w of x MS	Banking system of set S x MS

Yet, the same conclusion does not apply in the case of external debt servicing. Residents of W_w are forced to purchase MS to pay their foreign debt in a strong currency, thereby exerting a demand for MS which can obviously not be satisfied through monetary creation. The banking system of country W_w has not the power to issue money S, so that the residents' net demand refers to a limited quantity of MS (that corresponding to the country's trade surplus). This time the gap between supply and demand is positive and leads to a decrease in the price of MW_w relatively to MS.

If the servicing of foreign debt defined a reciprocal exchange between debtor and creditor countries, money W_w would simultaneously be supplied and demanded in terms of MS and vice versa. In this case, external debt servicing would not suffer from any anomaly and the indebted country could carry it out without having to take on both its financial and its monetary cost. More precisely still, this second cost would not even need to be mentioned, since every country could obtain the vehicular money required for its international payments gratuitously. The unilaterality of external debt servicing breaks down the symmetry, so that the vehicular money can only be obtained through an onerous purchase. In our example, residents of country W_w must give up part of their domestic resources in order to have access to a sum of bank deposits in money S equal to that obtained by the Central Bank because of W_w's trade surplus. Even though the Central Bank records a positive entry of money S, this does not mean that W_w's residents can obtain it gratuitously. On the contrary, they must buy it on the exchange market (a market in which Central Banks intervene only to safeguard the external value of their national currencies), by giving in exchange an equivalent sum of their domestic income. Now, besides the loss of purchasing power suffered by the indebted residents, this purchase has similar implications for their country. If external debt servicing entailed only a transfer of national income from the indebted residents to their Central Bank, everything would take place in accordance with monetary neutrality and there would be no reason to speak of a double payment. In reality, however, the purchase of money S carried out by the indebted residents of country W_w leads to the devaluation of their national currency. The second payment of the debt coincides thus with the sacrifice imposed on the whole country by the loss of value of MW_w relative to MS.

Besides having serviced its external debt in real terms, through the net exports of goods and services, country W_w is forced to suffer a loss in the value of its domestic currency. At this point only two alternatives are available to it: re-establishing the internal value of its currency through a new foreign loan, or sacrificing a double quantity of goods and services to obtain a single amount of foreign currency. In the second case, the country would avoid incurring a new debt, yet, in order to obtain a sum of MS equivalent to the one used to service its external debt, it has to transfer to the rest of the world a double quantity of goods and services, which amounts to the gratuitous transfer of the exports corresponding to external debt servicing (since, in exchange for 2 units of domestic goods and services, it only gets 1 unit of MS which, instead of increasing its wealth, simply restores the previous level of its domestic income).

Instead, in the first case devaluation would be avoided through the demand for MW_w exerted by the foreign purchasers of non-monetary claims newly exported by W_w. In contrast with commercial exports, the sale of domestic securities to the rest of the world does not imply a net emission of national money; the demand for MW_w would therefore not be matched by an equivalent increase in supply and would lead to a rise in the exchange rate of MW_w relative to MS. Devaluation due to external debt servicing would thus be avoided, but at the price of a new foreign loan which, despite the real sacrifice endured by W_w would take the country back to its previous level of indebtedness.

Let us develop this argument further and suppose country W_w to be able to finance the payment of interest and principal through a net sale of goods and services. Being paid through a transfer of bank deposits in money S, W_w's net commercial exports elicit an emission of domestic currency to the profit of the exporting agents. Let us refer to a numerical example, entering these transactions in the balance sheet of W_w's banking system (Table 14.2). Because of the monetisation of the external gain, the income available in

Table 14.2

Banking system of country W_w			
Liabilities			*Assets*
Income holders	100 MW	Domestic output	100 MW
Exporting firms	10 MW	Banking system of set S	1 MS
Income holders	100 MW	Domestic output	90 MW
		Banking system of set S	1 MS

country W_w remains unaltered despite the decrease in domestic output. After the payment of net commercial exports, the internal product (whose value is of 90 units) thus has a price of 100 MW_w.

Having supposed that the whole amount of net commercial exports is devoted to external debt servicing and that the exchange rate between money W_w and money S is of 10 MW_w for 1 MS, we now have to enter the transfer of 1 MS in favour of the creditor countries (Table 14.3). Being carried out on behalf of country W_w's residents, the transfer of the bank deposits in money S implies the loss of 10 units of domestic income, whose total amount is thus reduced from 100 to 90 units. However, it must not be forgotten that, despite being reduced because of commercial exports, domestic output has a price of 100 units. The domestic income still available after the servicing of external debt is therefore not enough to guarantee the sale of domestic output. Confronted with this situation, country W_w can only obtain the missing income from abroad. In other words, the indebted country is forced to incur a new debt to the extent that it sacrifices its external gains to the servicing of its previous debt: it is through this new debt that the country can recover the domestic income transferred abroad for the purchase of the bank deposits in money S carried out by the indebted residents (Table 14.4). Book-keeping entries show how the income available in country W_w corresponds to that required for the purchase of domestic output only on condition that the income devoted to external debt servicing is replaced through a new foreign loan. The new debt of country W_w is due to the fact that the servicing of the initial debt entails a double loss: that of the goods and services exported as a surplus and that of an equivalent amount of domestic income. Hence, while net commercial exports allow reduction of the external debt, the sacrifice of domestic income forces W_w to incur a new debt. Globally, W_w's debt remains unchanged although it pays the rest of the world in real goods and services.

If the system of international payments complied with logic, countries W would reduce their debts to the extent of their net commercial exports. The sacrifice of domestic income would not be added to that of the income

Table 14.3

Banking system of country W_w

Liabilities			*Assets*
Banking system of set S	1 MS	Indebted residents	10 MW
Income holders	90 MW	Domestic output (price 100 MW)	90 MW

Table 14.4

Banking system of set W			
Liabilities			*Assets*
Income holders	90 MW	Domestic output (price 100 MW)	90 MW
Income holders	10 MW	Banking system of set S (new debt)	1 MS

obtained from abroad, so that every single country would benefit from the entire amount of its national income. It is perfectly normal for a country to give up its external gain in order to service the debt incurred with the rest of the world, but it is illogical to force it to additionally give up that part of domestic saving which corresponds to its net exports of goods and services. As it is incurred by the country's residents, external debt must obviously be paid by them. Yet, it is obvious also that if it is the country (set of residents) which carries out the payment on their behalf, the residents' outlay must not be added to that of their country. Unfortunately, the present system of international payments is not always logical. The country's payment is added to that of its residents, which amounts to the double loss of a domestic income and an external one. The country's re-indebtedness is thus the unavoidable consequence of the loss of domestic income accompanying external debt servicing. As shown in Table 14.4, the internal equilibrium between output and national income can only be re-established by resorting to a new foreign loan, through which the banking system of W_w balances the loss of income due to external debt servicing with an equivalent import of foreign bank deposits.

Second possibility

Let us refer to our previous example and suppose that indebted residents, R_1, pay their foreign creditors by transferring to them a sum of bank deposits in national currency equivalent to the amount of money S earned by their country through the net export of goods and services (Figure 14.4). A foreign debt can effectively be serviced by the indebted country only if it is paid for with an income of external origin. In our example, country W_w has indeed at its disposal an income which it gets from the rest of the world in exchange for its net commercial exports (1). The positive servicing of the debt implies therefore the transfer of this income from W_w to the creditor country, C_c (2).

As far as the payment carried out by W_w's residents (3) is concerned we can observe that it leads to a reduction in the country's domestic income,

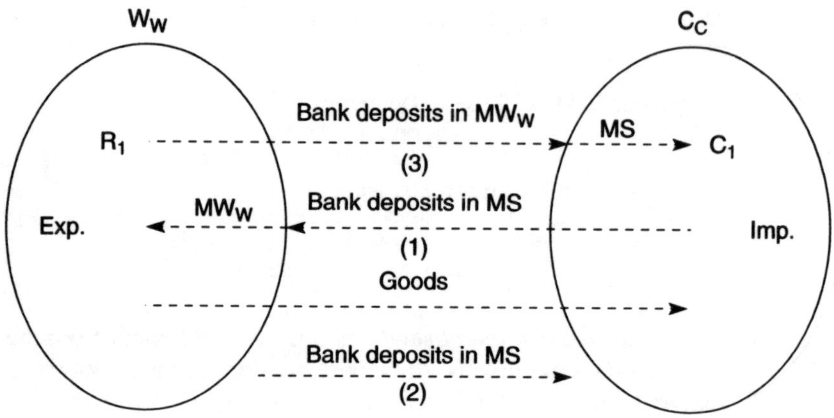

Figure 14.4

so that, on the whole, the servicing of external debt entails the loss of both an external and an internal income. Now, since every income transferred abroad is necessarily deposited in its country of origin, because of the payment made by W_w's residents the residents of C_c become the owner of part of their bank deposits. Country W_w can thus recover the domestic income paid to C_c only by incurring a new debt. In other words, since external debt servicing entails a reduction in national income, its reconstitution can be achieved only if the country can recover the rights over its bank deposits, that is, only if they are conveyed to it by a new loan in money S (Figure 14.5). Once the compensation between the bank deposits in money S held by W_w and those in MW held by C_c has been taken into account, transactions can be represented as shown in Figure 14.6. The new creditors of W_w, C_2, give part of their income in MS to their country, which transfers to residents R_2 of W_w the bank deposits previously obtained from R_1. Through the new sale of non-monetary claims country W_w is thus able to find the amount of national income needed for the purchase of its domestic output. Let us enter these transactions into the balance sheet of W_w's banking system (Table 14.5). Let us dispel a last doubt. From a superficial observation of the book-keeping entries of Table 14.5 it could be deduced that the foreign currencies obtained from the rest of the world in exchange for the country's net commercial exports (1) are definitively acquired by W_w, whose official reserves are thus increased correspondingly. External debt servicing would therefore be carried out by the indebted residents only, and not also by their set, a metaphysical entity with no match in factual reality. If this were true, the anomaly we have been denouncing so tenaciously would be disproved and the re-indebtedness needed to restore the level of domestic income would be balanced by an

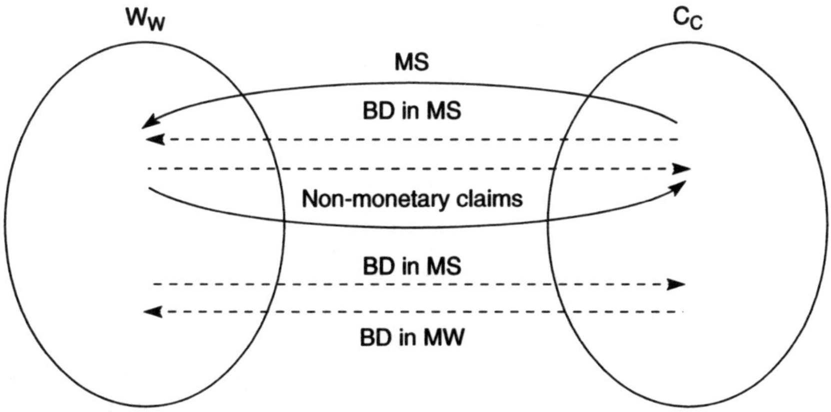

Figure 14.5

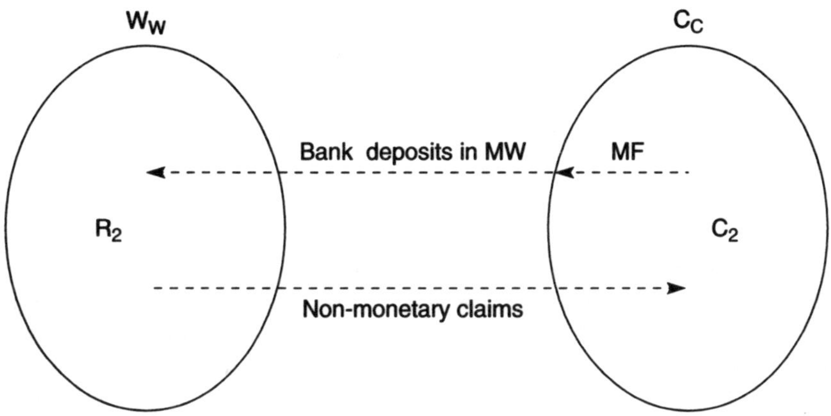

Figure 14.6

increase in the country's official reserves. Yet, the complexity of the problem requires a further analytical effort. An increase in official reserves is not enough to infer that the country does not suffer from any additional loss because of its residents' external debt servicing. On the contrary, the origin of the income which has to replace the one lost by residents R_1 leads us to the opposite conclusion. Having being lent to R_2, part of the income entered to the benefit of W_w's residents is owned by the creditor country C_c and will go on being part of its assets unless the bank deposits in money W_w owned by C_c can be compensated for by an equivalent sum of bank deposits in money S owned by W_w (Figure 14.7).

Table 14.5

Banking system of country W_w

	Liabilities			*Assets*
	Income holders	100 MW_w	Domestic output	100 MW_w
(1)	Exporting firms	10 MW_w	Rest of the world	1 MS
(2)	Creditor countries	10 MW_w	Residents R_1	10 MW_w
	Income holders	90 MW_w	Domestic output	90 MW_w
	Creditor countries	10 MW_w	Rest of the world	1 MS
(3)	Residents R_2	10 MW_w	Creditor countries	10 MW_w
	Income holders	100 MW_w	Domestic output	90 MW_w
			Rest of the world	1 MS

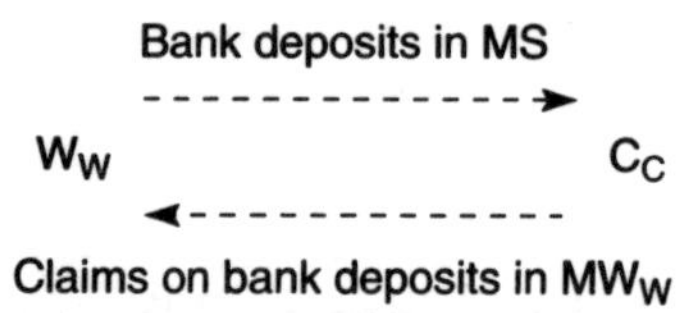

Figure 14.7

After compensation it appears that, in order to service its external debt and to restore the level of its domestic income, country W_w is bound to sacrifice the receipts of its trade surplus and to incur a new debt of 1 MS. This double sacrifice is the consequence of the anomaly inherent in today's external debt servicing. Having to transfer to foreign creditors part of its internal income, country W_w must convert the currency spent by its residents R_1 into money S, and it is this conversion (corresponding to the purchase of the vehicular money required to convey the payment of R_1) which is the source of the problem. If countries belonged to a single monetary area, international payments would imply only financial transfers similar to those taking place among regions of a single country. Monetary homogeneity would allow each of them to obtain the vehicle needed to carry out its payments (inclusive of external debt servicing) gratuitously. In this case, the conversion among incomes of different countries would take place through a perfectly neutral mechanism, and no country would be bound to service its debt both in real goods and in money. Unfortunately, the absence of an international Bank acting as a clearing house of national Central Banks sanctions the heterogeneity of domestic currencies and condemns the countries of set W to the double servicing of their external debt. As claimed by Keynes in his debate with Ohlin and Rueff on the payment of German war reparation, debtor countries must find the domestic resources required to finance their payment (budgetary problem) and, additionally, purchase the vehicle necessary to transfer them to the creditor countries (transfer problem). Because of this purchase indebted countries suffer from a further loss of domestic resources, which cancels the advantage derived from the positive servicing of their external debt.

> For I hold that the process of paying the debt has the effect of causing the money in which the debt is expressed to be worth a larger quantity of German-produced goods than it was before or would have been apart from the payment of the debt; so that the population of the debtor State suffers a loss of purchasing power greater than the original equivalent of the amount of the debt.
>
> (Keynes 1929c: 405)

Confronted with this loss of purchasing power, the indebted countries can restore the level of their internal income only through a new foreign loan, which takes them back to their starting point, thus transforming external debt servicing into a self-defeating process.

The case in which the country's net trade surplus is greater than its external debt servicing

Let us suppose that the amount of net commercial exports of country W_w is twice the size as the external debt servicing carried out by its residents. Since the analysis is not fundamentally different from that developed on p. 306, we shall only emphasise its peculiarities. Let us start with the payment of the residents. As in the previous case, this implies a transfer of domestic income which must be balanced by a new and equivalent entry of money S. Yet whereas the level of domestic resources was previously restored through a new foreign loan, now the country recovers its internal income through a further trade surplus. Instead of incurring a new debt, the country gives up an equivalent amount of goods and services (Figure 14.8). Half of the foreign exchange earned through net commercial exports is paid out by the country as external debt servicing, while the other half is used to recover the domestic income transferred to the rest of the world by the indebted residents. Globally, country W_w gives up the entire amount of its net trade surplus, equal to 20 units of MS, to see its foreign debt decrease by 10 units.

Once again, and despite appearances to the contrary, W_w incurs a new debt to the extent that it effectively services its debt. The only difference with the case analysed on p. 306 is that the new debt is now balanced by a further export of goods and services. It is not fundamentally different to

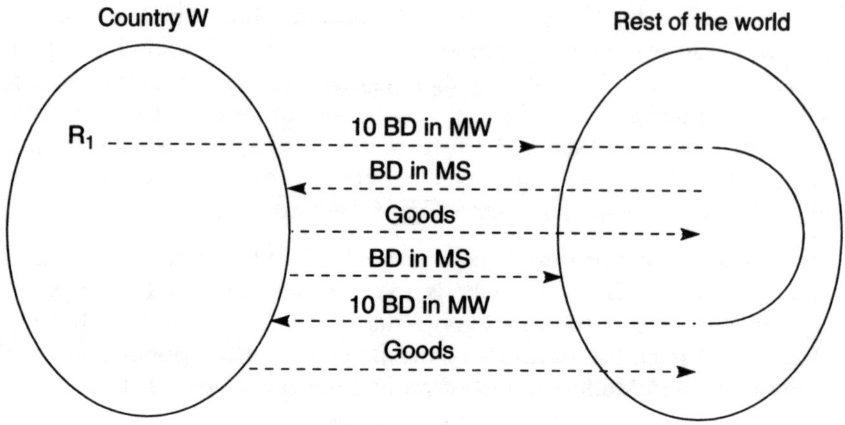

Figure 14.8

claim that, having been a net exporter and having serviced 10 units of its debt, the country incurs a new debt of 10, or that, having a trade surplus of 20 units and servicing its debt of 10, the country loses 10 units of its foreign income: while in the first case the country's global external debt does not decrease despite its positive real payment of 10 units, in the second case it decreases by 10 units even though the country's net real transfer to the rest of the world is of 20 units. In both cases the country suffers a loss of 10 units which increases its foreign debt (relative to the level it should reach because of the country's foreign earnings) and which confirms the exist- ence of the double servicing of external debt.

Before analysing the situation of those countries which can service their foreign debt only by raising a new loan with the rest of the world, let us stress the paradoxical nature of external debt servicing by examining its negative consequences over the external gain realised by trade surplus countries of set W.

Origin and consequences of the double servicing of external debt carried out by trade surplus countries

Let us reconsider the example in which external debt servicing is carried out by any country whatsoever of set W, W_w, whose net commercial exports amount to 1 MS (1 MS = 10 MW_w). The net sale of goods and services needed to obtain the bank deposits in money S required to pay the debt and their subsequent transfer to the creditor countries are represented in Figure 14.9. External debt servicing defines a unilateral transfer in favour of creditor countries which, being inconsistent with the principle of reciprocity developed in Chapter 13 (p. 300), forces country W_w to acquire at

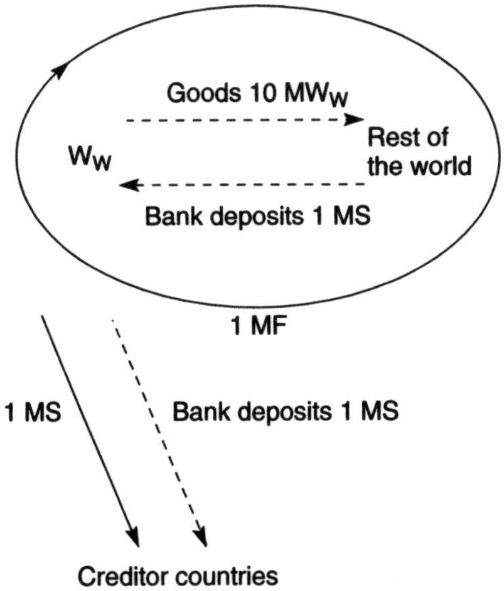

Figure 14.9

considerable cost the vehicular money necessary to convey bank deposits in money S. Hence, W_w has to sacrifice part of its domestic resources in order to transfer the deposit in MS already earned through the net export of an equivalent part of its national output to its foreign creditors. The fact is that the debt must also be paid for by the residents who have first incurred it. Even though the country earns a positive amount of foreign currencies with which it can service its external debt, its indebted residents must still transfer abroad an equivalent sum of domestic income. This second payment is redundant and implies the re-indebtedness of W_w, which, in order to restore the internal relationship between income and output, must either transfer new non-monetary claims to the rest of the world, or double its net commercial exports. Let us represent the loss of domestic income and the consequent new loan (new export of goods and services) by taking into account the fact that the payments of the residents are carried out by W_w's banking system (Figure 14.10). As can be noted, we have not specified if the money used in the sale of W_w's new financial claims (or goods) is that of set S or of set W. Since it plays a purely vehicular function (defined by its circular flow), it is irrelevant to identify it with one or the other. As far as foreign bank deposits are concerned, it is clear that they are defined in money S since the currency spent by the purchasers of W_w's securities (or goods) is MS. Yet it is also evident that the bank deposits in money S transferred to W_w by the rest of the world are equivalent to the bank deposits in money W_w paid to the rest of the world

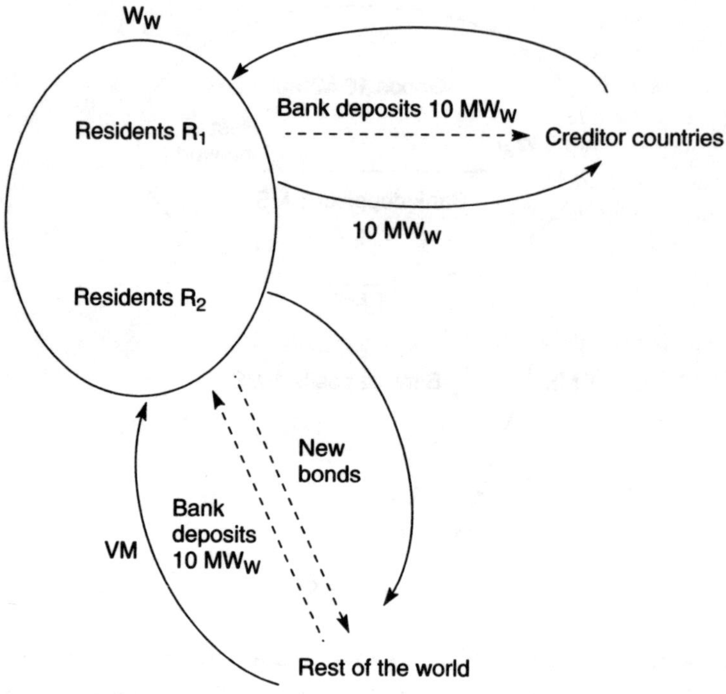

Figure 14.10

by W_w's indebted residents. After compensation it is therefore correct to enter the new debt (export) as an exchange between new non-monetary claims (goods) issued (produced) by W_w and the bank deposits in money W_w previously transferred to foreign creditors.

Because of the anomaly inherent in external debt servicing, the external income earned through net commercial exports is put in jeopardy. More precisely, it can be shown that the double charge put on the indebted countries cancels their foreign trade gains to the extent of their external debt servicing. In fact, being forced to incur a new debt to recover from the partial loss of its domestic income, country W_w allows creditor countries to import goods and services giving in exchange the very income transferred to them by its residents. In our example, country W_w transfers 1 MS of bank deposits in money S and 10 MW_w of bank deposits in money W_w to the rest of the world. The second transfer is unilateral. Thus, creditor countries obtain an income of W_w with which they can finance their net imports from that country. In other words, they get both the goods and the income needed to purchase them. Hence, since creditor countries can import without paying, the debtor country does not realise any positive gain out of its trade surplus.

Let us avoid any possible misunderstanding. To the extent that a country's exports of goods and services are greater than its imports, it realises an external gain: this is a fact. This does not mean, however, that if the country sacrifices this gain in order to service its foreign debt, the residents do not additionally transfer abroad an equivalent amount of their domestic income. Because of the double payment of external debts, part of W_w's internal income is gratuitously transferred to the rest of the world, which can thus finance its net commercial imports (Figure 14.11). Having obtained part of the domestic income of W_w without giving anything in exchange for it, the rest of the world can invest it to finance its net purchases of goods and services from W_w. Thus, external debt servicing cancels the external gain of the indebted country, leaving it in the absurd situation of having to incur a new debt or having to sacrifice new net commercial exports in order to effectively service its previous debt.

Let us reformulate the anomaly inherent in external debt servicing. Having to be covered both by the residents and by their own country, external debt servicing entails a double transfer of income to creditor countries. Residents transfer part of their domestic income, while the country has to transfer an equivalent income of external origin. Yet the first transfer cancels the gain in MS realised by the country because of its trade surplus. Hence, even though it has exported more goods and services than it has imported, the country does not obtain the currency required for the servicing of its external debt. Referring to the distinction between monetary and financial aspects of the payment we can say that the purchase of a vehicular money by W_w implies a loss of domestic income. Before servicing its debt, the country has the bank deposits needed to finance it but not the vehicular money required to convey it. Once it has purchased the vehicular money (that is, after the payment of the debt by the residents), it has the 'vehicle' but it is no longer capable of 'loading' it financially (since the bank

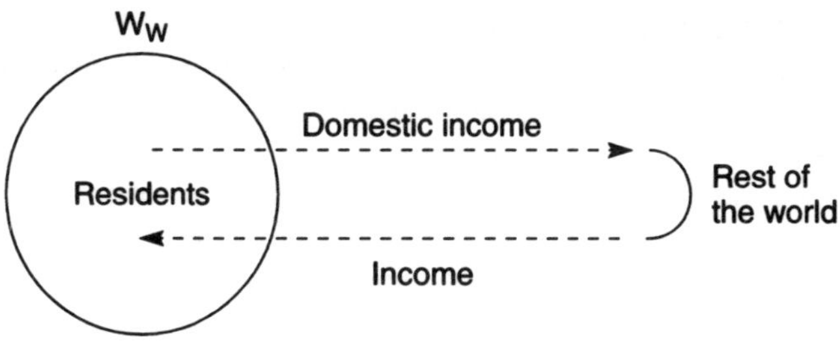

Figure 14.11

deposits in MS are compensated by those in MW_w transferred without counterpart to the creditor countries). In order to service its foreign debt, the country is thus forced to obtain a new loan from the rest of the world or to export new goods and services for an equivalent amount.

Finally, external debt servicing calls for a double payment, in kind (the net commercial exports) and in money (the residents' transfer of income). If the indebted country has a trade surplus, the anomaly of external debt servicing entails the cancellation of the gain in foreign currencies due to the commercial surplus. In its turn, the cancellation of the country's external gain leads either to the need to incur a new and equivalent debt, which takes the country back to its previous level of indebtedness, or to the cancellation of part of a new external gain, which corresponds to a relative increase in the country's debt. It is thus confirmed that, whether it leads to a re-indebtedness of countries of set W or to the sacrifice of new commercial exports, the double payment of external debt has as a consequence the cancellation of an equivalent part of the gain derived from net commercial exports.

External debt servicing when there is no trade surplus

Let us first show that the anomaly of external debt servicing is present even when the servicing of the debt is not based on a positive gain of external origin. The assumptions that must be complied with are two: the absence of an external gain and the necessity, for country W_w, to service its debt in a strong currency, MS. In this context, W_w is forced to get hold of bank deposits in MS through a new sale of non-monetary claims to the rest of the world. To incur a new debt in order to service an old one is a perfectly legitimate operation, which could even prove advantageous if the new loan were obtained at better conditions than the old. The anomaly can therefore not consist in replacing one debt with another one. The problem arises from external debt servicing itself, and not from the commercial and financial operations preceding it. As usual, the payment of the creditor country is carried out both by the indebted residents and by their own country. The former must sacrifice part of their income in domestic money, while the latter must transfer an equivalent sum of bank deposits in money S. Let us show how the two payments give rise to a transfer in favour of the creditor countries, C_c, and their residents.

Two arguments lead to the same result. According to the first, country W_w is forced to pay twice since, in addition to new bonds, it has to transfer the foreign exchange borrowed from the rest of the world *without counterpart*. As in the previous cases, the anomaly stands out better if it is compared with the orderly working of the operations. Let us thus represent, side by side, the actual, pathological scheme and the orderly one (Figure 14.12). For the sake of simplicity we have represented real flows only; the

Figure 14.12

reader will easily notice that, implicit in every transaction, monetary (vehicular) flows are similar to the real ones. Now, it is immediately clear that all the transactions in the right column are perfectly equilibrated, both financially and monetarily, whereas those in the left column show a unilateral transfer from W_w to the rest of the world. The difference between the two systems is already present in operation (2). In the actual key-currencies standard regime, the payment of net imports by countries who are members of set S is carried out through the transfer of bank deposits in money S, and not, as symmetry requires, through the equivalent transfer of goods, services or financial bonds. Hence, while the content of the payment of set W's net imports is made up of real goods (financial securities), that of set S consists of bank deposits.

If symmetry were effectively complied with, the rest of the world would pay for the purchase of W_w's non-monetary claims C_2 with an equivalent amount of non-monetary claims C_3. External debt servicing would thus take place through the exchange of claims C_1, previously transferred by W_w to the rest of the world in exchange for goods and services, with claims C_3, which the rest of the world transfers to W_w in exchange for claims C_2. After compensation it appears that, when the indebted country has no trade surplus, external debt servicing entails the substitution of one debt with another and, therefore, the simple exchange of non-monetary claims between W_w and the creditor countries.

According to the present scheme, on the contrary, the rest of the world acquires the new claims C_2 issued by W_w through a transfer of bank deposits in MS. Since it does not obtain financial claims from the rest of the world, country W_w cannot service its external debt through an exchange of bonds. It is true that even bank deposits are claims but, unlike those transferred by W_w, they are monetary claims whose content is a sum of money S; that is, a mere IOU of set S. Hence, the anomaly arises from the moment a promise to pay becomes the content of the payments carried out by countries S. Country W_w is forced to service its debt by unilaterally transferring the bank deposits obtained in exchange for its real goods (non-monetary claims) C_2. The anomaly is due to the unilaterality of this transfer; that is, to the fact that country W_w does not obtain anything in exchange for the bank deposits transferred to the creditor countries (since, precisely because of its payment, the claims which it gets back from C_c no longer have any positive value). Once it has been paid, the debt is cancelled and, deprived of their value, the corresponding claims cannot represent a counterpart to the bank deposits transferred by W_w.

Let us now analyse the second argument proposed earlier (p. 320). Since it is not linked to the choice of the money used to convey external debt servicing, the anomaly can be explained according to the following scheme, where W_w, C_c, R_1, R_2, C_1 and C_2 represent, respectively, the indebted country, the creditor countries, the indebted residents, the residents exporting new non-monetary claims, the creditors (residents of C_c) and the foreign purchasers of the claims exported by W_w (Figure 14.13). The servicing of external debt is carried out in money W_w by the indebted residents (1). The bank deposits in MW_w transferred by R_1 are entered on the asset side of C_c's banking system, which credits residents C_1, beneficiaries of the payment made by R_1, with an equivalent amount of bank deposits in money S (2). Since country W_w loses the domestic income paid by R_1 to the creditor countries, it has to sell new bonds to C_c in order to re-establish the level of domestic income needed for the sale of national output. Purchased by C_2, the new bonds give rise to a transfer of bank deposits in money S from C_2 to C_c's banking system (3), and of bank deposits in money W_w from C_c's banking system to residents R_2 of country

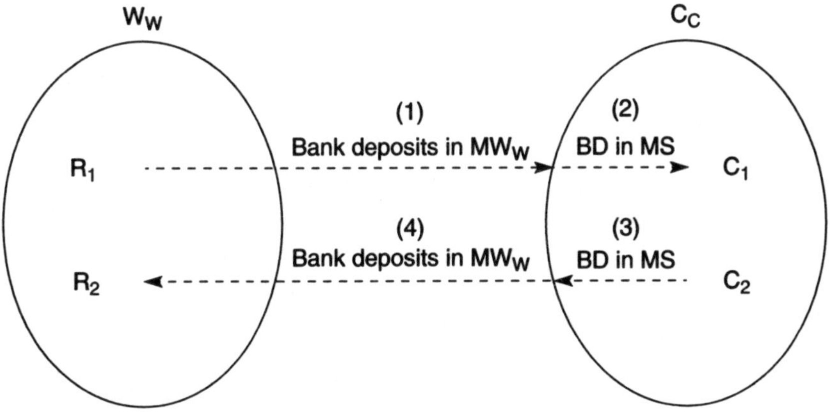

Figure 14.13

W_w (4). Yet this means that, having been borrowed from C_c, part of W_w's domestic income is owned by the rest of the world. Thus, besides re-establishing the previous level of its external debt by selling new financial claims, country W_w suffers an equivalent loss of national income which has been unilaterally transferred to the creditor countries.

Since country W_w must borrow the bank deposits transferred by its residents, the anomaly present in external debt servicing determines a loss of domestic income which cannot be justified by the conversion of the old debt incurred by R_1 into the new debt incurred by R_2.

Let us now show that, in the absence of net commercial exports, the negative effects of the anomaly are temporarily suspended.

The consequences of the double servicing of external debt in the absence of trade surplus

Unlike what happens when W_w has a trade surplus, the selling of bonds does not allow for the effective servicing of external debt. By transferring financial claims to C_c, country W_w merely promises a payment that will take place only when the inflow of bank deposits in MS corresponds to a true gain of external origin and not to a simple loan. Hence, if external debt servicing is postponed, so are the consequences of its anomaly. This does not mean that the anomaly is not already present when external debt servicing is financed by a new foreign loan. Yet its effects are 'frozen' waiting for the country to be effectively able to pay the rest of the world (through a trade surplus).

Let us verify this from an accounting point of view with reference to the two methods of payment analysed on p. 306.

First possibility

Let us record the entries inherent in the new loan incurred by W_w and in the external debt servicing carried out jointly by the country and its residents bearing in mind that, with this first method, the payment in domestic money carried out by the residents is immediately converted into money S through the purchase of foreign currencies on the international monetary market (Table 14.6). Since the inflow of the strong currency (1) is due to an export of financial claims, its domestic monetisation does not give rise to any net creation of national money. In conformity with the principle of the daily balance between loans and deposits, the banking system of country W_w confines itself to the transfer of part of the income deposited by IH to R_2. Hence, since it is not matched by an emission of MW_w, the demand exerted by MS provokes an increase in the value of W_w's national currency. Thus, instead of leading to a devaluation of MW_w, the demand for MS by residents R_1 re-establishes the exchange rate between the two currencies. The net demand for MW_w in terms of MS immediately balances the net demand for MS in terms of MW_w, which cancels its negative effects on the external value of W_w's money.

Second possibility

If external debt servicing implied the transfer of bank deposits in MW_w only, we would have the entries in the balance sheet of country W_w's banking system shown in Table 14.7. The reduction in domestic income caused by the external debt servicing carried out by residents R_1 (1) is matched by the foreign loan granted to residents R_2 (2). The anomaly does not consist in the fact, entirely justified in the absence of net commercial exports, that the country incurs a new debt in order to service its previous debt, but in the loss of domestic income which accompanies its re-indebtedness. The final equilibrium between national income and domestic output must not lead us astray: 10 out of the 100 units of domestic income are owned by the rest of the world, which lends them to W_w. The anomaly is thus confirmed by the fact that, besides incurring a new foreign debt, the country loses, simultaneously and additionally, an equivalent amount of

Table 14.6

Banking system of country W_w

	Liabilities		*Assets*	
	Income holders	100 MW_w	Domestic output	100 MW_w
(1)	Residents	10 MW_w	Rest of the world	1 MS
(2)	Rest of the world	1 MS	Residents R_1	10 MW_S

Table 14.7

	Banking system of country W_w			
	Liabilities			*Assets*
	Income holders	100 MW	Domestic output	100 MW
(1)	Rest of the world	10 MW	Residents R_1	10 MW
(2)	Residents R_2	10 MW	Rest of the world	10 MW
	Income holders	100 MW	Domestic output	100 MW

national income. Yet, despite the gravity of this anomaly, its negative effect is deferred until the country is effectively able to face its external commitments. The absence of trade surpluses puts the country in a kind of 'limbo' where it can momentarily avoid the negative effects of the double servicing of its external debt while constantly renewing its debt position towards the rest of the world.

The negative effect of external debt servicing is not cumulative in time

It is enough to refer to the analysis developed earlier (p. 315) to show that, although external debt servicing of weak-currency countries entails their pathological re-indebtedness, this effect is not produced more than once in the case of amortisation; that is, that, interest apart, external debt servicing implies a single anomalous sacrifice by W_w. If we suppose that the indebted country has a trade surplus of 20 units and that its residents service their foreign debt up to 10 units, the double servicing of the debt due to the conversion of a domestic into an external income leads to the cancellation of half of the gain corresponding to net exports and to the transfer of the other half. Globally, although country W_w sacrifices the whole amount of its foreign gain, 20 units, its debt to the rest of the world decreases by 10 units only. The loss inherent in the double payment is obvious. Yet it is also clear that the double sacrifice of country W_w is sufficient to cancel part of its debt. To the extent that W_w is effectively capable of paying 20 units to its foreign creditors, its debt is definitively reduced by 10 units. This means that the anomaly concerning external debt servicing is not cumulative in time. Every time that foreign debt is serviced, countries W get indebted because of this payment, but only in so far as external debt servicing does not concern the amortisation of the debt generated by the double payment itself.

Let us reconsider our numerical example by analysing what happens in period p_1, when country W_w services its external debt for the first time, and in period p_2, when it sacrifices a new amount of net commercial exports to service the debt generated by the previous double payment in favour of the rest of the world. The first servicing of the debt, carried out by country W_w

and by its residents simultaneously, leads to an equivalent new debt incurred by R_2 which is necessary to re-establish the initial level of domestic income (Figure 14.14). The second servicing of the debt carried out by W_w thanks to its new commercial exports is still related to the debt initially incurred by R_1 (and taken over by R_2 only because of the anomaly inherent in the payment of the debt of R_1). Hence, the indebted country transfers for a second time the income obtained from the rest of the world, which has the effect of momentarily cancelling the payment of the net imports carried out by the creditor countries. The residents of W_w (exporters) are thus still creditors to the rest of the world. This time the compensation can take place, so that the servicing of R_2's external debt (simple repetition of R_1's debt) does not lead to a further debt of W_w's residents (Figure 14.15).

Let us suppose that a country services its external debt of 100 by 10 units

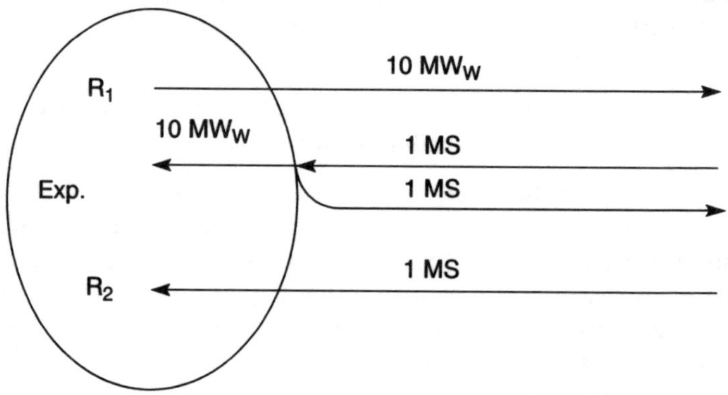

Figure 14.14

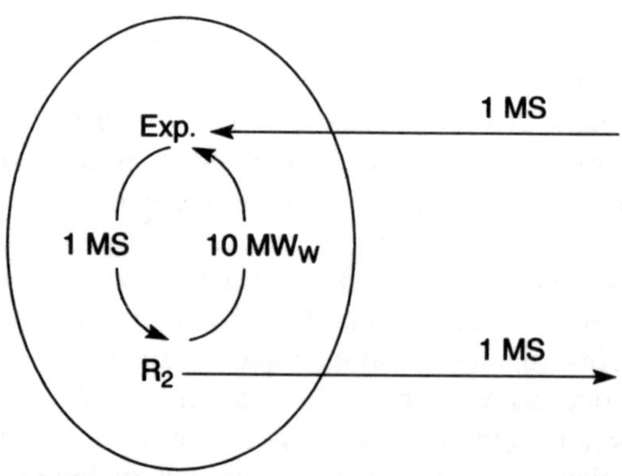

Figure 14.15

and that 7 of these 10 units pay interest and 3 amortisation. Since we assume that the country carries out its first effective debt servicing, because of this payment the country runs into a new debt for 10 units, which maintains its global debt at the level of 100 units. The following external debt servicing, which we suppose to be still equal to 10 units, again concerns the payment of interest and amortisation relative to 100 units. However, amortisation is partly that of the debt incurred because of the external debt servicing carried out in the previous period. According to our analysis, the new external debt servicing is thus only partially the cause of a new, pathological debt for the country: amortisation of the 10 units will not have any further negative effects. Moreover, since this argument applies to every external debt servicing, it follows that the part of amortisation which is not pathological is bound to increase with the increase in amortisation.

Despite the serious difficulties created by the double servicing of external debt it is thus possible for a given country, under favourable circumstances and at the price of huge sacrifice, to decrease the global amount of its foreign debt. Let us briefly show this by referring to our numerical example.

Double servicing and the reduction of debt

The proof that a country can cancel its external debt provided it amortises it twice is implicit in the pathological nature of external debt servicing. If the anomaly which characterises the present system of international payments forces the indebted countries to pay their debt twice, it is clear that every country which is able to pay twice is also able to cancel its foreign debt. The simplest illustration of this is given when a country succeeds in completely amortising its external debt.

Let us suppose that country W_w, whose external debt is of 100 MW_w, can finance, through its external gain, the payment of interest and the total amortisation of its debt. The global payment of W_w, which we assume to be equal to 120 MW_w (100 amortisation and 20 interest), is the cause of a new and equivalent debt, so that its total debt grows from 100 to 120 MW_w. Yet, of these 120 units, 100 have already been paid once. It thus follows that, if in the following period W_w succeeds in fully paying its debt again (for example paying 30 MW_w in interest and 120 in amortisation), its initial debt of 100 MW_w will be totally cancelled. Hence, it will still have to service a debt of 50 MW_w only, of which 20 units have already been paid once. Adding the interest on 50 MW_w (which we assume to be equal to 10 MW_w), in the third period country W_w can further reduce its debt to 40 units by paying 60 MW_w. Finally, if it obtains a new external gain of 110 MW_w country W_w will be able to completely cancel its debt to the rest of the world, the remaining debt (40 MW_w + interest) being entirely covered by the credit corresponding to its trade surplus. Let us summarise our argument in a simple table (Table 14.8).

Taking into account the mechanisms which lead to the re-indebtedness of those countries which are capable of servicing their external debt, we can now resume the statistical analysis sketched in the previous chapter.

A statistical approach to the double servicing of external debt

As the reader will remember, the analysis of the statistical data referring to Brazil, Mexico, Portugal, India and Nigeria between 1980 and 1991 shows the existence of a significant discrepancy between the effective amount of their external debt and that which can be explained on the basis of their economic transactions with the rest of the world. Despite all the reservations regarding the use of imperfect statistical data, it is interesting to compare those results with the amount of external debt servicing effectively carried out in those years by our five countries.

Because of the huge amounts these countries have to pay in interest, their external gains have almost never been enough to provide for the effective payment of amortisation (Nigeria in 1980 and 1990 is the only exception), so that their pathological re-indebtedness must be essentially attributed to the payment of interest. More precisely, the impact of the vice must be calculated taking into account that the payment of interest entails a new and equivalent debt only if the country has an external gain of twice as much as the sum paid in interest. If the indebted country has a current account surplus equal to the interest due, double payment can take place. The country is thus forced to incur a new debt in order to restore the level of its current account surplus pathologically decreased by the servicing of its external debt. If the balance of current accounts is even, only half of the interest can effectively be paid. Since the payment must be double, if 100 units are paid in interest only 50 of them correspond to an effective payment of the interest due, while the remaining 50, uncovered, give rise to a new debt. The anomalous re-indebtedness is only partial if the balance of current accounts is slightly negative and nil if the deficit is equal to or

Table 14.8

Initial debt	100	
External debt servicing		120 (20 interest + 100 amortisation)
New debt	120	
External debt servicing		150 (30 interest + 120 amortisation)
New debt	50	
External debt servicing		60 (10 interest + 50 amortisation)
New debt	40	

greater than the sum paid in interest (Table 14.9). The amount of Mexico's pathological re-indebtedness corresponds to the part of the interest which it has managed to pay twice. For example, in 1985 Mexico had a current account surplus of $1,130 million and paid $10,220 million in interest; this means that it was effectively able to pay $1,130 million twice while the remaining $9,090 million paid in interest entailed a positive debt servicing of only $9,090 ÷ 2 = $4,545 million. Globally, in 1985 Mexico's double payment was therefore of $5,675 millions, which was the amount of its anomalous re-indebtedness in that year. For the whole period taken into consideration, the total amount of the pathological debt incurred by Mexico is emblematically similar to that of the unjustified variation in debt pointed out in Chapter 13. The same result is reached by analysing the statistical data relating to Brazil (Table 14.10) and Portugal (Table 14.11). As in the case of Mexico, the double servicing of external debt has been calculated with reference to the effective payment of interest since, despite the current account surpluses of Brazil in 1984 and 1988 and of Portugal in 1985 and 1986, neither country has effectively been able to positively amortise its foreign debt. Once this is taken into consideration it appears that even in these two cases the global unjustifiable variation in debt can be explained statistically by referring to the data which measure, albeit approximately, the double servicing of external debt. Despite its important peculiarities, the case of India does not jeopardise this conclusion (Table 14.12). During the period that we have been considering, the total increase in India's external debt can be entirely explained by referring to its current account deficits,

Table 14.9 Mexico

		1980–91 *Total*
(1)	Unjustifiable variation in debt	+ 43,286
(2)	Effective interest payments	39,395
(3)	Effective principal repayments	0
(4)	Anomalous re-indebtedness (2) + (3)	39,395

Table 14.10 Brazil

		1980–91 *Total*
(1)	Unjustifiable variation in debt	+ 30,420
(2)	Effective interest payments	28,145
(3)	Effective principal repayments	0
(4)	Anomalous re-indebtedness (2) + (3)	28,145

Table 14.11 Portugal

		1980–91	*Total*
(1)	Unjustifiable variation in debt		+ 8,605
(2)	Effective interest payments		6,022
(3)	Effective principal repayments		0
(4)	Anomalous re-indebtedness (2) + (3)		6,022

Table 14.12 India

		1980–91	*Total*
(1)	Unjustifiable variation in debt		+ 3,534
(2)	Effective interest payments		1,132
(3)	Effective principal repayments		0
(4)	Anomalous re-indebtedness (2) + (3)		1,132

Table 14.13 Nigeria

		1980–91	*Total*
(1)	Unjustifiable variation in debt		+ 30,813
(2)	Effective interest payments		10,160
(3)	Effective principal repayments		3,021
(4)	Anomalous re-indebtedness (2) + (3)		13,181

the variation in its official reserves and the direct investments it has benefited from. Instead of representing an exception to the theory, the absence of any pathological re-indebtedness confirms it, since India's successive deficits have not allowed for the double payment of even a small fraction of interest. Statistical data are thus in accordance with the results of theoretical analysis and, as is also shown in the case of Nigeria (Table 14.13), it cannot be denied that this convergence is so striking that it cannot be considered as sheer chance.

Nigeria is one of the few countries which has succeeded in positively repaying part of the principal. In the years 1980, 1985 and 1990 its current account surpluses were of the order of \$5,127, \$2,566 and \$5,126 million respectively, while its interest payments were \$911, \$1,735 and \$1,793 million. In order to calculate the anomalous impact of external debt servicing we have also taken into consideration the effective double payment of the principal which Nigeria has been carrying out in these years, bearing in mind that, unlike interest payments, amortisation gives rise to a single pathological effect in time. For example, in 1980 Nigeria's current account surplus of $5,127 million was enough to allow for the double payment of interest ($911 million) and for an effective repayment of the principal of $2,103 million, while the surplus of 1985, $2,566 million, enabled the country to pay $1,735 million in interest but was not enough to allow for the effective amortisation of its external debt since the $831 million still available after interest payments was entirely absorbed by the payment of the pathological debt ($2,103 million) formed in 1980. Globally, the theory accounts for an anomalous re-indebtedness which is less than half the amount of the unjustified debt incurred by Nigeria between 1980 and 1991. Yet, despite this discrepancy, which is partially imputable to the insufficient precision of statistical data, even the case of Nigeria shows how the effective total amount of debt of the countries examined here can be significantly explained by taking into account the negative consequences of external debt servicing.

EXTERNAL DEBT SERVICING AS CARRIED OUT BY STRONG-CURRENCY COUNTRIES

Since the anomaly of external debt servicing is not contingent, it must apply even when the payment is carried out by countries of set S. The analysis is analogous to that worked out in the previous section and could easily be summarised if the use of a national currency as a vehicle of international payments did not put strong-currency countries in a particular situation which is worth examining in some detail. In this section we shall endeavour to show how a country of set S, S_w, can be confronted both with the formation of external debt and with its servicing in a totally different way from that which weak-currency countries are faced with.

The formation of S_w's external debt

It is useful to recall here that the pathology of external debt servicing originates from the fact that, lacking a common monetary area, national currencies are fundamentally heterogeneous. The need to convert heterogeneous currencies entails a double payment every time domestic income is transferred abroad. Thus, not only external debt servicing, but also the payment of net commercial imports is of a pathological nature. When their external debt is formed, weak-currency countries pay for their net imports of goods and services twice, both in domestic and in strong currency. However, in the same transaction countries of set W also benefit from a double payment which balances the one they are bound to carry out. The purchase of non-monetary claims issued by set W in order to finance its trade deficit implies in fact a transfer of domestic income by the rest of the world which corresponds to a double payment in favour of countries W. The final result is a reciprocal transfer of national income which neutralises the anomaly present in each unilateral transfer.

By referring to the distinction between the monetary and financial aspects of this transaction, we can say that the exchange between the commodities transferred by the rest of the world and the monetary claims transferred by countries W complies with the vehicular use of money. Hence, since the whole operation corresponds to an exchange and not to a unilateral transfer, the monetary cost is cancelled for both transactors, W and S, who can thus provide the reciprocal transfer of their domestic incomes by taking advantage of the circular use of a vehicular money. Let us represent the exchange between set W and set S and the unilateral (pathological) transfers which are thus compensated (Figure 14.16). The purchases of set W as well as that of set S are pathological since in both cases the transfer of bank deposits in domestic money implies a loss for the residents and for their country. The sacrifice is double since, despite the transfer of part of their domestic income, each country (whether it imports goods or non-monetary claims) incurs a debt towards the other. The joining of these two pathological operations allows for the compensation of their effects through the cancellation of the two countries' reciprocal debts brought about by the transfer of their bank deposits in foreign currency (Figure 14.17). Paying for their net commercial imports, weak-currency countries comply with the rule according to which it is the real content of the payment and not the instrument used to convey it that makes up its effectiveness. In the same way, strong-currency countries also comply with this rule to the extent that they finance their net purchases of goods and services through the sale of equivalent non-monetary claims.

When the debt of a strong-currency country S_w derives from the net sale of non-monetary claims carried out by its residents, the formation of its debt entails a reciprocal transfer similar to the one which is implied in the formation of weak-currency countries' debt and the analysis follows the same path as that applying to W_w. On the contrary, if S_w pays for its net purchases by simply transferring bank deposits in money S, its debt is formed through a unilateral transfer of income and is, therefore, of a pathological nature (Figure 14.18). The bank deposits in MS_w are monetary claims corresponding to the debt of the banking system in which they are formed. By transferring bank deposits in MS_w, country S_w acknowledges its debt to the rest of the world, postponing its effective payment until it becomes a net exporter of goods and services. The pathological nature of the operation thus consists in the fact that S_w's net commercial imports are simultaneously and additionally paid by the importers and by their country: the debt of S_w's banking system towards the exporting countries is added to the transfer of an equivalent sum of domestic income. Unlike what happens for weak-currency countries, however, S_w can avoid the negative

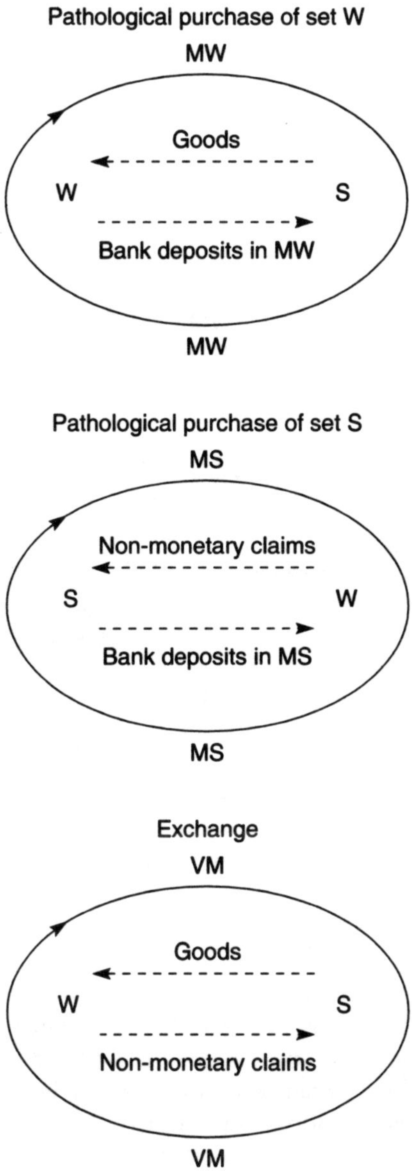

Figure 14.16

effects of the double payment as it can finance its net purchases of goods and services by transferring its monetary claims, that is, a sum of bank deposits in national money; while the countries of set W must purchase the monetary vehicle needed to transfer their internal income, S_w can use its

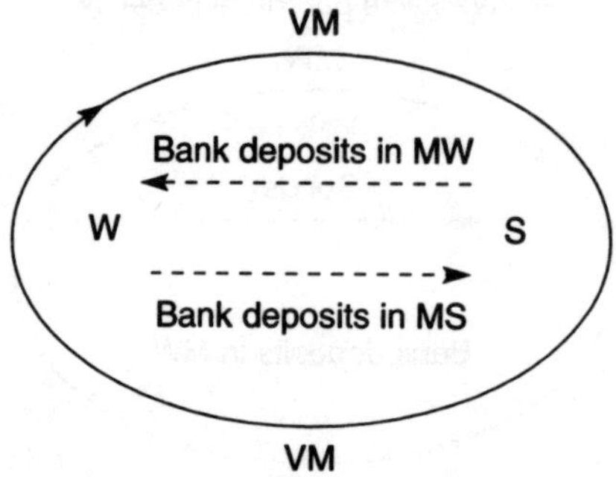

Figure 14.17

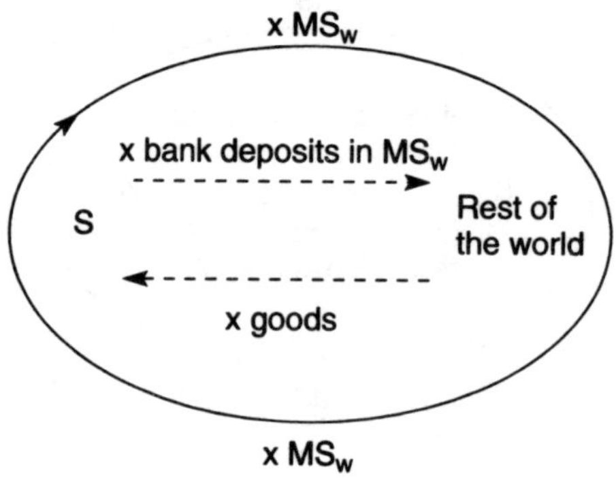

Figure 14.18

domestic money for this purpose. Hence, S_w can maintain the level of the income available within the country unchanged without having to transfer non-monetary claims to the rest of the world. Let us show, side by side, the book-keeping entries corresponding to the payment of the net commercial imports carried out by S_w and by a country of set W, W_w (Table 14.14). Both W_w and S_w lose part of their national income to the benefit of the rest of the world. Yet the income in money S paid by S_w is still entirely deposited in its own banking system, whereas that of W_w is spent in the purchase of the strong currency which must guarantee its conversion. For W_w equilibrium is re-established through the sale of non-monetary claims, which has the twofold function of maintaining national income at its previous level and compensating W_w's pathological payment with that carried out by the rest of the world. S_w, instead, can avoid the sale of non-monetary claims by limiting itself to acknowledging its monetary debt to the countries owning claims on its bank deposits.

Table 14.14

Banking system of country W_w			
Liabilities			*Assets*
IH	100 MW_w	Output	100 MWw
RW	1 MS_w	Importers	10 MW_w
Export of bonds	10 MW_w	RW	1 MS_w

Banking system of country S_w			
Liabilities			*Assets*
IH	100 MS_w	Output	100 MS_w
RW	1 MS_w	Importers	1 MS_w

This asymmetry among countries who are members of set W and S allows S_w not to have to compensate the pathological operation corresponding to the unilateral payment of its net commercial imports, an opportunity which has a beneficial effect on the anomaly related to external debt servicing.

The anomalous external debt servicing of strong-currency countries

Before analysing the case in which the anomaly concerning the formation of external debt is balanced by that accompanying external debt servicing, it is important to observe that when S_w gets indebted by giving non-monetary claims in exchange for foreign goods, its servicing of the debt cannot avoid a pathological double payment. Let us suppose that S_w's residents incur a foreign debt by selling bonds up to a value of 10 MS. As in every other case, external debt servicing is carried out by the indebted residents and by their country. Thus, while the country's debt servicing is effective only if S_w has a trade surplus, the payment made by the residents implies a reduction in the country's domestic income (Figure 14.19). The debt servicing carried out by residents R_1 transfers abroad x units of bank deposits in money S_w (1). In order to re-establish the level of internal income it is therefore necessary for country S_w (its residents R_2) to obtain a new foreign loan equivalent to x MS_w (2). Thanks to this, S_w can thus recover, directly or after compensation, the bank deposits initially transferred abroad by residents R_1. From a book-keeping point of view (and assuming that x corresponds to 10 units of money S_w and that the exchange rate between MS_w and the currency of the creditor countries, MS, is of 1 MS_w for 1 MS) we have the entries shown in Table 14.15. Since the analysis is analogous to that already worked out with regard to country W_w, we refer the reader back to the first section of the present chapter (p. 304), observing that the analogy is valid to the extent that S_w's residents incur a debt in a strong currency different from their own and are forced to pay it back in the same currency. Figure 14.19 can effectively be replaced by Figure 14.20, from which we can see that the new debt incurred by R_2 allows R_1 to service its external debt in the same reserve currency previously lent to it by the

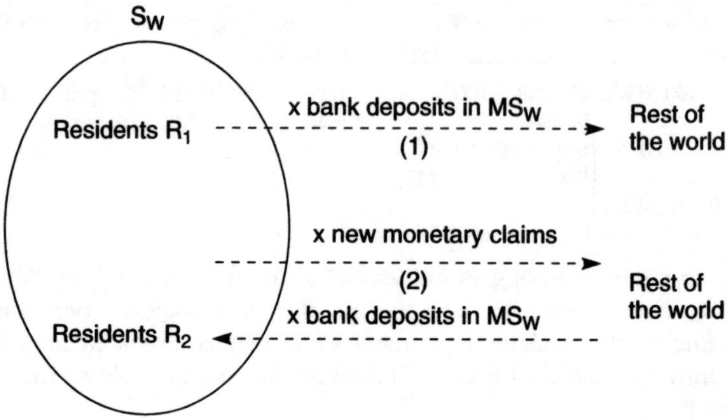

Figure 14.19

Table 14.15

Banking system of country S_w

Liabilities			*Assets*
Income holders	100 MS_w	Domestic output	100 MS_w
Exporting firms	10 MS_w	Rest of the world	10 MS
Income holders	100 MS_w	Domestic output (price 100 MS_w)	90 S_w
Rest of the world	10 MS	Rest of the world	10 MS
Residents R_2	10 MS_w	Residents R_1	10 MS_w
		Rest of the world	10 MS
Income holders (R_2 included)	100 MS_w	Domestic output (price 100 MS_w)	90 MS_w
		Rest of the world	10 MS

rest of the world. The internalisation of the transactions shows how the new sellers of bonds are paid by the indebted residents, to whom they transfer the currencies borrowed from the rest of the world.

If residents of country S_w incur their external debt by selling non-monetary claims and can pay it back by transferring an equivalent amount of their national currency, the analysis is as follows. Let us start from the formation of the debt. Since S_w's residents finance their net imports by selling bonds, the situation of their country is initially similar to that of any weak-currency country forced to get indebted in order to finance its net foreign purchases. This means that even in this case external debt servicing

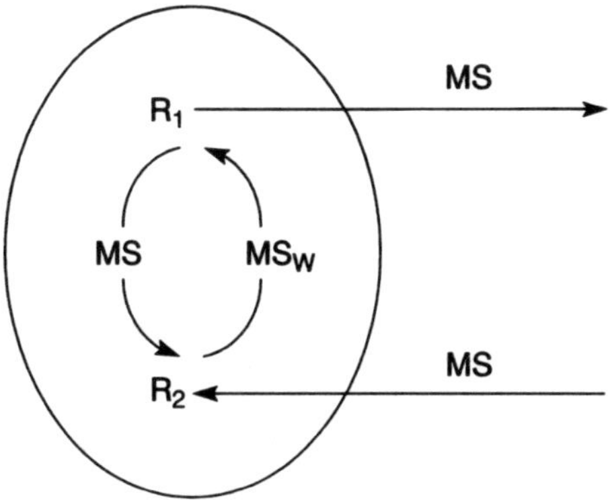

Figure 14.20

must be carried out both by country S_w and by its residents. Now, according to our initial assumption the indebted residents pay their foreign creditors in domestic money. If the country has no trade surplus, external debt servicing is thus carried out only by the residents, who transfer part of their national income abroad (Figure 14.21). Since every national income can only be deposited within the banking system from which it originates, the payment made by the indebted residents leads to the substitution of the currency transferred abroad (which flows back to S_w) with an equivalent amount of monetary claims (Figure 14.22). Because of the particular status of MS_w, the net imports obtained by R_1 through the sale of bonds can be paid through the transfer of monetary claims. In other words, external debt servicing has as a consequence the substitution of monetary claims for the financial claims previously transferred to the rest of the world. Instead of defining the effective servicing of S_w's debt, the payment made by R_1 has a

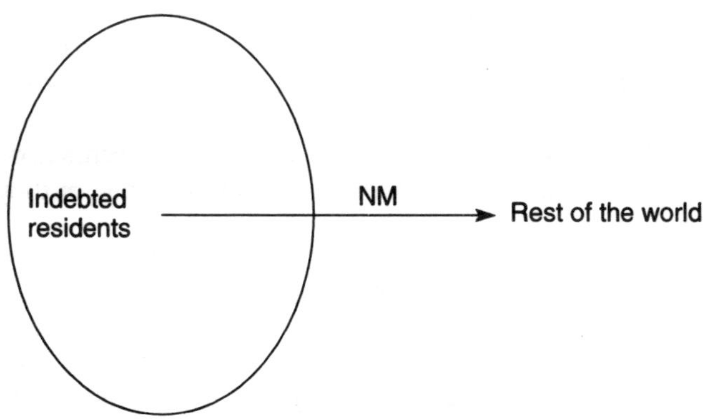

Figure 14.21

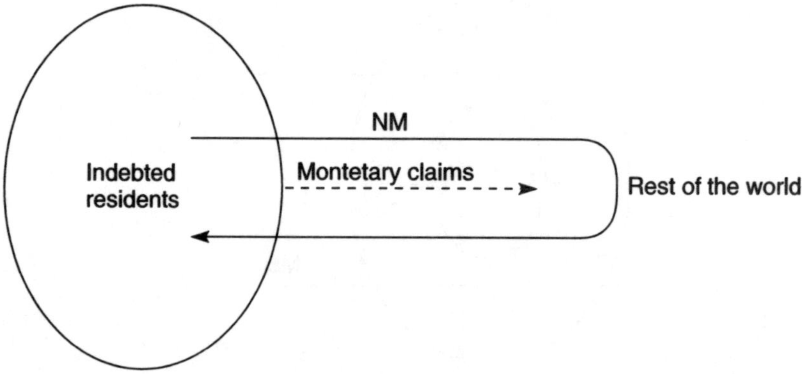

Figure 14.22

retroactive effect on its formation. Once the transfer of national money carried out by R_1 has been accounted for we observe that S_w's net commercial imports are 'paid for' through the transfer of monetary claims corresponding to its acknowledgement of debt. The formation of Eurocurrencies in MS_w, temporarily avoided by the sale of financial claims by R_1, is thus definitively sanctioned when R_1 replaces its IOUs with those issued by its country's banking system. Finally, the debt corresponding to S_w's net imports is transferred from the residents to the country, which, because MS_w is a reserve currency, leads to an equivalent increase in the amount of Eurocurrencies.

Let us now turn our attention to the case in which external debt servicing refers to the debt incurred by transferring monetary claims (bank deposits) in MS_w. As will be remembered, when S_w gets indebted by transferring monetary deposits formed within its banking system abroad, the operation is of a pathological nature since it entails a unilateral transfer of domestic income from S_w to the rest of the world (Figure 14.23). Since the debt is incurred by the country as a whole, its servicing can effectively take place only if S_w becomes a net exporter of goods and services. In this case the country benefits from a unilateral transfer of income by the rest of the world so that external debt servicing amounts to a simple compensation between the claims on S_w's bank deposits owned by the creditor countries and those

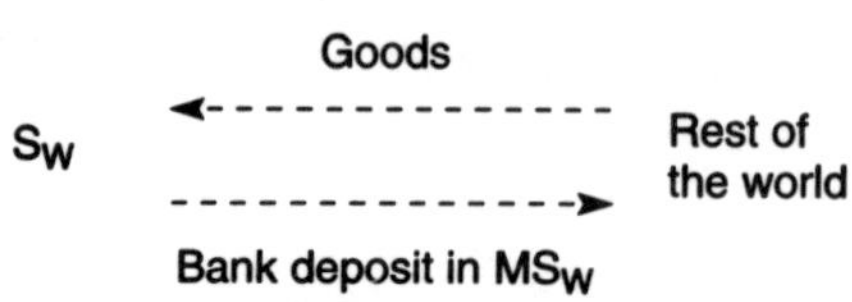

Figure 14.23

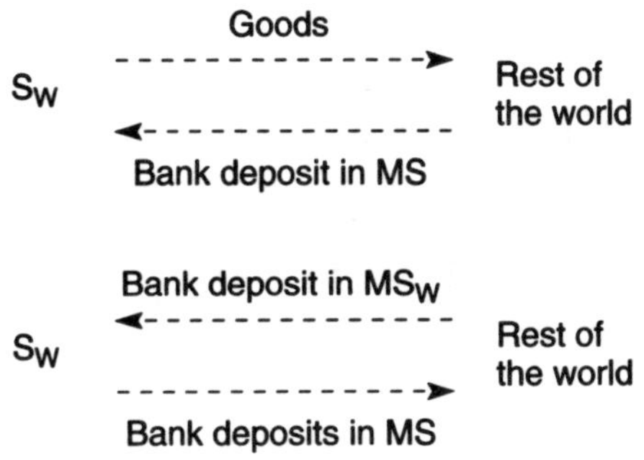

Figure 14.24

in MS obtained by S_w in exchange for its net commercial exports (Figure 14.24). Hence, although it leads to a pathological operation, external debt servicing has no negative effects since its anomaly is immediately balanced by that which originated from the formation of foreign debt. By operating a unilateral transfer of national income when it incurs its external debt, country S_w benefits from an equivalent unilateral transfer of foreign income when it services it. Through their unification the two opposed disequilibria are cancelled, which allows the country to limit the damage caused by the lack of a true international monetary system. Yet, until the country effectively services its external debt by becoming a net commercial exporter, the anomaly related to the payment of its net imports will go on exerting its negative effects on the whole monetary system (in particular by encouraging the expansion of the Euromarket through the pathological duplication of the bank deposits the rest of the world is credited with).

To summarise we can observe that the present system of international payments is the source of an anomaly which, when it is not reciprocal, leads to a double sacrifice. Implying a unilateral transfer of national income, external debt servicing fulfils the conditions for its concretisation: the double payment and the consequent re-indebtedness of debtor countries. The double servicing of external debt is thus a powerful obstacle towards the development of indebted countries as well as a serious threat to the growth of creditor countries. In this situation the only alternative is to find a solution implying the reform of the system of payments based on the key-currencies standard.

15

ELEMENTS FOR A SOLUTION TO THE EXTERNAL DEBT PROBLEM

In this last chapter we shall point out the principles on which every new attempt to solve the problem of international monetary disorder must be founded, with particular attention being paid to the problem of external debt servicing. Derived from the analysis developed in the previous chapters, these principles are closely related to the nature of bank money and can be considered the modern version of those already present, explicitly or implicitly, in the teaching of Smith, Ricardo and Keynes. Their implementation is a necessary requisite for the working out of a new system of international payments allowing for the creation of a single monetary area which, though respectful of monetary sovereignty, will free countries from the iniquitous double servicing of external debt and rescue national currencies from a regime of exchange rates (that of relative exchange rates) which deeply alter their nature. Referring back to the analysis developed in Chapter 12 we shall show how the new European Monetary System represents a model for a limited group of nations as well as for the whole international community. Finally, we shall indicate how the principles of the solution can also be implemented by a single country.

THE CENTRAL BANK AS 'BANK OF THE NATION'

As the analysis shows, external debt servicing has to be carried out by the indebted residents and by their country. Hence, the concept of nation acquires a centrality which has to be fully recognised through the institution of a specific department of the Central Bank which is given the task of representing the country from a book-keeping point of view. It is only if the economic existence of the nation is effectively accounted for that it is possible to reduce external debt servicing to a single payment carried out by the country on behalf of its residents.

Nation and residents

What is the relationship between the nation and its residents? Is it possible to consider a nation as the simple sum of its residents? Let us first note that, without residents, the nation would have no reason to exist. Yet is this enough to identify one with the other? Is it not true, on the contrary, that, given any number whatsoever of residents, the nation acquires an existence which cannot be reduced to that of the sum of its inhabitants? As observed in Chapter 14, factual considerations are essential in order to answer these questions. Let us consider the banking system of a given country. It cannot be denied that its existence presupposes the existence of people who make it work. It is also evident, however, that *vis-à-vis* the rest of the world it not only represents the situation of individual residents but also that of the whole country. Let us suppose the nation's money to be a reserve currency. If the residents are net importers and pay for their purchases by transferring part of their domestic income, they are discharged of any obligation. Now, if the nation amounted to the simple sum of its residents we should conclude that no debt subsists between the country and the rest of the world. Yet by definition, money is an acknowledgement of debt of the bank which issues it, so that, as soon as it is transferred abroad, a national currency represents the acknowledgement of debt of the whole banking system which has issued it. Thus, although residents have fully paid for their net foreign purchases, the nation still has a monetary relationship with the rest of the world.

Referring to a well-known concept of modern mathematics we can say that the nation corresponds to the set of residents, and not to their simple sum. In the same way as the set is richer than its constitutive elements, the nation is a whole which acquires an existence which is partially autonomous from that of its residents. As we have seen, the existence of the set 'nation' is particularly evident in the case of external debt servicing. The double payment of external debt shows how the nation represents the set (and not the sum) of its residents, whose foreign debt entails that of their country. However, if it is correct to claim that a set cannot be reduced to the sum of its elements, this does not mean that the situation of the set has to be cumulated with that of its elements. Thus, in our example, the economic existence of the nation is not enough to justify the fact that the debt of the country is added to that of its residents. On the contrary, analysis shows that the two debts are cumulative only within a pathological system of payments in which the book-keeping existence of the nation is not accounted for.

Nation, Central Bank and external debt servicing

Referring back to the analysis developed in Chapter 14, we can represent the anomaly of external debt servicing as in Figure 15.1, in which the payment of the country is added to that of its residents. By duplicating that carried out by the residents, country A's payment is entirely unjustified and entails a net loss of domestic income to the profit of international speculative capital. Order would be re-established only if the country's payments were made on behalf of its residents; in which case, by acting as a simple intermediary between indebted residents and foreign creditors, the country would give foreign currencies in exchange for an equivalent amount of domestic income. The residents would pay the nation in domestic money, and the nation would pay the rest of the world in foreign exchange (Figure 15.2). The national income spent by residents of A in the servicing of their external debt would thus remain entirely available within the country, whose payment would be carried out in foreign exchange.

For nation A to effectively play this role of intermediation between its indebted residents and the rest of the world it is necessary that its historical, cultural and juridical existence be matched by an economic one. In other words, the economic existence of the nation must be institutionalised through the creation of an entity entrusted with the structuring and managing of its book-keeping. It is true that countries already have national accounting, but this does not correspond to the accounts of the nation as such. Entries are the mere reflex of the transactions carried out by residents and the whole system is more like a statistical collection of data referring to national assets and real and monetary international flows (balance of payments) than double entry book-keeping. The present national accounting is, in a way, the mirror image of the financial position of residents relative to domestic resources and international transactions. The new book-keeping, instead, will have to refer to the nation considered as a set, taking into account those transactions which, though initially carried out by the residents, are taken over by their country.

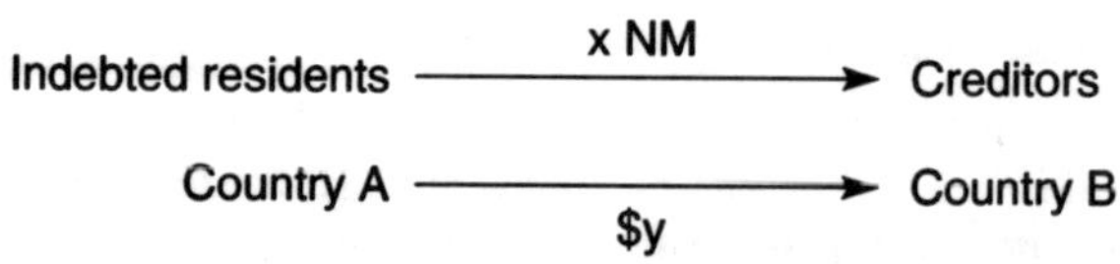

Figure 15.1

Figure 15.2

In the case of positive external debt servicing, for example, the book-keeping existence of the nation will be confirmed when the Central Bank is given the task of paying foreign creditors on behalf of the country. By giving rise to a positive entry of domestic income to the profit of the nation, external debt servicing will thus bring forth the formation of a domestic saving corresponding to the net commercial exports sacrificed to settle the debt with the rest of the world.

The main idea is that the 'monetary' existence of the nation must be matched by a book-keeping structure allowing for the country to play a role of intermediation. In the absence of such a structure, instead of taking the place of the payment carried out by the residents, the payment of the nation is added to it. As is confirmed by the double servicing of external debt: if the nation does not act on behalf of its residents the whole country loses both its external income and an equivalent amount of its domestic income. The conclusion is clear: monetary order requires the nation to be created as a book-keeping entity.

THE RIGOROUS SEPARATION OF INTERNAL AND EXTERNAL MONETARY CIRCUITS

As the reader will have observed, one of the distinctions introduced at the beginning of this volume and constantly re-proposed is that between vehicular and financial aspects of monetary circulation. Put forth by Smith and Ricardo (who speak of nominal and real money) and used by Keynes in his proposals for a reform of the international monetary system (when he speaks of monetary and financial bancor), this distinction plays a central role in the search for a solution to the problems of international monetary disorder. Yet it cannot be transposed from the national to the international level in a mechanical way. Since international transactions are not concerned with the monetisation of any new production, monetary and financial circuits must be related to those of every single country involved in international exchanges. However, to avoid the duplication of domestic currencies and their transformation from *means* into *objects* of exchange it is necessary to set up a structure where the interpenetration of internal and external monetary circuits is no longer allowed for. Let us specify the criteria of this separation both with regard to financial and to monetary (vehicular) circuits.

The circuits of vehicular money

Within every country vehicular (nominal) money is issued by banks, secondary and Central, making up the national banking system. The main purpose of this emission is the monetisation of domestic output and its distribution amongst the various economic agents. In order to fulfil this aim, banks perform a double operation: they acknowledge themselves spontaneously indebted to the economy and they carry out payments on behalf of its constitutive agents. Hence, every payment entails the intervention of banks as 'monetary intermediary' between its beneficiaries and its mandators.

However, the intermediation is such only if banks are not *monetarily* indebted to one another once the payment has taken place. The spontaneous acknowledgement of debt issued by a bank must flow back to its point of origin, in a circular flow that establishes a monetary circuit. As we have seen, the working of our national banking systems complies with the nature of vehicular money. Interbank clearing allows for the real settlement of net interbank imbalances, which proves that the content of domestic payments is rigorously distinct from the means used to carry them out. Being part of an economy of production, monetary circuits convey the financial ones. In every payment the circular flow of money leaves behind a book-keeping record which has national income as its object. Thus, being immediately recovered by the issuing bank, money leaves its place to a bank deposit which, directly or indirectly (through the transfer of financial bonds among secondary banks), stands for an equivalent amount of national output.

When it is transposed at the international level, the analysis confirms the centrality of the role played by vehicular money. The existence of a true international monetary system depends on the possibility of making use of a *means* of circulation and payment. Let us suppose that an international Bank is created, entrusted with the task of monetising international transactions. The money issued by this Bank must record, convey and settle international exchanges. The unit-of-account function can be achieved through the determination of parities between each domestic currency and the new international money. The second function requires the intervention of the international Bank as a multilateral clearing house, since the new international money plays a purely vehicular role only if national Central Banks are not monetarily indebted to one another. The task of the international Bank is precisely that of settling imbalances through multilateral clearing, thus avoiding the use of money as a final object of payment. In the same way as interbank imbalances are settled through the transfer of financial securities, those among Central Banks must imply a transfer of bonds from the debtor to the creditor countries. Carried out through the intermediation of the international Bank, these real flows guarantee the balance of payments equilibrium, allowing every country to balance its positive and negative movements of international money.

To summarise we can see that in our example the monetary equilibrium of every Central Bank is derived from the equality of their sales and their purchases. If countries are part of a system where every purchase is necessarily financed through an equivalent sale, monetary equilibrium is constantly maintained, which does not mean, of course, that commercial exports cannot differ from commercial imports. On the contrary, through the introduction of the financial market it is perfectly possible to conciliate monetary equilibrium with financial disequilibrium. Trade deficit can thus be financed through a foreign investment without modifying the equality of monetary flows which convey real exchanges through the intermediation of the international Bank (Figure 15.3). Resulting from the intermediation carried out by the international Bank, the rigorous separation of national and international circuits is the logical consequence of the use of a system complying with the banking nature of money. It is perfectly natural, in fact, for money to circulate only within the banking system from which it is created. The foundation of an international Bank would allow for the circulation of an extra-national money only at the international level, keeping it separate from the domestic circuits described by each national currency (Figure 15.4). According to the scheme represented in Figure 15.4

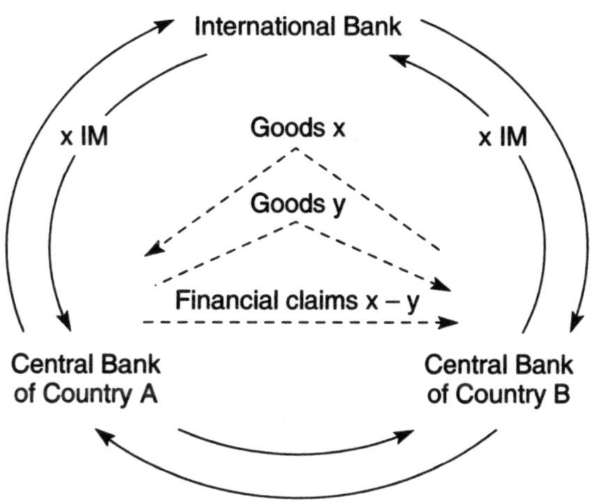

Figure 15.3

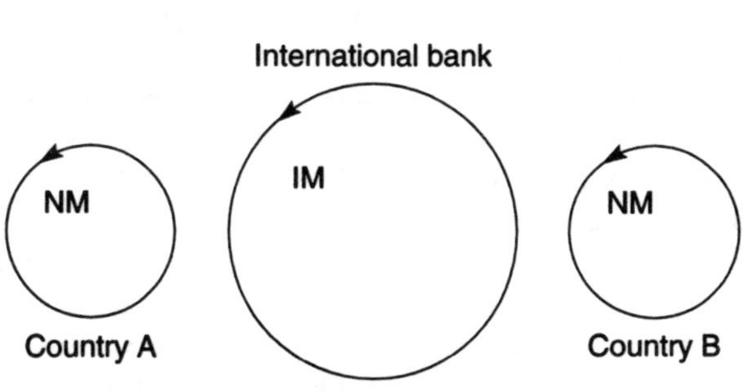

Figure 15.4

national currencies circulate only within their countries of origin, while the task of conveying international transactions is entrusted to the extra-national money. Thus, the national currency of any country whatsoever can never be entered as a net asset by any other country, which is the necessary condition to avoid the effect of duplication which is the mark of the present asymmetry between strong- and weak-currency countries.

While the vehicular use of the new international money provides for the monetary equilibrium of every transaction (so that countries cannot be monetarily indebted either to one another or to the international Bank), it still has to be shown how imbalances can be settled; that is, how net payments can be carried out using money as a simple instrument. Let us show this by referring back to the analysis of the financial circuits.

The financial circuits

Let us remember, first of all, that at the national level financial circuits owe their high degree of development to the intermediation played by secondary and Central banks. Whether it is carried out by secondary banks in favour of residents or by the Central Bank to the profit of secondary banks, financial intermediation is ruled by the principle according to which *purchases are financed by sales*. It is evident, in fact, that a resident can purchase a part of national output only if he has at his disposal an equivalent income, and that in order to be able to spend this income he has to sell a corresponding sum of monetary or non-monetary claims. The owners of national income hold it in the form of claims to bank deposits so that in order to spend their income they first have to sell these claims (give them back to their bank), while those who want to purchase goods and services, even though they do not own a positive income, must borrow it by giving in exchange (selling) financial bonds of the same value.

The real content of monetary transactions is vitally important. When a commodity is purchased within a national monetary system, what is given in exchange is not an empty monetary form, but its real content. If the purchase is final, the object of the payment is income and the transaction corresponds to an absolute exchange between the physical product and its monetary form. If the purchase is not final, income is given in exchange for a financial claim (that is, a claim on future output) and is simply transferred from its initial holder to the borrower. In both transactions money is used as a vehicle while payments are effective because of the transfer, from buyer to seller, of the content of vehicular money.

The principle of equality between sales and purchases is complied with even as far as secondary banks are concerned. In particular, when a bank is indebted to another bank the intervention of the Central Bank (or of another clearing house) transforms the monetary debt into a financial one through the transfer of bonds from the debtor to the creditor bank. It is thus generally true that, at the national level, exchanges have a real content so that purchases of any single economic agent are covered by equivalent sales of the same agent. Apart from the case in which the purchase is financed through the sale of claims on bank deposits (that is, from the expenditure of one's own income), we would like to stress here the fact that the net purchase of goods and services entails the net sale of equivalent financial bonds. When he does not own the income required for its net purchases, the buyer can exert an additional demand only if he sells an equivalent amount of bonds. Two financial circuits thus correspond to the exchange between commodities and bonds: that inherent to the sale of bonds – where resident A gives financial bonds B_2 in exchange for claims to bank deposits C_1 – and that inherent to the sale of goods and services – where A gives E the claims to bank deposits obtained from D in exchange for goods and services (Figure 15.5).

Let us now consider international transactions. The application of the same principle governing domestic transactions forces countries to finance their purchases through an equivalent sale of goods, services and bonds. It is only in this case that monetary payments have a real content and that no country is given the absurd privilege of paying its net purchases by giving its own IOU

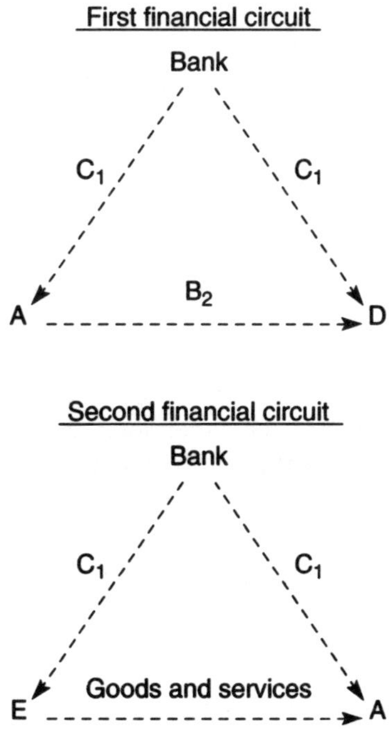

Figure 15.5

in exchange. This means that if a country wants to import more goods than it exports it must finance its net purchases through the net sale of financial securities. To the extent that its trade balance is in equilibrium, a country pays for its imports through its exports, while its net imports are possible only if it benefits from a net transfer of income from the rest of the world.

In the same way as happens within every national monetary system, the exchange between goods and bonds carried out by two countries whatsoever, W and S, requires the presence of two financial circuits. In the first, country W gives financial claims (private or public) in exchange for claims to bank deposits, while in the second it exchanges these latter claims for an equivalent amount of goods and services. Internationally, however, the financial intermediation is carried out by an institution which does not benefit from any deposit of income. Available incomes are all deposited with the various national banking systems and it would be useless to have them partially transferred to the international Bank. The role of intermediation does not imply any final transfer to the benefit of the international Bank. On the contrary, through its intermediation deficit countries can take advantage of a system of multilateral clearing allowing for their net commercial purchases to be financed by a loan from the surplus countries. In the simple example of a two-country system, the transfer of income from S corresponding to the sale of bonds carried out by W is thus balanced by an equivalent transfer to the benefit of S corresponding to W's net purchases of goods and services

In the balance sheet of the international Bank these two financial circuits give rise to entries as in Table 15.1. The first entry refers to the sale of financial bonds which allows country W to obtain a loan from S. Carried out through the intermediation of the international Bank, this transaction gives W a drawing right over S's domestic output, and S a drawing right over W's future output. The second entry corresponds to the purchase of goods and services that country W finances by transferring to S the income borrowed from it. Once again the transaction is mediated by the international Bank which, by debiting and crediting the Central Banks of W and S, matches the debit and credit of transaction (1). Globally, commercial imports are thus paid for by financial exports, through an exchange whose terms are the real contents of the international money (IM) used vehicularly by the two countries.

Table 15.1

International Bank

	Liabilities			*Assets*
(1)	CB of W	x IM	CB of S	x IM
(2)	CB of S	x IM	CB of W	x IM

The rule according to which every country finances its purchases through equivalent sales means that, by implying a transfer of income to the benefit of the importing country, net commercial exports are finally paid by the exporting country: it is the exporting country which, through the purchase of bonds, lends the importing country the income needed to pay for its net imports. The separation of national financial circuits thus acquires a special significance. By complying with the principle of bank money according to which the income formed in a given banking system can be deposited and spent only within that system, the new structure of international payments achieves the internalisation of every payment. The result which is aimed at is that of allowing for deficits to be effectively paid for, and there can be no doubt that this requires the expenditure of real income. Yet, this means that the whole of national output must be purchased through the expenditure of the income associated with it. Whether output is sold domestically or exported, its payment is effective only if it entails the final expenditure of the income generated by its production. The internalisation of the payment of exports is thus an essential requirement of every true international system, the only mechanism accounting for the real payment of every transaction. Let us verify it in the case of external debt servicing.

External debt servicing and the separation of monetary and financial circuits

As we have seen, the institution of an accounting department of the nation is the necessary condition for avoiding external debt servicing leading to the double loss of an external and a domestic income. Being carried out by the country as a whole, the servicing of foreign debt must allow the Central Bank to obtain in domestic money what it loses in foreign exchange, thus avoiding the problem that, besides transferring part of its national output (the net commercial exports corresponding to the external gain), the country is also forced to transfer an equivalent part of its domestic income. Let us again suppose that a general agreement is reached as to the creation of a supranational Bank. The new system of international payments would thus be composed of a series of Banks of the nations and an international Central Bank. In this system, the payment carried out by the indebted residents in domestic money is chanelled through the domestic circuit of the indebted country and leads to a transfer of income from the residents to the department of the Central Bank managing the internal accounts of the nation, whereas the payment of the creditor countries is carried out by the external department of the Central Bank in the new international money issued by the supranational Bank and earned through net commercial exports. The separation of the two circuits, national and international, leads to a threefold result:

1 by avoiding the inflow of foreign currencies into national monetary circuits it abolishes the actual asymmetry between strong- and weak-currency countries and, by forcing them all to give up financial bonds in exchange for net commercial imports, it puts an end to the process of Eurocurrency accumulation resulting from duplication;
2 by introducing a system of absolute exchange rates it takes national currencies out of the market, thus avoiding them being transformed from simple means of payment into objects of exchange whose price fluctuates on the basis of the erratic variations of supply and demand;
3 by keeping within the country the income spent by the indebted residents in their external debt servicing it allows indebted countries to service their creditors by sacrificing only an equivalent foreign income.

Finally, let us observe that this last result can be obtained because the vehicular money needed for the conversion of the domestic income spent by the indebted residents into the foreign income transferred by the country is freely provided by the international Bank. As will be remembered, the anomaly of the present system of international payments consists in the fact that weak currency countries are forced to pay to get the vehicle required for the transfer of the income earned through their net trade surplus. This purchase of vehicular money entails a re-indebtedness that the country can avoid only by sacrificing a further amount of net exports. In an orderly system, the monetary vehicle must be freely obtained by every country, a condition which can be satisfied only if an international Bank is created with the task of supplying the money needed to convey international transactions in a circulatory way. In short, the problem of external debt servicing is that of allowing for the free conversion of the domestic income spent by the indebted residents. Today this conversion is onerous, since the indebted country is forced to obtain both a foreign income and the vehicular money needed to transfer it to the creditor countries. The cost of the operation corresponds to a loss of domestic income which can be balanced only by incurring a new debt to the rest of the world. To avoid the present vicious circle of external debt servicing it is thus enough to allow for the free conversion of the domestic income spent by the residents into the foreign income spent by their country; a condition that would be complied with if, by giving away its external income, the country became the new holder of the domestic income spent by its residents.

In the present system, the conversion takes place on the exchange market and does not imply the country's intervention as an intermediary between indebted residents and foreign creditors. Hence, instead of being the extension of that carried out by the residents, the payment of the country is added to it. The two payments will stop being added to one another only when their conversion allows the country to become the beneficiary of the payment carried out by its residents. Since it takes their place in the payment of foreign creditors, it is normal for the country to be reimbursed in national money to the extent that it gives up its external income. The twofold requirement the new system of payments must comply with is that of allowing for both the internalisation and the internationalisation of external debt servicing. Taken on by the country as such, the first task is carried out thanks to the intermediation of the Central Bank, whose internal department prevents the outflow of income from the domestic circuit. The second task is carried out jointly by the external department of the country's Central Bank, which transfers to the creditor countries the external income obtained through the net sales of goods, services and bonds, and the international Bank, which supplies the monetary vehicle required for the transfer.

To illustrate what we have been claiming so far, let us refer to two examples based on the practical application of the principles enunciated in this chapter.

THE NEW EUROPEAN MONETARY SYSTEM AS AN EXAMPLE OF AN INTERNATIONAL SOLUTION TO THE PROBLEM OF EXTERNAL DEBT SERVICING

Let us start from a numerical example similar to that used in Chapter 12 and show how the European Central Bank and the external departments of the countries' Central Banks play their role of monetary and financial intermediation.

The European Central Bank and the monetary servicing of external debt

Let us suppose that transactions among Great Britain, Italy and Portugal are as shown in Figure 15.6 in millions of ECUs. Let us also suppose that, in the same period of reference, Italy uses the gain derived from its trade surplus with Portugal, equal to 2 million ECUs in order to service part of its debt to Great Britain, and that exchange rates between ECU and national currencies are £0.4 for 1 ECU, 1,000 lira for 1 ECU and 100 escudos for 1 ECU.

According to our numerical example, Portugal has a trade deficit of 20 million ECUs towards Great Britain which it balances through a net sale of bonds, while Italy has a trade surplus with Portugal of 2 million ECUs and balances its transactions with Great Britain through a net transfer of bonds equal to 10 million ECUs. External debt servicing carried out by Italy is financed through Portugal's net commercial purchases, that is, finally, through the new loan granted by Italy to Portugal. As we shall verify, external debt servicing does not entail any anomaly, so that it allows Italy to increase the level of its global debt only to the extent of its net trade deficit (ECU 8 million) while benefiting from the totality of its domestic income.

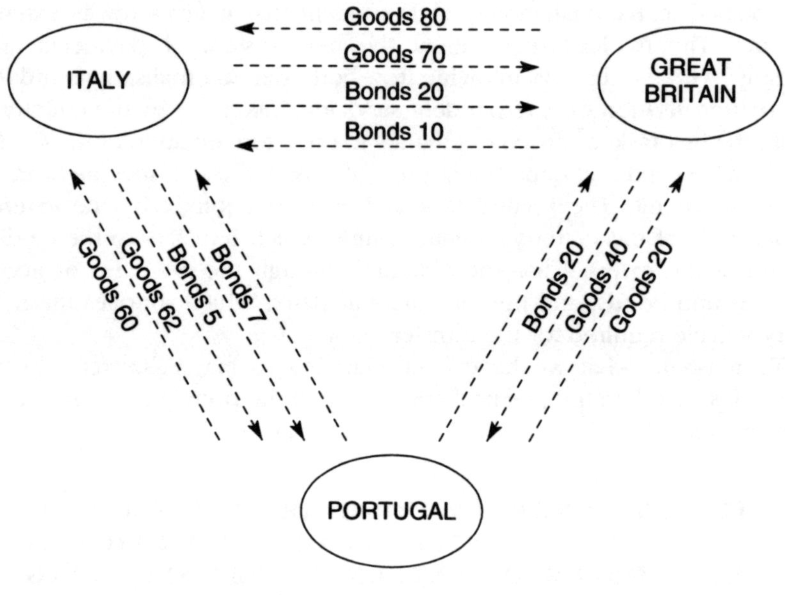

Figure 15.6

From a monetary point of view the European Central Bank intervenes in every payment supplying the three countries with the vehicular money needed to transfer goods, services and financial claims. In each of these interventions the vehicular money moves in a circular way as shown in Table 15.2. The vehicular use of the ECU is guaranteed by the equality between the inflows and the outflows concerning the commercial and financial transactions of every single country. In terms of supply and demand these equalities mean that the demand for ECUs exerted by each country's Central Bank is perfectly balanced by an equivalent demand for domestic currency. The stability of exchange rates, both absolute (between the ECU and each single domestic money) and relative, is thus one of the consequences of the ECB intervention as a multilateral clearing union. The equality between monetary inflows and outflows does not allow for any unilateral transfer of money, so that ECU and national currencies are only used as a means of payment. Being used as simple vehicles, currencies escape from the mechanisms of the free market and can thus reach a stability that the present non-system of payments can merely dream about.

As far as external debt servicing is concerned it is clear that, taking place within a mechanism of multilateral clearing, it no longer implies a loss of domestic income. In our example Italy is supplied free of cost with the vehicular money it needs to transfer to Great Britain the external income earned through its trade surplus with Portugal. Thus, since it is not forced

Table 15.2

European Central Bank			
Liabilities			*Assets*
Great Britain	80	Italy	80
Great Britain	10	Italy	10
Portugal	60	Italy	60
Portugal	7	Italy	7
Italy	70	Great Britain	70
Italy	20	Great Britain	20
Portugal	20	Great Britain	20
Portugal	20	Great Britain	20
Great Britain	40	Portugal	40
Italy	62	Portugal	62
Italy	5	Portugal	5

to purchase the vehicle of its inter-European payments, Italy can benefit entirely from its internal resources. The conversion of the domestic income spent by the indebted residents into an equivalent foreign income is carried out by the Bank of Italy; and it is the Bank of Italy who, as Bank of the nation, pays British creditors on behalf of Italian residents (Figure 15.7). The Italian nation becomes the new holder of that part of the country's domestic income which is sacrificed today in the double servicing of external debt, and can use it to pay the residents whose non-monetary claims (national or Portuguese) are transferred to Great Britain to pay the

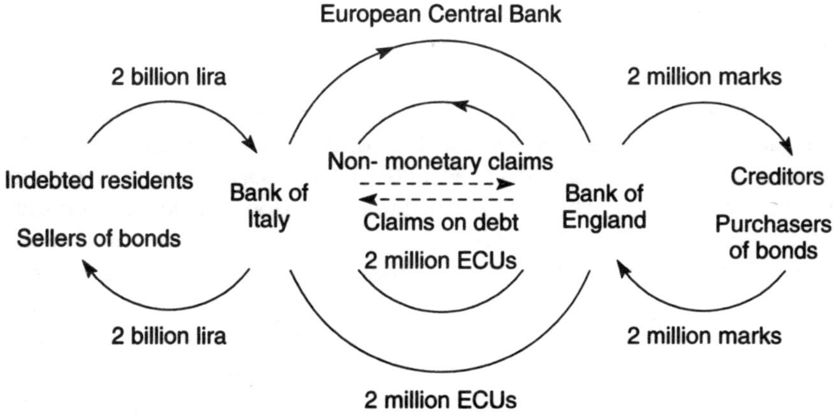

Figure 15.7

Italian debt. It must be remembered, in fact, that Italy services its debt to Great Britain thanks to its trade surplus with Portugal. The real content of the external income transferred from Italy to Great Britain as external debt servicing is represented by the financial claims transferred from Portugal to Italy (or, in the case of conversion, by equivalent Italian bonds). British creditors, in their turn, are paid by the Bank of England in pounds, which benefits from an equivalent inflow of pounds generated by the internal sale of the bonds transferred by Italy.

Let us now consider the book-keeping aspect of external debt servicing. To comply with the principles of monetary circulation it is useful to distinguish between two departments of the Bank of Italy: the external one and the internal one. The external department is given the task of entering the payments in favour of, and coming from the European Central Bank, while the entries of the internal department are concerned with the payments in domestic currency carried out by Italy's residents. While waiting for monetary order to be implemented at a planetary level, the European solution must take into account the existence of nations. In particular, the external debt must be assumed by the country so that its gradual amortisation will allow its Central Bank to recover the domestic income spent by the indebted residents and which, in the present system of international payments, is systematically lost in the double servicing of external debt. Hence, the debt accumulated by Italy's residents must be entered on the liability side of the external department of the Bank of Italy, where it is balanced by the goods, services and foreign exchange imported in excess during the same period. Taking into account the fact that the nation operates on behalf of its residents and, therefore, that the two departments of the Bank of Italy are both implied in every transaction, book-keeping entries relative to the external department are as in Table 15.3. Because of the vehicular function of European money, it is not surprising that the flows of ECUs in the external department of the Bank of Italy are matched by equivalent outflows. The only novelty with regard to the new European system of payments is represented by the last entry, where the decrease in the country's accumulated external debt gives rise to an equivalent gain immediately transferred to the internal department. To the extent that its foreign debt decreases, Italy benefits from a gain of external origin (corresponding to the domestic income which is no longer lost in the country's debt servicing) which, monetised by the internal department, can be transferred to the public authority (for example to the Treasury).

If we now shift our attention on the book-keeping entries of the internal department, we can represent their origin according to the scheme in Figure 15.8. As shown in Figure 15.8, domestic income spent by residents remains entirely available in Italy where, except for the part transferred to the Treasury (and corresponding to external debt servicing), it is used to

Table 15.3

Bank of Italy External department			
Liabilities			Assets
Accumulated debt	X	Goods and services	X – y
		Reserves	y
European Central Bank	80	Internal department	80
European Central Bank	10	Internal department	10
European Central Bank	60	Internal department	60
European Central Bank	7	Internal department	7
European Central Bank	2	Internal department	2
Internal department	2	European Central Bank	2
Internal department	70	European Central Bank	70
Internal department	20	European Central Bank	20
Internal department	62	European Central Bank	62
Internal department	5	European Central Bank	5
Internal department	2	Accumulated debt	2

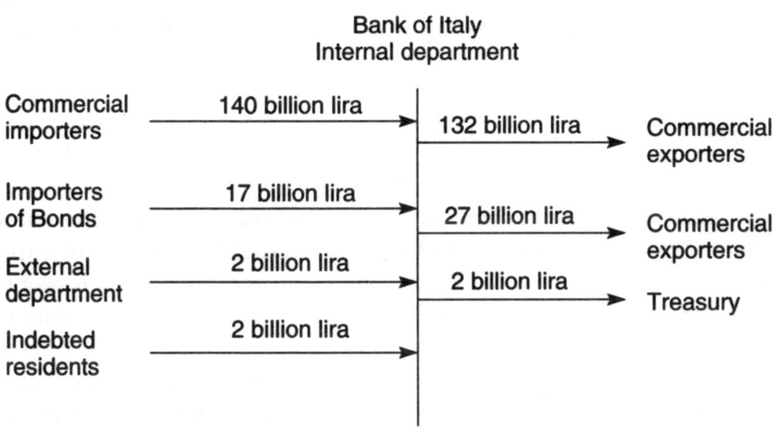

Figure 15.8

pay the exporters of goods, services and bonds (including those transferred to Great Britain as debt servicing). Contrary to what was observed in Chapter 14 (p. 323), external debt servicing does not decrease the amount of Italian domestic income, but only modifies its internal distribution. Once the transfers among importers, indebted residents, Treasury and exporters have been taken into account it appears that Italy's residents are the only holders of the income created within the country, which does not lose even a fraction of its domestic currency. Hence, the gain which the country derives from the new system of international payments is related to the lack of duplication of external debt servicing. Since no domestic income is spent in addition to that of external origin, Italy can service its debt without having to incur a new debt or lose an additional amount of its domestic output. As long as countries maintain their monetary sovereignty, the new system will thus allow nations to benefit from the external debt servicing carried out by their residents by providing a gain which, for example, can be used by the Treasury to decrease public debt.

Let us finally observe that, since in our numerical example Italy's trade balance is globally negative, external debt servicing goes side by side with a new debt corresponding to the net sale of bonds allowing Italy to finance its net imports of goods and services. This means that, although it services its previous debt, Italy increases its global indebtedness. In a way, Italy services its external debt by incurring a new debt which takes the place of the old one. Since external debt servicing amounts to 2 million ECUs and the new global debt to 10 million ECUs, Italy's final debt (old and new) is thus equal to X (the previously accumulated debt) – 2 + 10 = X + 8 million. Yet, whereas in the present system Italy gets indebted and (additionally) loses 2 million ECUs of its domestic income (see Chapter 14), in the new one, instead of being transferred abroad the payment carried out by the indebted residents is collected by their country, so that Italy obtains a positive gain of 2 million ECUs.

The European Central Bank and the financial servicing of external debt

Since the main elements of the analysis have already been worked out, we can only recall here that the ECB's financial intermediation does not imply its intervention as lender of last resort. The ECB certainly does not have the power to create riches, so that its financial activity is logically confined to the transfer of income, an operation which does not lead to any variation in the amount of income available in every national economy. Let us consider again the case of net commercial imports. Since it does not have at its disposal a sufficient external income, the importing country can pay for its net purchases only if it benefits from a loan. It is the ECB which must convey this loan, that is, which must transfer to the importing country the income of the exporting countries needed to pay for its net imports. In short, the financial intermediation amounts to a transfer of bonds, that is, of a drawing right over future output with which the importing country balances its net commercial purchases, whose updated payment is carried out by the exporting country.

Let us now consider the financial aspect of external debt servicing. If the indebted country has a trade surplus, it benefits from a net inflow of financial securities from the rest of the world. Then its external debt servicing amounts to a simple exchange between these bonds and those previously transferred to the creditor countries. Thus, the financial intermediation carried out by the ECB when the debt was initially formed is matched by that inherent in the payment of the country's net exports. The loan obtained from the rest of the world (sale of domestic bonds) is balanced by the loan granted to the rest of the world through the net sale of goods and services (purchase of foreign bonds) and the country's external debt servicing can take place without entailing any additional loss of domestic income. Thanks to the ECB, clearing has a multilateral character, so that a country can service its debt to another one by transferring the bonds obtained through its commercial transactions with other countries. In our previous numerical example, having a trade surplus with Portugal, Italy holds an external income which it can transfer to Great Britain as a settlement of part of the debt accumulated in the previous periods. Italian debt servicing corresponds thus to a transfer of Portuguese bonds, in a movement where Italian exports to Portugal balance part of the previous Italian imports from Great Britain.

What would happen, then, if Great Britain did not accept Portuguese bonds from Italy? This objection can easily be answered by observing that Portuguese bonds can be exchanged for Italian ones, so that Italy can pay Britain by transferring its domestic bonds without giving up the positive servicing of its external debt. The fact that Italy has a trade surplus with Portugal is enough for it to benefit from an external gain which balances part of the debt incurred by Italian residents to the rest of the world. Whether they are transferred to Great Britain or not, the bonds obtained from Portugal compensate part of those initially transferred to Britain by Italy, whose total debt is thus reduced to this extent. The multiplicity of combinations offered by multilateral clearing is confirmed by another observation. The European Central Bank can indeed be asked to play an active role on the financial market, raising funds for countries facing particular difficulties through the emission of ECU bonds. Hence, besides or instead of Portuguese bonds, in exchange for its net commercial exports to Portugal, Italy can benefit from a net inflow of ECU bonds issued by the ECB, which Great Britain will certainly accept for the (partial) settlement of the Italian debt.

Referring to our example let us consider the commercial transactions taking place between Italy and Portugal before external debt servicing. Expressed in millions of ECUs the monetary flows are as shown in Figure 15.9. Since transactions are all carried out through the monetary intermediation of the ECB, flows represented in Figure 15.9 cannot be final because they imply a net transfer of monetary ECUs, which the ECB carries out on behalf of Portugal and in favour of Italy. In order to fulfil monetary circulation the 2 million ECUs earned by Italy through its net sales to Portugal must instantaneously flow back to their point of origin (the ECB).

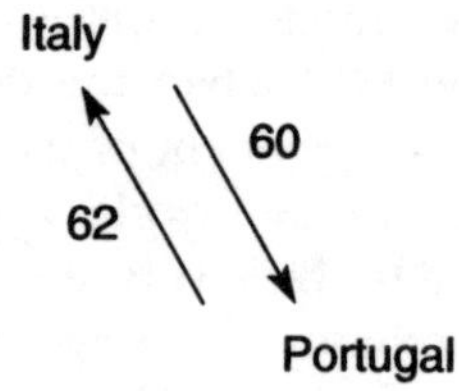

Figure 15.9

If we suppose that Italy uses its external gain to service part of its cumulated debt to Great Britain, we can represent the monetary flows as in Figure 15.10. The flow to Portugal of the 2 million ECUs obtained by Great Britain as a partial settlement of the Italian debt conforms both to the vehicular nature of European money and to the principle according to which money cannot be the object of any payment. This means that, although carried out in ECUs, external debt servicing must convey real goods to Great Britain, and not a mere IOU, whether of a particular country or of the ECB itself. In our example Italy's external debt servicing gives Great Britain ECU bonds whose real content is represented by the Portuguese bonds transferred by Portugal to the ECB to finance its trade deficit with Italy (Figure 15.11). The monetary intermediation of the ECB is thus carried out both with regard to commercial and financial transactions, including external debt servicing. As is shown by book-keeping entries in the ECB monetary department, the equality of ECU inflows and outflows is verified for each single country (Table 15.4). In order to underline the strict connection existing between monetary and financial intermediations we have introduced a distinction between the monetary department of the ECB, where all the movements relative to the vehicular use of the ECU are recorded, and its financial department, concerned with the debtor or creditor position of the various countries resulting from their multilateral transactions. According to the numerical example proposed here, Portugal suffers from a deficit which makes it a debtor to the financial department of the ECB. On the other hand, Great Britain benefits from a net inflow of

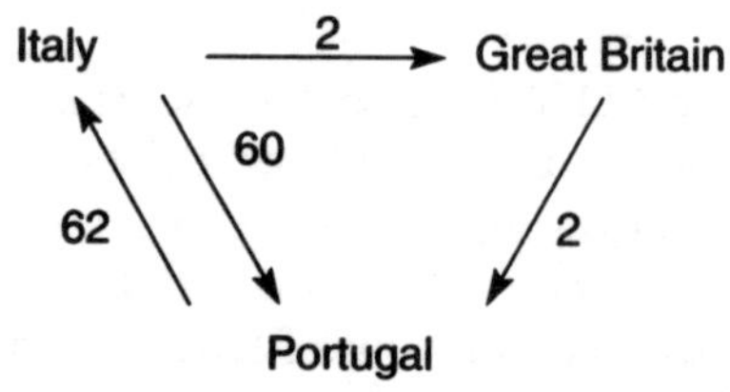

Figure 15.10

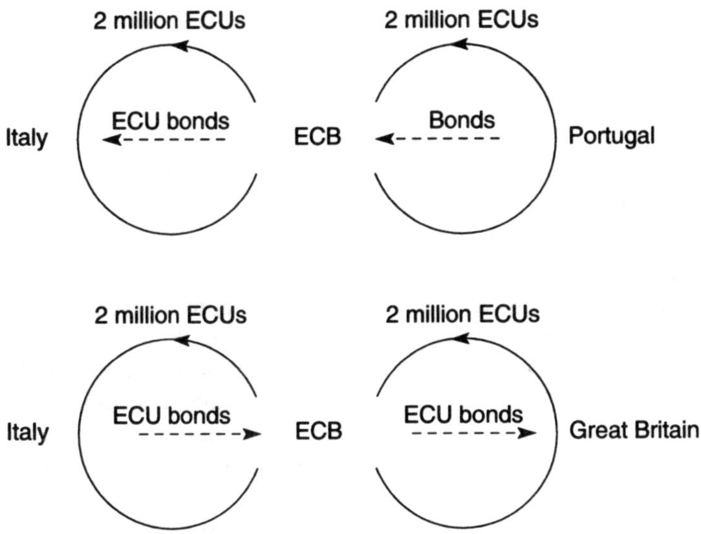

Figure 15.11

ECUs which makes it a creditor to the same department. Hence, the circular flow of ECUs (which flow instantaneously back to the ECB) makes Great Britain and Portugal the holders of a positive and a negative deposit with the ECB financial department. Through European Central Bank intermediation Great Britain lends Portugal the sum it receives as a payment from Italy. Whether this loan brings to Great Britain ECU bonds issued by the ECB or Portuguese bonds is of little relevance since, fundamentally, the ones are the basis for the others. In both cases it is Portugal which is the final holder of the debt, and it is Portugal which has to settle it. However, it is also true that, because of ECB intermediation within a system of multilateral clearing, the chances of providing countries with indirect loans

Table 15.4

European Central Bank Monetary department			
Liabilities			*Assets*
Portugal	60	Italy	60
Italy	62	Portugal	62
Great Britain	2	Italy	2
Financial department	2	Great Britain	2
Portugal	2	Financial department	2

are greatly increased, and the development of ECB financial intermediation will foster that of inter-European (as well as international) transactions.

Financial intermediation and multilateral clearing are therefore the two fundamental elements of the solution. Asymmetrical payments among European countries are avoided through the intervention of the ECB, which transforms external debt servicing into a simple exchange of financial claims. Basically, what has to be done is to work out a system of payments which respects the principle according to which a country gets indebted when it is a net importer and services its debt when it is a net exporter. Thus, the Central Bank of European Central Banks is given the task of monetising (conveying) inter-European transactions allowing for the real payment of each of them, including external debt servicing. No country is allowed to pay by getting indebted and no one is forced to purchase the money needed to transfer its external gain. Vehicular money is freely supplied by the ECB and its content determined by the real goods (commodities and bonds) obtained in exchange for commercial and financial exports.

To conclude, let us refer to the case of net commercial exports and show that, since the new system of multilateral clearing based on the monetary and financial intermediation of the ECB allows countries to service their external debt only once, it allows them to benefit from the whole amount of income spent by their residents. Let us start by analysing the situation in which a country does not sacrifice its external gain for the servicing of its external debt. According to the rules of the new system of payments, a country's trade surplus is necessarily balanced by an equivalent net import of bonds (either issued by the rest of the world or by the ECB). As shown in Figure 15.12, this means that the internal department of the country's Central Bank enters the sum paid by the net importers of foreign bonds as a saving of the nation; that is, as a sum which can immediately be transferred to the Treasury or to any other 'public' institution acting on behalf of the country's residents, who remain, directly or indirectly, the holders of the whole domestic income. In the example of Figure 15.12, we have assumed that the country's exports of goods and services amount to 110 million of national money (NM) and that its commercial imports are of NM 100 million. In the absence of external debt servicing, net commercial exports are paid for out of the revolving fund initially created by the Central Bank, while the payment made by the net importers of foreign bonds gives the internal department 10 million NM which is transferred to the Treasury.

Let us now suppose that the country sacrifices its trade surplus to external debt servicing. Since the country's external gain is used for the servicing of its external debt it could be thought that the saving of the nation is transferred abroad and that domestic income is thus correspondingly reduced. Yet it must be remembered that, having positively serviced its

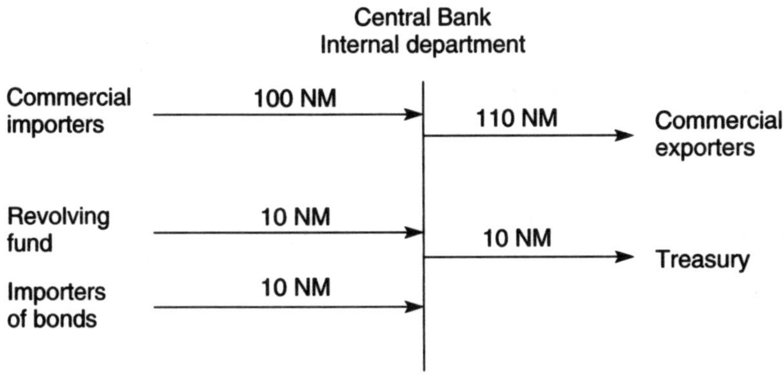

Figure 15.12

debt, the country benefits from a gain due to the reduction in its accumulated foreign engagements. Thus, the decrease in the external department liabilities amounts to a gain (the increase of an asset) which is transferred to the internal department and which is used to pay the net commercial exporters (who, since net commercial exports 'nourish' external debt servicing, are no longer paid out of the Central Bank revolving fund). On the other hand, the payment in NM carried out by the indebted residents takes the place of the payment made by the importers of foreign bonds in Figure 15.12. Because of the positive servicing of external debt, the foreign bonds earned through net commercial exports are transferred abroad in exchange for an equivalent amount of national claims. Thus, it is normal that the indebted residents replace the importers of bonds as a source of the inflow of domestic money which the internal department can benefit from and transfer to the Treasury (Figure 15.13). While waiting for the creation of an International Central Bank operating as a multilateral clearing union and allowing for the vehicular use of an international currency, countries seem trapped in the vicious circle of external debt servicing. Yet a solution exists which can be applied even in the absence of a true system of international payments. Let us end this chapter by showing how a single country can implement the principles of monetary circulation so as to avoid the double servicing of its external debt.

THE PRINCIPLES OF THE SOLUTION APPLIED TO A SINGLE COUNTRY

By referring to what has already been said, let us introduce the essential elements allowing for the correct servicing of a single country's external debt and for the implementation of its book-keeping solution.

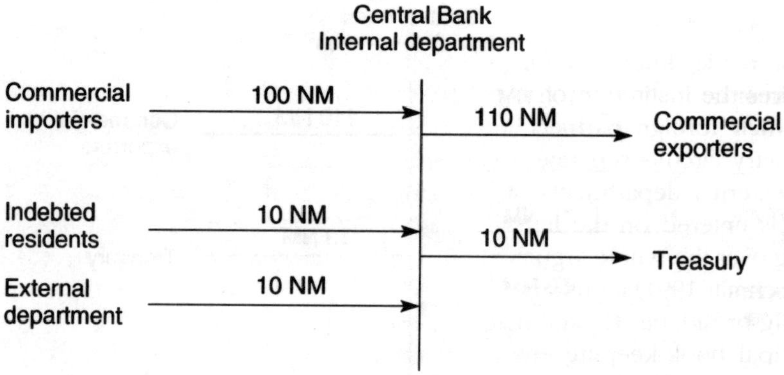

Figure 15.13

The logical rules of external debt servicing

Rule 1: external debt servicing must be carried out by the nation on behalf of its residents.
Corollary: residents must pay the nation, which extends the payment to the international area.

Rule 2: as Bank of the nation the Central Bank must provide for the circular use of foreign currencies.
Corollary: secondary banks must carry out their international payments through the intermediation of the Central Bank.

Rule 3: the loans in foreign exchange necessary for the servicing of external debt in the absence of net commercial exports must be obtained by the nation.
Corollary: the selling of domestic bonds on the international market must be carried out through the intermediation of the Central Bank.

Rule 4: imports and exports must be taken on by the nation.
Corollary: importers of goods, services and bonds must address their payments to the Central Bank, which is given the task of paying the exporters of domestic goods, services and bonds.

Rule 5: being carried out by the nation on behalf of its residents, external debt servicing is the source of a gain (corresponding to the reduction in foreign debt) which can be transferred to the Treasury.
Corollary: whether it entails a new loan or not, external debt servicing leads to a net transfer of internal resources to the benefit of the country as a whole.

The book-keeping implementation of the rules of external debt servicing

As the reader knows, the implementation of the new system of payments requires the institution of a monetary intermediary between the residents and their foreign partners. In order to keep national and international monetary circuits separate it is useful to distinguish between the internal and external departments of the nation. Then, the accumulated external debt is entered on the liability side of the external department. Without going over the whole argument once again (the reader can refer to Cencini and Schmitt 1991) let us simply reproduce the general scheme of payments amongst residents, Central Bank and foreign partners (Figure 15.14) and the principal book-keeping entries concerning the three cases in which the country servicing its external debt: (a) suffers from a trade deficit; (b) balances its commercial transactions; and (c) benefits from a trade surplus. The only point which is useful to emphasise here is the transfer to the Treasury of the sum of national money (NM) paid out by the indebted residents. The gain the whole country benefits from is due to the decrease in the nation's accumulated debt entered on the liability side of the Central Bank external department. Since a reduction on the liability side corresponds to an increase on the asset side, the external department enters a gain which, transferred to the internal department, is monetised in NM and used to pay the exporters either of goods and services (in the case of a trade surplus) or of bonds (in the other two cases). The amount paid by the indebted residents is thus entered as a gain by the internal department and

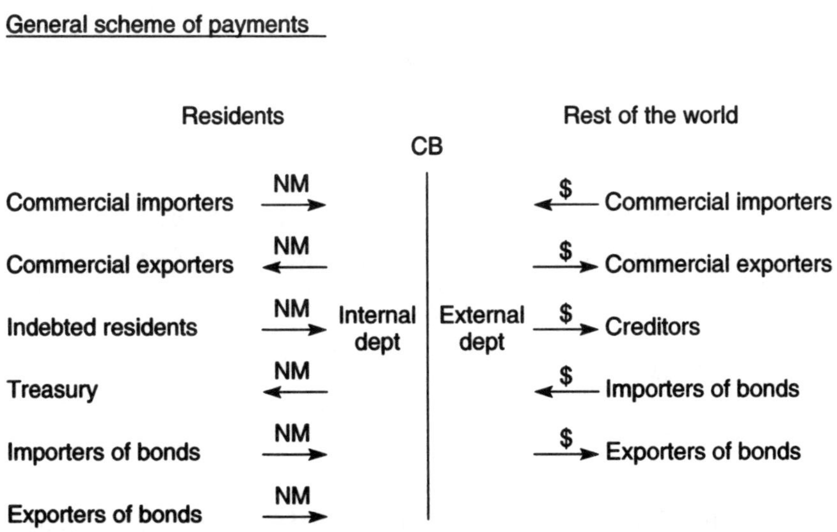

Figure 15.14

transferred to the Treasury. As far as the other operations are concerned, they are all carried out according to the rule of Central Bank intermediation between residents and non-residents.

To show the relationship existing between external debt servicing, a country's gain and its possible new indebtedness, let us briefly analyse the three cases separately.

Case 1: external debt servicing and the equilibrium of the balance of trade

Let us suppose that exports and imports of a given country C amount to $10 million and that its external debt servicing is $2 million. In this case, C can balance its trade account only if it is granted a new loan by the rest of the world. Thus, while part of the dollars earned through the export of goods and services is used in the servicing of external debt, those obtained through the new loan are used to finance an equivalent part of the country's commercial imports. By taking into account the fact that the inflow of dollars can be represented as an increase in reserves and that its counterpart pertains to the capital of the nation, the entries concerning commercial transactions and external debt servicing recorded by the external department of the Central Bank are as shown in Table 15.5. As the reader will observe, we have supposed that the external debt previously accumulated by C's residents and taken on by the Central Bank amounts to $X million and that y out of $X million corresponds to an increase in official reserves while the remaining X – y million corresponds to a commercial import. The inflows of dollars relative to the exports of goods and services, entry (3), and bonds, entry (1), are matched by equivalent outflows relative to commercial imports, entries (2) and (4), and external debt servicing, entry (5).

Table 15.5

Central Bank
External department

	Liabilities ($)		*Assets ($)*	
	External debt	X	Imported goods Reserves	X – y y
(1)	Capital	2	Reserves	2
(2)	Reserves	2	Capital	2
(3)	Capital	10	Reserves	10
(4)	Reserves	8	Capital	8
(5)	Reserves	2	Capital	2
(6)	Internal department	2	External debt	2

Entry (6), which corresponds to the decrease in the accumulated debt from \$X million to \$X – 2 million, stands for the gain the whole country benefits from and which is then transferred from the external department of the Central Bank to the internal department. As shown by the book-keeping entries recorded in this second department (Table 15.6), the sum transferred to the Treasury, entry (9), is derived from the payment carried out by the indebted residents, while the sum corresponding to the monetisation of the credit transferred by the external department is used for the partial payment of commercial exporters, entry (7). Finally, what is paid for by importers is transferred to the exporters of goods, services and bonds, entry (8). For the sake of clarity we have assumed the exchange rate between dollar and national money to be \$1 for 1 NM. It is immediately evident that inflows in national money are perfectly matched by outflows. In the case we are examining, external debt can effectively be serviced in dollars only if the country incurs a new debt on behalf of its residents. It is thus normal that, to the extent that it gets indebted to the rest of the world without getting any real counterpart in goods and services, the country finds an internal compensation. In the respect of monetary equilibrium the country benefits from a gain (transferred to the Treasury) whose justification is due to the fact that, having to pay the foreign creditors in dollars, the nation must be reimbursed in national currency by the residents who service their external debt.

Case 2: external debt servicing and trade deficit

Like the previous one, this case differs from it only as far as the amount of the new loan (which this time is greater than the amount of external debt servicing) is concerned. The logical succession of transactions is the same and the country's gain is always equal to \$2 million (corresponding to the decrease in the accumulated debt and compensating the new loan the country must incur to service foreign debt on behalf of its residents). That part of the new debt which exceeds external debt servicing and which is

Table 15.6

Central Bank
Internal department

	Liabilities (NM)		*Assets (NM)*	
(7)	Commercial exporters	2	External department	2
(8)	Commercial exporters	8	Importers	10
	Exporters of bonds	2		
(9)	Treasury	2	Indebted residents	2

used to match the trade deficit does not entail any monetary inflow for the country, whose compensation is represented by the net imports of goods and services.

Case 3: external debt servicing and trade surplus

Even in this third case the nation acts as an intermediary between residents and non-residents and carries out external debt servicing by transferring to foreign creditors the dollars obtained in exchange for its net commercial exports. The sacrifice in dollars is compensated for by an equivalent gain which takes the form of a transfer of domestic income from the indebted residents to the internal department of the Central Bank. Yet, while in the previous cases this gain was matched by a new debt incurred to the rest of the world, now net commercial exports allow the country to service its external debt positively, the global amount of which (accumulated debt + new debts) decreases from X to X – $2 million. Hence, although it is used for the servicing of external debt the domestic saving realised by the nation because of its trade surplus is not lost abroad. On the contrary, having paid the rest of the world in dollars, the country can still benefit from a net entry of NM corresponding to the income saved by its residents in their international transactions (Figure 15.15).

Let us record in the balance sheets of the two departments of the Central Bank (Table 15.7) the following entries:

1 the payment of commercial exports for $10 million,
2 the payment of commercial imports for $8 million,
3 the external debt servicing of $2 million,
4 the transfer to the internal department of the Central Bank of the gain derived from the reduction of the nation's foreign debt,
5 the monetisation of this gain by the internal department and

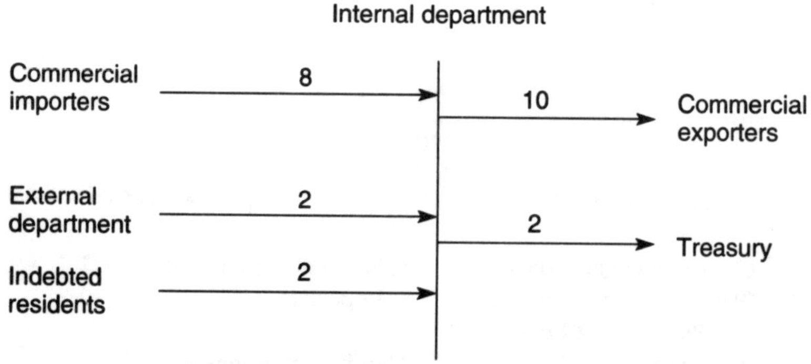

Figure 15.15

Table 15.7

Central Bank
External department

	Liabilities ($)		*Assets ($)*	
	External debt	X	Imported goods	X – y
			Reserves	y
(1)	Capital	10	Reserves	10
(2)	Reserves	8	Capital	8
(3)	Reserves	2	Capital	2
(4)	Internal department	2	External debt	2

Central Bank
Internal department

	Liabilities (NM)		*Assets (NM)*	
(5)	Capital	2	External department	2
(6)	Commercial exporters	2	Capital	2
(7)	Commercial exporters	2	Importers	2
(8)	Treasury	2	Indebted residents	2

6 its transfer to commercial exporters,
7 the payment carried out by national importers and its transfer to commercial exporters as a settlement of their global credit,
8 the payment carried out by the indebted residents and its transfer to the Treasury.

The analysis of the three cases provides an example of how the logical rules of external debt servicing can be implemented even by a single country. Apart from the advantages that the indebted country can derive from the adoption of the new system of payments, let us simply observe that without a book-keeping structure which allows the nation to play a function of intermediation, the pathological double servicing of external debt cannot be avoided.

Based on a rigorous inquiry into the nature of bank money and the mechanisms regulating its emission and its circulation, both nationally and internationally, the analysis of external debt servicing is the final stage of an itinerary littered with difficulties whose solution represents the exacting and urgent task of all those who put money at the centre of their scientific concern.

BIBLIOGRAPHY

Aglietta, M. (1989) 'Union monétaire et Banque centrale', *Revue d'économie financière*, no. 8/9, March–June.

Allen, P. R. (1986) *The ECU: Birth of a New Currency*, Occasional Papers 20, New York: Group of Thirty.

Altman, O. (1965) *Euro-Dollars: Some Further Comments*, Staff Papers, vol. 12, Washington: IMF.

Angelini, P. and Passacantando, F. (1992) 'Central Bank's Role in the Payment System and its Relationship with Monetary Policy and Supervision', in F. Bruni (ed.) *Prudential Regulation, Supervision and Monetary Policy: Theory, International Comparison and the European System of Central Bank's Role*, Proceedings of the Conference organized by the Paolo Baffi Centre for Monetary and Financial Economics, held at Bocconi University, Milan, *Giornale degli economisti e annali di economia*, vol. 51, September–December, Milan: Bocconi University.

Arcelli, M. (ed.) (1992) *Il ruolo della banca centrale nella politica economica*, Bologna: Il Mulino.

Arrow, K. J. and Boskin, M. J. (eds) (1988) *The Economics of Public Debt: Proceedings of a Conference held by the International Economic Association at Stanford, California*, London and Basingstoke: Macmillan.

Artis, M. J. and Brittan, S. (1989) *Europe without Currency Parities*, London: Social Market Foundation.

Artis, M. J. and Miller, M. M. (eds) (1981) *Essays in Fiscal and Monetary Policy*, Oxford: Oxford University Press.

Axilrod, S. H. and Wallich, H. C. (1992) 'Open-market Operations', in P. Newman, M. Milgate and J. Eatwell (eds) *The New Palgrave Dictionary of Money and Finance*, London and Basingstoke: Macmillan.

Bain, A. D. (1970) *The Control of the Money Supply*, Harmondsworth: Penguin.

Banca Nazionale Svizzera (1981) *BNS 75, gli anni dal 1957 al 1982*, Zürich: BNS.

Bank for International Settlements, *Annual Reports*, Basle: BIS.

—— (1992) *Recent Developments in International Interbank Relations*, Basle: BIS.

Baranzini, M. (ed.) (1982) *Advances in Economic Theory*, Oxford: Blackwell.

—— (1991) *Economia politica*, Lugano: Camera di commercio, industria e artigianato del Canton Ticino.

Baranzini, M. and Cencini, A. (eds) (1987) *Contributi di analisi economica*, Bellinzona: Casagrande.

Baranzini, M. and Scazzieri, R. (eds) (1986) *Foundations of Economics*, Oxford: Blackwell.

Barro, R. (1979) 'Money and the Price Level under the Gold Standard', *The Economic Journal*, no. 36, March.
Basevi, G. *et al.* (1975) 'The All Saints' Day Manifesto for European Monetary Union', *The Economist*, November.
Békerman, G. and Saint-Marc, M. (1991) *L'ECU*, Paris: Presses Universitaires de France.
Bernal, R. L. (1987) 'Resolving the Global Debt Crisis', *Economia internazionale*, May–August.
Bernstein, E. M. (1980) *Back to the Gold Standard?* Brookings Bulletin, vol. 17, Washington: Brookings Institution.
—— (1988) 'The Search for Exchange Stability: Before and After Bretton Woods', paper presented at a conference on The Future of the International Monetary System, at Glendon College, York University, Toronto.
Bernstein, E. M. *et al.* (1976) *Reflections on Jamaica*, Princeton Essays in International Finance, no. 115, April, Princeton: Princeton University Press.
Bini-Smaghi, L. (1990) *Progressing Towards European Monetary Unification: Selected Issues and Proposals*, Temi di discussione no. 133, Rome: Bank of Italy.
Black, S. W. (1989) *Transaction Costs and Vehicle Currencies*, Working Paper 89/96, November, Washington: IMF.
Bliss, C. and Braga de Macedo, J. (eds) (1990) *Economic Integration in the Enlarged EC*, Cambridge: Cambridge University Press.
Bloomfield, A. I. (1981) 'Gold Standard', in D. Greenwald (ed.) *Encyclopedia of Economics*, London and New York: McGraw-Hill
Bordo, M. D. and Eichengreen, B. (eds) (1993) *A Retrospective on the Bretton Woods System*, Chicago: University of Chicago Press.
Bordo, M. D. and Schwartz, A. J. (eds) (1984) *A Retrospective on the Classical Gold Standard, 1821–1931*, Chicago: University of Chicago Press.
Borio, C. E. V., Russo, D. and Van den Bergh, P. (1991) 'Payment System Arrangements and Related Policy Issues: A Cross-country Comparison', in F. Passacantando (ed.) *Prooceedings of the Workshop on Payment System Issues in the Perspective of European Monetary Unification*, Perugia, 22–23 November 1990, Roma: Banca d'Italia.
Britton, A. and Mayes, D. (1992) *Achieving Monetary Union in Europe*, Association for the Monetary Union of Europe, London: Sage Publications.
Bruni, F. (ed.) (1992) *Prudential Regulation, Supervision and Monetary Policy: Theory, International Comparison and the European System of Central Bank's Role*, Proceedings of the Conference organized by the Paolo Baffi Centre for Monetary and Financial Economics, held at Bocconi University, Milan, *Giornale degli economisti e annali di economia*, vol. 51, September–December, Milan: Bocconi University.
Byé, M. (1965) *Relations économiques internationales*, Paris: Dalloz.
Cagan, P. (1982) *Current Problems of Monetary Policy: Could the Gold Standard Help?*, Washington: American Enterprise Institute.
Caigdon, T. (1988) *The Debt Threat*, Oxford: Blackwell.
Cencini, A. (1984) *Time and the Macroeconomic Analysis of Income*, London: Pinter Publishers.
—— (1988) *Money, Income and Time*, London: Pinter Publishers.
—— (1990) 'The Specificity of the International Debt Problem', in *Studies in Economics*, Malaga: Annals of the Archive of Ferran Valls I Taberner's Library.
—— (1994) 'L'inflation: une approche théorique', *Encyclopaedia Universalis*, Paris: Pinter Publishers.
Cencini, A. and Schmitt, B. (1991) *External Debt Servicing: A Vicious Circle*, London: Pinter Publishers.

—— (1992) 'Per la creazione di uno spazio monetario europeo garante della sovranità di ogni singolo paese', in A.A.V.V. *Europa '93! E la piazza finanziaria svizzera?* Lugano: Centro di Studi Bancari/Meta-Edizioni.

Ciocca, P. L. (1990) 'Ancora sul credito di ultima istanza', *Moneta e credito*, no. 170, Juin.

Claassen, E.-M. (1974) 'Politique monétaire internationale: un bilan provisoire', in P. Salin (ed.) *L'unification monétaire européenne*, Paris: Calmann-Levy.

—— (ed.) (1990) *International and European Monetary Systems*, London: Heinemann.

Claassen, E.-M. and Salin, P. (eds) (1976) *Recent Issues in International Monetary Economics*, Amsterdam and New York: North-Holland.

Claassen, E.-M., Krul, N. and Salin, P. (1978) 'La crise monétaire européenne', in E.-M. Claassen and P. Salin (eds) *L'occident en désarroi. Turbulences d'une économie prospère*, Paris: Dunod.

Claudon, M. P. (ed.) (1986) *World Debt Crisis: International Lending on Trial*, Cambridge, MA: Ballinger Publishing Co.

Cline, W. R. (1976) *International Debt*, Cambridge, MA: The MIT Press.

—— (1985) *International Debt*, Cambridge, MA: The MIT Press.

—— (1988) 'International Debt: Progress and Strategy', *Finance and Development*, June.

Coats, W. L., Jr (1982) *The SDR as a Means of Payments*, Staff Papers, vol. 29, September, Washington: IMF.

Cohen, B. J. (1989) *Developing-country Debt: A Middle Way*, International Finance Section, Princeton: Princeton University Press.

Collins, M. (ed.) (1993) *Central Banking in History*, Aldershot: Elgar.

Communauté Européenne (1992) *L'union européenne: les Traités de Rome et de Maastricht*, Paris: La documentation française,

Cooper, R. (1987) *The International Monetary System, Essays in World Economics*, Cambridge, MA: The MIT Press.

Davidson, P. (1992) 'Reforming the World's Money', *Journal of Post-Keynesian Economics*, vol. 15, no. 2, Winter 1992–93.

De Grauwe, P. (1989) *International Money: Post-war Trends and Theories*, Oxford: Oxford University Press.

De Grauwe, P. and Peeters, T. (eds) (1990) *The ECU and European Monetary Integration*, London: Macmillan.

De Vries, M. G. (1977) *The International Monetary Fund 1966–71: The System under Stress*, Washington: IMF.

De Vries, T. (1980) *On the Meaning and Future of the European Monetary System*, Princeton Essays in International Finance, no. 138, Princeton: Princeton University Press.

Dell, S. (1988) 'The Future of the International Monetary System', paper presented at a conference on The Future of the International Monetary System, at Glendon College, York University, Toronto, June.

Delorme, C. D., Duncan, J. J., Kamerschen, D. R. (1987) 'A Compendium of Views on the Gold Standard', *International Review of the History of Banking*, Geneva: Librairie Droz.

Deschamps, C. and Soichot, J. (1980) 'Quelques aspects du nouveau système monétaire européen', *Revue d'économie politique*, no. 2, March–April.

Despres, E., Kindleberger, C. P. and Salant, W. S. (1966) 'The Dollar and World Liquidity: A Minority View', *The Economist*, February.

Dornbusch, R. (1987) *Dollars, Debts and Deficits*, Leuven and Cambridge, MA: Leuven University Press and The MIT Press.

—— (1990) *Problems of European Monetary Integration*, Cambridge, MA: The MIT Press.

Dow, J. C. R. and Saville, I. D. (1990) *A Critique of Monetary Policy*, Oxford: Oxford University Press.

Dudler, H.-J. (1984) 'Domestic Monetary Control in EC Countries under Different Exchange Rate Regimes: National Concerns and Community Options', in R. S. Masera and R. Triffin (eds) *Europe's Money, Problems of European Monetary Coordination and Integration*, Oxford: Clarendon Press.

Edwards, S. and Larrain, F. (eds) (1989) *The Latin American Debt Crisis: Perspectives and Solution*, Oxford: Blackwell.

Eichengreen, B. (1990) *Is Europe an Optimum Currency Area?* Discussion paper series, no. 478, London: Centre for Economic Policy Research.

—— (1992) *Should the Maastricht Treaty be Saved?* Studies in International Finance, no. 74, December, Princeton: Princeton University Press.

Eichengreen, B. and Lindert, P. H. (eds) (1989) *The International Debt Crisis in Historical Perspective*, Cambridge, MA: The MIT Press.

Ellyne, M. J. and Flinch, H. (1990) 'Issues in the Measurement of External Debt', *Finance and Development*, March, Washington: IMF and WB.

Emerson, M. and Huhne, C. (1991) *The ECU Report*, London: Pan Books.

European Community Commission (1977) *Optica Report '76: Inflation and Exchange Rates: Evidence and Policy Guidelines for the European Community*, Brussels: Commission for the European Communities

Fair, D. E. and de Boissieu, C. (eds) (1988) *International Monetary and Financial Integration – the European Dimension*, Dordrecht: Kluwer Academic Publishers.

Feldstein, M. (1992) 'The Case against EMU', *The Economist*, 13–19 June.

Fellner, W., Machlup, F., Triffin, R. and eleven others (1966) *Maintaining and Restoring Balance in International Payments*, Princeton: Princeton University Press.

Ferri, P. (ed.) (1990) *Prospects for the European Monetary System*, London and Basingstoke: Macmillan.

Fiorentini, R. (1990) *I tassi di cambio flessibili, teorie e verifiche*, Padova: CEDAM.

Fleming, J. M. (1964) *The Fund and International Liquidity*, Staff Papers, vol. 11, Washington: IMF.

Fraga, A. (1986) *German Reparations and Brazilian Debt: A Comparative Study*, Essays in International Finance, no. 163, Princeton: Princeton University Press.

Fraser, R. (1987) *The World Financial System*, Harlow, Essex: Longman.

Fratianni, M. and Peeters, T. (eds) (1978) *One Money for Europe*, London and Basingstoke: Macmillan.

Frenkel, J. A. and Johnson, H. G. (eds) (1974) *The Monetary Approach to the Balance of Payments*, London: Allen & Unwin.

Frenkel, J. A., Dooley, M. P. and Wickham, P. (eds) (1989) *Analytical Issues in Debt*, Washington: IMF.

Friboulet, J.-J. (1988) 'Ressources et emplois dans la comptabilité du commerce extérieur', Working Paper, Centre d'Etudes Monétaires et Financières, Dijon: University of Bourgogne.

Friboulet, J.-J. and Soichot, J. (1976) *Les 'monnaies'-paniers unités de compte ou unités de paiement?*, Cahier no. 1, Série Monnaie, Centre d'Etudes Monétaires et Financières, Dijon: Editions Universitaires de Dijon.

Friedman, M. (1953) *Essays in Positive Economics*, Chicago: University of Chicago Press.

—— (1963) 'Statement before the Joint Economic Committee', 88th Congress, 1st Session, *The United States Balance of Payments*, November.

Giavazzi, F., Micossi, S. and Miller, M. (eds) (1988) *The European Monetary System*, Cambridge: Cambridge University Press.

Giavazzi, F. and Giovannini, A. (1989) *The European Monetary System*, Cambridge, MA: The MIT Press.

Giovannini, A. and Mayer, C. (eds) (1990) *European Financial Integration*, Cambridge: Cambridge University Press.

Gnos, C. (1989) 'Faut-il abstraire l'ECU de ses monnaies composantes?' *Revue du Marché Commun*, no. 330, September–October.

—— (1992) *Production, répartition et monnaie*, Dijon: Editions Universitaires de Dijon.

—— (1992) 'La transition vers l'union économique et monétaire: les vertus négligées de la monnaie commune', *Revue du Marché Commun*, no. 360, July–August.

Gnos, C. and Rasera, J.-B. (1985) 'Circuit et circulation: une fausse analogie', *Cahiers de la Revue d'économie politique*, Paris: Sirey.

Gold, J. (1970) *Special Drawing Rights: Character and Use*, IMF Pamphlet Series no. 13, Washington: IMF.

—— (1971) *Special Drawing Rights: The Role of Language*, IMF Pamphlet Series no. 15, Washington: IMF.

Gomel, G. (1991) 'Il debito estero dei paesi in via di sviluppo: la situazione attuale e le prospettive', *Moneta e credito*, no. 173, March.

Goodhart, C. A. E. (1975) *Money, Information and Uncertainty*, London and Basingstoke: Macmillan.

—— (1991) *L'evoluzione delle banche centrali*, Roma and Bari: Laterza.

Goodhart, C. A. E. and Schoenmaker, D. (1992) 'Institutional Separation between Supervisory and Monetary Agencies', *Giornale degli economisti e annali di economia*, vol. 51, no. 9–12, September–December.

—— (1988) *The Evolution of Central Banks*, Cambridge, MA: The MIT Press.

Griffith-Jones, S. (ed.) (1988) *Managing World Debt*, New York: St Martin's Press.

Grubel, H. G. (ed.) (1963) *World Monetary Reform: Plans and Issues*, Stanford: Stanford University Press.

—— (1977) *The International Monetary System*, Harmondsworth: Penguin Books.

Habermeier, W. O. (1979) 'The SDR as an International Unit of Account', *Finance and Development*, March.

Hahn, F. (1982) *Money and Inflation*, Oxford: Blackwell.

Heldring, F. (1979) 'The Case for a World Central Bank', *Euromoney*, September.

Hirsch, F. (1971) *SDRs and the Working of the Gold Exchange Standard*, Staff Papers, vol. 18, Washington: IMF.

—— (1973) *An SDR Standard: Impetus, Elements and Impediments*, Essays in International Finance, no. 99, Princeton: Princeton University Press.

Hume, D. (1826) *The Philosophical Works*, vol. III, reprinted in E. Rotwein (1955) (ed.) *Writings on Economics*, Edinburgh: Nelson.

IMF (1974) *International Monetary Reform: Documents of the Committee of Twenty*, Washington: IMF.

—— (1977) *Balance of Payments Manual*, Washington: IMF.

—— (1991) *Balance of Payments Statistics Yearbook*, Washington: IMF.

—— (1992) *Report on the Measurement of International Capital Flows*, Washington: IMF.

—— (1993) *International Financial Statistics Yearbook*, Washington: IMF.

Jean, A. (1990) *L'ECU, le SME et le marché financier*, Paris: Les Editions d'Organisation.

Johnson, C. and Collignon, S. (1994) *The Monetary Economics of Europe*, London: Pinter Publishers.

Johnson, H. G. (1972) *Further Essays in Monetary Economics*, London: Allen & Unwin.

—— (1974) 'Towards a General Theory of the Balance of Payments', in J. A. Frenkel and H. G. Johnson (eds) *The Monetary Approach to the Balance of Payments*, London: Allen & Unwin.

Kenen, P. B. (1983) 'Use of the SDR to Supplement or Substitute for Other Means of Finance', in G. M. von Furstenberg (ed.) *International Money and Credit: the Policy Roles*, Washington: IMF.

Keynes, J. M. (1929a) 'The German Transfer Problem', *The Economic Journal*, March.

—— (1929b) 'A Rejoinder', *The Economic Journal*, June.

—— (1929c) 'A Reply by Mr. Keynes', *The Economic Journal*, September.

—— (1930) *A Treatise on Money*, vols V–VI of *The Collected Writings of John Maynard Keynes*, London and Basingstoke: Macmillan.

—— (1931) *Essays in Persuasion*, vol. IX of *The Collected Writings*, London and Basingstoke: Macmillan.

—— (1936) *The General Theory of Employment, Interest and Money*, vol. VII of *The Collected Writings*, London and Basingstoke: Macmillan.

—— (1973) *The Collected Writings*, vol. XIII, XIV, XXV, XXVI, London and Basingstoke: Macmillan.

Kindleberger, C. P. (1981) *International Money*, London: Allen & Unwin.

—— (1988) 'Il "lunedì nero" del 1987: considerazioni in prospettiva storica', *Rivista di storia economica*, no. 2, May.

Kindleberger, C. P. and Shonfield, A. (eds) (1971) *North American and Western European Economic Policies*, London: Macmillan.

Kloten, N. (1988) 'Towards European Monetary Union: The Role of ECU Coins and Bank Notes', *Deutsche Bundesbank: Auszüge aus Presserartikeln*, no. 4, January, Frankfurt am Main: Deutsche Bundesbank.

Kregel, J. A. (1988) 'Central Bank Monetary Control and Financial Structure: Some General Considerations', in B. Jossa and C. Panico (eds) *Teorie monetarie e banche centrali*, Napoli: Liguori Editore.

Kyriazis, N. (1987) 'L'ECU privé', *Revue du Marché Commun*, no. 307, May–June.

Lelart, M. (1988) 'L'ECU monnaie de règlement', *Revue du Marché Commun*, no. 321, November.

—— (1992) *Vers l'union monétaire européenne: rôle de l'ECU et d'une banque centrale européenne*, Paris: Commisariat Général du Plan.

Lidonni, I. (1984) *Dall'eurodollaro all'ECU*, Milano: SugarCo Edizioni.

Louw, A. (1988) 'The ECU and its Role on the European Monetary Scene', in D. E. Fair and C. de Boissieu (eds) *International Monetary and Financial Integration – the European Dimension*, Dordrecht: Kluwer Academic Publishers.

—— (1990) 'Le rôle de l'ECU dans le processus de l'union monétaire européenne et dans la réalisation du marché unique' *Revue du Marché Commun*, no. 334, February.

Machlup, F. (1976) 'Between Outline and Outcome the Reform was Lost', in E. Bernstein *et al. Reflections on Jamaica*, Essays in International Finance, no. 115, Princeton: Princeton University Press.

McKinnon, R. I. (1984) *An International Standard for Monetary Stabilization*, Washington: Institute for International Economics.

—— (1988) 'Monetary and Exchange Rate Policies for International Financial Stability: A Proposal', *Journal of Economic Perspectives*, February.

McKinnon, R. I. and Ohno, K. (1988) 'Purchasing Power Parity as a Monetary Standard', paper presented at a conference on *The Future of the International Monetary System*, at Glendon College, York University, Toronto.

Magee, S. P. and Rao, R. K. S. (1980) 'Vehicle and Nonvehicle Currencies in International Trade', *American Economic Review*, vol. 70, no. 2, May.

Magnifico, G. (1973) *European Monetary Unification*, London and Basingstoke: Macmillan.

—— (1976) *Una moneta per l'Europa*, Bari: Laterza.

—— (1979) 'Open Market Operation for Europe?' *The Journal of Commerce*, 26 April.

Malthus, T. R. (1986) *The Works of Thomas Robert Malthus*, E. A. Wrigley and D. Souden (eds), London: Pickering.

Marcuzzo, M. C. and Rosselli, A. (1986) *La teoria del gold standard, Ricardo e il suo tempo*, Bologna: Il Mulino.

Marx, K. (1969) *Theories of Surplus Value*, 3 vols, London: Lawrence & Wishart.

—— (1973) *Grundrisse*, Harmondsworth: The Pelican Marx Library.

—— (1979) *Capital*, 3 vols, Harmondsworth: The Pelican Marx Library.

Masciandaro, D. and Ristuccia, S. (eds) (1988) *L'autonomia delle banche centrali*, Milano: Edizioni di Comunità.

Masera, R. S. (1987) *L'unificazione monetaria e lo SME: l'esperienza dei primi otto anni*, Bologna: Il Mulino.

—— (1988) 'An Increasing Role for the ECU: A Character in Search of a Script', in D. E. Fair and C. de Boissieu (eds) *International Monetary and Financial Integration – the European Dimension*, Dordrecht: Kluwer Academic Publishers.

Masera, R. S. and Triffin, R. (eds) (1984) *Europe's Money, Problems of European Monetary Coordination and Integration*, Oxford: Clarendon Press.

Mauro, G. (1984) *Bilancia dei pagamenti e sistema monetario internazionale*, Torino: G. Giappichelli Editore.

Meier, G. M. (1982) *Problems of World Monetary Order*, Oxford: Oxford University Press.

Michie, R. C. (1986) 'The Myth of the Gold Standard: An Historian's Approach', *Revue Internationale d'Histoire de la Banque*, 32–33, Genève: Librairie Droz.

Micossi, S. (1985) 'The Intervention and Financial Mechanism of the EMS and the Role of the ECU', *Banca Nazionale del Lavoro Quarterly Review*, December.

Mill, J. S. (1893) *Principles of Political Economy*, 5th edn, New York: Appleton.

Mishkin, F. S. (1993) *Money, Interest Rates and Inflation*, Aldershot: Elgar.

Mundell, R. A. (1992) *EMU and the International Monetary System*, New York: Columbia University Press.

Mundell, R. A. and Polak, J. J. (eds) (1977) *The New International Monetary System*, New York: Columbia University Press.

Nowzad, B. (1990) 'Lessons of the Debt Decade: Will We Learn?' *Finance and Development*, March, Washington: IMF and WB.

Ohlin, B. (1929a) 'Transfer Difficulties, Real and Imagined', *The Economic Journal*, June.

—— (1929b) 'Mr. Keynes' Views on the Transfer Problem: A Rejoinder', *The Economic Journal*, September.

Padoa-Schioppa, T. (1987) *Efficiency, Stability and Equity: a Strategy for the Evolution of the Economic System of the European Community*, Oxford: Oxford University Press.

Peeters, T., de Grauwe, P. and Vaubel, R. (1978) 'Inflation-proof Europa: How it Might Work', in M. Fratianni and T. Peeters (eds) *One Money for Europe*, London and Basingstoke: Macmillan.

Polak, J.J. (1971) *Some Reflections on the Nature of Special Drawing Rights*, IMF Pamphlet Series, no. 16, Washington: IMF.

Poulon, F. (1985) (ed.) *Les écrits de Keynes*, Paris: Dunod.

Prissert, P. (1976) 'A propos d'un manifeste sur la monnaie européenne', *La Revue Banque*, no. 350, April.

Ricardo, D. (1951–5) *The Works and Correspondence of David Ricardo*, P. Sraffa (ed.), Cambridge: Cambridge University Press.

—— (1985) *Scritti monetari*, Istituto della Enciclopedia Italiana, Bibliotheca Biographica, Roma.

Ripa di Meana, A. and Sarcinelli, M. (1990) 'Il credito di ultima istanza e l'evoluzione dell'attività bancaria', *Giornale degli economisti e annali di economia*, Fasc. 7/8.

Rossi, S. (1994) *La moneta europea: utopia of realtà*, Lugano: Meta Edizioni and Centre for Banking Studies.

Rueff, J. (1929) 'Mr. Keynes' View on the Transfer Problem: A Criticism by M. Jacques Rueff', *The Economic Journal*, September.

—— (1963) 'Gold Exchange Standard a Danger to the West' in H. G. Grubel (ed.) *World Monetary Reform: Plans and Issues*, Stanford: Stanford University Press.

—— (1980) *Oeuvres complètes*, Paris: Plon.

Salin, P. (ed.) (1974) *L'unification monétaire européenne*, Paris: Calman-Lévy.

—— (1979) *L'unité monétaire européenne au profit de qui?* Paris: Economica.

Sarcinelli, M. (1985) 'Lo SME e il sistema monetario internazionale: verso una maggiore stabilità', *Moneta e Credito*, no. 152, December.

—— (1992) 'La Banca Centrale Europea: istituzione concettualmente "evoluta" o all'inizio della sua "evoluzione"?' *Moneta e credito*, no. 178, June.

Sayers, R. S. (1957) *Central Banking after Bagehot*, Oxford: Oxford University Press.

—— (1958) *Modern Banking*, Oxford: Oxford University Press.

Schmitt, B. (1966) *Monnaie, salaires et profits*, Paris: Presses Universitaires de France.

—— (1973) *New Proposals for World Monetary Reform*, Albeuve: Castella.

—— (1977) *La monnaie européenne*, Paris: Presses Universitaires de France.

—— (1984) *Inflation, chômage et malformations du capital*, Paris and Albeuve: Economica and Castella.

—— (1985) 'Un nouvel ordre monétaire international: le plan Keynes', in F. Poulon (ed.) *Les écrits de Keynes*, Paris: Dunod.

—— (1988) *L'ECU et les souverainetés nationales en Europe*, Paris: Dunod.

Schumacher, E. F. (1943) 'Multilateral Clearing', *Economica*, May.

Schweitzer, P.-P. (1967) *The New Arrangements to Supplement World Reserves and Their Implications for the Developing Countries*, Washington: IMF.

Singer, H. W. and Sharma, S. (eds) (1989) *Economic Development and World Debt*, London and Basingstoke: Macmillan.

Smith, A. (1776/1978) *The Wealth of Nations*, Harmondsworth: Pelican Classics.

Steinherr, A. and Weiserbs, D. (1991) *Evolution of the International and Regional Monetary Systems: Essays in Honour of Robert Triffin*, Macmillan: London and Basingstoke.

Sweeney, R. J. and Willet, T. D. (1976) 'Eurodollars, Petrodollars, and World Liquidity and Inflation', *Journal of Monetary Economics*, Amsterdam: North-Holland.

Swoboda, A. K. (1991) 'The Road to European Monetary Union: Lessons from the Bretton Woods Regime', the 1991 Per Jacobson Lecture, Washington: IMF.

Tarshis, L. (1988) 'A Return Visit to the International Debt Problem of the LDCs', paper presented at a conference on *The Future of the International Monetary System*, at Glendon College, York University, Toronto.

Thornton, H. (1939/1965) *An Enquiry into the Nature and Effects of the Paper Credit of Great Britain*, New York: A. M. Kelly.

Timberlake, R. H. (1984) 'The Central Banking Role of Clearinghouse Associations', *Journal of Money, Credit and Banking*, vol. 16, February.

Tobin, J. (1971) *Essays in Economics*, vol. I: *Macroeconomics*, Amsterdam: North-Holland.

—— (1978) 'A Proposal for International Monetary Reform', *The Eastern Economic Journal*, vol. 3, July–October.

—— (1980) 'Discussion of Overlapping Generations Models', in J. H. Kareken and

N. Wallace (eds) *Models of Monetary Economics*, Minneapolis: Federal Reserve Bank of Minneapolis.

Tower, E. and Willet, T. (1976) *The Theory of Optimum Currency Areas and Exchange-Rate Flexibility*, Princeton: Princeton University Press.

Traité de Maastricht, mode d'emploi (1992), *Paris: 10/18.*

Triffin, R. (1961) *Gold and the Dollar Crisis*, revised edn, New Haven: Yale University Press.

—— (1966) 'The Balance-of-payments Seesaw', in W. Fellner, F. Machlup, R. Triffin and eleven others, *Maintaining and Restoring Balance in International Payments*, Princeton: Princeton University Press.

—— (1968) *Our International Monetary System: Yesterday, Today and Tomorrow*, New York: Random House.

—— (1980) 'The Future of the International Monetary System', *Banca Nazionale del Lavoro Quarterly Review*, March, Rome.

—— (1984) 'How to End the World "Infession": Crisis Management or Fundamental Reforms?' in R. S. Masera and R. Triffin (eds) *Europe's Money, Problems of European Monetary Coordination and Integration*, Oxford: Clarendon Press.

Triffin, R. and Swings, A.A.L. (1980) *The Private Use of the ECU*, Brussels: Kredietbank.

Vaggi, G. (ed.) (1993) *From the Debt Crisis to Sustainable Development: Changing on North–South Relations*, New York: St Martin's Press.

Van Ypersele, J. and Koeune, J.-C. (1985) *The European Monetary System*, Brussels: The European Perspectives Series.

Vaubel, R. (1978) *Strategies for Currency Unification, The Economics of Currency Competition and the Case for a European Parallel Currency*, Kieler Studien no. 156, Tübingen, J.C.B. Mohr (Paul Siebeck).

Villiaz, P. (1991) 'La question de l'ECU: plaidoyer pour la simplicité', *Problèmes économiques*, no. 2.226, 23 May.

Wallich, H. C. (1979) 'The International Monetary and Cyclical Situation', remarks at a meeting sponsored by the Landenszentralbank in Berlin, Monday, 18 June, Berlin.

Walras, L. (1965) *Elements of Pure Economics*, London: Allen & Unwin (first published 1874).

WB, IMF, BIS, OECD (1988) *External Debt, Definition, Statistical Coverage and Methodology*, Paris: OECD Publications.

Werner, P. (1971) *Vers l'union monétaire européenne*, Lausanne: Centre de recherches européennes.

White, H. D. (1943) 'Preliminary Draft Outline of a Proposal for an International Stablization Fund of the United and Associated Nations', in J. K. Horsefield (ed.) (1969) *The International Monetary Fund 1945–1965, vol. III: Documents*, Washington: IMF.

Williamson, J. (1992) 'On Designing an International Monetary System', *Journal of Post Keynesian Economics*, vol. 15, no. 2, Winter 1992–93.

World Bank (1987–93) *World Debt Tables*, Washington: World Bank.

—— (1987–93) *World Development Report*, Washington: World Bank.

AUTHOR INDEX

SUBJECT INDEX